Essentials of Blockchain Technology

Essentials of Blockchain Technology

Edited by

Kuan-Ching Li
Xiaofeng Chen
Hai Jiang
Elisa Bertino

CRC Press
Taylor & Francis Group
Boca Raton London New York

CRC Press is an imprint of the
Taylor & Francis Group, an **informa** business

A CHAPMAN & HALL BOOK

CRC Press
Taylor & Francis Group
6000 Broken Sound Parkway NW, Suite 300

Boca Raton, FL 33487-2742
© 2020 by Taylor & Francis Group, LLC

CRC Press is an imprint of Taylor & Francis Group, an Informa business

No claim to original U.S. Government works

International Standard Book Number-13: 978-0-367-02771-1 (Hardback)

International Standard Book Number-13: 978-0-429-67445-7 (eBook)

Library of Congress Cataloging-in-Publication Data

Names: Li, Kuan-Ching, editor. | Chen, Xiaofeng, 1976- editor. |
Jiang, Hai, editor. | Bertino, Elisa, editor.
Title: Essentials of blockchain technology / edited by Kuan-Ching Li, Xiaofeng Chen,
Hai Jiang, Elisa Bertino.
Description: Boca Raton : CRC Press, [2020] | Includes bibliographical references and index.
Identifiers: LCCN 2019024843 (print) | LCCN 2019024844 (ebook) |
ISBN 9780367027711 (hardback) | ISBN 9780429674457 (ebook)
Subjects: LCSH: Blockchains (Databases) | Database security.
Classification: LCC QA76.9.B56 E77 2020 (print) | LCC QA76.9.B56 (ebook) | DDC 005.8/24–dc23
LC record available at https://lccn.loc.gov/2019024843
LC ebook record available at https://lccn.loc.gov/2019024844

Visit the Taylor & Francis Web site at
www.taylorandfrancis.com

and the CRC Press Web site at
www.crcpress.com

Contents

Foreword I

At present blockchain is, perhaps, one of the most promising technologies, and it possesses a very high potential to change today's business models. It is essentially a distributed database of records, or a public ledger of all transactions (or digital events) that have been executed and shared among participating parties. Each transaction in the public ledger is verified by the consensus of a majority of the participants' computing power in the entire system. Therefore, blockchain has the potential to significantly change the way financial institutions, for example, operate today. As an early evidence note that Bitcoin is one of the most commonly used applications based on blockchain technology. Also, due to the attractive characteristic of decentralization, persistency, anonymity, and auditability, it has further far-reaching implications in a wide range of industries, sectors, and application areas, such as Internet of Things (IoT), medical health, and smart contracts, respectively. As a result, blockchain technology has received considerable attention in both the academic and the industrial communities.

The current book, *Essentials of Blockchain Technology*, covers the significant technical aspects and applications of blockchain technology. As such, it gives real value for individuals or organizations that attempt to understand the foundations and practical applications in the field. The field, in turn, includes the areas of fundamental study, practical applications, and other related areas on issues such as regulatory approaches. Specifically, the fundamental study mainly consists of distributed consensus mechanisms, validation services for permissioned blockchain, and privacy in blockchain; the practical applications covers, among other areas, the areas of IoT, global health, car registration, electronic voting machine.

In the field of fundamental study, this book includes a survey of distributed consensus, which is at the heart of the blockchain-based systems. Distributed consensus protocols glue individual computers together to provide a reliable service to the outside world. According to the failure model, there are two types of distributed consensus, fail-stop-tolerant consensus, and Byzantine-fault-tolerant consensus. Paxos and Raft, two fail-stop-tolerant consensus protocols, are suitable for fail-stop systems in which the nodes either work correctly or stop working. Practical Byzantine fault tolerance (PBFT) and Nakamoto Consensus, two Byzantine-fault-tolerant consensus systems, are suitable for Byzantine-fault system in which faulty nodes may even send malicious messages. Since the Blockchain-based system should be Byzantine-fault-tolerant since motivation of participants are unknown, the PBFT and Nakamoto protocols are highlighted in this book. This is even more so, since public blockchain systems, such as Bitcoin and Ethereum, allow anyone to join and contribute to their networks.

In contrast, permissioned blockchain is built to grant special permissions for each participant to perform specific functions, for example, read, write, and access operations. With the features of privacy, scalability, and fine-grained access control, most of the enterprise blockchain systems are classified as permissioned blockchain. This book focuses on the permissioned blockchain setting and explains how to validate transactions using robotic process automation (RPA). Next, note that despite tremendous benefits, protection of private information in the blockchain framework is still a challenge. This book introduces different concepts of blockchain privacy, provides an overview of major attacks, and discusses specific solutions to ensure privacy in the blockchain network. Further, a variant of blockchain, the Directed Acyclic Graph (DAG), has revolutionized the blockchain technology. This book, therefore, also discusses the details of DAG technology and makes a comparison between the classical linked-list based blockchain and popular DAG-based blockchains.

In the field of practical application, as noted above, blockchain technology is facilitating applications in a wide range of areas, both financial and non-financial. Due to the primary attributes of transparency, speed of settlement, security, and automation, blockchain has great potential in significantly changing the way the financial sector operate today. This book covers how the blockchain technology should be appropriately implemented within the financial services industry while noting that the opportunities for blockchain practical applications in the non-financial area are also plentiful. Recently, blockchain-based smart contracts have gained increasing attention, as they seem to offer tantalizing possibilities to automate and better control the deployment, execution, management, and governance of collaborative processes. This book presents details of blockchain-based smart contracts and provides an in-depth survey of some recent examples and applications of smart contracts. The book also addresses security issues concerning the IoT using blockchain technology and designs blockchain-based secure IoT infrastructure and systems for managing cybersecurity in the IoT area. In addition, a secure and reliable blockchain-based method of recording and sharing sensitive data in the health sector, a car registration system based on the Hyperledger Fabric Blockchain technology, and an implementation of the electronic voting machine (EVM) based on blockchains, are also included in this book.

The book also covers the legal aspects of blockchain technology. Typically, novel technologies conflict with existing regulations, which may be too slow or rigid to adapt to the explored innovative functionalities, and blockchain is no exception to this. This book provides a general understanding of how the blockchain technology is seen to interact with three major fields of law: (smart) contracts, intellectual property, and data protection. Also, the prediction of the cryptocurrency market price is vital, since Bitcoin and Ethereum are concretely operating in the present financial market. Thus, this book provides an introduction on how to predict the accuracy of both Bitcoin and Ethereum currencies using a deep learning algorithm operating over blockchain information.

Overall, in this book, authors are dedicated to providing the state-of-art studies on blockchain technology, including in the areas of fundamental studies, typical applications, and other challenging issues. Additionally, this book is well organized, novel in its content, and comprehensive in coverage. These facts, in turn, have excellent potential in providing long-lasting values, when serving both the academic and the industrial communities, in their efforts to understand the challenging technical and scientific field of blockchain.

Moti Yung
Google and Columbia University, USA

Foreword II

B lockchain is a decentralized, shared and public digital ledger that is used to record transactions across many computers so that any involved record cannot be altered retroactively without the alteration of all subsequent blocks. It provides us a new system to record a public history of transactions without relying on any centralized trusted party. The property of decentralization, openness, permissionless and tamper-resistant has attracted considerable interest in both academic and industrial communities.

As a promising technology to achieve decentralized consensus, blockchain is not only limited in cryptocurrency but also critical to enterprises and creates extraordinary opportunities for Digital Health, Supply Chain, Energy, IoT, Fintech, etc. Although blockchain can maintain a secure public ledger by all participants through the distributed network, how to apply in different industrial sectors flexibly is still a big challenge. The current book, *Essentials of Blockchain Technology*, comes at the right time with the right purpose and contains the following research ideas:

The chapter "Distributed Consensus and Fault Tolerance Mechanisms" discusses consensus problems and consensus protocols in distributed systems, fault-tolerant mechanisms in blockchain-based systems and tradeoff between consensus and performance. Moreover, the related research on scalable consensus protocols for blockchain-based systems is discussed.

The chapter "Validation Services for Permissioned Blockchains" discusses the needs, methods, and implications of validating transactions before record on a permissioned blockchain. It also compares permissioned and permissionless blockchains and discusses why permissioned blockchains need validation services. Finally, implications for accounting, auditing, and technology services are discussed.

The chapter "From Byzantine Consensus to Blockchains" introduces state-of-the-art in the area of Byzantine consensus and its application in blockchains, from classical algorithms to those used in blockchains and those that combine both approaches.

The chapter "Application of Blockchain and Smart Contract: Approaches and Challenges" performs an in-depth survey of some recent examples and applications of Blockchain and smart contracts. Moreover, the applications of Blockchain for Vehicular Ad-hoc Network (VANET) and some current applications of blockchain in the cloud and education area are also elaborated.

The chapter "Towards Preserving Privacy and Security in Blockchain" introduces a privacy-preserving model for ensuring privacy in blockchain. The proposed approach based on White-Box Cryptography (WBC) ensures privacy in smart contracts. By introducing the new system, the most severe attacks including MatE and white-box attacks can be resisted.

The chapter "Smart Contracts: State of the Art versus the State of Practice" introduces smart contract as an emerging distributed computing enterprise technology to enact collaborative processes, and contrasts the state-of-the-art, cutting-edge developments in R&D and puts with the actual state-of-practice in the industry at large.

The chapter "Blockchain Application for IoT Cybersecurity Management" reviews the IoT concept and definitions, generalized IoT architecture and reference model proposed, and IoT standardization issues. Moreover, two main directions of applying Blockchain technologies on the IoT are represented.

The chapter "IoT Security using Blockchain" introduces the security issues concerning the Internet of Things (IoT) and in particular, investigates the use of Blockchain technology to address these issues. It also depicts how to integrate smart contracts, verifiable claims and self-sovereign identity with Blockchain to address the security issues of IoT. Finally, a secure IoT architecture based on Blockchain technology is presented.

The chapter "Blockchain in Global Health – An appraisal of Current and Future Applications" synthesizes some current applications of Blockchain technology in the global healthcare sector and offers an outlook. It also introduces relevant global health landscape and role of various stakeholders, latest developments, pilots and opportunities in the application of Blockchain. Finally, an outlook, the proliferation of Blockchain technologies in healthcare enable further by MIoT that can better support public health around the world, is presented.

The chapter "A Blockchain Use Case for Car Registration" provides a car registration system based on the Hyperledger Fabric Blockchain technology. The system considers several government entities in a single country, but possibly supports car data sharing at the level of the European Union. Moreover, the system can simplify the information exchange among multiple states as the car registration information is distributed to each government entity in a single decentralized system.

The chapter "Advancing the Cybersecurity of EVM Using Blockchain" presents an implementation of the Electronic Voting Machine (EVM) illustrating the applicability of emerging blockchain-based solutions to address current and emerging cybersecurity threats.

The chapter "Implementing Blockchain Technology in the Financial Services Industry" shows how to implement the blockchain technology in the financial services industry. Blockchain, with attributes of transparency, speed of settlement, security, and automation, has the potential to significantly change the way financial institutions operate today. Moreover, the implication of moving towards a blockchain general ledger and the hurdles are also discussed.

The chapter "Blockchain and the Financial Industry" provides a contextual background of blockchain technology in the financial industry, as well as an overview of the

ICO regulatory frameworks and the developments concerning the recent trend of launching security token offerings (STOs), by analyzing how regulators from different countries decided to handle the phenomenon.

The chapter "Legal Aspects of Blockchain Technology: Smart Contracts, Intellectual Property, and Data Protection" reviews the promised benefits of blockchain from the legal perspective to provide a general understanding on how the technology interacts with three major fields of law. Moreover, intellectual property law aspect, covering the potential benefits brought about by blockchain-based systems to holders – and users – of copyright, registered and unregistered trademarks and designs, as well as trade secrets are also introduced.

The chapter "Prediction of Cryptocurrency Market Price Using Deep Learning and Blockchain Information: Bitcoin and Ethereum" introduce the prediction accuracy of both Bitcoin and Ethereum currencies using historical data. Moreover, by undertaking a descriptive analysis for blockchain attributes, the deep learning prediction approach was found to be very effective for analyzing blockchain and cryptocurrency data set. The price prediction of the cryptocurrency market price is vital as Bitcoin and Ethereum are effective in the present financial market.

The editors have assembled an impressive book consisting of 16 chapters, written by 45 authors. Although authors come from different disciplines and subfields, their journey is the same: to discover the essentials of blockchain technology. The chapters are well-written by various authors who are active researchers or practical experts in the area related to or in blockchain technology. *Essentials of Blockchain Technology* will contribute tremendously to the blockchain technology and help to find an appropriately implemented in the financial services industry. Also, it will have a high impact on the Internet, IoT, cloud computing and big data.

I would like to thank and congratulate the editors for their energy and dedication in putting together this significant volume. Recently, a number of enterprises, and institutions have launched their study in the field of blockchain. This book has great potential to provide original idea to apply the blockchain in health, IoT, Fintech, as well as other segments of the industry and our society.

Joseph K. Liu
Monash University, Australia

Acknowledgments

First and foremost, we would like to thank and acknowledge the contributors to this volume for their support and patience, and the reviewers for their useful comments and suggestions that helped in improving the earlier outline of the book and presentation of the material. We extend our deepest thanks to Randi Cohen from CRC Press (USA) for her collaboration, guidance, and most importantly, patience in finalizing this book. Finally, we would like to acknowledge the efforts of the team from CRC Press's production department for their extensive efforts during the many phases of this project and the timely fashion in which the book was produced. Lastly, the support in part by Overseas Expertise Introduction Center for Discipline Innovation and China 111 project (No. B16037) is acknowledged.

Editors

Kuan-Ching Li is a professor of computer science and information engineering at Providence University, Taiwan. He is a recipient of distinguished chair professorships from universities in China and other countries. He has also received awards and funding support from a number of agencies and industrial companies. He has been actively involved in many major conferences and workshops in program/general/steering conference chairman positions and has organized numerous conferences related to high-performance computing and computational science and engineering. He is a fellow of IET, a senior member of the IEEE, and a member of the AAAS. Besides the publication of more than 200 research papers, he is co-author/co-editor of several technical professional books published by CRC Press, Springer, McGraw-Hill, and IGI Global. His research interests include GPU/many-core computing, Big Data, and Cloud.

Xiaofeng Chen is a professor of school of cyber engineering at Xidian University. His research interests include applied cryptography and cloud computing security. He has published over 200 research papers in refereed international conferences and journals. His work has been cited more than 8000 times at Google Scholar. He is in the Editorial Board of IEEE Transactions on Dependable and Secure Computing, Security and Privacy, and Computing and Informatics (CAI). He has served as the program/general chair or program committee member in over 30 international conferences.

Hai Jiang is a professor in the Department of Computer Science at Arkansas State University, Jonesboro, Arkansas. His current research interests include Parallel and Distributed Systems, Computer and Network Security, High-Performance Computing and Communication, Big Data, and Modeling and Simulation. He has published one book and research papers in major international journals and conference proceedings. He has served as a U.S. National Science Foundation proposal review panelists and a U.S. DoE (Department of Energy) Smart Grid Investment Grant (SGIG) reviewer multiple times. He has served as a general or program co-chair as well as member of the program committee for some major conferences/workshops (CSE, HPCC, ISPA, GPC, ScaleCom, ESCAPE, GPU-Cloud, FutureTech, GPUTA, FC, SGC). He is a professional member of ACM, IEEE computer society, and U.S. NSF XSEDE (Extreme Science and Engineering Discovery Environment) Campus Champion for Arkansas State University.

Elisa Bertino joined Purdue in January 2004 as a professor of computer science and research director at CERIAS, Purdue University. Her research interests cover many areas in the fields of information security and database systems. Her research combines both theoretical and practical aspects, addressing applications on a number of domains, such as medicine and humanities. Current research includes access control systems, secure publishing techniques, and secure broadcast for XML data; advanced RBAC models and foundations of access control models; trust negotiation languages and privacy; data mining and security; multi-strategy filtering systems for Web pages and sites; security for grid computing systems; integration of virtual reality techniques and databases; and geographical information systems and spatial databases. Professor Bertino has served on the editorial boards of several journals, and general or program co-chair as well a member of the program committee of many conferences related to security. Professor Bertino is a fellow of the IEEE and ACM. She received the IEEE Computer Society Technical Achievement award in 2002 for outstanding contributions to database systems and database security and advanced data management systems and received the 2005 Tsutomu Kanai Award by the IEEE Computer Society for pioneering and innovative research contributions to secure distributed systems.

Contributors

Mamun Abu-Tair
Ulster University
Coleraine, UK

Aftab Ali
Ulster University
Coleraine, UK

Aranka Anema
Globalhealthpx
Vancouver, Canada

Muhammad Rizwan Asghar
Department of Computer Science
The University of Auckland
Auckland, New Zealand

Paolo Balboni
ICT Legal Consulting
Milan, Italy
Maastricht University
Maastricht, The Netherlands

Martim Taborda Barata
ICT Legal Consulting
Milan, Italy

Elizabeth Bautista
Lawrence Berkeley National Laboratory
Berkeley, California

Giacomo Bocale
DWF
Milan, Italy

Vladimir Budzko
National Research Nuclear University
   MEPhI
Moscow, Russian Federation

Bert-Jan Butijn
JADS
The Netherlands

Edward Chen
University of Massachusetts Lowell
Massachusetts

Miguel Correia
Department of Informatics
   Engineering
Instituto Superior Técnico (IST)
   of Universidade de Lisboa
   (ULisboa)
Lisboa, Portugal

Giovanni Cucchiarato
DWF
Milan, Italy

Joshua Daniel
British Telecom
Newport, United Kingdom

Maniklal Das
Dhirubhai Ambani Institute of
   Information and Communication
   Technology (DA-IICT)
Gandhinagar, Gujarat, India

Gery Ducatel
British Telecom
Newport, United Kingdom

Dr. David R. Firth
College of Business
University of Montana
Missoula, Montana

Hisham Haddad
Department of Information Technology
Kennesaw State University
Marietta, Georgia

Malka Halgamuge
University of Melbourne
Melbourne, Australia

Ullah, Hanif
Ulster University
Coleraine, UK

Irfan Ul Haq
Pakistan Institute of Engineering and
    Applied Sciences
Islamabad, Pakistan

Mohammad Mustafa Helal
Department of Computer Science
The University of Auckland
Auckland, New Zealand

Willem-Jan van den Heuvel
Tilburg University
Tilburg, The Netherlands

Alexander Houghton
Globalhealthpx
Vancouver, Canada

Muhammad Usama Irfan
Pakistan Institute of Engineering and
    Applied Sciences
Islamabad, Pakistan

Victoria Lemieux
University of British Columbia
Vancouver, Canada

Zhiwei Lin
Ulster University
Coleraine, UK

Natalia Miloslavskaya
National Research Nuclear University
    MEPhI
Moscow, Russian Federation

Philip Morrow
Ulster University
Coleraine, UK

Muhammad Muneeb
Pakistan Institute of Engineering and
    Applied Sciences
Islamabad, Pakistan

Huma Pervez
Pakistan Institute of Engineering and
    Applied Sciences
Islamabad, Pakistan

Feiyang Qu
Department of Information
    Technology
Kennesaw State University
Marietta, Georgia

Kashif Rabbani
Ulster University
Coleraine, UK

Joe Rafferty
Ulster University
Coleraine, UK

Liuyang Ren
University of Waterloo
Ontario, Canada

Tiago António Baptista Cabrita Arriegas Rosado
Department of Informatics Engineering
Instituto Superior Técnico (IST) of
  Universidade de Lisboa (ULisboa)
Lisboa, Portugal

John-George Sample
Slippery Rock University of Pennsylvania
Pennsylvania

Gulani Senthuran
Charles Sturt University
Melbourne, Australia

Hossain Shahriar
Department of Information Technology
Kennesaw State University
Marietta, Georgia

Nitin Sukhija
Slippery Rock University of Pennsylvania
Pennsylvania

Isho Tama-Sweet
College of Business
University of Montana
Missoula, Montana

Alexander Tolstoy
National Research Nuclear University
  MEPhI
Moscow, Russian Federation

Chandana Unnithan
Torrens University Australia
Adelaide, Australia

André Vasconcelos
Department of Informatics Engineering
Instituto Superior Técnico (IST) of
  Universidade de Lisboa (ULisboa)
Lisboa, Portugal

Paul A.S. Ward
University of Waterloo
Ontario, Canada

Essentials of Blockchain Technology

A ll types of transactions such as purchase orders, payments, account tracking, and delivery tracking may take place every single second. The business goal is to ensure the smooth completion of end-to-end transactions and reduce vulnerabilities. More and more people are looking at new technology – blockchain. A blockchain – originally block chain – is a continuously growing list of records, called blocks, which are linked and secured using cryptography. Each block contains a hash pointer typically as a link to a previous block, a timestamp and transaction data. By design, blockchains are inherently resistant to modification of the data. A blockchain is an open, distributed ledger that can record transactions between two parties efficiently and in a verifiable and permanent way. As a promising technique to achieve decentralized consensus, blockchain helps achieve benefits critical to enterprises and create extraordinary opportunities for businesses to come together in new ways. Particularly in finance, it has been successfully applied to digital cryptocurrencies, and blockchain-based systems have received significant attention in both academia and industry. Inspired by this challenging paradigm, this book covers the significant technical aspects and applications of blockchain technology. In the following, we will describe the chapters contained in the book.

Chapter 1, "Distributed Consensus and Fault Tolerance Mechanisms," by Liuyang Ren and Paul A.S. Ward, focuses on distributed consensus, the heart of blockchain-based systems. Distributed consensus protocols glue individual computers together to provide a reliable service to the outside world. This necessitates the fault-tolerant property of consensus protocols—faults may occur within the system but should not be noticed by clients. Although Nakamoto Consensus Protocol of Bitcoin allows tens of thousands of nodes to participate in the consensus process, the system performance does not increase as more nodes join the network. This is also the common issue of, if not all, most consensus protocols no matter they are Byzantine-fault-tolerant or not. This chapter elaborates the consensus problem and consensus protocols in distributed systems, fault-tolerant mechanisms in blockchain-based systems, and the tradeoff between consensus and performance. Based on the knowledge, this chapter also introduces related research on scalable consensus protocols for blockchain-based networks.

Chapter 2, "Validation Services for Permissioned Blockchains," by David Firth and Isho Tama-Sweet, covers the needs, methods, and implications of validating transactions prior to recording on a permissioned blockchain. It begins with a comparison of permissioned and permissionless blockchains, explains why the differences in blockchain format lead to different methods of transaction validation and discuss why permissioned blockchains require validation services. Next, it explains how to validate transactions using robotic process automation (RPA), and details the three underlying technologies RPA uses: optical character recognition, advanced Excel macros, and proprietary tools based on application program interfaces. Finally, the implications for accounting, auditing, and technology services are discussed. A detailed example of customer-supplier transactions is used throughout the chapter to facilitate comprehension.

Chapter 3, "From Byzantine Consensus to Blockchains," by Miguel Correia, has pointed out that blockchains trade performance and resource-usage efficiency for security. They are implemented by a set of nodes that store the same state and run an algorithm to make consensus over the order of transactions, even if some of the nodes misbehave (are "Byzantine"). This aspect work—replication plus consensus despite misbehavior work—is a constant topic of research since the late 1970s. Interestingly, despite all this research effort, Nakamoto, the author or authors of Bitcoin, decided to use an entirely different approach to achieve consensus—proof-of-work—in the system that implements that cryptocurrency. This chapter presents state of the art in the area of Byzantine consensus and its application in blockchains, from classical algorithms to those used in blockchains and those that combine both approaches.

Chapter 4, "Smart Contracts: State of the Art versus State of Practice," by Bert-Jan Butijn and Willem-Jan van den Heuvel, indicates that recently blockchain-based smart contracts have attracted increasing attention of practitioners and scholars alike as they seem to offer tantalizing possibilities to automate and better control the deployment, execution, management, and governance of collaborative processes. While blockchain currently suffers from healthy skepticism, the authors proclaim that with blockchain-based smart contracts will emerge from the dust as the de-facto enabler of digital transformation. This chapter introduces smart contract as an emerging distributed computing enterprise technology to enact collaborative processes, and contrast the state-of-the-art, cutting-edge developments in R&D and puts with the actual state-of-practice in the industry at large.

Chapter 5, "Towards Preserving Privacy and Security in Blockchain," by Mohammad Mustafa Helal and Muhammad Rizwan Asghar, aims at presenting a privacy-preserving model for ensuring the privacy in the blockchain. The proposed approach is based on White-Box Cryptography (WBC) to ensure privacy in smart contracts. The authors aim to transform the smart contract into an obfuscated smart contract, shipped to the blockchain node along with the private assets hidden within the contract implementation. In this way, a system is introduced to protect sensitive data. First, the new system is resistant to the most severe attacks including MatE and the white-box attacks, which enable the attacker to gain full control of the execution environment. Furthermore, storing sensitive data in an encrypted form within the obfuscated smart contract prevents information leakage.

Chapter 6, "Application of Blockchain and Smart Contract: Approaches and Challenges," by Feiyang Qu, Hisham Haddad and Hossain Shahriar, states that blockchain technology enables sharing information between individual computers. The potential of blockchain application is not only in e-currency but also in secure data sharing and identity management. Ethereum is a representative example of a blockchain-based platform. Created by Vitalik Buterin, Ethereum is an open software construct based on smart contracts. The contract is one kind of account in Ethereum. The contract can not only read codes and currency in a transaction but also create another contract for reading code and writing into storage. In this book chapter, the authors perform an in-depth survey of some recent examples and applications of blockchain and smart contracts.

Chapter 7, "Blockchain Application for IoT Cybersecurity Management," by Natalia Miloslavskaya, Alexander Tolstoy, Vladimir Budzko and Maniklal Das, covers three interdisciplinary, observable, and rapidly developing areas of research, namely the Internet of Things (IoT) technologies, the blockchain (BC) technologies (BCT), and cybersecurity management for the IoT. The chapter is organized as follows: after a short introduction, the IoT technologies are discussed, including the IoT concept and definitions, generalized IoT architecture and reference model proposed, and the IoT standardization issues. The second part of the chapter is devoted to the BCT and their application areas, as well as to a BC glossary worked by the authors and the list of standards for the BCT. On this basis, two main directions of applying the BCT to the IoT are represented, namely for designing BC-based secure IoT infrastructure and BC-based system for managing cybersecurity in the IoT. Final discussion and future research areas conclude the Chapter.

Chapter 8, "IoT Security using Blockchain," by Hanif Ullah, Mamun Abu-Tair, Aftab Ali, Kashif Rabbani, Joshua Daniel, Joe Rafferty, Zhiwei Lin, Philip Morrow and Gery Ducatel, addresses security issues with respect to the Internet of Things (IoT) and in particular investigates the use of blockchain technology to address these issues. Some foundational concepts, related to the topic are highlighted, including smart contracts, verifiable claims, self-sovereign identity, along with General Data Protection Regulation (GDPR) and Network and Information Security (NIS) principles. Beyond the block chain-based solution, a secure IoT architecture based on blockchain technology is also presented.

Chapter 9, "Blockchain in Global Health – An appraisal of Current and Future Applications," by Chandana Unnithan, Victoria Lemieux, Alexander Houghton, and Aranka Anema, introduces a secure and reliable Blockchain-based method of recording and sharing sensitive data in the health sector. This chapter aims at synthesizing some current applications of this technology in the global health sector and offers an outlook. Initially, readers are introduced to the relevant global health landscape through relevant policy and regulatory frameworks, notably the United Nations Sustainable Development Goals (UN SDGs) pertaining to health. Subsequently, it describes the role of various stakeholders, latest developments, pilots and opportunities in the application of blockchain to health that can benefit patients, providers, payers and researcher communities. A critical appraisal follows synthesizing the challenges leading into an outlook where the proliferation of blockchain technologies in health enabled further by MIoT can better support public health around the world.

Chapter 10, "A Blockchain Use Case for Car Registration," by André Vasconcelos, Miguel Correia and Tiago Rosado, presents a car registration system based on the Hyperledger Fabric blockchain technology. This system considers several government entities in a single country, but might be extended to a cross-border scenario, possibly supporting car data sharing at the level of the European Union. The system – Bcar – handles the processes related to car registration management, e.g., registering a vehicle, changing ownership status, and registering a leasing contract between a lessor and a lessee. This system can simplify the information exchange among multiple states as the car registration information is distributed to each government entity in a single decentralized system. The authors analyze the benefits and implications of the blockchain technology application and present an evaluation of the system's performance.

Chapter 11, "Advancing the Cybersecurity of EVM Using Blockchain," by Nitin Sukhija, John-George Sample and Elizabeth Bautista, points out that blockchain is one of the powerful emerging technology that is diverse, dynamic and promises substantial resiliency against malicious adversaries when employed in the advanced, unpredictable, and heterogeneous computing ecosystems, such as financial services industry, national cyberinfrastructures and more. One of the most significant benefits of blockchain technology is its inherent resiliency to cyber-attacks. While blockchain is not immune to all forms of cyber risk, its exceptional configuration facilitates cybersecurity features that are not currently present in the traditional ledgers and other legacy technologies. Consequently, a comprehensive study of how blockchains may fit within broader cybersecurity objectives is of paramount importance, especially for researchers from both academic and industrial domains dealing with facilitating innovative solutions for enabling cybersecurity in their respective domains. This chapter presents an implementation of the electronic voting machine (EVM) illustrating the applicability of emerging blockchain technology-based solutions to address current and emerging cybersecurity threats.

Chapter 12, "Implementing the Blockchain Technology in the Financial Services Industry," by Edward T. Chen, focuses on how this blockchain technology should be appropriately implemented in the financial services industry. Once widely overlooked by many due to its association with the controversial digital currency Bitcoin, the underlying technology, the blockchain, has become a large area of focus for most major financial institutions. At its core, the blockchain serves as an immutable, secure, distributed ledger shared amongst the participants connected to it. The primary attributes of the blockchain, including transparency, speed of settlement, security, and automation, have the potential to significantly change the way financial institutions operate today. This chapter will also address the implications of moving towards a Blockchain general ledger and the hurdles that must be overcome.

Chapter 13, "Blockchain and the Financial Industry," by Giovanni Cucchiarato and Giacomo Bocale, shows that Blockchain has experienced impressive growth and has expanded beyond its initial close ties with Bitcoin. Moreover, it has clearly demonstrated its ability to operate as an autonomous technological innovation in the eyes of both investors and institutions. One of the areas in which Blockchain has emerged as a particularly important player, is that of initial coin offerings (ICOs). ICOs offer an innovative new way of raising capital for companies based on the emission of "digital tokens" through blockchain-based platforms. This shift in market practice, together with the development and widespread adoption of innovative finance-related tools and services (commonly identified as "FinTech") has prompted global regulators and national supervisory authorities to play a more prominent regulatory role. This is a significant change from the soft regulatory approach (that can be traced back to the "*Do no harm approach*" pursued by the US Commodity Future Trading Commission) that was averse to stifling the FinTech-related stream of innovation. It is now clear, however, that a more sophisticated regulatory approach will look towards designing comprehensive regulatory frameworks that guarantee investor protection and market integrity. This chapter provides a contextual background of blockchain technology in the financial industry, as well as an overview of the ICO regulatory frameworks and of the developments concerning the recent trend of launching security token offerings (STOs), by analyzing how regulators from different countries decided to handle the phenomenon.

Chapter 14, "Legal Aspects of Blockchain Technology: Smart Contracts, Intellectual Property and Data Protection," by Paolo Balboni and Martim Taborda Barata, expresses that in the field of law, particularly, novel technologies often collide with existing regulations, which may be too slow or rigid to adapt to the innovative functionalities explored, and blockchain is no exception to this. In this chapter, the authors take a look at blockchain's promised benefits from the legal perspective in order to provide a general understanding on how the technology is seen to interact with three major fields of law. Firstly, with respect to contract law they analyze, in particular, the implications blockchain technology may bring for smart contracts. Secondly, they deal with intellectual property law aspect, covering the potential benefits brought about by blockchain-based systems to holders – and users – of copyright, registered and unregistered trademarks and designs, as well as trade secrets). Thirdly, concerning personal data protection law they focus on the contradictions between blockchain and the European General Data Protection Regulation – some merely apparent, while others unavoidable – and explore the ways in which the use of blockchain allows for, and even potentially enhances, the practical implementation of the principles of data protection by design and, more specifically, fairness by design.

Chapter 15, "Prediction of Cryptocurrency Market Price Using Deep Learning and Blockchain Information: Bitcoin and Ethereum," by Gulani Senthuran and Malka N. Halgamuge, points out that Bitcoin and Ethereum are widely used at present in global financial markets and so far, have received a significant value improvement and market capitalization with Ethereum being more impervious to downgrading than the other cryptocurrencies. The main aim of this chapter is to ascertain the prediction accuracy of both Bitcoin and Ethereum currencies using historical data (Blockchain data with cryptocurrency data). This is the first study that the authors are aware of that predicts cryptocurrency prices using a Deep learning algorithm and blockchain information (Bitcoin and Ethereum). To accomplish this task, the blockchain data (2015–2018) of both Bitcoin and Ethereum currencies were collected to enhance the security and the prediction rate. Further, the market price of Bitcoin and Ethereum currencies were retrieved online. The effectiveness of the prediction accuracy was investigated using Deep learning approach with cryptocurrency data and blockchain data. The results of data analysis showed that when the blockchain data were used together with Bitcoin and Ethereum Prices, the prediction performance is high for both currencies. In addition, the comparison between Bitcoin and Ethereum revealed that Ethereum currency has the highest percentage of the prediction accuracy and the lowest error rate. Moreover, descriptive analysis was undertaken for blockchain attributes such as difficulty, hash rate, number of transactions, average block size and miner's revenue. The blockchain data directly influenced the prediction accuracy of these both currencies (Bitcoin and Ethereum). The deep learning prediction approach was found to be very effective for analyzing blockchain and cryptocurrency data set. The price prediction of the cryptocurrency market price is vital as Bitcoin and Ethereum are effective in the present financial market.

Overall, this book represents a substantial research contribution to state-of-the-art studies on blockchain technology and practical achievements in the Internet of Things and financial sectors. The editors are confident that this book will help university students, researchers, and professionals understand the significant issues in Blockchain technology as well as the corresponding strategies to tackle them in real cases.

CHAPTER 1

Distributed Consensus and Fault Tolerance Mechanisms

Liuyang Ren and Paul A. S. Ward

University of Waterloo, Ontario

CONTENTS

B lockchain-based systems are essentially distributed systems, at the heart of which lies distributed consensus. Distributed consensus protocols glue individual computers together to provide a reliable service to the outside world. This necessitates the fault-tolerant property of consensus protocols—faults may occur within the system but should not be noticed by clients.

1.1 INTRODUCTION

The goal of consensus is to increase system reliability. Unreliability in a distributed system comes from two sources: (1) communication channels, e.g., messages may be delayed, duplicated, lost, or reordered and (2) nodes, e.g., a node may crash or behave maliciously. Malicious behavior includes but not restricted to: send inconsistent messages to different nodes; tamper with messages sent by other nodes; sniff network traffic.

Depending on the failure model, a distributed system can be either a fail-stop system or a Byzantine-fault-tolerant system. In a fail-stop system, communication channels can be unreliable but nodes behave in a predictable way—they either work correctly or stop working. In contrast, both communication channels and nodes are unreliable in a Byzantine-fault-tolerant system.

Paxos and Raft are consensus protocols tolerating fail-stop failures and widely used to coordinate computers in a cluster because a cluster is usually under the control of a single entity and hence Byzantine-fault-free. However, these protocols do not apply to blockchain-based systems, where nodes may fail arbitrarily (Byzantine failure). Conventional Byzantine-fault-tolerant consensus protocols, such as Practical Byzantine Fault Tolerance (PBFT), require message exchange among nodes, and this communication overhead increases quickly as the network grows. Nakamoto Consensus of Bitcoin is arguably the first Byzantine-fault-tolerant consensus protocol that scales to 10,000 nodes.

Although Nakamoto Consensus allows tens of thousands of nodes to participate in the consensus process, the system performance does not increase as more nodes join the network. This is also the common issue of, if not all, most consensus protocols no matter they are Byzantine-fault-tolerant or not. Actually, searching for high-throughput and low-latency consensus protocols is currently a hot research topic.

In this chapter, we elaborate the consensus problem and consensus protocols in distributed systems, fault-tolerant mechanisms in blockchain-based systems, and the tradeoff between consensus and performance. Based on the knowledge, we introduce related research on scalable consensus protocols for blockchain-based systems.

1.2 DISTRIBUTED CONSENSUS

Computers forming a consensus group can be modeled as a Replicated State Machine (RSM), where state machines on different processors execute the exact same deterministic commands in the same order and, therefore, produce the same result. One way to achieve this is to employ a replicated log. Every command has to be replicated to all the logs before it can be executed, so the state machines will be in the same state as long as the logs are identical. Figure 1.1 illustrates that five steps are involved to execute the command *set x as 4*:

1. A client submits the command $x \leftarrow 4$ to Server S1;

2. S1 forwards the command to both S2 and S3;

3. S1, S2 and S3 append the command to the end of their logs;

4. State machines on S1, S2 and S3 execute the command;

5. S1 return the result back to the client.

Step 3 is the most challenging one because servers must communicate with each other to discover whether others agree to append the command to their logs.

In this section, we first introduce consensus protocols used in fail-stop systems, Paxos and Raft, to provide a good background of the consensus problem, and then we discuss Byzantine-fault-tolerant consensus protocols. You will see Raft and Nakamoto Consensus directly resort to the replicated log approach; Multi-Paxos and PBFT also adopt this approach indirectly.

1.2.1 Paxos

Paxos was a family of consensus protocols for fail-stop systems first published in 1998 by Leslie Lamport [2], a Turning Award winner. Paxos decomposes the consensus problem as [3]:

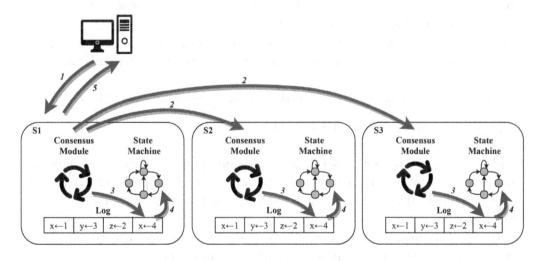

FIGURE 1.1   Replicated State Machine (RSM) [1]

1. Basic Paxos
   One or more servers propose values;
   The system must agree on one single value;
   Once the single value is chosen, it cannot be changed.

2. Multi-PaxosThe system agrees on a series of values, which together form a log, by runninga Basic Paxos instance for each value.

1.2.1.1 Basic Paxos

The goal of Basic Paxos is to achieve consensus on a single value among processes, and once this value is chosen, it cannot be changed in the future. Paxos defines three roles: *Proposer, Acceptor*, and *Learner*. A proposer receives client requests asking for a specific value (e.g., a state machine command) to be chosen, proposes the value to acceptors, and actively moves forward the protocol in order to convince acceptors to choose the value. Acceptors vote for a proposed value from proposers, and their votes are collected by proposers to decide which value has been chosen. Learners take action (e.g., execute a code piece) based on the chosen value and return results to clients and, therefore, must be informed once a value is chosen. A single processor can play one or more roles at the same time.

Paxos is a two-phase protocol, a prepare phase followed by a commit phase. Figure 1.2 illustrates message exchanges between a client and the three roles. The two round trips between the proposer and the acceptors can be subdivided into four stages.

Phase 1a: Prepare. A proposer chooses a proposal identifier number n, higher than any previous numbers it used, for this request. Then the proposer sends *Prepare* (n) message to a majority of acceptors.

Phase 1b: Promise. Each acceptor maintains a variable *minId*, which is the highest proposal identifier it has ever seen and, also, the minimum proposal identifier it can accept. If receiving a *Prepare* (n) message whose n is greater than *minId*, an acceptor promises the proposer that it will not accept any proposals numbered less than n by setting *minId* $= n$ and returning (*acceptId, acceptValue*) to the proposer. Otherwise, the acceptor just ignores the *Prepare* (n) message.

Phase 2a: Accept Request. If the proposer receives responses from a majority of acceptors, it then sends an accept request *accept_req(n, value)* to those acceptors where *value* is:

(a) *acceptValue* with highest *acceptId* returned by acceptors in Phase 1b; or

(b) *V* if all *acceptId* and *acceptValue* are *null*

Therefore, if a value has been chosen (case a), all future proposers will not be allowed to request acceptors to accept other values. In the case that the proposer receives not enough responses, the proposer restarts the protocol restart from Phase 1a with a higher n.

Phase 2b: Accepted. An acceptor check if the n in a received *accept_req(n, value)* message is greater than or equal to its local *minId*. If so, it sets

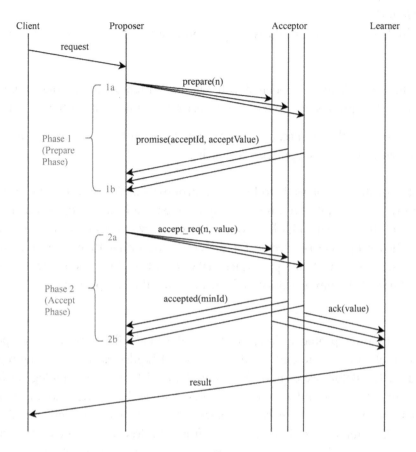

FIGURE 1.2   Message exchange of Basic Paxos. Three acceptors can tolerate one faulty acceptor.

$acceptId = n$;
$acceptValue = value$;
$minId = n$.

Then it sends back an *accept(minId)* message with *minId* to acknowledge the proposer. Otherwise, the acceptor directly returns *minId* without updating its local states (*acceptId, acceptValue,* and *minId*) to inform the proposer it has promised not to accept any proposals with identifier lower than *minId*.

Finally, the proposer waits for *accepted (minId)* from a majority of acceptors. If any returned *minId* is greater than *n*, then the proposer knows acceptors failed to accept the proposal and it has to restart from Phase 1a and choose a proposal identifier number higher than *minId*. Otherwise, the *value* has been successfully agreed on. Learners will hear the value from a majority of acceptors, take action, and return the result to the client.

The majority rule guarantees that at least one acceptor can see conflicting proposals. Paxos demands $2f + 1$ acceptors to tolerate f faulty ones such that when all faulty nodes fail, the remaining $f + 1$ nodes still constitute a majority allowing the protocol to advance.

1.2.1.2 Multi-Paxos

Using multiple Basic Paxos instances to agree on a series of values forming a log has two problems:

1. Conflicts are likely to happen due to the co-existence of multiple proposers. For example, two proposers may attempt to place their proposals in the same log entry.

2. Running both phases (Prepare and Accept) for each log entry results in significant overhead (a four-message delay for each entry).

The purpose of the first phase is to block old proposals and discover any chosen values. When one relatively stable proposer is designated as the leader without other contending proposers, the Prepare phase becomes unnecessary. In other words, a leader (i.e., a distinguished proposer) is selected for the entire log rather than a specific entry. The leader can send the next accept request (Phase 2a) as long as it receives *accepted* messages (Phase 2b) from a majority of acceptors for the last proposal.

1.2.2 Raft

Raft is a consensus protocol designed for understandability [4]. It decomposes the consensus problem in a different way than Paxos: (1) Leader election, (2) Log replication, and (3) Safety [1]. Before we explore the details, let us define the terminology of Raft.

Server states—*Leader, Candidate*, and *Followers*. A leader is a server who interacts directly with clients. There is always at most one leader in the system, and leaders typically operate until they fail. A follower receives messages from the leader and responds accordingly. Followers are completely passive and never add or remove log entries independently. A candidate is a server who assumes itself to be the leader and asks for confirmatory votes from other servers. The transition among the three states is shown in Figure 1.3.

System states—*Leader-election* and *Log-replication*. In the *Leader-election* state, no leader is established and the cluster does not respond to client requests. Servers keep running a leader-election protocol until a leader emerges, and then the system enters the

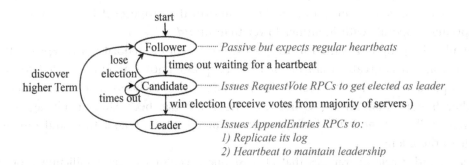

FIGURE 1.3 Server states and transitions. "Lose election" means a candidate receives heartbeats from some server that has already won the election or it discovers a higher Term number [1]

Log replication state and is able to service clients. If the leader crashes, the system goes back to the *Leader-election* state.

Messages—*RequestVote* and *AppendEntries* Remote Procedure Calls (RPCs). *RequestVote* RPCs are initiated by candidates to request votes from other servers. *AppendEntries* are initiated by a leader to replicate its log on followers, as well as send heartbeats to followers to maintain its leadership.

Log entry identification—*Term and Index. Each log entry has a Term number and Index number associated with it. Index is an incremental natural number indicating the position of a specific log entry. Based on leader changes, time is divided into arbitrarily long slots called Terms. No more than one leader can exist in a Term.*

1.2.2.1 Leader Election

Some Terms have no leader (Term 3 in Figure 1.4) because of a failed leader election, e.g. in a 5-server cluster, 3 servers transition to the Candidate state, splitting votes into 2, 2, 1 (no one receives votes from a majority). To ensure that split votes are rare and are resolved quickly, Raft uses randomized election timeouts. Followers choose timeouts randomly from a fixed interval (e.g., 150–300 ms) and transition to the Candidate state once they have timed out. With high probability, one server times out first, wins the election, and sends heartbeats to other servers before any other server times out. If a rare split vote occurs, each candidate increments its Term number, restarts its randomized election timeout, waits for the timeout to elapse, and then sends out RequestVote RPC again.

Terms, increasing monotonically over time, act as a logical clock in Raft and enable servers to detect lags among them. Servers include Term numbers in both the two types of RPCs. If a follower finds that its current Term number is smaller than those of any other server, it brings itself up-to-date by increasing its Term number to the largest one it has seen; if a candidate or leader discovers a higher Term number, in addition to updating the local Term number, it also reverts to the follower state because a higher Term number means there is at least one more updated server in the cluster who is more eligible to be a leader. Servers receiving RPCs with obsolete Term numbers do not fulfill the call and instead return an error message.

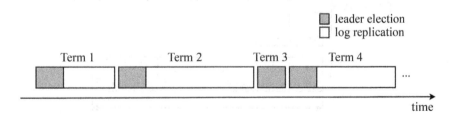

FIGURE 1.4 Time is divided into Terms. Each Term starts with leader election, followed by log replication if a leader emerges. If servers fail to reach consensus on who should be the leader of a Term due to, for example, split votes, the current Term will have no log replication part [4].

1.2.2.2 Log Replication

Figure 1.5 shows the Raft log structure. In addition to a client request (e.g., $x \leftarrow 3$ command at the first log entry), each log entry also stores the Term number when the leader of the cluster receives this command from the client. A leader sends AppendEntries RPC with client requests as an argument to followers. As long as it receives responses from a majority of the servers (including the leader itself), the leader executes the request on its local state machine and returns the result to the client. This procedure leads to optimal performance—one RPC to each server of the majority to commit a request. The leader does not wait for the execution results from followers, because once the log entry reaches a majority of servers in the current Term, it will definitely be executed by the system. This execution is carried out even if the leader crashes after replying to the client because a future leader sees this entry and replicates it to all servers. This action is ensured by certain additional requirements on winning an election, which will be explained in 1.2.2.3. Similar to Basic Paxos, the majority rule also justifies why $2f + 1$ servers are necessary to tolerate f faulty servers.

Whenever a follower's log differs from the leader's, the leader replicates its own log to the follower. In an AppendEntries RPC, the leader includes the Index and Term of the immediately proceeding entry of the entry to be replicated. If the follower does not have an entry with the same Index and Term number, it refuses to append the new entry. Figure 1.6 illustrates a follower's log may miss some entries, contain stale entries, or both. To accomplish log replication, the leader first finds the latest log entry that it and the

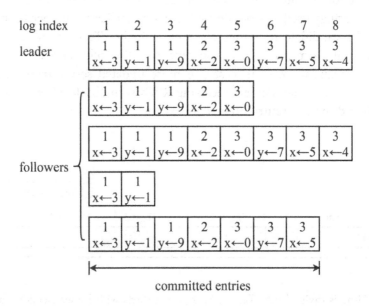

FIGURE 1.5 Log entries are numbered by indices. Each log entry includes a Term number and a command [4].

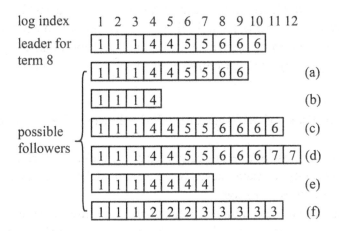

FIGURE 1.6   Possible follower logs [4]

follower agree on, and then sends all following entries in its own log to the follower to replace the follower's log entries. A leader maintains a *nextIndex* for each follower, which is the next log entry the leader will send to the follower. If the AppendEntries RPC fails, the leader decrements *nextIndex* and issue AppendEntries RPC again until the RPC returns successfully. At this point, the leader knows that the follower's log is identical to its own log up through the *nextIndex*, so it can send succeeding entries to bring the follower's log up-to-date.

1.2.2.3 Safety (Leader Crash Handling)
As described in 1.2.2.2, a leader replicates its log to followers provided any discrepancy exists. This mechanism assumes the leader's log is always perfectly correct (hold all committed entries). Additional election restrictions are added to guarantee this property.

Log entries are ranked by $\langle LastTerm, LastIndex \rangle$. For example, if two logs have last entries with different Terms, the one with the higher Term is more up-to-date; if two logs end up with the same Term, the one with larger last entry Index (i.e., longer) is more up-to-date. A server denies its vote if it has a more up-to-date log than that of the candidate requesting votes. Each server votes for one leader per Term in a first come, first serve fashion. Since committed entries have been replicated on a majority of servers, and a candidate must contact a majority of the cluster in order to win the election, every committed entry must be present in at least one of the contacted servers. If the candidate's log is equally or more up-to-date than this server, then it also holds all committed entries and is eligible to become a leader.

Followers do not know if a log entry is committed, even if it returns successfully for the AppendEntries RPC from the leader. This is solved by incorporating a "learderCommit" argument, which is the Index of the highest log entry that the leader knows is committed, in AppendEntries RPCs. Therefore, the leader is able to inform followers up to which entry is committed when it requests followers to append more entries in their log. In the scenario that the leader continuously functions without failure, this is equivalent to piggybacking the commit decision of an entry (or entries) on the request for appending the next entry (or entries).

1.2.2.4 Properties

The above mechanisms of Raft guarantee the following five properties are always true [4].

Election Safety: at most one leader can be elected in a given Term.

Leader Append-Only: a leader never overwrites or deletes entries in its own log; it only appends new entries in its log.

Log Matching: if two logs contain an entry with the same Index and Term, then the logs are identical in all entries up through the given Index. This property implies log entry Index and Term number uniquely define the log up to this entry. Consequently, the last log entry uniquely identifies the entire log.

Leader Completeness: if a log entry is committed in a given Term, then that entry will be present in the logs of the leaders for all higher-numbered Terms.

State Machine Safety: if a server has applied a log entry at a given Index to its state machine, no other server will ever apply a different log entry for the same Index.

1.2.3 Practical Byzantine Fault Tolerance (PBFT)

PBFT is used in HeperLedger Fabric, a permissioned blockchain-based project led by IBM. Proposed in 1999, PBFT is the first efficient solution to the Byzantine fault tolerance in a weakly synchronous environment, e.g., the Internet [5]. We will describe the normal-case operation and view changes of PBFT. PBFT experiences scalability problems and may limit the performance of blockchain-based systems.

1.2.3.1 Overview

The goal of PBFT is to ensure that honest replicas can reach consensus about the service state even in the presence of Byzantine replicas, which may send inconsistent messages to different replicas. Cryptography involvement is almost inevitable in a Byzantine tolerant system to prevent spoofing and replays and to detect corrupted messages. All exchanged messages are signed in PBFT.

In the original PBFT paper, servers are called *replicas*; the one that interacts with clients is called *primary,* and others are called *backup*. PBFT demands at least $3f + 1$ replicas to tolerate f faulty nodes. Assume the total number of replicas is $|R|$ and f of them are faulty. The f Byzantine faulty replicas may not respond, yet the protocol must be able to proceed. However, it is possible the f non-responding replicas are not faulty, but their messages are delayed or dropped by the network instead. In this scenario, the remaining $|R| - f$ responding replicas contain the f faulty ones. Faulty replicas and non-fault replicas may respond to a client with conflicting responses. The client must be able to decide which response is correct; therefore, among the $|R| - f$ responses, responses from non-faulty replicas must outnumber those from faulty ones (i.e., $|R| - f - f > f$). Thus, $|R| > 3f$.

1.2.3.2 Normal-Case Operation

In normal cases, a primary has already been established and continuously functions. A client c sends a signed request $\langle REQUEST, o, t, c \rangle_{\sigma_c}$ to the primary to request the execution of a state machine command o. Timestamp t is included to guarantee the request will be processed exactly once. The primary, p, then starts the three-phase (*pre-prepare*, *prepare*, and *commit*) PBFT protocol as follows.

Pre-prepare. The primary multicasts a pre-prepare message in the form of $\langle\langle PRE - PREPARE, v, n, d \rangle_{\sigma_p}, m \rangle$ to all other replicas and appends it to its own log. v is the view number when p sends out this pre-prepare message. *view* is a concept similar to the *Term* in Raft. When and how view number changes will be depicted in 1.2.3.3. n is the sequence number (resembling the proposal identifier number of Paxos) assigned by p to the request. m is the client request message, and d is the digest of m (e.g., d is the hash of m).

Prepare. A backup i accepts the pre-prepare message and enters the prepare phase by: (1) multicasting $\langle PREPARE, v, n, d, i \rangle_{\sigma_i}$ to all replicas and (2) appends both the pre-prepare and prepare messages to its log if the following conditions are true:

(1) for the pre-prepare message, the signature is valid and d is indeed the digest of m;

(2) i is in view v;

(3) i has not accepted a pre-prepare message with the same v and n but different d;

(4) n is within a specific range. This condition prevents a faulty primary from exhausting the sequence number space by choosing a very large n.

Otherwise, i does nothing.

Commit. A replica r (may be the primary or a backup) accepts a received prepare message by appending it to its log. If r has collected $2f$ prepare messages from different backups and they all match the pre-prepare message in its log, r knows that there are at least $f + 1$ non-faulty replicas ($2f$ backups plus one primary minus at most f faulty replicas) have agreed to assign the sequence number n to the request m and, thus, it is safe to enter the commit phase. Matching means two messages have the same view number, sequence number, and digest. r enters the commit phase by multicasting $\langle COMMIT, v, n, d, r \rangle_{\sigma_r}$ to all replicas. Other replicas also send out commit messages once they enter the commit phase. A replica accepts a commit message by appending it to its log and executes the requested command o if

1) $2f + 1$ matching commit messages (possibly including its own) from different replicas are collected;

2) its state reflects the sequential execution of all requests with a sequence number lower than *n*. This ensures all non-faulty replicas execute requests in the same order and, thus, end up with the same state.

A replica *r* sends a reply $\langle REPLY, v, t, c, r, res \rangle_{\sigma_r}$ back to the client *c* after executing *o*. *c* waits for $f + 1$ replies with the same *t* and *res* from different replicas, certainly also with valid signatures, before accepting the result *res*. Since at most *f* replicas can be faulty, $f + 1$ consistent replies guarantee the client a valid result.

Figure 1.7 illustrates the message exchange of PBFT. The pre-prepare and prepare phases together guarantee that non-faulty replicas agree on the total order of requests in a view. The prepare phase allows PBFT to tolerate a faulty primary.

1.2.3.3 View Changes
The view change protocol allows the system to progress even when the primary fails. A backup *i* starts a timer when it receives a request. If *i* is currently in view *v* and the timer expires, *i* multicasts a view-change message to all replicas to move the system to view $v = 1$. The primary of view *v* is the replica *p* such that $p = v \ mod \ |R|$, so each replica knows who is the primary of view $v + 1$. When the primary p_{v+1} of view $v + 1$ receives $2f$ view-change messages from other replicas, it multicasts a new-view message to all other replicas. A backup accepts a new-view message by appending it to its log. Then the system starts to proceed as described in 2.3.2.

During a view change, replicas stop accepting pre-prepare, prepare, and commit messages. Requests half-way through the three-phase protocol must be migrated to the new view. This involves the checkpointing mechanism of PBFT.[1]

1.2.4 Nakamoto Consensus of Bitcoin
A blockchain system can also be modeled as RSM; the blockchain maintained by every node is essentially a replicated log with entries (i.e., transactions) batched in blocks [5]. Since log entries are transactions that can be verified by any nodes, it is reasonable to call the log *public ledger*. Nodes process the transactions recorded in the blockchain

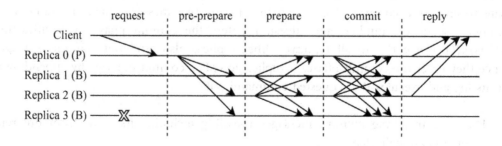

FIGURE 1.7   PBFT normal-case operation. Replica 0 is the primary; others are backups [6].

sequentially and end up with the same state, i.e., the Unspent Transaction Output (UTxO) database.

1.2.4.1 Leader Selection Algorithm—PoW

In Raft, we say a leader is *elected* because it obtains votes from a majority of nodes. However, PoW probabilistically selects a leader based on the computational power of miners. Miners do not need any votes or consents from others to propose a block, so it is more appropriate to call PoW a leader *selection* algorithm.

Miners compete in solving a PoW puzzle for block rewards. Figure 1.8 shows the relation between the header hash and the enclosed content of a block. Since hashing is a one-way function, miners have to adjust some fields and calculate block header hash repetitively. The three adjustable fields in a block are: the *nonce* and *timestamp* in the block header, and the *extraNonce* in the coinbase transaction. A block is valid only if the following inequality is satisfied.

$$SHA256^2\left(H_{prev}||root||nBits||ver||nonce||ts\right) < target \qquad (1.1)$$

where $SHA256^2(\cdot)$ stands for performing the $SHA256$ hash calculation twice; $H_{prev}, root, nBits, ver, nonce, ts$ are the previous block header hash, Merkle root, nBits, version, nonce, and timestamp respectively; "$||$" represents the concatenation operation. *target* is stored in the *nBits* field, which is a 32-bit scientific-notation-like representation of a 256-bit unsigned integer.

Unlike Multi-Paxos, Raft, and PBFT, where leader election protocol is only executed if the current leader fails (or a node lost connection with the leader due to network partition and wrongly presumes the leader fails), Nakamoto Consensus run PoW for every block.

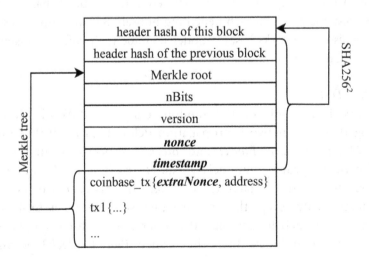

FIGURE 1.8 Bitcoin block structure with highlighted adjustable fields

1.2.4.2 Log Replication

Log replication is achieved by combining gossip protocol, hash chaining, and the longest-chain rule. When a leader is selected, it sends its block to all of its peers, who then forward the block to their peers. Malicious nodes may tamper with the block, but this will invalidate the PoW and, thus, be detected by others. A node accepts a block by appending it to its log/blockchain and referring to it as the previous block in the header of the next block.

PoW does not guarantee exactly one leader is selected every round. If a node receives more than one valid blocks in a round, it will temporarily accept the first one it hears about but also keep the second one in its storage. Future blocks may extend either of the two branches, and the states of nodes may diverge if some nodes execute transactions on one branch whereas other nodes execute those on the other branch. The longest-chain rule eliminates this kind of risk by requiring nodes to only accept blocks on the longest chain. This forking issue and resolving strategies will be further elaborated in Section 1.3.

1.3 FAULT TOLERANCE IN BLOCKCHAIN-BASED SYSTEMS

Forking is an erroneous state of the blockchain, so any cause of forking is a fault. In this section, we analyze three types of fault–imperfection of leader selection rules, malicious attacks, and software updates–and how a blockchain-based system recovers from forks resulted from these faults.

1.3.1 Fork Taxonomy

We say blocks are of the same round if they have the same parent/previous block. PoW does not guarantee only one leader is selected each round; two miners may each find a valid block extending the same parent block. This is called a natural fork since it is a consequence of the randomness of the leader selection mechanism rather than human manipulation. An adversary can also deliberately fork the blockchain with the aim of switching the best chain to a branch benefiting himself. Software upgrades changing the consensus rule also incur forks if some nodes upgrade their software instances to a new version whereas others do not.

1.3.1.1 Natural Fork

A natural fork is a result of the randomness of a PoW-like leader selection algorithm together with network propagation delay. Figure 1.9 illustrates a natural fork where *M* and *N* mine *Block1* and *Block2*, respectively, in the same round. Because of network propagation delay, *Block1* reaches *M, A* and *B* earlier than *Block2* but reaches *N* and *C* later than *Block2*. In this scenario, nodes keep both blocks and temporarily accept the first one they see. The tie is broken by the next block making one branch longer than the other one. If, for example, *Block3* refers to *Block1* as its parent block, then the branch *Block1*←*Block3* becomes the best chain.

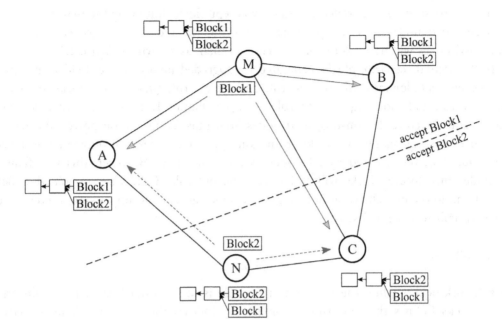

FIGURE 1.9   Network topology when a fork happens. *M, A* and *B* think *Block1* is the tip of current best chain while *N* and *C* think *Block2* is the tip of current best chain.

1.3.1.2 Malicious Fork

Adversaries may deliberately fork the blockchain provided it is lucrative. One example is selfish mining analyzed by Ittay Eyal [8]. To perform selfish mining, an attacker maintains a secret branch and releases all the secret blocks at once when the public branch is about to be as long as the secret one. Since the secret chain is longer, the attacker can get the block rewards of all the secret blocks. Selfish mining enables an attacker to subvert a blockchain-based system with only 25% of the overall computation power of the network [8].

1.3.1.3 Software Upgrade Fork

A software upgrade can introduce forks if it changes the consensus rule. The situation where upgraded nodes and non-upgraded nodes work on two permanently diverging branches is coined as *hard fork*; the situation where they finally agree on the same best chain is coined as *soft fork*.

1. Hard fork

A hard fork occurs when: 1) the new consensus rule and the old consensus rule are completely incompatible or 2) the new consensus rule is less restrictive than the old one (i.e., blocks following the old rule automatically satisfy the new rule).

In the first scenario, upgraded nodes only accept blocks following the new rule, while non-upgraded nodes only accept blocks following the old rule. Upgraded and non-upgraded nodes will never agree on the same branch, as shown in Figure 1.10.

In the second scenario, blocks generated by upgraded nodes can be divided into two classes: blocks following both the new rule and the old rule (new_{old}) or blocks following the new rule but violating the old rule ($new_{!old}$). Figure 1.11 illustrates one possible blockchain structure. If non-upgraded nodes hold most computation power, the upper branch consisting mainly of blocks from non-upgraded nodes will outgrow the lower one and, thus, be accepted by all nodes as the best chain. However, this is a failing upgrade since future blocks will still follow the old rule. Otherwise, upgraded nodes accept the lower branch while non-upgraded nodes accept the upper one, thereby the network fails to reach consensus.

1. Soft fork

A soft fork occurs when the new consensus rule is more restrictive than the old one (i.e., blocks follows the new rule automatically follows the old rule). This scenario

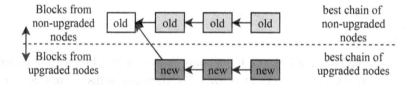

FIGURE 1.10 An example of the blockchain structure where the new consensus rule and the old consensus rule are completely incompatible. Light grey blocks are on the best chain of non-upgraded nodes; dark grey blocks are on the best chain of upgraded nodes.

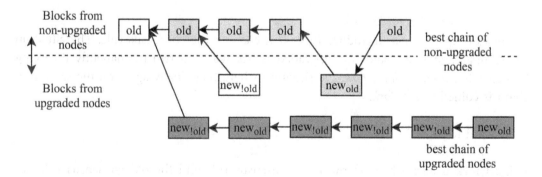

FIGURE 1.11 An example of the blockchain structure where the new consensus rule is less restrictive than the old one. Upgraded nodes hold most computation power. Light grey blocks are on the best chain of non-upgraded nodes; dark grey blocks are on the best chain of upgraded nodes.

"flips" the second case incurring hard forks. Blocks generated by non-upgraded nodes can be divided into two classes: blocks following both the old rule and the new rule (old_{new}) or blocks following the old rule but violating the new rule ($old_{!new}$). Figure 1.12 illustrates one possible blockchain structure, As long as upgraded nodes hold most computation power, the lower branch consisting mainly of blocks from upgraded nodes will outgrow the upper one and be accepted by all nodes. In other words, despite the existence of non-upgraded nodes, the whole network can still agree on one replicated log following the new rule.

1.3.2 Fork Tolerance

The longest-chain rule can resolve forks but does not take advantage of stale blocks to secure the best chain. Attackers playing selfish mining can switch the best chain to their secret chain with just 25% of the overall computation power. Another chain selection rule—Greedy Heaviest-Observed Sub-Tree (GHOST)—can tolerate a higher fork rate and malicious computation power.

1.3.2.1 Greedy Heaviest-Observed Sub-Tree (GHOST)

GHOST starts from the genesis block. At each step, it computes the subtree sizes of each child block and advances to the child with the heaviest subtree, until it reaches a leaf block. The advantage of the GHOST rule is that it guarantees the irreversibility of the selected best chain even when facing natural forks because stale blocks also contribute to the sub-tree size of blocks on the best chain. Figure 1.13 illustrates how off-chain blocks help to secure the best chain against a selfish mining attack. In the diagram, blocks with the same number are of the same height, and capital letters are used to distinguish them from each other. At the first step, GHOST selects 1B as part of the best chain because its subtree size is twelve (2B:2D, 3B:3F, 4B:4C, 5B and 1B itself), while the subtree size of 1A is only six. Therefore the attacker's secret chain cannot subvert the best chain selected according to GHOST though it is enough to override the longest chain. A modified version of GHOST has already been adopted by Ethereum.

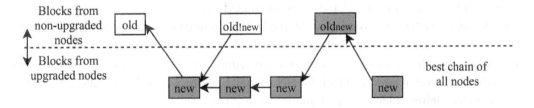

FIGURE 1.12 An example of the blockchain structure where the new consensus rule is more restrictive than the old one. Upgraded nodes hold the majority computation power. Grey blocks belong to the best chain of all nodes.

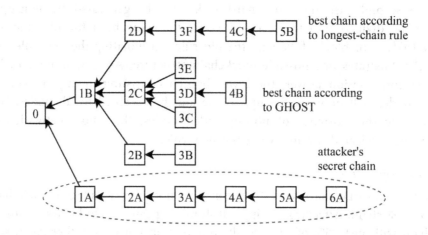

FIGURE 1.13 A block tree where the longest chain and the chain selected by GHOST differ. An attacker's chain is able to switch the longest chain, but not the one selected by GHOST [9].

1.4 TRADEOFF BETWEEN CONSENSUS AND PERFORMANCE

With the assumption that an average transaction takes 250 bytes, Bitcoin can achieve at most 7 transactions per second on average due to the 1MB maximum block size and 10-minute average block interval. However, these parameters are chosen with consensus and security issues in consideration. We explain the tradeoff in this section and show that improving performance by tuning block size and block interval has an upper bound far from satisfactory.

The two most straightforward approaches to improve throughput are: (1) increase block size and (2) reduce block interval. The former has already been taken by BitcoinCash with 8MB maximum block size [10].

However, if a node has not learned all blocks on the best chain by the time it finds a valid block, it could extend an alternative branch other than the best chain or even create a new fork. Consequently, larger block size and faster block creation increase fork rate and attackers' chance to sabotage the best chain under the longest-chain rule because more honest nodes waste their computational power on stale blocks. In other words, increases in the block size or decreases in the block interval do not translate to linear increases in throughput as fork rate also increases and all transactions enclosed by off-chain blocks are not considered to be in the ledger.

Decker et al. established a model for Bitcoin fork rate and proved that network propagation delay is the primary cause for blockchain forks [11]. They also verified that connecting one node to all the other nodes in the network can reduce fork rate by 53.41%. Based on this research, Croman et al. observed that there is a throughput limit of scaling blockchain systems by parameter tuning—block size and interval must satisfy:

$$\frac{block\ size}{X\%\ effective\ throughput} < block\ interval \qquad (1.2)$$

where the metric "X% effective throughput" is defined as X% effective throughput = (block size)/(time taken for X% of the nodes to receive a full block) [12]. In 2016, 90% effective throughput of Bitcoin corresponds to merely 55 Kbps (27.5 tx/sec). Parameter tuning is also subject to network size and connectivity. X% effective throughput drops if new nodes join the network by connecting to only one peer. Therefore, it is a widely held view that significant throughput improvement demands changes in the fundamental consensus rule.

1.5 RELATED WORKS ON IMPROVING BLOCKCHAIN PERFORMANCE

As described in 1.4, parameter tuning tends to increase fork rate. Profound performance improvement requires consensus protocol adjustment. We give an introduction of related research in the section.

1.5.1 Bitcoin-NG

The ultimate goal of PoW is to randomly select a leader who gets the privilege to propose the next one block. Intuitively, if one leader can propose multiple blocks, the blockchain can extend at a higher rate.

Bitcoin-NG (Next Generation) is such a protocol. The protocol introduces two types of blocks: *key blocks* for leader selection and *microblocks* for appending ledger entries [13]. Figure 1.14 illustrates the structure of blockchain under Bitcoin-NG protocol. The header structure of a key block is the same as that of a normal Bitcoin block except for a leader's public key field. The leader is supposed to append and sign all subsequent microblocks until the next key block emerges. Other nodes can detect imposters using the public key field in the key block. Microblocks contain no PoW and thus can be generated fairly fast (e.g., 10 seconds per microblock) by the leader specified in the last key block. Miners compete with each other to become a new leader and may refuse to accept microblocks proposed by the previous leader. The remuneration strategy alleviates this issue by distributing 40% block reward to the current leader and 60% to the subsequent leader.

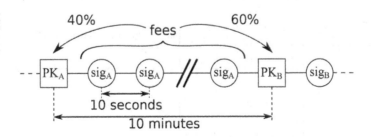

FIGURE 1.14 Structure of the Bitcoin-NG chain. Squares represent key blocks; circles represent microblocks [13].

1.5.2 The Inclusive Protocol

Forking is inevitable as long as leader selection is randomized because there is always the chance that two leaders co-exist. However, if transactions on two branches are compatible, there is no need to invalidate one branch completely. Furthermore, the higher fork rate introduced by larger block size or shorter block interval can be tolerated if forks are handled effectively.

The goal of the Inclusive Protocol is to add transactions not conflicting with the best chain to the ledger so that less computational power is wasted due to forking, hence throughput improvement. To select eligible transactions, the forked blockchain is modeled as a directed acyclic graph (DAG), allowing one block reference multiple predecessors with preference order.

Figure 1.15 illustrates the principle of Inclusive-longest-chain Protocol. Assume *Block1* arrives earlier than *Block2*, so the longest-chain rule selects *Genesis← 1← 3* as the best chain. Then the "inclusive" rule selects non-conflicting transactions from *Block2* (i.e., *tx3: coin3 →Charlie*) as a valid transaction in the ledger. *tx4: coin 2 →David* is invalid since it conflicts with *tx2: coin 2 →Bob* and *Block1* has a higher preference order in the parent list of *Block3*.

1.5.3 Elastico

ELASTICO is a sharding protocol for permissionless blockchain-based systems [14]. It divides nodes into small concurrently operating committees, and each committee operates on a subset of transactions. This sharding approach is a very effective way to improve throughput and widely used in conventional distributed systems such as Google Spanner. The consensus protocol of ELASTICO has two hierarchies: (1) intra-committee consensus to agree on a transaction set and (2) inter-committee consensus to merge transaction sets from all committees.

Identities must be established so that a node knows which committee it is in and who are in the same committee. To prevent Sybil attacks, identity creation incorporates PoW. A node first solves a PoW puzzle, and the last s bits of the output hash value represents the identifier of its committee.

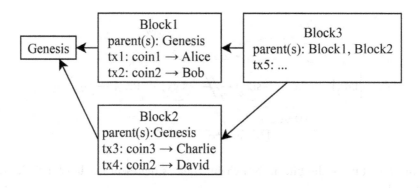

FIGURE 1.15   Inclusive-longest-chain Protocol

PBFT is used as the intra-committee consensus protocol. Once a node receives enough signatures ($2f + 1$ in PBFT commit phase) on a transaction set from other members of the same committee, it sends the transaction set to the final committee. The final committee verifies transaction sets received from each committee, merges and signs them, and broadcasts the combined block to the entire network.

Although ELASTICO can scale up the throughput nearly linearly in network size, PBFT poses a limit on the committee size. In [14], the authors mentioned that running PBFT among 320 nodes did not terminate within an hour, and they set committee size as 100 nodes in their experiments.

1.5.4 Bitcoin Lightning Network

A Bitcoin transaction has a field named *locktime*, which specifies the earliest time (expressed either in UNIX timestamp or block height) that this transaction can be included in a block. Usually, *locktime* has the value of zero, indicating this transaction can be added to the blockchain immediately. When *locktime* is greater than 0, the transaction's commit is intentionally delayed, and this transaction can be superseded by another transaction spending the same UTxO but having a smaller *locktime*. Figure 1.16 illustrates this process. *Tx2* is broadcast later than *Tx1* with *timelock* $T - \Delta T < T$, so *Tx2* becomes valid once the time $T - \Delta T$ is reached. This situation invalidates *Tx1* since *Tx1* claims *coin1* that is already spent in *Tx2*.

A payment channel takes advantage of *locktime* and allows two parties, typically Payment Service Provider (PSP) such as PayPal, to transfer money multiple times without adding burden on the blockchain [15]. A channel is set up by freezing money owned by two parties and creating a shared account that needs the signatures of both parties to claim its balance. The frozen money is transferred in small quantities, and update transactions are created to reflect the aggregate payment amount. For example, in Figure 1.16, assume a channel has been set up between some sender and Alice (the receiver). The sender first buys a product from Alice and creates transaction *Tx1* to pay her *coin1*. Later, the sender buys another product whose price is *coin2*, so an update

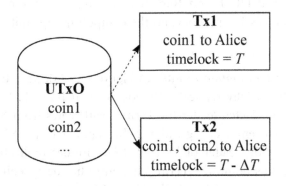

FIGURE 1.16   Transaction Superseding

transaction *Tx2* is created to reflect that the sender needs to pay Alice *coin*1 + *coin*2 in total. In the end, only the most recent transaction is committed to the blockchain to reflect the final aggregate amount.

One payment channel connects only two parties, so there will be a high volume of on-chain transactions if one payment channel is set up for each pair of users. Bitcoin Lightning Network offers a solution by setting up a network of payment channels between big users who transact very frequently (e.g., PSPs). Then a payment from a small user can be "routed" to the receiver in the network.

1.6 SUMMARY

Having consistent states among nodes is essential for any distributed system. In a Byzantine-failure-free environment, protocols tolerating only crash failures (e.g., Paxos and Raft) can provide the desired consistency using $2f + 1$ nodes, where f is the maximum possible crashing nodes. If Byzantine failure must be tolerated but nodes cannot forge identities (possibly with the help of Public Key Infrastructure (PKI)), PBFT-like protocols can instead tolerate up to f malicious nodes with $3f + 1$ nodes. In other words, PBFT works with pre-configured memberships and is vulnerable to Sybil attacks. The robust PoW-based Nakamoto Consensus sacrifices energy and hardware resources for its Sybil-attack-tolerance. Unlike Paxos, Raft, and PBFT, Nakamoto Consensus does not require a node to know all the other nodes.

Paxos, Raft, and PBFT all suffer from scalability issue due to the high-volume message exchange between nodes. In practice, these protocols run only among no more than a handful of nodes to avoid performance degradation and only where consistency is in desperate need [16]. Bitcoin has demonstrated that PoW has the capability of scaling to tens of thousands of nodes. However, the tradeoff between security and performance limits the performance of Bitcoin to one-hour latency and 7-transactions-per-second throughput.

Researchers are dedicating their efforts to designing scalable, high-performance, Sybil-attack-resistant, and Byzantine-failure-tolerant consensus protocols. The most straight-forward and promising approach is to modify Nakamoto Consensus. Bitcoin-NG enables a miner to verify transactions at the speed of its processing power, whereas the Inclusive Protocol, ELASTICO, and Bitcoin Lightning Network have the potential to achieve transaction processing rate beyond the computing capability of one single node.

Exercises

1.1 *Commitment determination in Raft.* In Figure 1.17 (a), *S1* is the leader of Term 1 and Term 2. It partially replicates the log entry at Index 2. In Figure 1.17 (b) *S1* crashes; *S5* is the elected leader for Term 3 with votes from *S3, S4*, and itself. *S5* accepts a different entry at log Index 2. In Figure 1.17 (c) *S5* crashes; *S1* restarts and is elected as the leader of Term 4. *S1* continues replicating the Term-2 log entry to *S3*. At this point, the Term-2 log entry has been replicated on a majority of the servers (*S1, S2*, and *S3*). Is the Term-2 log entry committed? Why?

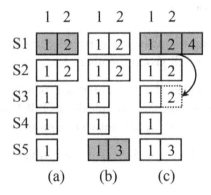

FIGURE 1.17   Server S1 replicates a Term-2 log entry to a majority of server during Term 4 [4].

Solution: No. A future leader may overwrite the Term-2 log entry. For example, in Figure 1.18 (d1), *S1* crashes; *S5* is the elected leader of the next Term (Term 5 or higher). *S5* will replicate the Term-3 log entry at index 2.

A leader cannot immediately conclude that an entry from a previous Term is committed once it is stored on a majority of servers. Raft never commits log entries from previous Terms by counting replicas. Only log entries from the leader's current Term are committed by counting replicas, as the Term-4 log entry in Figure 1.18 (d2) where *S1* manages to replicate the Term-4 log entry to *S2* and *S3* as the leader of Term 4.

1.2 *PBFT application.* PBFT has been used in permissioned blockchain systems, such as HyperLedger Fabric. Why it does not apply to permissionless blockchain systems?

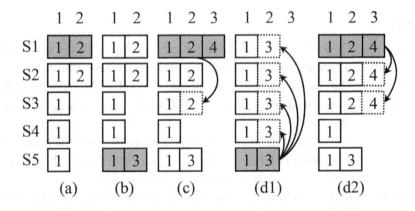

FIGURE 1.18   An example of a leader (S1) overwriting a log entry replicated by a previous leader on a majority of servers (S1) [4].

Solution: There are three reasons:

1) There is no fixed group member in a permissionless blockchain system, but PBFT needs the public keys of all group members.

2) The all-to-all multicasts in the Prepare Phase (except for the primary) and the Commit Phase make the message complexity of PBFT as high as $O(n^2)$, where n is the number of replicas. This significantly constrains the scalability of PBFT.

3) PBFT is vulnerable to Sybil attack because one adversary can vote twice with two different identities.

1.3 Assume the block size in Bitcoin is 1 MB and we want to increase it to 2 MB. Does this take a hard fork or soft fork?

Solution: Hard fork. Because non-upgraded nodes will not accept blocks whose size is between 1 MB and 2 MB generated by upgraded nodes. The new rule is less restrictive.

1.4 *Multi-Paxos and Bitcoin-NG*. Is there any similarity between Multi-Paxos and Bitcoin-NG?

Solution: Yes. In Multi-Paxos, one leader can coordinate the value-choosing process for multiple log entries; in Bitcoin-NG, one leader can append multiple blocks to the blockchain. They both reduce message overhead by avoiding unnecessary leader election.

Think About It...

It is impossible to have a deterministic protocol that solves consensus in a message-passing asynchronous system in which at most one process may fail by crashing.

FLP Impossibility of Consensus

GLOSSARY

Consensus:	The state where all nodes in a network agree on the same decision.
Byzantine Fault:	A type of fault where faulty nodes may behave arbitrarily.
Best Chain:	The branch should be accepted as the blockchain when forks occur according to a specified chain selection rule (e.g., longest-chain rule).
Block Height:	The number of blocks on the best chain between the genesis block and a specific block (the genesis block is included while the specific block is not). The block height of the genesis block is zero [17].
Orphan Block:	A block whose previous (parent) hash field points to an unknown block, meaning the orphan cannot be validated [17].
Stale Block:	A block which was successfully mined but is not included on the current best blockchain, likely because of natural fork [17]. Stale

blocks have known parents in the blockchain, whereas orphan blocks do not.

Off-chain Block: A block that is not part of the best chain, including orphan blocks and stale blocks.

NOTES

1   For further reading, please refer to the paper "Practical Byzantine Fault Tolerance" [6].
2   The actual field name is *coinbase* and the value of this field is a script. The value can vary because coinbase transaction has no input and hence no need to include a valid script redeeming previous transaction output [7].

FURTHER READING

Castro, M. and Liskov, B., 1999, February. Practical Byzantine Fault Tolerance. In *OSDI* (Vol. 99, pp. 173–186).

Narayanan, A., Bonneau, J., Felten, E., Miller, A. and Goldfeder, S., 2016. *Bitcoin and Cryptocurrency Technologies: A Comprehensive Introduction.* Princeton University Press.

Croman, K., Decker, C., Eyal, I., Gencer, A. E., Juels, A., Kosba, A., Miller, A., Saxena, P., Shi, E., Sirer, E. G. and Song, D., 2016. On Scaling Decentralized Blockchains. In *International Conference on Financial Cryptography and Data Security* (pp. 106–125). Springer, Berlin, Heidelberg.

Cachin, C. and Vukolić, M., 2017. *Blockchains Consensus Protocols in the Wild.* arXiv preprint arXiv:1707.01873.

REFERENCES

[1] John Ousterhout. Designing for Understandability: The Raft Consensus Algorithm: www.youtube.com/watch?v=vYp4LYbnnW8.
[2] Leslie Lamport. The Part-Time Parliament. *ACM Transactions on Computer Systems (TOCS)*, 16(2): 133–169, 1998.
[3] John Ousterhout. Paxos Lecture: www.youtube.com/watch?v=JEpsBg0AO6o&t=914s.
[4] Diego Ongaro and John K. Ousterhout. In Search of an Understandable Consensus Algorithm. In USENIX Annual Technical Conference, pp. 305–319, 2014.
[5] Satoshi Nakamoto. *Bitcoin: A Peer-to-Peer Electronic Cash System*, 2008: https://bitcoin.org/en/bitcoin-paper.
[6] Miguel Castro, Miguel Castro, Barbara Liskov and Barbara Liskov. Practical Byzantine Fault Tolerance. OSDI –'"99: Proceedings of the Third Symposium on Operating Systems Design and Implementation, (February): 173–186, 1999.
[7] Bitcoin.org. Coinbase Input: The Input of the First Transaction in a Block: https://bitcoin.org/en/developer-reference{\#}raw-transaction-format.
[8] Ittay Eyal and Emin Gun Sirer. Majority Is Not Enough: Bitcoin Mining Is Vulnerable. *Communications of the ACM*, 61(7): 95–102, 2018.
[9] Yonatan Sompolinsky and Aviv Zohar. Secure High-Rate Transaction Processing in Bitcoin. International Conference on Financial Cryptography and Data Security, pp. 507–527. Springer, Berlin, Heidelberg, 2015.
[10] Bitcoincash.org. Bitcoincash: www.bitcoincash.org/.
[11] Christian Decker and Roger Wattenhofer. Information Propagation in the Bitcoin Network. *IEEE P2P 2013 Proceedings*, pp. 1–10, September 9–11, 2013. Trento, Italy. DOI: 10.1109/P2P.2013.6688704

[12] Kyle Croman, Christian Decker, Ittay Eyal, Adem Efe Gencer, Ari Juels, Ahmed Kosba, Andrew Miller, Prateek Saxena, Elaine Shi, Emin Gun Sirer, et al. On Scaling Decentralized Blockchains. International Conference on Financial Cryptography and Data Security, pp. 106–125. Springer, Berlin, Heidelberg, 2016.

[13] Ittay Eyal, Adem Efe Gencer, Emin Gun Sirer and Robbert Van Renesse and Implementation Nsdi. Bitcoin-NG: A Scalable Blockchain Protocol. 13th {USENIX} Symposium on Networked Systems Design and Implementation ({NSDI} 16), pp. 45–59. 2016.

[14] Loi Luu, Viswesh Narayanan, Chaodong Zheng, Kunal Baweja, Seth Gilbert and Prateek Saxena. A Secure Sharding Protocol for Open Blockchains. Proceedings of the 2016 ACM SIGSAC Conference on Computer and Communications Security - CCS'16, pp. 17–30, 2016.

[15] Christian Decker and Roger Wattenhofer. A Fast and Scalable Payment Network with Bitcoin Duplex Micropayment Channels. Distributed Computing Group, ETH Zürich, Zürich, Switzerland. pp. 3–18, August 4, 2015. DOI: 10.1007/978-3-319-21741-3_1

[16] Marko Vukolić. The quest for scalable blockchain fabric: Proof-of-work vs. BFT replication. In *International workshop on open problems in network security*, pp. 112-125. Springer, Cham, 2015.

[17] Bitcoin.org. Bitcoin Developer Glossary: https://bitcoin.org/en/developer-glossary.

CHAPTER 2

Validation Services for Permissioned Blockchains

David Firth and Isho Tama-Sweet

CONTENTS

Double-Entry book keeping dates all the way back to Genoa, Italy, in 1340 when the Messari, Treasurer of the Republic of Genoa, kept a ledger of debits and credits to record transactions. In the intervening 700 years, little has changed with the system, with companies maintaining a ledger of debits and credits. Distributed ledger technology (DLT), more commonly known as Blockchain, is set to transform this single ledger system. As its name implies, DLT allows for two (or more) companies to share a ledger, or more likely just parts of a ledger, between them securely. This chapter will discuss what happens in the accounting and auditing industry and by extension almost every company that is audited, when this DLT matures. These shared ledgers should not and will not open the entire general ledger of a company to other companies. Instead, companies will carve-out (select) parts of their general ledger that they will share with other companies.

For example, a company could establish a permissioned blockchain in which it shares a portion of its general ledger with its customers and supplies. Each individual supplier or customer would only be allowed to view the transactions in which it participated. To join the blockchain, a customer or supplier would need permission (i.e., an invitation) from the company, and therefore this is considered a permissioned blockchain. In contrast, permissionless, or public, blockchain, such as bitcoin, is available to anyone.

As we know, blockchains are immutable, unchangeable. Therefore, it is essential that every transaction going on to the permissioned blockchain is valid, and this means that permissioned blockchains will need validation services. As discussed in detail later, differences in the structure of permissioned and permissionless DLT lead to different requirements and methods of transaction validation. For permissioned DLT, these validation services are going to combine automated and human checks. Automated checks are most commonly embedded in RPA, a field which has come a long way since the late 1980s when you could have a macro run a series of steps for you in Excel. Even with RPA handling much of the transaction validation, humans will need to examine exceptions and more complex cases that fall outside the usual operating parameters of the business.

2.1 BLOCKCHAINS AND DISTRIBUTED LEDGER TECHNOLOGY (DLT)

For our purposes, we define blockchain and distributed ledger technology (DLT) the following way:

> A **blockchain** is a *distributed ledger* that can record transactions between two (or more) parties efficiently and in a *verifiable* and *permanent way*.

A ledger is a principal book (originally) or computer file (now predominantly) for recording transactions. A "distributed ledger" simply means that the record of those transactions is not kept in one place, but on each computer that is part of the blockchain network. This notion of what "distributed" means is important, as there are two possible definitions. One definition of "distributed" is that one whole ledger is divided up and spread across the network. This would be like having a jigsaw puzzle where each piece is given to a different person (or computer) on the network. This is *not* how blockchain works. The second definition of "distributed" is that an *identical* copy of the entire ledger is kept on each computer on the network. This would be like having multiple copies of a jigsaw puzzle and giving the entire puzzle to each person (or computer) on the network. This is how blockchain works: a copy of the entire ledger is on each computer on the network.

For businesses, what this means is that a customer (or customers) and a supplier could share a ledger covering their transactions: purchases and sales, shipments and deliveries, invoices and payments, credit memos and refunds, and so on. A bank and their client could share a ledger for a loan, and that shared ledger could cover the loan documents, collateral details, interest and principal payments, and so on.

Once a transaction has been entered into the blockchain, it is permanent and cannot be changed. It cannot be altered by the members of the chain, nor can it be changed by hackers. This is achieved by using a mathematical function that provides a "hash" (sort of like a total) of everything on the blockchain using a one-way mathematical function, the SHA-256 cryptographic hash, where SHA stands for secure hash algorithm. For the purposes of this chapter, it is not important how this cryptography works, just that it does work, and it makes entries on the distributed ledger permanent and very secure.

Given the permanence of transactions on the distributed ledger, it is imperative that transactions are put on to the distributed ledger in a "verifiable" way. This means that, for permissioned DLT, only a permissioned member of the blockchain may enter a transaction, and even an authorized person has to have the transaction checked for authenticity before it can be recorded. We will discuss this "verifiability" later in this chapter when we cover who might provide distributed ledger technology.

2.2 PERMISSIONED DLT

Now that we have a definition of DLT, and have briefly discussed "permissioned" and "permissionless" versions, we will discuss the use of permissioned DLT in greater detail.

Once you are on a permissioned blockchain, depending on your access, you can either see a subset of transactions, see all transactions, or see all transactions and add new transactions. In most business applications of blockchain, a permissioned blockchain would be a carve-out of specific sections of the ledger to specific people or entities to either view only or view and make additional entries.

In our customer/supplier example above, both the customer and supplier have a general ledger that keeps all their account transactions and balances. Within that general ledger is a part of the ledger that relates just to that particular customer/supplier relationship. The customer records purchases from the supplier, and the supplier records sales to the customer. With blockchain/distributed ledger technology, we could have a permissioned blockchain where just the supplier and just the customer had access to just the purchase and sales transactions between just this supplier and this customer.

Figure 2.1 illustrates a particular customer/supplier relationship that is highly typical. At left, the arrow shows a contract between the customer and the supplier. The contract contains term agreements including lines of credit, payment terms, return handling terms and other conditions. Currently, both the customer and supplier would hold a copy of this agreement in four places: supplier attorney, supplier in-house counsel, customer attorney, and customer in-house counsel. This is inefficient and wasteful of time and effort.

The second arrow from the left in Figure 2.1 shows the company placing a purchase order with the supplier. This is Purchase Order number 1, P.O.#1. This purchase order impacts the ledger of the company by a purchase being recorded, a change to future inventory being recorded as the company awaits delivery of their purchase, efforts by the accounting department at the company to record all these transactions, and efforts and entries in the company ledger by the finance department to make sure funds are available to pay for the purchase when payment is due.

The second arrow from the right (third from the left) in Figure 2.1 shows the supplier who has received the purchase order from the company. The supplier will do almost the same things as the purchasing company, first setting up a Supply Order number 1, S.O.#1. This supply order impacts the ledger of the supplier by a sale being recorded, a change to

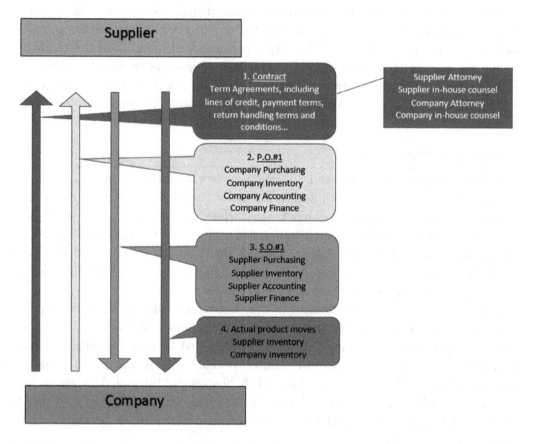

FIGURE 2.1   A typical customer/supplier relationship

future inventory being recorded as the company awaits delivery of their sale, efforts by the accounting department at the supplier to record all these transactions, and efforts and entries in the company ledger by the finance department to make sure funds are received for the sale when payment is due.

The first arrow from the right (fourth from the left) in Figure 2.1 shows the supplier actually moving product to the customer. This causes a reduction in the supplier's inventory and a corresponding increase in the customer company's inventory.

As described, you can already see that much of what the purchasing company does and records in its ledgers are the exact same (or more correctly the exact opposite, but exactly same amounts and dates) as the supplier. There is an enormous duplication of efforts and ledger entries to record just the one sale. This duplicative effort and duplicative ledger entries are the same across all routine sales between the company and the supplier. Further, these duplicative efforts and duplicative ledger entries are the same across all routine sales between all other companies that the supplier does business with, and across all suppliers that the company does business with.

Figure 2.2 captures the level of duplicative efforts and ledger entries across this typical customer/suppler relationship. As the figure shows, almost all of the effort and entries are the same across the two entities. Indeed, only the physical movement of goods is not the same.

It is important to highlight that we do recognize that actual general ledger entries for the supplier and customer are reversed. When a purchase of $500 is made by the company from the supplier, the general ledger entries for the company are as follows:

Dr *Purchased Items Receivable Account* $500

Cr *Accounts Payable Account* $500

The general ledger entries for the supplier are as follows:

Dr *Accounts Receivable Account* $500

Cr *Items Sold Account* $500

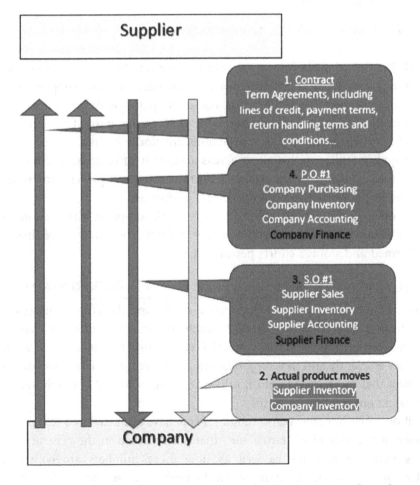

FIGURE 2.2   Duplicative efforts and ledger entries in a typical customer/supplier relationship

The amounts are exactly offsetting, and the accounts for the debits and credits are well-known and also offsetting.

When the item actually moves, the general ledger entries for the supplier are as follows:

Dr *Cash* $500

Cr *Accounts Receivable Account* $500

Dr *Items Sold Account* $500

Cr *Sales* $500

The general ledger entries for the customer are as follows:

Dr *Accounts Payable Account* $500

Cr *Cash* $500

Dr *Items Purchased* $500

Cr *Purchased Items Receivable Account* $500

Since all these entries are known in advance, are for the same amounts and for the same item, a permissioned blockchain between the customer and supplier could record these transactions once, and the work could be performed just once, rather than duplicated at the company and supplier. This reduces the amount of accounting work by half and also reduces the places transactions are stored by half.

As the supplier replicates this effort across a number of customers, the economies of scale from the reduction of duplicative efforts across multiple customers more than halves the work performed and storage efforts performed.

As a customer replicates this effort across multiple suppliers, the economies of scale from the reduction of duplicative efforts across multiple customers more than halves the work performed and storage efforts performed.

2.3 VALIDATION SERVICES ON PERMISSIONED BLOCKCHAINS

The move of businesses to reduce duplicative efforts and therefore transaction costs by recording transactions on permissioned blockchains brings about other changes too. As we discussed earlier, the blockchain or DLT can record transactions between two (or more) parties efficiently and in a *verifiable* and *permanent way*. The permanent nature of DLT requires that transactions put on to the DLT are valid and correctly recorded. This is where validation services come in.

For well over one hundred years, auditing firms have evaluated and tested the accuracy and validity of the individual transactions that are recorded in the general ledger of the companies they are auditing, as well as how those numbers are consolidated into companies' financial statements to represent the health and well-being of those companies.

In almost all companies, there are far too many transactions for the audit firm to check every one so statistical samples are taken. Coupled with work to support the access to, security of, and integrity of the systems running the general ledger, these statistical samples provide support for and evidence that the transactions of the companies have been recorded properly. In addition to the limitations of looking at a statistical sample of transactions, auditors have also only been able to render an opinion on those transactions and the financial statements several months after the end of the fiscal year.

For decades, auditors have been talking about real-time audits where they can actually check transactions as they are happening, and as such be able to give an opinion on the related financial statements in near-real time. Such a change would revolutionize auditing, as well as investing and other financial-related issues.

DLT and permissioned blockchains bring us much closer to real time audits since DLT requires each transaction be validated before recording instead of several months after recording. In addition, since the DLT transactions record is viewable by everyone with permission, the stakes are higher than they used to be when a company kept its own private (unshared) ledgers, and those ledgers got audited just once a year.

Fortunately, other recent technological developments are facilitating the validation of transactions prior to recording. The technology delivering real-time ability to check every transaction is typically called "robotic process automation", and it is this RPA that forms the backbone of validation services on permissioned blockchains.

While not the focus of this chapter, we note that the validation of transactions for permissionless blockchains is fundamentally different that permissioned blockchains. Permissionless blockchains (often with hundreds or thousands of members) require consensus "proof of work" (solving a complex mathematical algorithm) by a majority of members of the network in order to add a transaction. This can be slow and requires significant computing and energy resources. Security when adding transactions (i.e., ensuring transactions are valid) is at least partially due to the large number of members of the network. The different underlying structure of permissioned and permissionless blockchains thus require different validation approaches.

2.4 ROBOTIC PROCESS AUTOMATION

RPA is a combination of a number of different technological improvements over the last 30 years into a single tool that can perform many of the tasks that humans have traditionally done.

The first part of RPA technology is optical character recognition (OCR). OCR actually dates back to 1931 when the first patent was issued for searching microfilm archives using an optical code recognition system. Massive advances were made in the mid-1970s, and by 2000 OCR was mainstream and so achievable by computers that its original definition as "artificial intelligence" is now forgotten. OCR allows the RPA tool to read contracts, purchase orders and supply orders with near-perfect accuracy, to extract all salient details from them, and to put all those details into the correct fields in the RPA's database.

The second part of RPA technology is essentially "Excel-macros on steroids". Macros have been available in Excel from the very first version in 1985, and are a way to program a series of steps to be completed by Excel. Macros are an efficient method to complete a repetitive task, often involving some logic functions that have defined steps to complete. Then a simple keyboard combination would run the macro allowing Excel to quickly complete that repetitive task. RPA technology has integrated this ability into its toolkit, making it simple, intuitive and graphic for users to configure (unlike traditional programming of Excel macros).

The final part of RPA technology is built-in tools to allow the RPA to open business software packages, securely enter login credentials, and then either enter information or collect information from those software packages and do something with it. Much of this builds on already existing technology called application programming interfaces (APIs). APIs have been around since 1968 and have developed enormously since then in conjunction with developments in business software. RPA technology can open, read and write to almost every business software you can think of, including all the Microsoft software (Outlook email, Word, Excel, PowerPoint), almost any database, Software as a Service (SaaS) packages such as Salesforce, and ERP packages including SAP and Oracle. In sum, virtually all business software can be accessed, written to, read from and used by RPA technology.

Packaged together, advanced OCR, improvements in Excel-macros on steroids, and better APIs means that provided you can logically break down a sequence of tasks, you can have RPA complete those tasks for you. Additionally, RPA can perform those tasks faster than humans can, with more reliability and accuracy, and on a 24×7 basis.

2.5 USING ROBOTIC PROCESS AUTOMATION FOR VALIDATION SERVICES ON PERMISSIONED BLOCKCHAINS

Back to our customer/supplier example, we can see how RPA can be applied to validation services on permissioned blockchains. Figure 2.3 shows the permissioned blockchain between the supplier and customer. The purchase order created by the customer and sent to the supplier is shown as P.O. #1. Both the customer and the supplier want to know that P.O. #1 is valid, and the steps to ensure validity are frequently incredibly similar for both companies. The auditors need to make sure that purchase orders are valid, and ask a series of standard questions to make sure they are.

Figure 2.4 shows the sorts of questions asked. The first question is: how does the company know itself that a purchase order is valid? Typically, they will have a series of controls to make sure purchase orders sent out to suppliers are valid. These will include things such as whether or not the purchase order is on official company headed notepaper, or from an official company email address. Most companies set limits on what can be ordered. These limits can be both physical quantities and monetary values. Frequently both these limits will be set, and be different, for different items the company purchases. For instance, a company might have a limit of 100 for items $1,000 or over, and a limit of 500 for items below $1,000. Most companies will also limit what can be ordered and what can be ordered from which suppliers. For example, most companies

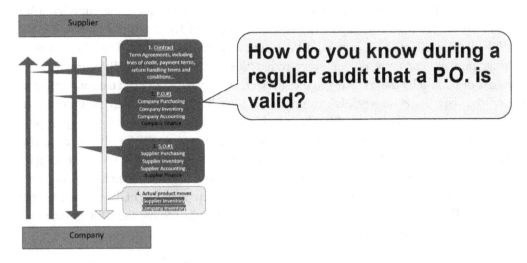

FIGURE 2.3   What makes a purchase order valid on a permissioned blockchain

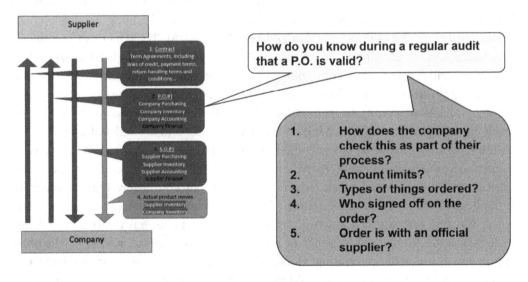

FIGURE 2.4   Things to consider that makes a purchase order valid on a permissioned blockchain

do not have a usual order process for company cars or trucks – these are one-off high-value purchases that require special attention. On the other end of the scale, the same company might have no limit on the number of nuts or bolts that can be ordered (subject to other monetary or quantity limits). Most companies have sign-off processes for various items, quantities of items, prices of items, or a combination of those. Companies also often only allow items to be purchased from an approved vendor list. The supplier on the other side of this transaction will almost certainly have the same sorts of controls, although sizes and limits may vary (for instance, the supplier might have a limit of 200 for items $2,000 or over, and a limit of 1,000 for items below $2,000).

With all this business logic in hand, RPA technology can be configured to take over much of what humans currently do for every transaction. OCR within the RPA can read the purchase order sent by the company to the supplier, be it on paper or via email, and can check it is official. The "Excel on steroids" within the RPA can be configured with both the supplier and customer limits. Should anything be out of limit, emails can be sent to the appropriate person at the appropriate company – that person is guided in to the RPA software to approve, or not, the order. The RPA software can then open any business software for either company (SAP, Oracle, Salesforce, etc.) to make updates as necessary. Email confirmations can be sent to show that everything was approved, or for things that were not. One of the premier vendors of RPA is UIPath. A video of just such a process being handled inside the RPA software is at this weblink: www.youtube.com/watch?v=gp3hG9UFFk4

2.6 HOW ROBOTIC PROCESS AUTOMATION FOR VALIDATION SERVICES ON PERMISSIONED BLOCKCHAINS CHANGES WHAT AUDITORS AND ACCOUNTANTS DO

There is plenty of hype about how technology will disrupt what people will do at work. Many professions may be set to change, and accounting and auditing are likely to be impacted early (see, for example, Latham and Humbred, 2018). The American Institute of CPAs (AICPA) and the United States State Boards of Accountancy that regulate CPAs within the United States have come out with position statements including that "tech fluency leads profession's needs" (Accounting Today, 2018). Our discussion above about RPA and validation services on permission blockchains, and the need for tech fluency, provide insight into some of the changes that may face accountants and auditors.

A move to a permissioned blockchain environment could potentially reduce the need for many corporate accountants. As we have covered in our example of a supplier and a customer, a permissioned blockchain environment can completely remove much of the duplicative work accountants perform in the two companies. An accountant is still needed, but just one, rather than two. As this scales up to several customers and one supplier, it could be that the supplier provides all the accounting, with each customer needing much reduced accounting work. The reverse is also true: if we have one customer with several suppliers, it could be that the customer provides all the accounting, with each supplier needing much reduced accounting work. The possibility also exists that an accounting firm could step in and provide accounting services for permissioned blockchain environments. This could largely eliminate the role of the traditional accountant within companies and suppliers.

The auditing profession could see wholesale changes as well. A move to validation services on permissioned blockchain environments would fundamentally change the traditional audit. Auditors would have to work with companies and suppliers using permissioned blockchain environments to fully understand how the RPA was configured. In other words, instead of financial audits, the primary role of the auditor may develop into an RPA auditor. Additionally, auditors could possibly set up the RPA technology for companies and suppliers, unless this gets done by the RPA technology provider. Although auditors have for years had to understand the risks and controls of the technology environment that supports the general ledger, in many cases, this has been a small part of the audit. Auditors have relied on other audit processes and sampling and confirmations of balances to make sure the transactions being recorded and the numbers in the general ledger are correct. In an RPA environment, auditors might be pushed to actually certify (or attest, or sign-off on the accuracy of) the controls configured within the RPA and whether they are designed properly and operating effectively all the time. The AICPA has standards to support auditors doing this, which they called Systems and Organization Controls, SOC (www.aicpa.org/interestareas/frc/assuranceadvisoryservices/serviceorganiza tion-smanagement.html). Specifically, AICPA standards outline ways for auditors to

report on the fairness of the presentation of management's description of the service organization's system and the suitability of the design and operating effectiveness of the controls to achieve the related control objectives included in the description throughout a specified period

and calls them Type 2 – SOC 1 reports.

However, few accounting programs teach students these skills, and only the biggest firms (so-called Big 4, which includes KPMG, PwC, Deloitte and EY) and the larger mid-tier firms (including the likes of Moss Adams, Grant Thornton) have specialized practices that deliver these services or routinely provide these services to clients in other ways. As a result, firms that currently do not provide these services at all may be at a grave competitive disadvantage, and firms that do currently provide these services will struggle to find new talent from college accounting programs. Thus these firms will incur substantial expense, to train new hires to understand RPA and how to audit in an RPA environment.

2.7 WHO PROVIDES PERMISSIONED BLOCKCHAINS?

One question arising from our extensive discussion of permissioned blockchain technology is: who provides the permissioned blockchain technology? The answer to this question might be partly wrapped up in the fact that a key part of blockchain technology is that the ledger of transactions (the actual blocks on the chain that make up the blockchain) is "distributed", leading to the distributed ledger technology (DLT) terminology. Part of what makes blockchain so trusted is that everything on the blockchain is replicated across all the different computers on the network. Provided more than 50% of the computers on the network are independent of each other, then you have certainty in what is on the blockchain.

In a permissioned blockchain environment, suppliers and companies probably don't want to share their transactions across a wide network of computers. Indeed, the whole idea of "permissioned" is that access is limited. To inject trust in to the blockchain, it seems logically that there has to be a third party who both the supplier and company trust to be the provider and keeper of the blockchain. This trusted third party would also provide the "verifiability" service of the transaction being put on the permissioned blockchain. This is different, but highly related, to the validation services we have already discussed. The validation services make sure that a particular transaction meets the business-rules of the customer and supplier. As we have discussed, most of these will be provided by RPA. Once the validation services give us a valid transaction, then it has to be put on to the permissioned blockchain in trusted, verifiable, way. The providers of permissioned blockchain technology would have to provide a verifiable way to show the customer/supplier that only transactions that should go on the blockchain actually go on the blockchain. Technology solutions such as digital certificates can provide this trust.

Some possible providers of permissioned blockchain technology would be accounting or auditing firms, or a new firm that they establish themselves (individually or as a coalition) to provide the technology. This is a departure from the usual role of accounting and auditing firms, but given their trusted status and their proximity to the configuration and use of the RPA technology that is the front end to transactions being put on to the permissioned blockchain, it makes a lot of sense for them to be the technology provider. This closely mirrors what JP Morgan Chase did in the financial services industry. "The firm launched Quorum, an open-source enterprise-ready distributed ledger and smart contracts platform specifically to meet the needs of the financial services industry." (Deloitte Insights, Tech Trends, 2018: www2.deloitte.com /insights/us/en/focus/tech-trends/2018/blockchain-integration-smart-contracts.html).

More likely, however, is that a company such as Amazon or IBM will provide this technology, and do so as a service. Both Amazon and IBM are pushing aggressively into blockchain technology (IBM calls their offering Hyperledger: www.ibm.com/blockchain/ hyperledger, Amazon has it as part of AWS: https://aws.amazon.com/blockchain/). Other providers such as Ethereum (www.ethereum.org/), which is developed by a worldwide team of developers for the Ethereum Foundation, a Swiss nonprofit organization, are also trying to push their solution.

As Deloitte Insights, Tech Trends 2018 report notes (www2.deloitte.com/insights/us/ en/focus/tech-trends/2018/blockchain-integration-smart-contracts.html) the next stop for blockchain technology is standardization, and "the need for standardized technologies, platforms, and skillsets becomes more pressing each day." What that would mean is that IBM, Amazon and Ethereum come together to standardize their offerings, which would make it easier for our supplier/customer to go to permissioned blockchain technology as choices would not need to be made on technical specifications, but more on price and service. The history of technology suggests that this is not likely – Microsoft Windows and Apple OS still don't talk to each other after 30 years of sharing the marketspace. As a result, customers and suppliers will need professional advice, consulting services, and technical sales to help them make technology choices around permissioned blockchains.

2.8 CONCLUSION

The idea that blockchain is a technology disrupter and a disruptive innovation is well known and has been widely discussed. In this chapter, we have dug down into the details of what this likely means for the accounting and auditing industry, and by extension almost every company that is audited. We have also described what will likely happen when blockchain technology matures to a point that companies can share a portion of their ledgers on a permissioned blockchain.

With its ability to provide a distributed, immutable ledger, blockchain technology is well placed to replace existing ledgers, usually called general ledgers, inside companies. Currently, two companies who conduct business with each other simply replicate the accounting of transactions between them – debits for one company for accounts receivable are recorded as credits for accounts payable in the other company, for instance. This duplication is wasteful of resources, as it requires duplicative efforts of bookkeeping and the subsequent audit of those transactions. If the two companies could share a distributed, immutable ledger between themselves, they could halve the total work needed, leading to cost and time savings. Blockchain technology provides that capability in the form of permissioned blockchains. A permissioned blockchain is one which is not open to all, as is the case for bitcoin, for example, but instead has access restricted to those who have been given permission to be on that blockchain.

Since the blockchain ledger is immutable and now shared with trading partners (customers and suppliers, say), it becomes imperative that every transaction put on to the shared ledger is audited before it hits the blockchain so that there are no disputes over shared unchangeable transactions.

RPA will provide this real-time full-sample audit capability, and we have described the three elements that make RPA possible: optical character recognition (OCR), Excel-macros on steroids that are simple to configure, and the built-in tools to allow the RPA to open business software packages, securely enter login credentials, and then either enter information or collect information from those software packages and do something with it. With a solid understanding of the business processes and controls already in place, RPA can be used to effectively monitor every single transaction a company and supplier transact before it goes on to the permissioned blockchain.

But who provides this permissioned blockchain technology? Although it makes sense that accounting firms charged with auditing the permissioned blockchains could also be primary providers of that technology, we believe it is much more likely that existing technology companies like IBM or Amazon, or newly-formed technology consortiums like Ethereum, will be the technology providers. Users of the permissioned blockchain technology will be faced with a disparate array of different technologies, with a lack of standards for blockchain technology itself, never mind permissioned blockchain technology, making choosing the right permissioned blockchain technology a potentially arduous task. Professional advisors such as the accounting and auditing firms themselves, consulting services, and technical sales people from the technology vendors will step into this fray seeking to guide potential users to hopefully the most appropriate technology solutions.

All this means that the adoption of permissioned blockchain, and validation services for those blockchains, is likely to proceed in fits and starts. We are likely to see technology adoption characterized by the technology vendors themselves finding interesting use cases for their technology where they can get quick wins for their clients, and use those wins to persuade others to become adopters. Accounting and auditing firms can also provide meaningful advice to their clients about when and where it makes sense to adopt this technology.

REFERENCE

Rogowski, T. "Tech fluency leads profession's needs", October 2018, www.accountingtoday.com/opinion/technology-fluency-is-top-required-skill-set-for-new-cpas

CHAPTER 3

From Byzantine Consensus to Blockchain Consensus

Miguel Correia

CONTENTS

3.1 INTRODUCTION

Blockchain is an exciting new technology that is making headlines worldwide. The reasons behind the success of a technology are often unclear, but in the case of blockchain it is safe to say that an important factor is that it has two killer apps, not one. The first killer app are cryptocurrencies, as the *original blockchain* is the core of Bitcoin [1]—the first cryptocurrency and the one that is fostering the adoption of cryptocurrencies. The second killer app are *smart contracts*, first introduced in the Ethereum system [2], with their promise of computerizing legal contracts and of supporting a countless number of applications [3–5]. Moreover, the sky seems to be the limit for the applications people are imagining for blockchain.

A blockchain is essentially a secure, unmodifiable, append-only, log of transactions. The word *transaction* should be taken in a broad sense; in Bitcoin, a transaction is a transfer of currency between accounts, but in smart contracts, transactions do not necessarily involve money. Blockchains trade performance and resource-usage efficiency for security, in the sense that they are implemented by a set of redundant nodes that store the same state and run an algorithm to make *consensus* over the order of transactions (more precisely of blocks of transactions), even if some of the nodes misbehave in some way.

3.1.1 Byzantine Consensus

This last aspect—replication plus consensus despite misbehavior—is a topic of research since the late 1970s [6, 7]. The problem of reaching consensus in such conditions was first proposed by Pease, Shostak, and Lamport in 1980 [6], but popularized by the same authors when they explained it as a story of Byzantine generals that have to agree on a common attack plan by exchanging messages [7]. The problem considers the existence of *arbitrary faults*, i.e., some nodes deviating from the algorithm they are supposed to execute, both in the domain of time (e.g., delaying messages or stopping to communicate) and the domain of value (e.g., sending wrong values in messages) [8], but that later work led to the term *Byzantine faults* being used to mean the same. These works considered a fully connected network (all nodes can communicate with all), but Dolev generalized the model to consider a mesh network, in which faulty nodes may corrupt and discard messages [9]. Consensus can be used to replicate a service in a set of nodes in such a way that clients of that service observe a correct (non-faulty) service even if some nodes are faulty [10].

These earlier works consider a synchronous model, i.e., they assume that the communication and processing delays are bounded (they do not state it this way, but they assume it is possible to know if a message was not received, which is equivalent). However, this kind of model is inadequate for most distributed systems due to the uncertainty of communication delays in the Internet and of processing in typical nodes (workstations, mobile devices, servers, etc.). Moreover, they had a theoretical vein. In the 1990s, there was a line of work on algorithms for reliable communication between nodes assuming an asynchronous model, i.e., there are no time bounds. Notable examples are the work by Reiter et al. [11, 12] and by Kihlstrom et al. [13, 14]. This work has led to the first efficient asynchronous Byzantine fault-tolerant replication algorithm, often designated PBFT, due to Castro and Liskov. [15] After PBFT, many other algorithms appeared [16–28], including our own. [29–33] All these algorithms provide well-defined safety and liveness properties [34] under well-defined assumptions. We will designate the problem solved by these algorithms informally as *Byzantine consensus*.

3.1.2 Blockchain

Interestingly, despite all this research effort, Satoshi Nakamoto, the author(s) of Bitcoin, decided to use an entirely different approach to achieve consensus in the system that implements that cryptocurrency [1]. This consensus algorithm, often designated *Nakamoto consensus*, is based on the notion of *proof-of-work* (PoW). Nodes flood the network with transactions, which they collect and add to blocks. When a block is appended to the chain (in the log), nodes close the block they were creating and start solving a cryptopuzzle in order to obtain a PoW for their block. When a node solves the cryptopuzzle, it broadcasts its block with the PoW, which is validated, then appended by all nodes to the chain in the other nodes. The time needed to solve the cryptopuzzle throttles the addition of blocks to the chain, which is a requirement when there are many competing nodes, which may pretend to be even more (a Sybil attack [35]). Moreover, the randomness of the time to solve it provides a sort of consensus, as it supports the assumption that no two nodes will obtain PoWs concurrently. However, this process does allow two different PoWs to be obtained concurrently, leading different subsets of the network of nodes to append different blocks to the chain, breaking agreement, which is an important property of any consensus algorithm. This is a clear disadvantage of Nakamoto consensus in relation to Byzantine consensus algorithms. On the positive side, the Nakamoto consensus is more scalable, as it can be used on top of a mesh network, using a peer-to-peer dissemination protocol, as in the case of Bitcoin [1, 36–38].

The potential of the blockchain technology has led to an increase in research in this area and in the actual implementation of blockchain systems and applications. In terms of research, a large number of papers have been published on improved consensus algorithms [39–42], blockchain scalability [37, 38, 43, 44], attacks against cryptocurrencies and blockchains [45–48], among many other topics. In relation to implementations, for example, there are now more than 2,000 cryptocurrencies with a global value of more than 100 billion euros (around 50% due to Bitcoin) [49]; in 2016, during a period of a few months there were around 15,000 smart contracts deployed in Ethereum [50].

3.1.3 This Chapter

This chapter presents a state-of-the-art in the area of Byzantine consensus and its application in blockchains. The chapter is organized as follows. Section 3.2 presents the first part of the state-of-the-art, about Byzantine consensus. Section 3.3 presents the second part, on blockchain based on the Nakamoto consensus and related schemes. Section 3.4 presents the third part, about blockchain based on Byzantine consensus. Finally, Section 3.5 concludes the chapter.

3.2 BYZANTINE CONSENSUS

This section presents a state-of-the-art in what we call *Byzantine consensus*, which excludes the Nakamoto consensus based on PoW. As already mentioned, research in the area started in the late 1970s [6, 7, 9] with synchronous algorithms, and evolved to asynchronous algorithms later. This section is about more recent work, starting with the FLP impossibility result, then with practical algorithms starting with PBFT.

3.2.1 On System Models

Consensus algorithms depend strongly on the system model, i.e., on the assumptions made about the environment and the system. In this chapter, we consider a basic system model: message-passing communication, Byzantine (or arbitrary) faults, and asynchrony. We say that this is the *basic* system model because all the algorithms considered refine it somehow.

The reason for this model is that it expresses well the conditions that exist in today's distributed systems, such as those based on the Internet:

- *Message-passing* is a convenient communication model as in the Internet, and any other modern network, communication is broken down into some sort of messages: packets, datagrams, application-layer messages, etc. Even network technologies that use virtual circuits in the lower layers (e.g., SDH/SONET and ATM) are used to transmit messages in the upper layers. Except when noticed, we consider that communication is done using *authenticated channels* that authenticate messages (prevent impersonation of the sender) and ensure their integrity (detect and discard modified messages). These characteristics are easy to implement with protocols such as SSL/TLS [51]. An alternative system model would be *shared memory* [52–56], but in the Internet the shared memory itself would have to be implemented using message-passing algorithms.

- Assuming *Byzantine faults* means to make no assumptions about how individual nodes fail. Poor assumptions may be vulnerabilities, so making no assumptions about faults is convenient when the objective is to make a system dependable and secure. Byzantine faults can be intentional, malicious, so tolerating such faults allows improving the security of the system, e.g., of the blockchain. A particularly pernicious subclass of Byzantine faults are inconsistent value faults that happen, e.g., when a faulty process sends two messages with the same identifier and different contents to two subsets of processes.

- *Asynchrony* means also to make no assumptions, but about bounds on communication and processing delays. This non-assumption is also convenient because, otherwise, adversaries might do attacks that cause delays on purpose. In fact, attacks against time, namely denial-of-service attacks, are very common because they tend to be easier to do than attacks against integrity or confidentiality.

A system model that considers Byzantine faults and asynchrony is very generic in the sense that algorithms designed for this model are correct even if the environment is more benign, e.g., if nodes can only crash or delays are bounded. Unfortunately, consensus is not solvable in this basic model, a problem that we explain in Section 3.2.3.

3.2.2 Byzantine Consensus Definitions

There is no single definition of Byzantine consensus, also denominated *Byzantine agreement*. In fact there are many, with significative differences.

Consider the basic system model above and that the consensus algorithm is executed by a set of n nodes or *processes*. We say that a process is *correct* if it follows its algorithm until termination, otherwise it is said to be *faulty*. We assume that there are at most $f < n$ faulty processes. Each process *proposes* a value (sometimes called the *initial value*) and *decides* a value.

Two common and similar definitions of consensus are *binary consensus* and *multi-valued consensus*. They differ in terms of the range of admissible value, respectively, binary or arbitrary. Otherwise, the definition is similar [14, 57–60]:

- *Validity:* If all correct processes propose the same value v, then any correct process that decides, decides v.

- *Agreement:* No two correct processes decide differently.

- *Termination:* Every correct process eventually decides.

The first two properties are *safety properties*, i.e., properties that say that bad things cannot happen, whereas the last is a *liveness property* that states that good things must happen [61]. A weaker validity property is the following [62–64]:

- *Validity':* If a correct process decides v, then v was proposed by some process.

Although Validity is stronger than Validity', it does not say much about the value decided in case not all correct processes propose the same value. This limitation leads to the definition of *vector consensus* in which processes decide on the same vector with one value per process, for at least n-f processes [62, 65]. This definition of consensus is related to the *interactive consistency* problem, which however considered a synchronous system model [6]. In terms of definition, the difference between vector consensus and multi-valued consensus is the validity property that becomes:

- *Vector validity:* Every correct process that decides, decides on a vector V of size n:

- $\forall_{p_i}$: if pi is correct, then either $V[i]$ is the value proposed by pi or $\perp$;

- at least f+1 elements of V were proposed by correct processes.

A different solution to the same difficulty with the validity properties is given by the *validity predicate-based consensus* [66]. We will come back to this definition as it was written with blockchains in mind. The definition is similar to the previous ones, but the validity property depends on an application-specific *valid()* predicate:

- *Predicate-based validity:* If a correct process decides *v*, then *v* satisfies the *valid()* predicate.

These definitions of consensus consider that all processes play the same role: all propose a value and all decide a value (at least if they are correct). Lamport introduced an alternative definition in an algorithm known as Paxos [67, 68], which has been thoroughly studied and modified [16, 69, 70, 71]. In Paxos, processes play one or more of the following roles: *proposers*, which propose values; *acceptors*, which choose the value to be decided; and *learners*, which receive the chosen value. The problem can be defined in terms of five properties [68, 71]:

- *Safety 1:* Only a value that has been proposed may be chosen.

- *Safety 2:* Only a single value may be chosen.

- *Safety 3:* Only a chosen value may be learned by a correct learner.

- *Liveness 1:* Some proposed value is eventually chosen.

- *Liveness 2:* Once a value is chosen, correct learners eventually learn it.

This definition is related to *state machine replication* (SMR) or the state machine approach [10, 72], but first let us introduce *atomic broadcast* or total order broadcast. Atomic broadcast is a problem that is different from consensus, but the two have been shown to be equivalent in several system models [73–76]. The problem essentially states that all processes deliver the same messages in the same order, which is equivalent to running a sequence of consensus instances to decide what message(s) to deliver next. Atomic broadcast can be defined in terms of four properties [77]:

- *Validity:* If a correct process broadcasts a message *m*, then some correct process eventually delivers *m*.

- *Agreement:* If a correct process delivers a message *m*, then all correct processes eventually deliver *m*.

- *Integrity:* For any identifier *id* and sender *p*, every correct process *q* delivers at most one message *m* with identifier *id* from sender *p*, and if *p* is correct then *m* was previously broadcast by *p*.

- *Total order:* If two correct processes deliver two messages m_1 and m_2, then both processes deliver the two messages in the same order.

State machine replication is related to Paxos because it involves two kinds of processes: clients that make requests and receive replies (similarly to Paxos' proposers and learners); servers that provide a service to the clients and do consensus about the order of execution of the requests (similarly to Paxos' acceptors). This approach involves ordering requests using an atomic broadcast protocol, which, as explained, is equivalent to consensus. Consider a *state machine* that provides a service and that is characterized by a set of state variables that define its state, and by a set of commands that modify the state variables. All correct servers follow the same history of states if four properties are satisfied:

- *Initial state:* All correct servers start in the same state.

- *Agreement:* All correct servers execute the same commands.

- *Total order:* All correct servers execute the commands in the same order.

- *Determinism:* The same command executed in the same initial state in two different correct servers generates the same final state.

If these properties are satisfied, the service is correct as long as no more from f servers are faulty. The relation between n and f depends on the algorithm, e.g., it can be $n \geq 3f+1$ [15–17, 20] or $n \geq 2f+1$ [18, 29, 31, 32]. SMR is a problem different from consensus, but we will abuse the language and call it *consensus* as it involves solving consensus. We prefer to use this term because it is common in the blockchain domain.

The Paxos definition of consensus is interesting because it allows a simple implementation of SMR in the crash failure model [10, 68]. However, in the Byzantine failure model, this is more complicated because faulty processes can deviate from the algorithm arbitrarily [15, 70].

There are several other consensus variants. In the *k-set consensus* problem, correct processes can decide at most k different values [78, 79]. The *Byzantine generals with alternative plans* problem takes into account the fact that processes may have several views about what decisions/actions are acceptable and unacceptable [80]. Each process has a set of good decisions and a set of bad decisions. The problem is to make all correct processes agree on good decisions proposed by a correct process, and never on a bad decision.

All these definitions of consensus consider that the algorithm is executed by a fixed set of n known processes. There are a few works on consensus in dynamic systems in which the set of processes is unknown and varying [81–84]. The single Byzantine algorithm of this kind, BFT-CUP, is based on an oracle called participant detector that provides hints about the active processes [83, 84].

Table 3.1 presents a summary of the consensus definitions.

3.2.3 FLP Impossibility

A problem with consensus in the basic system model is that it is not solvable. This fact derives trivially from an impossibility result known as FLP, after the names of its proponents [85]. FLP considers binary consensus and a different, weaker, system model (let us call it the FLP system model). This system model also considers message-passing communication and asynchrony, but only that a single process can fail simply

TABLE 3.1 Definitions of consensus and related problems.

Definition	Characteristics	References
Binary consensus	Agreement about a binary value	[57, 58]
Multi-valued consensus	Agreement about an arbitrary value	[14, 59, 60]
Vector consensus	Agreement about a vector with values from at least n-f processes	[62, 65]
Interactive consistency	Similar but for synchronous system models	[6]
Validity predicate-based consensus	Validity property depends on an application-specific *valid()* predicate	[66]
Paxos	Multi-valued consensus with 3 roles: proposers, acceptors, learners	[16, 67, 68, 69, 70, 71]
Atomic broadcast	Processes broadcast and deliver the same messages in the same order	[73–77]
State machine replication	Servers implement a replicated service; clients request that service	[10, 18, 29, 31, 32, 72]
k-set consensus	Correct processes can decide at most k different values	[78, 79]
Consensus with unknown processes	For dynamic systems in which the set of processes is unknown	[81–84]

by crashing (neither any process, nor arbitrarily). It also excludes the existence of random numbers, so the statement is actually about deterministic algorithms. An intuition of this result is that the combination of uncertainty in terms of time (asynchrony) and uncertainty in terms of failure (a process may fail) does not allow an algorithm to distinguish if a process is slow or faulty.

This result is inconvenient because it requires modifying the system model, but, interestingly, has also fostered research on consensus. Specifically, there has been a lot of research on system models that are similar to the FLP system model and the basic system model and allow solving consensus. These new conditions in which the problem is solvable are often said to *circumvent* FLP, whereas, in fact, they change its premises.

The main ways of circumventing FLP are the following [86]:

1. *Add time assumptions to the model,* thus partially sacrificing asynchrony. The idea is to add these assumptions in a way that is realistic in the Internet and other networks. Dwork et al. presented two partial synchrony models that add such time assumptions and allow solving consensus [59]. A partial synchrony model captures the intuition that systems may behave asynchronously (i.e., with variable/unknown processing/communication delays) for some time interval, but that they tend to eventually stabilize. Therefore, the idea is to let the system be mostly asynchronous but to make assumptions about timing properties that are eventually satisfied. Algorithms based on this model are typically guaranteed to terminate only when these timing properties are satisfied. Chandra and Toueg proposed a third partial synchrony model that is similar

but weaker [87]: for each execution, there is an unknown global stabilization time GST, such that an unknown bound on the message delivery time Δ is always satisfied from GST onward. When designing PBFT, Castro and Liskov used an even weaker model in which delays are assumed not to grow exponentially forever [15]. This last model has been adopted by many Byzantine consensus and SMR algorithms [16, 21, 22, 30]. NewTOP [88] and XPaxos [89] consider stronger time assumptions, respectively that pairs of nodes and correct replicas can communicate within a known delay Δ.

2. *Add oracles to the model* that provide hints about process failure, thus partially sacrificing asynchrony. This idea was introduced by Chandra and Toueg [87]. The FLP result derives from the impossibility of distinguishing if a process is faulty or simply very slow, therefore, intuitively, having a hint about the failure/crash of a process may be enough to circumvent FLP. The idea is to associate an unreliable failure detector (UFD) to each process, which provides hints about other processes failures. Chandra and Toueg presented eights classes of UFDs based on properties of accuracy and completeness [87]. They also proved that extending the FLP system model with a rather weak UFD was enough to solve consensus [90]. These oracles are an elegant construct, but, at the end of the day, they hide time assumptions that are necessary to implement them (the system cannot be asynchronous). There are other oracles that allow solving consensus and are not failure detectors, e.g., the Ω detector, which provides hints about who is the leader process [90], and ordering oracles, which provide hints about the order of messages broadcasted [91].

3. *Use a hybrid system model* that includes a subsystem with stronger time assumptions, again partially sacrificing asynchrony. A *wormhole* is an abstraction that system-wise is a component of the system, but model-wise is an extension to the system model [92, 93]. The first work on wormholes to solve consensus [94] considers the basic system model extended with a wormhole called *Trusted Timely Computing Base* (TTCB) [95]. The TTCB is a secure, real-time, and fail-silent distributed component, which provides enough timeliness to circumvent FLP. Applications implementing the consensus algorithm run in the normal system, i.e., in the asynchronous Byzantine system, but use the services provided by the wormhole. In this case, the consensus algorithm relies on the Trusted Block Agreement Service, which essentially makes an agreement on small values (typically hashes) proposed by a set of processes. Later, a simpler multi-valued consensus algorithm and a vector consensus based on the TTCB were also proposed [65, 96]. There are other consensus and SMR algorithms based on wormholes, although most authors do not use the term "wormhole" [18, 25, 29, 31, 32, 77, 97, 98].

4. *Add randomization to the model*, partially sacrificing determinism. FLP applies to deterministic algorithms, so a solution to circumvent this result is to add randomization to the system model—the ability to generate random numbers—and

design probabilistic algorithms [58, 75, 99–106]. This involves changing one of the properties that define consensus and make it probabilistic.

These ways of circumventing FLP are also a form of classifying algorithms in the area. Table 3.2 presents a summary of the techniques to circumvent FLP.

3.2.4 Byzantine Consensus Patterns

The consensus algorithms mentioned in the previous section follow two major communication patterns: *decentralized* and *leader-based*. In this section, we use these patterns to present briefly how Byzantine consensus algorithms work. Moreover, this will become useful later to understand blockchain consensus algorithms.

The two patterns are represented in Figure 3.1. In decentralized consensus algorithms, all processes play the same role and try to individually reach a decision. In leader-based (or coordinator-based or primary-backup) consensus algorithms, there is a leader (or primary or coordinator) that tries to impose a decision; if the leader is faulty, a new leader has to be elected. The fact that in decentralized consensus algorithms all processes communicate with all others imposes a quadratic message complexity ($O(n^2)$). On crash fault-tolerant leader-based consensus algorithms it is possible to achieve linear message complexity ($O(n)$) [87, 111, 112], but in Byzantine leader-based consensus algorithms the need to deal with inconsistent value faults imposes a quadratic message complexity.

Decentralized consensus algorithms work basically the following way (Figure 3.1(a)). In the first step, every process broadcasts a proposal, and waits for n-f messages. In the second step, every process picks a proposal with enough votes or a default value, broadcasts it, and waits for n-f messages. In the third step every process picks a proposal if it has enough votes, broadcasts it, waits for n-f messages, and decides the value if it received enough copies. Otherwise, the whole process is repeated. This explanation and the figure are based on Bracha's algorithm [113]. In that algorithm the broadcast primitive is not standard, unreliable, network broadcast, but *reliable broadcast* [76, 113]. The reliable broadcast problem consists in guaranteeing that when a process sends a message, all processes deliver that message, or possibly no message at all if the

TABLE 3.2 Techniques to circumvent FLP.

Technique	Positive/Negative	References
Add time assumptions	Algorithms efficient if network stable/delayed otherwise	[15, 16, 21, 22, 30, 59, 87]
Add oracles	Same as previous	[87, 90, 91]
Hybrid model	Efficient algorithms/additional assumptions	[18, 25, 29, 31, 32, 65, 77, 95–97]
Allow randomization	No assumptions/less efficient algorithms	[58, 75, 99–106]
		[107–108]

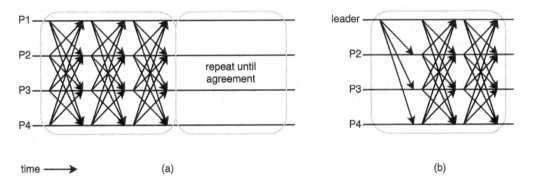

FIGURE 3.1   The two main organization patterns of Byzantine consensus algorithms: (a) decentralized and (b) leader-based.

sender is faulty. This problem is weaker than atomic broadcast (no ordering) and also weaker than consensus, but requires three communication steps and $O(n^2)$ messages in the basic system model. Therefore, there are many more messages being actually sent than those represented in the figure; Bracha's algorithm has $O(n^3)$ message complexity.

Leader-based consensus algorithms work essentially, as shown in Figure 3.1(b). In the first step, the leader broadcasts a proposal and in the following two steps the other processes agree on accepting it and confirm their acceptance. This pattern corresponds to the normal mode operation of PBFT, omitting the interaction with the clients (recall that PBFT is an SMR algorithm). In that algorithm, as in many others, in case the leader is suspected, a new leader may have to be elected (also not represented in the figure). There is another class of leader-based consensus algorithms that rotate the leader, so there is no need for electing a new one, including some our own [22, 30, 31, 59, 77].

3.2.5 Hybrid Models to Reduce Processes

After defining consensus and explaining the main ways to circumvent FLP, we present two areas in which we did much work related to the topic (this and the next section).

Most Byzantine consensus and SMR algorithms consider the basic system model extended with time assumptions (e.g., the same as PBFT [15]) or failure detectors (1 and 2 in Section 3.2.3). In these models, the relation between the number of processes n and the maximum number of faulty processes f is $n \geq 3f+1$ [15–17, 20]. This means that 4 processes are needed to mask 1 that is faulty, 7 to mask 2, and so on. In the 1990s and 2000s, these numbers were considered high, and the folklore in the area said that many companies refused to use such algorithms due to the costs involved. At the time many companies used crash fault-tolerant algorithms, which required only $n \geq 2f+1$, e.g., as part of Chubby [114] or Zookeeper [115]. Interestingly, the concern with the number of replicas vanished with Bitcoin and blockchain (Section 3.3), but reducing the number of processes is clearly an important goal. Notice that in SMR, more processes (server replicas in that context) mean more hardware, more software licences, and more administration costs. Moreover, it is important to avoid common mode failures, which requires different replicas, i.e., diversity [116].

We were the first to show that it is possible to reduce the minimum number of replicas in Byzantine SMR from $3f+1$ to $2f+1$ using a hybrid failure model (3 in Section 3.2.3) [29, 97]. That algorithm, BFT-TO, is based on a wormhole called Trusted Ordering Wormhole (TO wormhole).[1] This wormhole is distributed (has a component in each replica) and provides an ordering service, so it solves consensus. It has to be implemented in a way that it satisfies two security properties: integrity (its service and data cannot be tampered with by an adversary) and confidentiality (of the cryptographic material used to protect the communication). Therefore, the TO wormhole fails only by crashing, so it can solve consensus with only $2f+1$ replicas, e.g., using Schiper's algorithm [112]. BFT-TO uses the TO wormhole to order hashes of the requests, so it is not bound by the $n \geq 3f+1$ relation of other Byzantine consensus algorithms.

A few years later, Chun et al. proposed the *Attested Append-Only Memory* (A2M), another wormhole used to implement state machine replication with only $2f+1$ replicas [18]. This Byzantine SMR algorithm was called A2M-PBFT-EA. Like the TO wormhole, A2M has to be tamperproof, but it is local to the computers, not distributed, which is a significant improvement. Replicas using the A2M are forced to commit to a single, monotonically increasing sequence of operations. Since the sequence is externally verifiable, faulty replicas cannot present different sequences to different replicas.

Later, we presented an even simpler wormhole that also allows implementing state machine replication with only $2f+1$ replicas, the *Unique Sequential Identifier Generator* (USIG) [31, 32]. This component contains only a counter and a few cryptographic functions that are used to associate sequence numbers to certain operations done by the replicas, e.g., producing a signed certificate that proves unequivocally that the number is assigned to that message. The USIG has been used to implement three SMR algorithms: MinBFT and MinZyzzyva that are inspired on PBFT and Zyzzyva [17] but with less replicas [32]; and EBAWA that uses a rotating leader and has other characteristics adequate for wide-area networks [31]. The USIG is also the basis for a methodology to transform consensus algorithms that tolerate crash faults and require $2f+1$ processes, into similar algorithms that tolerate Byzantine faults also with $2f+1$ processes [77].

We implemented the USIG as a thin layer on top of the Trusted Platform Module (TPM), a security chip designed by the Trusted Computing Group and now present in the mainboard of most PCs [32, 117]. Our implementation was based on one of the TPM's monotonic counters and signatures. Abraham et al. presented a Byzantine consensus based on the TPM that uses one of the TPM's Platform Configuration Registers (PCRs) instead of the monotonic counter [118]. Our experiments have shown that using the TPM was a bad option, as the signature implementation was quite slow (approximately 0.4s to obtain a signature). Both USIG and Abraham et al.'s abstraction are similar to Trinc [119].

Kapitza et al. implemented our USIG service on an FPGA and called it Counter Assignment Service in Hardware (CASH) [25]. Then, they designed CheapBFT, a Byzantine SMR architecture and algorithm that tolerates that all but one of the replicas active are faulty in normal-case operation. CheapBFT runs only $f+1$ replicas in normal-case operation and keeps the other f replicas on hold; it activates these f replicas in case there is disagreement between the active replicas because one or more are faulty. In total, it uses $2f+1$ replicas, similarly to MinBFT in which it is based. This reduction of the number of replicas is interesting but comes at the cost of having a trusted infrastructure to detect disagreement between replicas and activate the replicas on hold, which is much more complex than the USIG service.

Hybster parallelizes consensus instances to be able to order more than 1 million operations per second, increasing one order of magnitude the performance of algorithms in the area [98]. That scheme is based on TrInX, a software version of USIG/Trinc/CASH implemented in Intel SGX enclaves [120, 121]. These enclaves are trusted execution environments that run software components isolated from the rest of the platform, including the operating system. This isolation is enforced by the CPU itself. TrInX is different from similar components in two ways. First, for parallelization purposes, it can implement an arbitrary number of counters and provide multi-counter certificates. Second, for performance, it uses message authentication codes based on cryptographic hash functions instead of digital signatures.

Table 3.3 summarizes the works on using hybrid models to reduce the number of processes.

3.2.6 Randomization

Another area in which we did significant work was on solving Byzantine consensus using randomization. As mentioned in Section 3.2.3, adding randomization to the model allows circumventing FLP and involves making one of the properties that defines the consensus problem probabilistic, instead of deterministic. Most authors choose to make a liveness property probabilistic (e.g., Termination), as the algorithm may run until this property is satisfied, so its probabilistic nature becomes irrelevant. The Termination property becomes:

- *Probabilistic termination:* Every correct process eventually decides with probability 1.

Curiously there are a few papers that sacrifice a safety property instead of liveness. Specifically, these algorithms satisfy an agreement property with a certain probability

TABLE 3.3 Byzantine consensus algorithms based on hybrid models.

Algorithm	Subsystem	Characteristics	References
BFT-TO	TO wormhole	Distributed subsystem	[29, 97]
A2M-PBFT-EA	A2M	Local subsystem	[18]
MinBFT, MinZyzzyva, EBAWA	USIG	Local and simple subsystem	[31, 32]
	TPM/PCRs	Based on common hardware, slower	[118]
CheapBFT	CASH	Hardware implementation of USIG	[25]
Hybster	TrInX	Alternative implementation of USIG	[98]

[101, 103]. This is arguably a bad idea, but is also the option taken in several blockchains, starting with Bitcoin's.

Randomized Byzantine consensus algorithms have been around since 1983 [57, 58]. All randomized consensus algorithms are based on a random operation, typically picking randomly 0 or 1, something that is often designated *tossing a coin*. Randomized consensus algorithms can be classified in two classes, depending on how the coin tossing operation is done:

- *Local coin*: algorithms in which each process tosses its own coin. The first algorithm is due to Ben-Or [57]. Local coin tossing is trivial to implement: it requires just a random number generator that returns binary values. However, when consensus algorithms based on local coins require tossing a coin, there tends to be disagreement about the coin values in each process, so these algorithms terminate in an expected exponential number of communication steps [57, 113].

- *Shared coin*: algorithms in which processes toss coins cooperatively. The first algorithm is due to Rabin [58]. Shared coin tossing is more complicated because it requires a distributed algorithm that provides the same coin value to all non-faulty processes. However, these algorithms can terminate in an expected constant number of steps, as all processes see the same sequence of coins tossed [58, 99–103].

Randomized consensus algorithms have raised a lot of interest from a theoretical point of view. However, on the practical side, they have often been assumed to be inefficient due to their probabilistic nature, which leads to high *expected time complexity* (number of rounds to terminate) and high *expected message complexity* (number of messages sent). However, those assumptions miss the fact that consensus algorithms are not usually executed in oblivion, but in the context of a higher-level problem (e.g., atomic broadcast) that can provide a context that promotes fast termination (e.g., many processes proposing the same value can lead to a quick termination). Moreover, adversary models usually consider a strong adversary that completely controls the scheduling of the network and decides which processes receive which messages and in which order, whereas in practice, an adversary is not able or interested in doing such attacks (it would be simpler to block the whole communication instead). Therefore, in practice, the network scheduling may also foster fast termination.

A second, more real, reason for inefficiency is that these algorithms are not executed alone but stacked to solve a relevant problem, such as SMR. Most randomized consensus algorithms in the literature solve binary consensus [58, 99–103], as the expected time complexity becomes much worse if the random number has more than one bit [122]. Therefore, to do something useful, we need *transformations*, e.g., from binary consensus and broadcast primitives into multi-valued consensus and from multi-valued consensus into vector consensus or atomic broadcast [75, 104, 105]. This stacking of algorithms can lead to large expected time and message complexities.

We have shown that randomized consensus can be efficient in two steps. As a first step, we developed a set of transformations from binary randomized consensus to multi-valued consensus, vector consensus and atomic broadcast [75]. The proposed transformations have a set of properties that we believed had the potential to provide good performance. First, they do not use digital signatures constructed with public-key cryptography, a well-known performance bottleneck in such algorithms at the time. Second, they make no synchrony assumptions, since these assumptions are often vulnerable to subtle but effective attacks. Third, they are completely decentralized, thus avoiding the cost of detecting faulty leaders that exists in leader-based protocols like PBFT [15, 22, 30]. Fourth, they have optimal resilience, i.e., $n \geq 3f+1$. In terms of time complexity, the multi-valued consensus protocol terminates in a constant expected number of rounds, while the vector consensus and atomic broadcast protocols have $O(f)$ complexity.

The second step involved implementing minor variations of these algorithms and evaluating their performance experimentally [105, 106]. The algorithms were implemented as a protocol stack called RITAS. At the lowest level of the stack, there are two broadcast primitives: reliable broadcast and echo broadcast (essentially weaker versions of atomic broadcast that do not require ordering or consensus). On top of these primitives, stands Bracha's binary consensus [113]. Building on the binary consensus layer, multi-valued consensus allows the agreement on values of arbitrary range. At the highest level there is vector consensus that lets processes decide on a vector with values proposed by a subset of the processes, and atomic broadcast that ensures total order. The algorithms have shown good performance, e.g., with latencies in the order of milliseconds and throughput of a few thousand messages per second delivered by the atomic broadcast primitive [106].

ABBA was a major step in randomized consensus algorithms [100]. This binary consensus algorithm is based on a shared coin created using a novel combination of cryptographic schemes, mainly threshold signatures and a threshold coin-tossing scheme, which has lead to constant expected time complexity ($O(1)$) and expected message complexity $O(n^2)$. This algorithm theoretically performs better than Bracha's (which uses local coins), but resorts to expensive public-key cryptography, so we made a thorough experimental comparison of the two [123]. In a nutshell, Bracha's algorithm performed always better, but we considered only 4, 7, and 10 processes, and ABBA seemed to scale much better, so with a few more processes it would start performing better and stay that way.

When further experimenting with these algorithms on Wi-Fi networks (802.11a/g at 54 Mb/s and 802.11b at 11 Mb/s), both with PDAs (circa 2006 there were no smartphones) and laptops, we observed that the performance was much worse than in wired networks, possibly due to the lower bandwidth [124]. Later, we concluded that the reasons were more profound and that the *basic system model* was inadequate for wireless networks, most especially wireless ad-hoc networks [107, 108]. In the basic system model every pair of processes is connected by an authenticated channel, so when a process broadcasts a message to all others—a common communication pattern in these algorithms—it actually sends $n - 1$ messages; as the medium is shared, it becomes occupied for the period of sending all these individual messages. Moreover, there are several effects in wireless networks that lead to retransmissions: loss of signal due to mobility, interference from other wireless networks, electromagnetic interference from other sources, reflection and blocking caused by objects. Therefore, the problem is not only that in theory the bandwidth is lower than in typical wired networks, but that in practice the available bandwidth is even further reduced.

This leads us to investigate an adequate system model for wireless networks [107, 108]. In this system model, processes broadcast messages to all others and there can be dynamic omission faults that prevent any number of processes from receiving the message sent in a round. Interestingly, Santoro and Widmayer have proved that, even with strong synchrony assumptions, there is no deterministic solution to any non-trivial form of agreement if *n-1* or more messages can be lost per communication round [125]. We proposed two binary consensus algorithms that circumvent this impossibility result using randomization. The first tolerated only crash faults [107, 108], so we focus on the second, Turquois, which tolerates Byzantine faults [109, 110]. Turquois works in rounds, similarly to Bracha's algorithm, but does progress only in rounds when processes receive enough messages. Moreover, it uses a novel message validation scheme that has two aspects: authenticity validation and semantic validation. Turquois was evaluated experimentally and proved to be much faster than ABBA and Bracha's algorithm.

Despite our work in the early 2010s, randomized consensus algorithms continued not to raise much practical interested until very recently with the appearance of HoneyBadgerBFT [126]. This algorithm is inspired on SINTRA, a protocol stack that builds on ABBA [104] (our own stack, RITAS, was inspired on SINTRA, but avoided public-key cryptography for efficiency). HoneyBadgerBFT solves atomic broadcast and manages to improve over SINTRA by resorting to an efficient transformation from multi-valued consensus to vector consensus (that they call common subset agreement) using batching. The algorithm solves atomic broadcast with time complexity $O(n)$.

Table 3.4 summarizes the works on randomized consensus.

3.2.7 Summary

This section provided a brief state-of-the-art on Byzantine consensus. We started with a discussion on the system models that are relevant in this context, and then presented

TABLE 3.4 Randomized Byzantine consensus algorithms and stacks.

Algorithm/Stack	Characteristics	References
several with local coin	binary consensus	[57, 113]
several with shared coin	binary consensus	[58, 99–103]
SINTRA	protocol stack; builds on the ABBA binary consensus algorithm	[104]
RITAS	protocol stack; avoids public-key cryptography for efficiency	[75, 105]
HoneyBadgerBFT	efficient atomic broadcast based on an efficient transformation from multi-valued consensus to vector consensus	[126]

several definitions of consensus protocols, including related notions such as state machine replication and atomic broadcast. Then, we presented the influential FLP impossibility result and the main approaches to circumvent it. Next, the organization patterns used in most algorithms are presented. Finally, we presented two areas in which we did significant work: using hybrid models to solve consensus with less processes, and efficient randomized consensus algorithms. The next section presents the notions of blockchain and Nakamoto consensus, as well as several related algorithms.

3.3 BLOCKCHAINS WITH NAKAMOTO CONSENSUS

As mentioned in the introduction, the original blockchain—the one at the core of Bitcoin—runs a consensus algorithm based on the notion of *proof-of-work* (PoW) [1], which we denominate *Nakamoto consensus*. This section presents the original blockchain, its consensus algorithm, the killer applications (cryptocurrencies and smart contracts), and variants of PoW-based consensus. It does not present more recent blockchains that use Byzantine consensus related to those presented in the previous section (Section 3.4).

3.3.1 Bitcoin's Blockchain and Consensus

This section presents Bitcoin's blockchain and consensus. They were not introduced in a scientific paper, but on a white paper that presents how they work in an informal way [1]. In a sense, that paper presents a brilliant piece of work, which puts together several previously existing concepts to create a novel, highly successful, system. However, it misses important aspects such as a clearly defined system model, properties, communication protocol, and consensus algorithm. Moreover, the Bitcoin system is not static, but a system in production, with frequent software updates and conceptual changes. Fortunately, there is more rigorous documentation from the Ethereum project [2, 127] (Ethereum in many aspects is very close to Bitcoin), from Garay et al. [128], and others [129].

Bitcoin's blockchain is a secure, unmodifiable, append-only, log of transactions, as mentioned before. This blockchain is executed in a set of nodes that run Bitcoin's software and form a *peer-to-peer network* (P2P). This network is decentralized, i.e., it has no central control or authority, although the team that develops that software has some control, at least as far as they manage to convince the nodes to install the new versions of the software (complete autonomy is a myth). The nodes run a consensus algorithm to decide which transactions to log. Every consensus decides the next *block* (or set) of transactions that is added to the log.

Each node stores locally a *chain of blocks* or blockchain (Figure 3.2). This chain is a linked list that contains the log itself. The first block is called genesis block. Each record contains the following items:

- *Version:* a non-trivial combination of version of the Bitcoin software used to create the block and a bitmask [130];

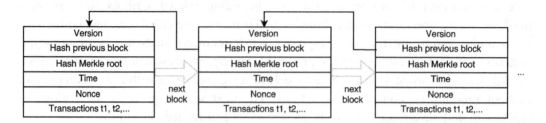

FIGURE 3.2   Chain of blocks in Bitcoin's blockchain.

- *Hash previous block:* cryptographic hash (SHA-256) of the header of the previous block (i.e., the previous block except the transactions);

- *Hash Merkle root:* the cryptographic hash that is at the root of the Merkle tree that summarizes the transactions;

- *Time:* a timestamp that indicates when the block was created;

- *Nonce:* a number that has the property of making the cryptographic hash of the header to be below a certain threshold (related to PoW, explained later);

- *Transactions:* list of the block's transactions (the only item that is not part of the header).

A Merkle tree is a binary tree where the root and every node is a hash of its two children, except the leafs that are, in this case, transactions. The use of such a tree allows nodes to delete or not download the transactions that are not relevant to them, as the Merkle tree allows nodes to verify transactions individually (instead of needing all the transactions to check the hash of a block).

Notice that the consensus algorithm also defines the order in which the nodes are appended to the chain. Therefore, it would be more consistent with the original distributed algorithms nomenclature (Section 3.2) to say that the algorithm solves atomic broadcast or SMR. Nevertheless, we will stick to the term consensus, as it is the one that is used in the blockchain and cryptocurrency literature. One aspect in which the consensus used in blockchains differs from these two other problems is that each block depends on the previous, as it includes its hash.

There are several types of nodes in Bitcoin. Each type of node implements a subset of the following four *roles* [129]:

- *Wallet:* storing the data necessary to access the coins (BTC) of the node's owner (including cryptographic material);

- *Miner:* solving the cryptopuzzle necessary to obtain PoWs for blocks;

- *Full blockchain:* storing the full chain of blocks;

- *Network routing:* implementing Bitcoin's P2P protocol, making the node part of the Bitcoin network.

When a node (with wallet and network routing roles) wants to do a transaction, it disseminates that transaction in the P2P network. All nodes (with mining role) collect transactions and add them to blocks. When a node (with mining role) appends a block to the chain, it closes the block it was creating and starts solving the cryptopuzzle in order to obtain a PoW for that block. A node appends a block to the chain when it receives a block that has the hash of the last block in the chain and a valid PoW.

The cryptopuzzle is the problem of finding a nonce that makes the hash of the block lower than a certain *target*, or, equivalently, to start with a number of 0-bit values. The target number is defined dynamically, in order to tune the difficulty of the problem (the target may be, e.g., 2^{187}). This process of solving the cryptopuzzle is called *mining*, involves a huge amount of energy, and is compensated with two forms of incentives in coins: new minted coins created by the block itself (50 coins in the beginning of Bitcoin, but periodically reduced), and a transaction fee (payed by everyone that has a transaction in the block). Today (successful) mining is not done by individual nodes, but by large groups of nodes: *mining pools* where ad-hoc sets of nodes share mining work and split the reward [131] or *mining datacenters* dedicated to mining Bitcoin [132].

This algorithm is clearly not a classical Byzantine consensus as those presented in Section 3.2:

- *Validity* is ensured by the nodes that receive the block, which do not add it to the chain unless the two hashes are correct, the timestamp is within certain bounds, and the transactions satisfy certain conditions (e.g., they do not spend money already spent).

- *Agreement* can be violated, as the algorithm allows PoWs for two different blocks to be obtained concurrently by competing groups, leading different subsets of the network of nodes to append different blocks to the chain (blocks from different groups of nodes must be different, as the first transaction of the block is a special transaction that creates a number of coins to reward the effort of the group of nodes). Such *temporary forks* are healed by letting the chains grow and pruning the smallest subchain(s), effectively undoing the transactions in all blocks in these smallest chains since the fork point (Figure 3.3).

- *Termination* is only eventually satisfied because in case there is a temporary fork it has to be healed for consensus on a block to terminate. Moreover, Nakamoto claims that as long as a majority of the CPU power—*mining power*—is controlled by nodes that are not faulty, they will generate the longest chain and the properties of the blockchain will be assured [1]; however, Eyal and Sirer have shown an attack in which colluding miners obtain a revenue larger than their fair share, making it rational to collude and create a pool with more than half of the mining power. [45]

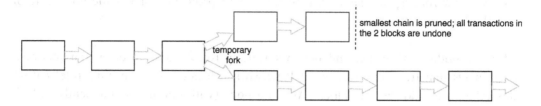

FIGURE 3.3 Temporary fork in Bitcoin's blockchain.

Bitcoin's blockchain may be said to implement a *speculative* variation of *validity predicate-based consensus* (Section 3.2.2). There are several speculative versions of SMR algorithms [17, 32, 133, 134]. These algorithms reply faster to clients in normal conditions, but in some cases servers may have to rollback part of the execution. This is essentially what happens also with Bitcoin's blockchain, which may have to remove from the chain some previously added blocks, undoing many transactions.

This *speculative validity predicate-based Byzantine consensus* can be defined in terms of the following properties:

- *Predicate-based validity:* If a correct process decides v, then v satisfies the *valid()* predicate.

- *Eventual agreement:* Eventually no two correct processes decide differently.

- *Termination:* Every correct process eventually decides.

In Bitcoin the *valid()* predicate checks if: the previous block referenced by the block exists; the timestamp of the block is greater than the timestamp of the previous block and less than 2 hours in the future; the PoW of the block is valid; no transaction causes an error (tries to spend unavailable money or is wrongly signed).

Vukolic formalizes the necessity that consensus is not undone in terms of the following property, which is not satisfied by consensus algorithms based on PoW [38]:

- *Consensus finality:* If a correct node p appends block b to its copy of the blockchain before appending block b', then no correct node q appends block b' before b to its copy of the blockchain.

These properties define the consensus variation. A *blockchain* has to satisfy a set of additional properties, which are particularly challenging when consensus is based on PoW [135]:

- *Exponential convergence:* The probability of a fork of depth d is $O(2^{-d})$.

- *Liveness:* New blocks containing new transactions will continue to be appended to the chain.

- *Correctness:* All blocks in the longest chain will only include valid transactions.

- *Fairness:* A miner with a ratio α of the total mining power will mine a ratio α of the blocks when time tends to infinite.

The first property is important to give users confidence that waiting for a number of blocks being appended to the chain after the one containing their transaction will ensure this transaction is permanently part of the chain.

As mentioned above, there are different types of Bitcoin nodes, that implement different subsets of the four roles. The most important types of nodes are the following [129]. A *reference client* implements the four roles, i.e., it provides the full functionality. A *full blockchain node* is a node that keeps a copy of the chain, so it implements the full blockchain and the network routing roles. A *solo miner* is a node that is concerned only with mining, so it implements all roles except the wallet. A *lightweight wallet* or *simplified payment verification node* is a basic user wallet that provides only the wallet and network routing roles. Notice that these are the original types of nodes; mining pools and mining datacenters have servers that play mainly two roles: miner and routing (using another protocol, typically Stratum [136]).

There is no trivial matching between these node types and SMR's client and server, but it is reasonable to say that nodes that implement the wallet and network routing roles correspond to clients, whereas nodes that implement the miner, full blockchain, and network routing roles correspond to servers. Interestingly, the reference node type includes all these roles, so such nodes are both clients and servers.

Figure 3.4 represents the Bitcoin's consensus communication pattern. Major differences in relation to Byzantine consensus patterns (Figure 3.1) are that there are less communication steps and servers do not communicate all-with-all. These differences are associated to a much lower message complexity, but also to a weakening of the agreement and termination properties.

This does not mean that Bitcon's blockchain performs well. Quite on the contrary, as the threshold of the cryptopuzzle is configured for miners to take 10 minutes to find a solution and there is a maximum of transactions per block (imposed by a maximum block size of 1 MB), the throughput is limited (7 transactions per second until recently). The latency is also huge due to those 10 minutes, plus the existence of a queue of about 1 hour of pending transactions, plus about 1 hour for 6 blocks to be inserted in the chain, providing some assurance that the block with the relevant transaction will no longer be removed (recall that termination is not guaranteed). It is also noteworthy that the energy consumed by the Bitcoin network is estimated to be in the order of a few tens of TWh per year and raising due to the PoW mechanism, which corresponds to the energy spend by a medium-sized European country [137]. On the positive side, the Bitcoin network supports a large number of nodes—more than 10,000 currently [138]—whereas Byzantine consensus algorithms support only some 10 to 100 servers or so.

In the context of Bitcoin and generically blockchain, the term fork is also used with two other meanings. There is a *soft fork* when there is a new version of the node software that is backwards compatible with the previous version. A *hard fork* is similar except that the new version is not backwards compatible. When there is a hard fork, two

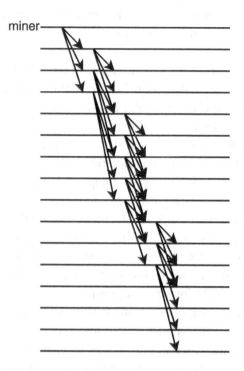

FIGURE 3.4   Communication pattern in Bitcoin and other blockchains.

subnetworks may start existing as some users may change to the new versions while others do not. In fact, although we talk simply about Bitcoin in this chapter, today there are several co-existing Bitcoin networks created by hard forks: Bitcoin, Bitcoin Cash, Bitcoin SV, Bitcoin Gold, etc.

3.3.2 Blockchain Applications

This section deviates from the line of the rest of the chapter on consensus algorithms. The objective is to present briefly what we called the two blockchain's killer apps: cryptocurrencies and smart contracts, as this is important to better understand the notion of blockchain.

The first *cryptocurrency*, in the sense we use the term, was Bitcoin [1], which we use as example. As already explained, Bitcoin is based on the original blockchain. Bitcoin's blockchain does not store the amount of money owned in users's *accounts*, but transactions involving accounts. The money in an account is designated the unspent transaction output (UTXO) [2].

An account is identified by a 20-byte address that is the hash of a public key K_u of an elliptic curve public-key cryptographic (ECC) scheme. The corresponding private key K_r is kept by the account's owner in a wallet. There are many wallet implementations, from those more secure that use specific hardware, to others less secure in software an even at the cloud.

A transaction contains one or more inputs. Each input contains a reference to a UTXO (a transaction in a block of the chain) and a signature produced by the owner of the account. That signature has two components: a real signature, obtained with the ECC scheme with K_r; and the public key K_u.

Every coin is created by a special transaction; every time a new block is mined and added to the chain, the first transaction of the block is such a transaction that creates coins.

Bitcoin's ledger can be considered a *state machine*: the state is the ownership of every coin (the UTXO of every account) and the transactions are commands that modify the state, either creating coins or transferring currency to other accounts (Section 3.2.2). On the contrary of most state machine implementations, in Bitcoin the state is not stored explicitly, but implicitly, i.e., in terms of an initial empty state and commands that modify it. The outcome of a transfer transaction can be the transfer of currency or an error (because the account does not have enough money or the signature is invalid), but recall that blocks with transactions that return error are not stored in the blockchain (Section 3.3.1). The major objective is to avoid *double spending*, i.e., that the same owner uses the same coins more than once.

The notion of *smart contracts* was introduced by Szabo in 1997 [139]. The general idea is the one of contracts that are automatically executed and, to the possible extent, automatically enforced. The author gives as example a vending machine, which can be considered to be a legacy, automatically executed and enforced, smart contract: a person inserts coins and automatically receives from the vendor a product. According to Szabo, "smart contracts go beyond the vending machine in proposing to embed contracts in all sorts of property that is valuable and controlled by digital means". However, there was no solution for implementing the concept at large scale in the late 1990s.

Buterin created Ethereum as a platform for the implementation of smart contracts in a blockchain, using a cryptocurrency when necessary [2]. Ethereum provides a cryptocurrency called *ether* that is similar to Bitcoin's. The way it works is very similar to what we just described, except that the part of the state that is modified by the transactions in a block is stored in the chain, at the end of that block. However, Ethereum did not aim to be just another cryptocurrency, but to support the execution of distributed applications, designated by Dapps.

Besides a cryptocurrency, Ethereum provides support for the execution of smart contracts. In Ethereum an *account* is more complex than in Bitcoin. An account has four data items:

- *Nonce:* a counter used to guarantee that each transaction is processed only once;
- *Ether balance:* the currency in ether held by the contract;
- *Contract code:* the program that implements the contract;
- *Storage:* space to store data persistently.

Ethereum supports two types of accounts. *Externally owned accounts* have no contract code, are controlled by private cryptographic keys, and serve to do payments, just like Bitcoin's accounts.

Contract accounts are controlled by their contract code. When a contract account receives a *message*, its contract code is executed, possibly reading and writing the account's storage, sending messages, and creating new contracts. A message can come in a transaction from an externally owned account or from a contract. Notice that by *receiving* a message/transaction we actually mean the moment when a node accept there is consensus on a block and triggers that transaction for processing.

A message contains the following fields:

- *Nonce:* the nonce of the externally owned account that sent the message;

- *Recipient:* the recipient account for the message;

- *Ether:* the amount of currency (ether) to transfer from the sender's account to the recipient's account (if any);

- *Data:* an opaque data field with input(s) for the contract;

- *Startgas:* the maximum number of computational steps the transaction is allowed to execute;

- *Gasprice:* the *transaction fee* the sender account pays per computational step to the miner (the node that created the PoW for the block).

The *startgas* and *gasprice* have the purpose of preventing accidental or intentional denial of services. In practice, they force users to pay for the execution of contracts, limiting the amount of code they can execute. The term *gas* denominates the unit of computation. Ethereum executes smart contract code written in the Ethereum virtual machine (EVM) code language. For every EVM opcode there is a gas cost defined, varying from 0 (e.g., for the STOP opcode that halts the execution) to 32,000 (for the CREATE opcode that created a new account with code) [140]. There is an additional fee (5 gas) per byte in the transaction data field. The objective of this mechanisms is to make the sender—potentially an attacker—to pay the miner for the computational resources it uses.

Transactions containing a message from a contract to another contract have the same fields as a message (above), plus a *signature* created by the sender with its private key.

When a transaction for a contract account is received, Ethereum checks if: its syntax is correct, the signature is valid, and the nonce matches the sender's account nonce. If not, it returns an error, else it calculates the transaction fee (*startgas* × *gasprice*), subtracts the fee from the sender's account balance (if enough, otherwise returns an error), and increments the sender's nonce. Then, it transfers the transaction's ether from the sender's account to the recipient's and executes the contract code until it terminates or runs out of gas. If the value transfer fails because the sender does not have enough money or the code runs out of gas, all state changes are reverted, except the fees that are added to the miner's account. Otherwise, the fee corresponding to the remaining gas is transferred back to the sender's account.

EVM is a low-level programming language that is inconvenient for humans to write. Therefore, smart contracts are written in a higher-level language, typically Solidity [141], although there are other options (e.g., Serpent and LLL). The approach is, therefore, similar to Java and .NET: a high-level language (Java, C#, VB.NET, etc.) is compiled to a lower-level language (bytecodes, Common Intermediate Language) that is interpreted or goes through just-in-time compilation. EVM has the important characteristic of being Turing-complete. Bitcoin already supported basic programming in a language that was not Turing-complete (Script). Hyperledger Fabric uses an interesting alternative: smart contracts—*chaincode* in their lingo—are executed in Docker containers, so they can be programmed in several different languages [142].

3.3.3 Nakamoto Consensus Variants

Creating variants of Bitcoin and Nakamoto consensus is one of the more prolific research topic in the blockchain area, so this section will focus on some of the most relevant works.

Many works improve the Nakamoto consensus with the goal of solving problems of *fairness* (Section 3.3.1). One of the first works in this line points out that nodes that receive transactions directly from non-miner nodes (lightweight wallets) benefit from keeping information about these transactions to themselves, so that they can put them in a block and receive the associated reward [143]. Babaioff et al. augment the Nakamoto consensus with a scheme to reward information propagation with fees, and prove that it can achieve an equilibrium using a game-theoretic model.

A *selfish mining attack* starts from the same idea of a node withholding transactions [45]. The attack consists in a (selfish) mining pool to withhold transactions, privately mine blocks with these transactions, and, when the length of the public chain gets shorter than the length of the private chain, the pool disseminates their blocks, intentionally forking the chain and making non-faulty nodes do useless computation. This attack makes all nodes waste resources, but the selfish pool looses less and earns more reward than what corresponds to its mining power. Moreover, it is rational for the non-selfish nodes to join the selfish mining pool, increasing its share of the total mining power. Eyal and Sirer show that Bitcoin is not *incentive-compatible*, as it is vulnerable to selfish mining. They propose a modification to the Bitcoin algorithm to resist this attack: all (non-faulty) nodes shall propagate information about all competing blocks that lead to branches of the same length and pick randomly the one to which they will start mining the next block.

Sompolinsky and Zohar have shown that blockchains with many nodes and in which blocks are mined fast have high fork rates, allowing reasonably weak attackers to reverse payments they made [46]. To solve this problem, they present the *greedy heaviest-observed sub-tree* (GHOST) mechanism. Recall that in Bitcoin temporary forks are healed by pruning the smallest subchain(s). GHOST does not prune the smallest but the lightest subchains, i.e., it selects the heaviest subchain (or "sub-tree"). The weight of a subchain is the number of blocks it contains, counting all its branches. Ethereum implements a version of GHOST that considers only 7 generations of blocks, to simplify implementation and to keep the incentive of mining blocks for the longest chain [2].

Miller et al. recognize the problems of fairness created by large mining pools, referring that in 2014 the largest mining pool, GHash.IO, exceeded 50% of the mining power [47]. To deal with this problem, they introduce the notion of *strongly nonoutsourceable puzzles* (SNP), which are alternatives to PoW that are not amenable for mining pools. Specifically, a SNP is a cryptopuzzle that satisfies the following property: if a pool operator outsources mining work to a worker, then the worker can steal the reward without producing any evidence that can potentially implicate itself [47]. The authors present a SNP scheme called *scratch-off puzzles*. The scheme involves creating puzzles that are solvable in parallel, in such a way that the workers retain a signing key that can later be used to obtain their reward. Moreover, it provides a zero-knowledge spending option that allows workers to spend their reward in a way that does not reveal information.

The PoW mechanism provides the benefit of allowing arbitrary nodes to participate in a blockchain at the cost of consuming much energy (tens of TWh per year in Bitcoin, as mentioned before). Therefore, there is a quest for alternative mechanisms that solve the same problem without such a cost. The *proof-of-stake* (PoS) mechanism is one of the first. The idea is that nodes have a certain *stake* in the network, instead of having done a certain work. Nodes are called *stakers* or *minters*, no longer miners. Stakers do not get a reward for mining a block, only transaction fees. PPCoin uses a hybrid scheme in which there are two types of blocks: PoW blocks, the same as in Bitcoin; and PoS blocks that contain a single transaction called coinstake [39]. Its authors introduce the notion of *coin age* that is the number of coins the user holds multiplied by the time he holds them. In a coinstake transaction an user pays himself an amount, effectively reducing his coin age. Producing a PoS block involves solving a cryptopuzzle similar to obtaining a PoW, but requiring low effort and low energy consumption (the search space is limited). Their scheme uses PoW blocks in the beggining but substitutes them by PoS blocks at some stage (undefined). The difficulty of the cryptopuzzle is variable and is lower the higher the coin age consumed. Casper the Friendly Finality Gadget (Casper FFG) is a PoS mechanism being develop for Ethereum [144]. Casper FFG does not aim to create chains of blocks—in Ethereum these will continue to be created using PoW for now—but to select which subchain to maintain and which to prune, in case there are conflicting subchains. The main idea is to use Casper FFG to produces periodic checkpoints (1 every 100 blocks) using PoS. Moreover, it provides an accountability scheme that allows punishing faulty nodes. In the context of Ethereum a complementary mechanism called Casper the Friendly GHOST (Casper TFG) is being designed, but less information about it is available. Activating Casper in Ethereum will involve a hard fork of that blockchain.

There is a line or research on *useful puzzles*, i.e., on alternatives to PoW that spend energy solving useful tasks. The challenge is to find puzzles that are hard to compute, but with solutions that that can be verified efficiently. Primecoin seems to be the first cryptocurrency based on such an puzzle [145]. Its puzzles involve finding chains of prime numbers that are large enough to be hard to find, but not to verify. These prime numbers might be useful as cryptographic keys. Permacoin substitutes

TABLE 3.5 Nakamoto consensus variants.

Algorithm	Mechanism	Problem Handled	References
Bitcoin	proof-of-work (PoW)	double spending	[1]
Ethereum	PoW/PoS	efficiency, using PoS	[2]
Bitcoin variant	PoW	fairness, by rewarding	[143]
Bitcoin variant	PoW	selfish mining	[45]
Bitcoin variant	greedy heaviest-observed sub-tree (GHOST)	high fork rate	[46]
Bitcoin variant	strongly nonoutsourceable puzzles (SNP)	large mining pools	[47]
PPCoin	proof-of-stake (PoS)	PoW inefficiency	[39]
Ethereum	Casper FFG/TFG	PoW inefficiency	[144]
Primecoin	useful puzzles	useless spending of energy	[145]
Permacoin	proofs-of-retrievability (PoR)	distributed storage of data	[146]
Bitcoin variants	several countermeasures	mining power isolation	[48]

PoW by *proofs-of-retrievability* (PoR) to support distributed storage of data [146]. The purpose of a PoR is to certify that a node is using storage space to store a file. Therefore, Permacoin is a peer-to-peer file storage system in which nodes have an incentive to provide storage space, instead of mere altruism.

Apostolaki et al. show that by hijacking less than 100 BGP prefixes it is possible to isolate more than 50% of the Bitcoin mining power, even when considering that mining pools are strongly multi-homed [48] They present several countermeasures to reduce the impact of these attacks on Bitcoin, most of them related to increasing the number or diversity of connections between nodes (8 by default in Bitcoin) and to protect the communication (by default not encrypted or integrity-protected).

Table 3.5 summarizes the works on variants of Nakamoto consensus presented.

3.3.4 Summary

This section provided a brief state-of-the-art on blockchain with Nakamoto consensus and its variants. We started with a presentation of the Bitcoin blockchain and its consensus algorithm. Then, we presented two major applications for blockchains: cryptocurrencies and smart contracts. Finally, we presented several variants of the Nakamoto consensus and PoW, such as proof-of-stake and other related schemes. The next section presents blockchains based on Byzantine consensus algorithms (Section 3.2), some of them also with PoW and other mechanisms related to Nakamoto consensus.

3.4 BLOCKCHAINS WITH BYZANTINE CONSENSUS

The previous section presented the original blockchain (Bitcoin's), Ethereum, and several variants of Nakamoto consensus. These consensus algorithms have essentially the same goal of the Byzantine consensus algorithms of Section 3.2—doing agreement—but trade scalability for performance and weaker versions of the agreement and termination properties (Section 3.3.1). However, one of the evolutions of these first blockchains are the so-called *permissioned blockchains*, which require a different trade-off. This section starts by presenting such permissioned blockchains, then presents a new generation of *permissionless* blockchains that provide a service similar to Bitcoin and Ethereum, but better performance. The former are based on variants of Byzantine consensus algorithms such as BFT-SMaRt, whereas the later are based on *hybrid* consensus algorithms.

3.4.1 Permissioned Blockchains with Byzantine Consensus

Around 2014 many private companies started to understand the potential benefits of blockchain technology. That year, a group of major financial institutions formed a consortium called R3 with the objective of understanding the benefits of blockchain for their operation, e.g., to support payments between them [147]. These companies and institutions soon understood that the *permissionless* nature of Bitcoin or Ethereum—the lack of need of permission to participate—was not what they needed. In fact, it was even unacceptable to put customer information in such infrastructures, from the point of view of compliance, privacy, etc.

This scenario has led to the appearance of *permissioned blockchains*, in which nodes must authenticate themselves and be authorized to become peers. This allowed the creation of *consortia blockchains* (managed by a group of institutions) and *private blockchains* (managed by a single institution) [148]. Permissioned blockchains have important differences in relation to permissionless: they do not need the PoW mechanism to throttle appends to the blockchain; the number of nodes is typically much lower (e.g., 5 to 20 instead of hundreds or thousands); they can be implemented using Byzantine consensus algorithms (Section 3.2) and made much more efficient. In relation to consensus definitions, they can use validity predicate-based consensus, no longer *speculative* validity predicate-based consensus as Bitcoin and other permissionless blockchains.

Next, we review some of the existing permissioned blockchains based on Byzantine consensus:

Hyperledger is a blockchain project of the Linux Foundation that is developing several blockchains. The most popular of these blockchains seems to be Hyperledger Fabric, a modular blockchain focused on running smart contracts [149, 150]. Hyperledger Fabric does not provide a cryptocurrency and runs smart contracts (chaincode) in Docker containers (Section 3.3.2). Fabric considers two types of nodes: *validating peers* that run the consensus algorithm, validate the transactions, and maintain the chain; and *non-validating peers* that function as proxies to connect clients that issue transactions, possibly validating but not executing these transactions. Despite these nodes being called peers, Fabric is not peer-to-peer, as all validating peers communicate with all the others directly.

The consensus algorithm used is configurable; when version 1.0 was published, there was a fault-tolerant consensus algorithm based on the Apache Kafta stream processing platform; recently a Byzantine consensus algorithm based on the BFT-SMaRt library [26, 42] has been included. This later algorithm is a variant of PBFT so it solves SMR, is leader-based, has optimal resilience ($n \geq 3f+1$), and assumes the basic system model extended with a weak time assumption to circumvent FLP. Unlike the blockchains presented in the previous section (Bitcoin's, Ethereum), it provides strong agreement and termination properties, not their eventual versions. BFT-SMaRt's default algorithm is quite efficient, with a throughput of tens of thousands of transactions per second and latency below 1s [42]. BFT-SMaRt provides another consensus algorithm called WHEAT that uses speculative executions and other mechanisms to be more efficient in large-scale deployments, at the cost of becoming slower if not all replicas reply within certain time bounds.

Corda was developed by the R3 consortium [151]. Corda is similar to Hyperledger Fabric in many aspects. Its purpose is also to support the execution of smart contracts, although the motivation of the consortium is specifically financial agreements. In Corda, the consensus algorithm is executed by nodes called *notaries* and is also not peer-to-peer. This algorithm is again configurable and the Byzantine fault-tolerant version is also based on the BFT-SMaRt library.

Tendermint provides its own consensus algorithm, but it is similar to PBFT and BFT-SMaRt's default algorithm [152]. There is, however, a major difference in relation to Fabric and Corda: Tendermint's communication is peer-to-peer, as each node sends messages (gossip) only to a subset of the existing nodes. This in theory might allow a better throughput than using BFT-SMaRt, but the experimental results suggest their performance is similar [152], although it is not fair to compare experiments done in different settings.

The Red Belly Blockchain is a permissioned blockchain based on an efficient Byzantine consensus algorithm [153, 154]. The algorithm has two components. The first is a Byzantine binary consensus that, as the previous algorithms, assumes the basic system model extended with a weak time assumption. Moreover, it is also leader-based, although it rotates the leader so there is no leader election involved (similarly to our Spinning algorithm [30]). The second is a transformation from binary consensus into multi-valued consensus. The overall algorithm has optimal resilience and terminates in $O(f)$ steps (or $O(1)$ if there are no faulty nodes). Red Belly Blockchain supports some hundreds of nodes and a throughput of several hundred thousand transactions per second [153].

These works do not consider a hybrid model (Section 3.2.5), so nodes do not require trusted components (wormholes) and their resilience is $n \geq 3f+1$. In large blockchains like Bitcoin's there is no need to improve this resilience, but in consortium or private blockchains there may be a benefit on having only $n = 2f+1$ nodes, e.g., only 5 or 7 instead of 7 or 10, which we have shown to be possible with trusted components [29, 32]. Moreover, with a trusted component it is also possible to reduce the number of communication steps and messages exchanged, which is beneficial in terms of latency and throughput [32]. Interestingly, the Hyperledger project is implementing a version of our MinBFT algorithm based on Intel SGX [155].

For completeness, we mention that there are many other permissioned blockchains available, although they use different approaches to do consensus: Quorum, an enterprise version of Ethereum; Hyperledger Burrow, from the Hyperledger project; Guardtime's KSI blockchain, developed for the Estonian government; Ripple, that provides a money transfer service; Stellar, that supports the deployment of financial products; and others.

3.4.2 Permissionless Blockchains with Hybrid Consensus

The blockchains presented in the previous section are unsuitable for permissionless operation for at least two reasons. First, they become less efficient when the number of nodes grow; in fact they certainly cannot support a number of nodes similar to Bitcoin (more than 10,000 [138]) or Ethereum (also more than 10,000 [156]). Second, they reach consensus based on node votes, so they need the nodes that can vote to be clearly identified, otherwise they would be vulnerable to Sybil attacks (a node that pretends to be several) [35] or to collusions of faulty nodes.

There are some recent proposals of permissionless blockchains that leverage the benefits of Byzantine consensus algorithms, whereas also using PoW and related mechanisms to allow any node to be part of the system. These blockchains are based on what some authors call *hybrid* consensus algorithms, in the sense that they mix the two types of algorithms [157]. Next, we present briefly some of these systems.

Bitcoin-NG aims to provide a more scalable version of Bitcoin [158]. The idea is to use a leader-based Byzantine consensus algorithm to order blocks of transactions; to deal with the fact that any node can be part of the blockchain, Bitcoin-NG uses PoW to elect the leader. However, this use of PoW allows the existence of temporary forks, as in Bitcoin's blockchain.

PeerCensus [159] and Hybrid consensus [160] are based on a similar idea: they use PoW to limit the rate at which nodes can join the blockchain, and run a Byzantine consensus algorithm among the blockchain nodes to order blocks. Again, the possibility of temporary forks remains. PeerCensus is used to build a cryptocurrency called Discoin. More importantly, the Hybrid Consensus work studies the conditions in which a permissionless consensus can satisfy the property of *responsiveness*, i.e., in which the latency for a transaction to be confirmed is a function of the network delay. They prove that permissionless consensus is impossible in partially synchronous models, and that their hybrid consensus is responsive (by leveraging PoW).

Byzcoin is based on the same idea of using a variation of Byzantine consensus for ordering and PoW for defining the committee of nodes that run the consensus [161]. However, its authors introduce two interesting ideas for performance reasons. First, they substitute PBFT's vectors of MACs by signatures and use a *collective signing* protocol (nodes jointly produce signatures) to avoid the leader to check O(n) signatures during consensus. Second, they use the notion of *communication trees* from multicast protocols to reduce the number of messages sent.

Algorand is a cryptocurrency that introduces several new mechanisms and is not based on PoW [41]. First, it considers *weighted users*, i.e., the voting power of a node depends on the amount of money it holds. In that sense, there is some relation to PoS. Second, it does *consensus by committee*, i.e., only a subset of the nodes (committee) run the Byzantine consensus algorithm, greatly reducing the number of messages exchanged. The committee members are chosen randomly, but the probability of a node being chosen is not constant, depends on its weight. Third, it uses a *cryptographic sortition scheme* for committee members to be chosen in a private and non-interactive way (i.e., without communication), making it harder for adversaries to do denial of service attacks against these nodes. Fourth, it uses *participant replacement* again to mitigate denial of service attacks. The idea is that once a committee member sends a message, it stops being a member, so it is no longer useful to do denial of service against it.

Solida is inspired by Byzcoin and Hybrid consensus [162]. Transactions are ordered by a committee using an adaptation of the PBFT algorithm. The number of members of the committee is fixed, so when a new member joins, the oldest leaves. A node joins the committee by presenting a PoW and, when it does so, it becomes the leader. If two nodes obtain a PoW concurrently, a leader election protocol is executed to select which one becomes the leader, avoiding the creation of temporary forks.

Other more recent algorithms that follow similar principles are Chainspace and Omniledger [44, 163].

Table 3.6 summarizes both the permissioned and permissionless blockchains presented.

3.4.3 Summary

This section presents a set of recent blockchains based on Byzantine consensus. First, it presents permissioned blockchains, which run essentially a Byzantine consensus algorithm, typically a SMR algorithm. Then, it presents permissionless blockchains that require a more complex consensus algorithm to deal with the fact that participants are unknown and Sybil attacks may exist.

TABLE 3.6 Blockchains with Byzantine consensus algorithms.

Algorithm	Type	Characteristics	References
Fabric w/BFT-SMaRt	Permissioned	modular, efficient, not peer-to-peer	[42, 150]
Corda w/BFT-SMaRt	Permissioned	similar to the previous	[151]
Tendermint	Permissioned	peer-to-peer	[152]
Red Belly Blockchain	Permissioned	based on an efficient Byzantine consensus algorithm	[153, 154]
Bitcoin-NG	Permissionless/ Hybrid	use PoW to elect the leader of a leader-based consensus	[158]
PeerCensus, Hybrid consensus	Permissionless/ Hybrid	use PoW to throttle nodes joining the committee that runs consensus	[159, 160]
Byzcoin	Permissionless/ Hybrid	similar but uses multicast trees	[161]
Algorand	Permissionless/ Hybrid	committee members selected using a cryptographic sortition scheme	[41]
Solida	Permissionless/ Hybrid	when node joins the committee it becomes leader and another leaves	[162]
Chainspace, Omniledger	Permissionless/ Hybrid	similar	[44, 163]

3.5 CONCLUSION

The objective of the chapter was to present a state of the art in the area of Byzantine consensus and its application in blockchains.

Section 3.1 introduces the notions explored in the chapter, including those related to blockchain and Byzantine consensus.

Section 3.2 presents a state-of-the-art in what we call Byzantine consensus, which excludes the Nakamoto consensus based on PoW. The area started in the late 1970s with synchronous algorithms, but the section is about more recent work, starting with the FLP impossibility result, then with practical algorithms starting with PBFT.

Section 3.3 presents the original blockchain, its consensus algorithm, the killer applications (cryptocurrencies and smart contracts), and variants of PoW-based consensus.

Section 3.4 starts by presenting permissioned blockchains, then presents a new generation of permissionless blockchains that provide a service similar to Bitcoin and Ethereum, but better performance. The former are based on variants of Byzantine consensus algorithms such as BFT-SMaRt, whereas the later are based on hybrid consensus algorithms.

Acknowledgements. This work was partially supported by the EC through project 822404 (QualiChain), and by national funds through Fundação para a Ciência e a Tecnologia (FCT) with reference UID/CEC/50021/2019 (INESC-ID).

NOTE

1   This explanation is based on the most recent, more refined, version of the algorithm [97], instead of the original [29].

REFERENCES

[1] Satoshi Nakamoto. *Bitcoin: A Peer-to-peer Electronic Cash System*, 2008.

[2] Vitalik Buterin and Ethereum team. *Ethereum - a Next-generation Smart Contract and Decentralized Application Platform*. White Paper, 2014–17.

[3] World Economic Forum. *The Future of Financial Infrastructure. An Ambitious Look at How Blockchain Can Reshape Financial Services*, 2016.

[4] UK Government Office for Science. *Distributed Ledger Technology: Beyond Block Chain*. A report by the UK Government Chief Scientific Adviser, London, UK, 2016.

[5] Garrick Hileman and Michel Rauchs. *Global Blockchain Benchmarking Study*. Cambridge Centre for Alternative Finance, Cambridge, UK, 2017.

[6] Marshall Pease, Robert Shostak, and Leslie Lamport. Reaching agreement in the presence of faults. *Journal of the ACM*, 27(2):228–234, April 1980.

[7] Leslie Lamport, Robert Shostak, and Marshall Pease. The Byzantine generals problem. *ACM Transactions on Programming Languages and Systems*, 4(3):382–401, July 1982.

[8] Algirdas Avizienis, Jean-Claude Laprie, Brian Randell, and Carl E. Landwehr. Basic concepts and taxonomy of dependable and secure computing. *IEEE Transactions on Dependable and Secure Computing*, 1(1):11–33, January-March 2004.

[9] Danny Dolev. The Byzantine generals strike again. *Journal of Algorithms*, 3:14–30, 1982.

[10] Fred B. Schneider. Implementing fault-tolerant services using the state machine approach: A tutorial. *ACM Computing Surveys*, 22(4):299–319, December 1990.

[11] Michael K. Reiter. Secure agreement protocols: Reliable and atomic group multicast in Rampart. In *Proceedings of the 2nd ACM Conference on Computer and Communication Security*, pp. 68–80, November 1994.

[12] Michael K. Reiter. A secure group membership protocol. In *Proceedings of the 1994 IEEE Symposium on Research in Security and Privacy*, pp. 176–189, May 1994.

[13] Kim Potter Kihlstrom, Louise E. Moser, and Paul M. Melliar-Smith. The SecureRing group communication system. *ACM Transactions on Information and System Security*, 4(4):371–406, November 2001.

[14] Kim Potter Kihlstrom, Louise E. Moser, and Paul M. Melliar-Smith. Byzantine fault detectors for solving consensus. *The Computer Journal*, 46(1):16–35, January 2003.

[15] Miguel Castro and Barbara Liskov. Practical Byzantine fault tolerance. In *Proceedings of the 3rd USENIX Symposium on Operating Systems Design and Implementation*, pp. 173–186, February 1999.

[16] James Cowling, Daniel Myers, Barbara Liskov, Rodrigo Rodrigues, and Liuba Shrira. HQ-Replication: A hybrid quorum protocol for Byzantine fault tolerance. In *Proceedings of 7th USENIX Symposium on Operating Systems Design and Implementation*, pp. 177–190, November 2006.

[17] Ramakrishna Kotla, Lorenzo Alvisi, Mike Dahlin, Allen Clement, and Edmund Wong. Zyzzyva: Speculative Byzantine fault tolerance. In *Proceedings of 21st ACM SIGOPS Symposium on Operating Systems Principles*, October 2007.

[18] Byung-Gon Chun, Petros Maniatis, Scott Shenker, and John Kubiatowicz. Attested append-only memory: Making adversaries stick to their word. In *Proceedings of the 21st ACM Symposium on Operating Systems Principles*, pp. 189–204, October 2007.

[19] Marco Serafini and Neeraj Suri. The fail-heterogeneous architectural model. In *Proceedings of the 26th IEEE International Symposium on Reliable Distributed Systems*, pp. 103–113, 2007.

[20] Yair Amir, Brian Coan, Jonathan Kirsch, and John Lane. Byzantine replication under attack. In *Proceedings of the IEEE/IFIP 38th International Conference on Dependable Systems and Networks*, pp. 197–206, June 2008.

[21] Allen Clement, Edmund Wong, Lorenzo Alvisi, Mike Dahlin, and Mirco Marchetti. UpRight cluster services. In *Proceedings of the 22nd ACM Symposium on Operating Systems Principles*, October 2009.

[22] Allen Clement, Edmund Wong, Lorenzo Alvisi, Mike Dahlin, and Mirco Marchetti. Making Byzantine fault tolerant systems tolerate Byzantine faults. In *Proceedings of the 6th USENIX Symposium on Networked Systems Design & Implementation*, pp. 153–168, 22–24 April 2009.

[23] Marco Serafini, Péter Bokor, Dan Dobre, Matthias Majuntke, and Neeraj Suri. Scrooge: Reducing the costs of fast Byzantine replication in presence of unresponsive replicas. In *Proceedings of the IEEE/IFIP 40th International Conference on Dependable Systems and Networks*, pp. 353–362, July 2010.

[24] Yair Amir, Brian A. Coan, Jonathan Kirsch, and John Lane. Prime: Byzantine replication under attack. *IEEE Transactions on Dependable and Secure Computing*, 8(4):564–577, 2011.

[25] Rüdiger Kapitza, Johannes Behl, Christian Cachin, Tobias Distler, Simon Kuhnle, Seyed Vahid Mohammadi, Wolfgang Schröder-Preikschat, and Klaus Stengel. Cheapbft: Resource-efficient byzantine fault tolerance. In *Proceedings of the 7th ACM European Conference on Computer Systems*, pp. 295–308, 2012.

[26] Alysson Bessani, João Sousa, and Eduardo E. P. Alchieri. State machine replication for the masses with BFT-smart. In *Proceedings of the IEEE/IFIP International Conference on Dependable Systems and Networks*, pp. 355–362, June 2014.

[27] Daniel Porto, Joao Leitao, Cheng Li, Allen Clement, Aniket Kate, Flavio Junqueira, and Rodrigo Rodrigues. Visigoth fault tolerance. In *Proceedings of the 10th ACM European Conference on Computer Systems*, 2015.

[28] Johannes Behl, Tobias Distler, and Rüdiger Kapitza. Consensus-oriented parallelization: How to earn your first million. In *Proceedings of the 16th Annual Middleware Conference*, pp. 173–184, 2015.

[29] Miguel Correia, Nuno F. Neves, and Paulo Verssimo. How to tolerate half less one Byzantine nodes in practical distributed systems. In *Proceedings of the 23rd IEEE Symposium on Reliable Distributed Systems*, pp. 174–183, October 2004.

[30] Giuliana Santos Veronese, Miguel Correia, Alysson N. Bessani, and Lau Cheuk Lung. Spin one's wheels? Byzantine fault tolerance with a spinning primary. In *Proceedings of the 2009 28th IEEE International Symposium on Reliable Distributed Systems*, pp. 135–144, 2009.

[31] Giuliana Santos Veronese, Miguel Correia, Alysson N. Bessani, and Lau Cheuk Lung. EBAWA: Efficient Byzantine agreement for wide-area networks. In *Proceedings of the 12th IEEE International Symposium on High-Assurance Systems Engineering*, pp. 10–19, November 2010.

[32] Giuliana Santos Veronese, Miguel Correia, Alysson N. Bessani, Lau Cheuk Lung, and Paulo Verssimo. Efficient Byzantine fault tolerance. *IEEE Transactions on Computers*, 62(1):16–30, 2013.

[33] Ray Neiheiser, Daniel Presser, Luciana Rech, Manuel Bravo, Lus Rodrigues, and Miguel Correia. Fireplug: Flexible and robust n-version geo-replication of graph databases. In *Proceedings of the 32nd International Conference on Information Networking*, January 2018.

[34] Bowen Alpern and Fred B. Schneider. Recognizing safety and liveness. *Distributed Computing*, 2(3):117–126, 1987.

[35] John R. Douceur. The Sybil attack. In *International Workshop on Peer-to-Peer Systems*, pp. 251–260, 2002.

[36] Christian Decker and Roger Wattenhofer. Information propagation in the Bitcoin network. In *Proceedings of the IEEE 13th International Conference on Peer-to-Peer Computing*, pp. 1–10, 2013.

[37] Kyle Croman, Christian Decker, Ittay Eyal, Adem Efe Gencer, Ari Juels, Ahmed Kosba, Andrew Miller, Prateek Saxena, Elaine Shi, Emin Gün Sirer, et al. On scaling decentralized blockchains. In *International Conference on Financial Cryptography and Data Security*, pp. 106–125, 2016.

[38] Marko Vukolić. The quest for scalable blockchain fabric: Proof-of-work vs. BFT replication. In *International Workshop on Open Problems in Network Security*, pp. 112–125, Springer, Cham, 2015.

[39] Sunny King and Scott Nadal. *PPCoin: Peer-to-peer Crypto-currency with Proof-of-stake*. self-published paper, 2012.

[40] Iddo Bentov, Charles Lee, Alex Mizrahi, and Meni Rosenfeld. Proof of activity: Extending Bitcoin's proof of work via proof of stake. *ACM SIGMETRICS Performance Evaluation Review*, 42(3), pp. 34–37, 2014.

[41] Yossi Gilad, Rotem Hemo, Silvio Micali, Georgios Vlachos, and Nickolai Zeldovich. Algorand: Scaling Byzantine agreements for cryptocurrencies. In *Proceedings of the 26th ACM Symposium on Operating Systems Principles*, pp. 51–68, 2017.

[42] João Sousa, Alysson Bessani, and Marko Vukolic. A Byzantine fault-tolerant ordering service for Hyperledger Fabric. In *Proceedings of the 48th Annual IEEE/IFIP International Conference on Dependable Systems and Networks*, 2018.

[43] Rami Khalil and Arthur Gervais. Revive: Rebalancing off-blockchain payment networks. In *Proceedings of the 2017 ACM SIGSAC Conference on Computer and Communications Security*, pp. 439–453, 2017.

[44] Eleftherios Kokoris-Kogias, Philipp Jovanovic, Linus Gasser, Nicolas Gailly, Ewa Syta, and Bryan Ford. OmniLedger: A secure, scale-out, decentralized ledger via sharding. In *Proceedings of the 39th IEEE Symposium on Security and Privacy*, 2018.

[45] Ittay Eyal and Emin Gün Sirer. Majority is not enough: Bitcoin mining is vulnerable. In *International Conference on Financial Cryptography and Data Security*, pp. 436–454, 2014.

[46] Yonatan Sompolinsky and Aviv Zohar. Secure high-rate transaction processing in Bitcoin. In *International Conference on Financial Cryptography and Data Security*, pp. 507–527, 2015.

[47] Andrew Miller, Ahmed Kosba, Jonathan Katz, and Elaine Shi. Nonoutsourceable scratch-off puzzles to discourage Bitcoin mining coalitions. In *Proceedings of the 22nd ACM SIGSAC Conference on Computer and Communications Security*, pp. 680–691, 2015.

[48] Maria Apostolaki, Aviv Zohar, and Laurent Vanbever. Hijacking Bitcoin: Routing attacks on cryptocurrencies. In *Proceedings of the 2017 IEEE Symposium on Security and Privacy*, pp. 375–392, 2017.

[49] coinmarketcap. https://coinmarketcap.com/, March 2018.

[50] Loi Luu, Duc-Hiep Chu, Hrishi Olickel, Prateek Saxena, and Aquinas Hobor. Making smart contracts smarter. In *Proceedings of the 2016 ACM SIGSAC Conference on Computer and Communications Security*, pp. 254–269, 2016.

[51] Tim Dierks and Christopher Allen. The TLS Protocol Version 1.0 (RFC 2246). *IETF Request For Comments*, January, 1999.

[52] Paul C. Attie. Wait-free Byzantine consensus. *Information Processing Letters*, 83(4):221–227, August 2002.

[53] Roy Friedman, Achour Mostefaoui, Sergio Rajsbaum, and Michel Raynal. Distributed agreement and its relation with error-correcting codes. In *Proceedings of the 16th International Conference on Distributed Computing*, pp. 63–87, October 2002.

[54] Dahlia Malkhi, Michael Merrit, Micheal Reiter, and Gadi Taubenfeld. Objects shared by Byzantine processes. *Distributed Computing*, 16(1):37–48, February 2003.

[55] Noga Alon, Michael Merrit, Omer Reingold, Gadi Taubenfeld, and Rebeca Wright. Tight bounds for shared memory systems accessed by Byzantine processes. *Distributed Computing*, 18(2):99–109, November 2005.

[56] Alysson Neves Bessani, Miguel Correia, Joni Da Silva Fraga, and Lau Cheuk Lung. Sharing memory between byzantine processes using policy-enforced tuple spaces. *IEEE Transactions on Parallel and Distributed Systems*, 20(3):419–432, 2009.

[57] Michael Ben-Or. Another advantage of free choice: Completely asynchronous agreement protocols. In *Proceedings of the 2nd ACM Symposium on Principles of Distributed Computing*, pp. 27–30, August 1983.

[58] Michael O. Rabin. Randomized Byzantine generals. In *Proceedings of the 24th Annual IEEE Symposium on Foundations of Computer Science*, pp. 403–409, November 1983.

[59] C. Dwork, N. Lynch, and L. Stockmeyer. Consensus in the presence of partial synchrony. *Journal of the ACM*, 35(2):288–323, April 1988.

[60] Dahlia Malkhi and Michael Reiter. Unreliable intrusion detection in distributed computations. In *Proceedings of the 10th Computer Security Foundations Workshop*, pp. 116–124, June 1997.

[61] Bowen Alpern and Fred Schneider. *Defining Liveness*. Technical report, Department of Computer Science, Cornell University, Ithaca, NY, 1984.

[62] Assia Doudou, Bernoit Garbinato, Rachid Guerraoui, and Andre Schiper. Muteness failure detectors: Specification and implementation. In *Proceedings of the Third European Dependable Computing Conference*, pp. 71–87, September 1999.

[63] Assia Doudou, Bernoit Garbinato, and Rachid Guerraoui. Encapsulating failure detection: From crash-stop to Byzantine failures. In *International Conference on Reliable Software Technologies*, pp. 24–50, May 2002.

[64] Roberto Baldoni, Jean-Michel Helary, Michel Raynal, and Lenaik Tanguy. Consensus in Byzantine asynchronous systems. *Journal of Discrete Algorithms*, 1(2):185–210, 2003.

[65] Nuno F. Neves, Miguel Correia, and Paulo Verssimo. Solving vector consensus with a wormhole. *IEEE Transactions on Parallel and Distributed Systems*, 16(12):1120–1131, 2005.

[66] Tyler Crain, Vincent Gramoli, Mikel Larrea, and Michel Raynal. (leader/randomization/ signature)-free Byzantine consensus for consortium blockchains. *arXiv preprint arXiv: 1702.03068*, February 2017.

[67] Leslie Lamport. The part-time parliament. *ACM Transactions Computer Systems*, 16(2):133–169, May 1998.

[68] Leslie Lamport. Paxos made simple. *ACM SIGACT News*, 32(4):51–58, 2001.

[69] Butler Lampson. The ABCD's of Paxos. In *Proc. Of the 20th Annual ACM Symp. on Principles of Distributed Computing*, Newport, Rhode Island, 2001.

[70] Piotr Zielinski. *Paxos at War*. Technical Report UCAM-CL-TR-593, Univ. of Cambridge Computer Laboratory, Cambridge, UK, June 2004.

[71] Jean-Philippe Martin and Lorenzo Alvisi. Fast Byzantine consensus. In *Proceedings of the IEEE/IFIP 35th International Conference on Dependable Systems and Networks*, pp. 402–411, June 2005.

[72] Alysson Neves Bessani and Eduardo Alchieri. A guided tour on the theory and practice of state machine replication. In *Tutorials of the 32nd Brazilian Symposium on Computer Networks and Distributed Systems*, 2014.

[73] Gabriel Bracha and Sam Toueg. Asynchronous consensus and broadcast protocols. *Journal of the ACM*, 32(4):824–840, October 1985.

[74] Cristian Cachin, Klaus Kursawe, Frank Petzold, and Victor Shoup. Secure and efficient asynchronous broadcast protocols. In *Advances in Cryptology: CRYPTO 2001, Volume 2139 of Lecture Notes in Computer Science*. Springer, Berlin, Heidelberg, 2001.

[75] Miguel Correia, Nuno F. Neves, and Paulo Verssimo. From consensus to atomic broadcast: Time-free Byzantine-resistant protocols without signatures. *Computer Journal*, 41(1):82–96, January 2006.

[76] Vassos Hadzilacos and Sam Toueg. *A Modular Approach to Fault-tolerant Broadcasts and Related Problems*. Technical Report TR94-1425, Cornell University, Department of Computer Science, Ithaka, NY, May 1994.

[77] Miguel Correia, Giuliana Santos Veronese, and Lau Cheuk Lung. Asynchronous byzantine consensus with 2f+1 processes. In *Proceedings of the 2010 ACM Symposium on Applied Computing (SAC)*, pp. 475–480, 2010.

[78] Soma Chaudhuri. More choices allow more faults: Set consensus problems in totally asynchronous systems. *Information and Computation*, 105(1):132–158, July 1993.

[79] Roberto De Prisco, Dahlia Malkhi, and Michael Reiter. On k-set consensus problems in asynchronous systems. In *Proceedings of the 18th ACM Symposium on Principles of Distributed Computing*, pp. 257–265, May 1999.

[80] Miguel Correia, Alysson Neves Bessani, and Paulo Verssimo. On Byzantine generals with alternative plans. *Journal of Parallel and Distributed Computing*, 68(9): 1291–1296, September 2008.

[81] Achour Mostefaoui, Michel Raynal, Corentin Travers, Stacy Patterson, Divyakant Agrawal, and Amr El Abbadi. From static distributed systems to dynamic systems. In *Proceedings of the 24th IEEE Symposium on Reliable Distributed Systems*, pp. 109–118, October 2005.

[82] Marcos K. Aguilera. A pleasant stroll through the land of infinitely many creatures. *ACM SIGACT News*, 35(2):36–59, 2004.

[83] Eduardo Adlio Pelinson Alchieri, Alysson Neves Bessani, Joni Da Silva Fraga, and Fabola Greve. Byzantine consensus with unknown participants. In *Proceedings of the 12th International Conference on Principles of Distributed Systems*, pp. 22–40, 2008.

[84] Eduardo Adilio Pelinson Alchieri, Alysson Bessani, Fabiola Greve, and Joni Da Silva Fraga. Knowledge connectivity requirements for solving Byzantine consensus with unknown participants. *IEEE Transactions on Dependable and Secure Computing*, 15(2):246–259, 2018.

[85] Michael J. Fischer, Nancy A. Lynch, and Michael S. Paterson. Impossibility of distributed consensus with one faulty process. *Journal of the ACM*, 32(2):374–382, April 1985.

[86] Miguel Correia, Giuliana Santos Veronese, Nuno Ferreira Neves, and Paulo Verssimo. Byzantine consensus in asynchronous message-passing systems: A survey. *International Journal of Critical Computer-Based Systems*, 2(2):141–161, 2011.

[87] Tushar Deepak Chandra and Sam Toueg. Unreliable failure detectors for reliable distributed systems. *Journal of the ACM*, 43(2): 225–267, March 1996.

[88] D. Mpoeleng, P. Ezhilchelvan, and N. Speirs. From crash tolerance to authenticated Byzantine tolerance: A structured approach, the cost and benefits. In *Proceedings of the IEEE/IFIP 33rd International Conference on Dependable Systems and Networks*, pp. 227–236, June 2003.

[89] Shengyun Liu, Paolo Viotti, Christian Cachin, Vivien Quéma, and Marko Vukolic. XFT: Practical fault tolerance beyond crashes. In *12th USENIX Symposium on Operating Systems Design and Implementation*, pp. 485–500, 2016.

[90] Tushar Deepak Chandra, Vassos Hadzilacos, and Sam Toueg. The weakest failure detector for solving consensus. *Journal of the ACM*, 43(4):685–722, July 1996.

[91] Fernando Pedone, André Schiper, Péter Urbán, and David Cavin. Solving agreement problems with weak ordering oracles. In *Proceedings of the 4th European Dependable Computing Conference*, pp. 44–61, 23–25 October 2002.

[92] Paulo Verssimo. Uncertainty and predictability: Can they be reconciled?. In *Future Directions in Distributed Computing, Volume 2584 of Lecture Notes in Computer Science*, pp. 108–113, Springer, Berlin, Heidelberg, 2003.

[93] Paulo Verssimo. Travelling through wormholes: A new look at distributed systems models. *SIGACT News*, 37(1):66–81, 2006.

[94] Miguel Correia, Nuno F. Neves, Lau Cheuk Lung, and Paulo Verssimo. Low complexity Byzantine-resilient consensus. *Distributed Computing*, 17(3):237–249, 2005.

[95] Miguel Correia, Paulo Verssimo, and Nuno F. Neves. The design of a COTS real-time distributed security kernel. In *Proceedings of the 4th European Dependable Computing Conference*, pp. 234–252, October 2002.

[96] Nuno F. Neves, Miguel Correia, and Paulo Verssimo. Wormhole-aware Byzantine protocols. In *2nd Bertinoro Workshop on Future Directions in Distributed Computing: Survivability - Obstacles and Solutions*, June 2004.

[97] Miguel Correia, Nuno Ferreira Neves, and Paulo Verssimo. BFT-TO: Intrusion tolerance with less replicas. *Computer Journal*, 56(6):693–715, 2013.

[98] Johannes Behl, Tobias Distler, and Rüdiger Kapitza. Hybrids on steroids: SGX-based high performance BFT. In *Proceedings of the 12th ACM European Conference on Computer Systems*, pp. 222–237, 2017.

[99] Michael Ben-Or. Fast asynchronous Byzantine agreement. In *Proceedings of the 4th ACM Symposium on Principles of Distributed Computing*, pp. 149–151, August 1985.

[100] Cristian Cachin, Klaus Kursawe, and Victor Shoup. Random oracles in Contanstinople: Practical asynchronous Byzantine agreement using cryptography. In *Proceedings of the 19th ACM Symposium on Principles of Distributed Computing*, pp. 123–132, July 2000.

[101] Ran Canetti and Tal Rabin. Fast asynchronous Byzantine agreement with optimal resilience. In *Proceedings of the 25th Annual ACM Symposium on Theory of Computing*, pp. 42–51, 1993.

[102] Roy Friedman, Achour Mostefaoui, and Michel Raynal. Simple and efficient oracle-based consensus protocols for asynchronous Byzantine systems. *IEEE Transactions on Dependable and Secure Computing*, 2(1): 46–56, January 2005.

[103] Sam Toueg. Randomized Byzantine agreements. In *Proceedings of the 3rd ACM Symposium on Principles of Distributed Computing*, pp. 163–178, August 1984.

[104] Christian Cachin and Jonathan A. Poritz. Secure intrusion-tolerant replication on the Internet. In *Proceedings of the Conference on Dependable Systems and Networks*, pp. 167–176, 2002.

[105] Henrique Moniz, Nuno Ferreira Neves, Miguel Correia, and Paulo Verssimo. Randomized intrusion-tolerant asynchronous services. In *Proceedings of the IEEE/IFIP 36th International Conference on Dependable Systems and Networks*, pp. 568–577, 25–28 June 2006.

[106] Henrique Moniz, Nuno Ferreira Neves, Miguel Correia, and Paulo Verssimo. RITAS: Services for randomized intrusion tolerance. *IEEE Transactions on Dependable and Secure Computing*, 8(1):122–136, 2011.

[107] Henrique Moniz, Nuno Ferreira Neves, Miguel Correia, and Paulo Verssimo. Randomization can be a healer: Consensus with dynamic omission failures. In *Distributed Computing, 23rd International Symposium*, pp. 63–77, 2009.

[108] Henrique Moniz, Nuno Ferreira Neves, Miguel Correia, and Paulo Verssimo. Randomization can be a healer: Consensus with dynamic omission failures. *Distributed Computing*, 24(3–4):165–175, 2011.

[109] Henrique Moniz, Nuno Ferreira Neves, and Miguel Correia. Turquois: Byzantine consensus in wireless ad hoc networks. In *Proceedings of the 2010 IEEE/IFIP International Conference on Dependable Systems and Networks*, pp. 537–546, 2010.

[110] Henrique Moniz, Nuno Ferreira Neves, and Miguel Correia. Byzantine fault-tolerant consensus in wireless ad hoc networks. *IEEE Transactions on Mobile Computing*, 12(12):2441–2454, 2013.

[111] Michel Hurfin and Michel Raynal. A simple and fast asynchronous consensus protocol based on a weak failure detector. *Distributed Computing*, 12:209–223, 1999.

[112] André Schiper. Early consensus in an asynchronous system with a weak failure detector. *Distributed Computing*, 10:149–157, October 1997.

[113] Gabriel Bracha. An asynchronous -resilient consensus protocol. In *Proceedings of the 3rd ACM Symposium on Principles of Distributed Computing*, pp. 154–162, August 1984.

[114] Mike Burrows. The Chubby lock service for loosely-coupled distributed systems. In *Proceedings of the USENIX 7th Symposium on Operating Systems Design and Implementation*, pp. 335–350, 2006.

[115] Patrick Hunt, Mahadev Konar, Flavio Paiva Junqueira, and Benjamin Reed. Zookeeper: Wait-free coordination for internet-scale systems. In *USENIX Annual Technical Conference*, USENIX, 2010.

[116] Bev Littlewood. The impact of diversity upon common mode failures. *Reliability Engineering & System Safety*, 51(1):101–113, 1996.

[117] Trusted Computing Group. TPM main specification level 2 version 1.2, revision 116. https://trustedcomputinggroup.org/tpm-main-specification/, 2011.

[118] Ittai Abraham, Marcos Kawazoe Aguilera, and Dahlia Malkhi. Fast asynchronous consensus with optimal resilience. In *Proceedings of the 24th International Symposium on Distributed Computing*, pp. 4–19, 2010.

[119] Dave Levin, John R. Douceur, Jacob R. Lorch, and Thomas Moscibroda. Trinc: Small trusted hardware for large distributed systems. In *Proceedings of the 6th USENIX Symposium on Networked Systems Design and Implementation*, USENIX, pp. 1–14, 2009.

[120] Frank McKeen, Ilya Alexandrovich, Alex Berenzon, Carlos V. Rozas, Hisham Shafi, Vedvyas Shanbhogue, and Uday R. Savagaonkar. Innovative instructions and software model for isolated execution. In *Proceedings of the 2nd International Workshop on Hardware and Architectural Support for Security and Privacy*, 2013.

[121] Ittai Anati, Shay Gueron, Simon Johnson, and Vincent Scarlata. Innovative technology for CPU based attestation and sealing. In *Proceedings of the 2nd International Workshop on Hardware and Architectural Support for Security and Privacy*, 2013.

[122] Paul Ezhilchelvan, Achour Mostefaoui, and Michel Raynal. Randomized multivalued consensus. In *Proceedings of the 4th IEEE International Symposium on Object-Oriented Real-Time Computing*, pp. 195–200, May 2001.

[123] Henrique Moniz, Nuno Ferreira Neves, Miguel Correia, and Paulo Verissimo. Experimental comparison of local and shared coin randomized consensus protocols. In *Proceedings of the 25th IEEE Symposium on Reliable Distributed Systems*, pp. 235–244, October 2006.

[124] Henrique Moniz, Nuno Ferreira Neves, Miguel Correia, Antonio Casimiro, and Paulo Verissimo. Intrusion tolerance in wireless environments: An experimental evaluation. In *Proceedings of the 13th IEEE Pacific Rim Dependable Computing Conference*, December 2007.

[125] Nicola Santoro and Peter Widmayer. Time is not a healer. In *Proceedings of the 6th Symposium on Theoretical Aspects of Computer Science*, pp. 304–313, 1989.

[126] Andrew Miller, Yu Xia, Kyle Croman, Elaine Shi, and Dawn Song. The honey badger of BFT protocols. In *Proceedings of the 2016 ACM SIGSAC Conference on Computer and Communications Security*, pp. 31–42, 2016.

[127] Gavin Wood. *Ethereum: A Secure Decentralised Generalised Transaction Ledger*. Ethereum Project Yellow Paper, EIP-150 Revision, 2014.

[128] Juan A. Garay, Aggelos Kiayias, and Nikos Leonardos. The Bitcoin backbone protocol: Analysis and applications. *Advances in Cryptology – EUROCRYPT 2015*, LNCS, 9056, 281–310, Springer, Berlin, Heidelberg, 2015.

[129] Andreas Antonopoulos. *Mastering Bitcoin*. O'Reilly, 2nd edition, 2017.

[130] Pieter Wuille, Peter Todd, Greg Maxwell, and Rusty Russell. *Version Bits with Timeout and Delay*. BIP-0009, October.

[131] Arthur Gervais, Ghassan O Karame, Karl Wüst, Vasileios Glykantzis, Hubert Ritzdorf, and Srdjan Capkun. On the security and performance of proof of work blockchains. In *Proceedings of the 2016 ACM SIGSAC Conference on Computer and Communications Security*, pp. 3–16, 2016.

[132] Morgen E. Peck. Why the biggest Bitcoin mines are in China. *IEEE Spectrum*, 54(10), 2017.

[133] Rachid Guerraoui, Nikola Knežević, Vivien Quéma, and Vukolić Marko. The next 700 BFT protocols. In *Proceedings of the 5th ACM SIGOPS/EuroSys European Systems Conference*, pp. 363–376, 2010.

[134] Dan RK Ports, Jialin Li, Vincent Liu, Naveen Kr Sharma, and Arvind Krishnamurthy. Designing distributed systems using approximate synchrony in data center networks. In *12th USENIX Symposium on Networked Systems Design and Implementation*, pp. 43–57, 2015.

[135] Joseph Bonneau, Andrew Miller, Jeremy Clark, Arvind Narayanan, Joshua A. Kroll, and Edward W. Felten. SoK: Research perspectives and challenges for Bitcoin and cryptocurrencies. In *2015 IEEE Symposium on Security and Privacy*, pp. 104–121, 2015.

[136] Slushpool. Stratum mining protocol. https://slushpool.com/help/manual/stratum-protocol.

[137] Digiconomist. Bitcoin energy consumption index. https://digiconomist.net/bitcoin-energy-consumption, December 2017.

[138] Global Bitcoin nodes distribution. https://bitnodes.earn.com/, January 2018.

[139] Nick Szabo. The idea of smart contracts. http://szabo.best.vwh.net/smart_contracts_idea.html.

[140] Ethereum VM (EVM) opcodes and instruction reference. https://github.com/trailofbits/evm-opcodes, 2018.

[141] Ethereum team. Solidity. https://solidity.readthedocs.io/en/develop/, 2016–2017.

[142] Hyperledger Fabric team. Hyperledger fabric documentation. https://hyperledger-fabric.readthedocs.io/.

[143] Moshe Babaioff, Shahar Dobzinski, Sigal Oren, and Aviv Zohar. On Bitcoin and red balloons. In *Proceedings of the 13th ACM Conference on Electronic Commerce*, pp. 56–73, 2012.

[144] Vitalik Buterin and Virgil Griffith. Casper the friendly finality gadget. *arXiv preprint arXiv:1710.09437*, 2017.

[145] Sunny King. *Primecoin: Cryptocurrency with Prime Number Proof-of-work*, 2013.

[146] Andrew Miller, Ari Juels, Elaine Shi, Bryan Parno, and Jonathan Katz. Permacoin: Repurposing Bitcoin work for data preservation. In *Proceedings of the IEEE Symposium on Security and Privacy*, pp. 475–490, 2014.

[147] Morgen E Peck. Blockchains: How they work and why they'll change the world. *IEEE Spectrum*, 54(10):26–35, 2017.

[148] Vitalik Buterin. On public and private blockchains. https://blog.ethereum.org/2015/08/07/on-public-and-private-blockchains/, August 2015.

[149] Christian Cachin. Architecture of the hyperledger blockchain fabric. In *Workshop on Distributed Cryptocurrencies and Consensus Ledgers*, 2016.

[150] Elli Androulaki, Artem Barger, Vita Bortnikov, Christian Cachin, Konstantinos Christidis, Angelo De Caro, David Enyeart, Christopher Ferris, Gennady Laventman, Yacov Manevich, et al Hyperledger fabric: A distributed operating system for permissioned blockchains. In *Proceedings of the 13th ACM EuroSys Conference*, 2018.

[151] Richard Gendal Brown, James Carlyle, Ian Grigg, and Mike Hearn. Corda: An introduction. *R3 CEV*, August 2016.

[152] Ethan Buchman. *Tendermint: Byzantine Fault Tolerance in the Age of Blockchains*. Master's thesis, The University of Guelph, Canada, 2016.

[153] Tyler Crain, Vincent Gramoli, Chris Natoli, Gary Shapiro, Michael Spain, and Guillaume Vizier. Red Belly Blockchain. http://csrg.redbellyblockchain.io/rbbc/.

[154] Tyler Crain, Vincent Gramoli, Mikel Larrea, and Michel Raynal. Blockchain consensus. In *ALGOTEL 2017-19èmes Rencontres Francophones Sur Les Aspects Algorithmiques Des Télécommunications*, 2017.

[155] Implementation of MinBFT consensus protocol. https://github.com/hyperledger-labs/minbft, 2018.

[156] ethernodes.org: Network number 1. www.ethernodes.org/network/1, January 2018.

[157] Shehar Bano, Alberto Sonnino, Mustafa Al-Bassam, Sarah Azouvi, Patrick McCorry, Sarah Meiklejohn, and George Danezis. SoK: Consensus in the age of blockchains. *arXiv preprint arXiv:1711.03936*, 2017.

[158] Ittay Eyal, Adem Efe Gencer, Emin Gün Sirer, and van Renesse Robbert. Bitcoin-ng: A scalable blockchain protocol. In *Proceedings of the 13th USENIX Symposium on Networked Systems Design and Implementation*, 2016.

[159] Christian Decker, Jochen Seidel, and Roger Wattenhofer. Bitcoin meets strong consistency. In *Proceedings of the 17th International Conference on Distributed Computing and Networking*, 2016.

[160] Rafael Pass and Elaine Shi. Hybrid consensus: Efficient consensus in the permissionless model. In *LIPIcs-Leibniz International Proceedings in Informatics, Volume 91*. Schloss Dagstuhl-Leibniz-Zentrum fuer Informatik, 2017.

[161] Eleftherios Kokoris Kogias, Philipp Jovanovic, Nicolas Gailly, Ismail Khoffi, Linus Gasser, and Bryan Ford. Enhancing Bitcoin security and performance with strong consistency via collective signing. In *25th USENIX Security Symposium*, pp. 279–296, 2016.

[162] Ittai Abraham, Dahlia Malkhi, Kartik Nayak, Ling Ren, and Alexander Spiegelman. Solida: A blockchain protocol based on reconfigurable Byzantine consensus. In *Proceedings of the 21st International Conference on Principles of Distributed Systems*, 2017.

[163] Mustafa Al-Bassam, Alberto Sonnino, Shehar Bano, Dave Hrycyszyn, and George Danezis. Chainspace: A sharded smart contracts platform. In *Proceedings of the Network and Distributed System Security Symposium*, 2018.

CHAPTER 4

Smart Contract-Driven Business Transactions

Bert-Jan Butijn, Willem-Jan van den Heuvel, and Indika Kumara

Jheronimus Academy of Data Science

CONTENTS

A utomating business processes across a network of untrusted business parties are increasingly problematic due to the inherent lack of mutual trust between parties. Blockchain provides a promising solution to enact business processes in a trustworthy manner in untrusted business environments. Blockchain includes a shared ledger that provides a trusted, privacy-preserving, immutable data repository that can store business objects and events, enabling provenance and transparency. It also supports the decentralized execution of computations on it in the form of programs called smart contracts. This chapter describes the role of the smart contract and shared ledger in automating collaborative business processes. In particular, we present a meta-model, a life cycle model, and a reference architecture for smart contract-driven business transactions and processes.

4.1 INTRODUCTION

Business processes that span organization boundaries pose a number of significant business and system level challenges [1–3]. Once the legal contracts between the trading partners are established, those should be monitored, enforced, and managed (including handling contract violations, termination, and update). As there exists often a lack of trust among the organizations, they face the delicate situation of trusting a specific partner for enforcing contractual obligations. To avoid relying on one trusted party, the business transactions need to be made transparent across partners. The transaction data including business interaction states, business objects and events should be shared among partners using a trustworthy, privacy-preserving, non-repudiable medium.

Blockchain is an emerging digital technology that can execute and verify transactions between multiple parties without involving a trusted third party and can record the transactions permanently [4–10]. It can provide a promising solution to address the contract enforcement and management challenges in untrusted business networks [7]. The two key enabling features of Blockchain are the distributed shared ledger, and computer programs (so-called smart contracts) that run on the ledger [2, 3]. The former can store immutable records of transactions in a peer-to-peer network of machines. Every allowed participant can access the data. The smart contracts are executed by all consensus nodes in the network. A participant can invoke the coded functions of a deployed contract by sending messages. The outcomes of the contract innovations are stored in the shared ledger, providing transparency to all relevant parties if conflicts arise. Note that while these computer programs are called "smart contracts", they are generally not very smart, and lacks the contracts to represent legal contracts [11].

Blockchain is gaining popularity in enterprises. According to Gartner Hype Cycle for Emerging Technologies for 2018 blockchain will reach Maturity within 10 years. According to Gartner, by 2022, smart contracts will be adopted by more than 25% of global enterprises. There are already several blockchain providers, such as Hyperledger, Ethereum, BigChainDB, and Kadena. Blockchain have promising use cases in areas such as trade finance, insurance, security industry, digital properties and rights management, organizational management, Internet of Things (IoT), and energy [9].

The transparency and accountability enabled by the blockchain make it suitable to implement a (*logical*) trusted third party that can execute business transactions in untrusted business networks. The business transactions are much more complex operations than sending monetary resources from one party to the other [12, 13], and require enforcing the legal contractual obligations and rights of the involved parties [14].

In this chapter, we discuss the roles of the blockchain for enabling decentralized collaborative business processes across untrusted business partners. In particular, we present a meta-model that captures the key abstractions and constructs of smart contract-driven business transactions. It maps the business-related aspects of business transactions to the system-related aspects that are necessary for executing transactions using the blockchain. We also describe the life cycle of smart contract-driven business transactions, from the negotiation of legal contracts to the enactment of the transactions on a blockchain platform. To guide the implementation of the smart contract-driven business processes, we also provide a reference architecture that supports our meta-model and life cycle model.

4.2 MOTIVATING EXAMPLE

In this section, we present a simple supply chain scenario (adopted from [2]) to motivate the smart contract-driven the business transactions in the collaborative business processes.

As shown in Figure 4.1, the supply chain business network consists of four business entities: the Bulk Buyer, the Manufacturer, the Supplier, and the Special Carrier. Each entity can perform some business functions. For example, the Manufacturer can produce products and calculate the demands for products, and the Supplier can produce raw materials. The supply chain business processes are often carried out as a set of multi-step business transactions. In a business transaction, an initiating partner requests the business functions from one or more partners, who perform the requested business functions, and may in turn request the business functions from some other partners. For example, the Bulk Buyer places a new order with the Manufacturer, which either accepts or rejects the order. If the order is accepted, the Manufacturer calculates the product demands and orders the raw materials from the Supplier. Once the raw materials are ready, the Supplier asks the Special Carrier to transport them to the Manufacturer, which produces the products and delivers the produced products to the Bulk Buyer.

The business transactions (and thus processes) are governed by the legal contracts between the business entities. Typically, the contracts express the obligations of the contract parties to each other, and outlines services provided, business interactions allowed, performance, resources, conditions of providing services, and handling of contract violations. For example, the contract between the Bulk Buyer and the Manufacturer can state that the Manufacturer must deliver the requested products within 7 days after the order.

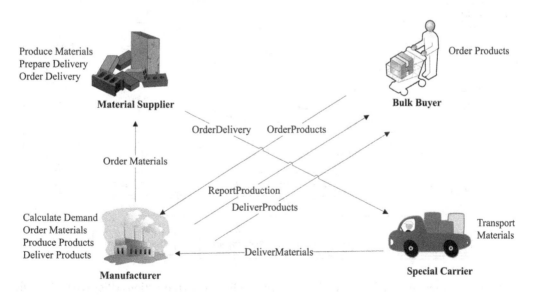

FIGURE 4.1 Supply Chain Example, Adopted from [2]

In business collaborations, as there often exist lack of trust between parties, the resolution of the conflicts between them can be challenging. Consider the case that the Buyer receives the products that do not match the requested product specifications, and thus refuse to accept the products. As the product is tailor-made for the Buyer, and cannot be sold to another buyer, the Manufacturer argues that the products are exactly matched with what were ordered. To resolve this conflict, the business interactions between parties must be made transparent while preserving privacy and security constraints, so that the malicious behaviors of parties can be readily spotted and legally penalized. Blockchain can help to build a trusted coordination environment for automating business collaborations between the untrusted business entities.

4.3 A META-MODEL FOR SMART CONTRACT-DRIVEN BUSINESS TRANSACTIONS

This section describes the key concepts of smart contract-driven business transactions. Note that by smart contracts, we do not mean the contracts of Ethereum blockchain platform. Smart contracts govern and dictate the business transactions occurred in business processes. Figure 4.2 presents a meta-model of smart contracts, including their relation to business transactions and processes. We base our meta-model from

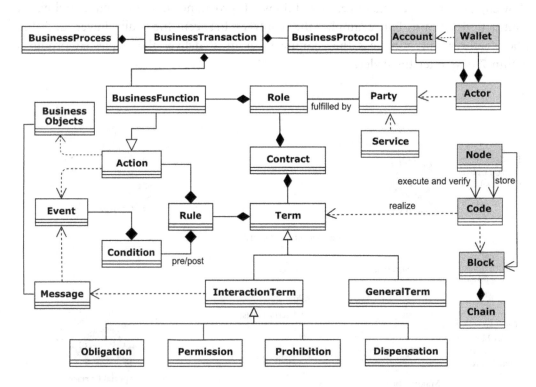

FIGURE 4.2   A Meta-model for Smart Contract-Driven Business Transactions (Blockchain Specific Concepts are Shaded)

the works on business transaction modeling [1], contract-based system modeling [15–17], and ontologies for blockchain [18, 19].

In business collaborations, the participants relate to each other by contractual agreements and interact at runtime by requesting and/or providing business functions (atomic units of works). A business process in such environments consists of a collection of business functions or tasks that are performed by business partners (parties) in order to achieve the shared business objectives of the stakeholders. A business process can be decomposed into a set of business transactions among business entities. A business transaction represents a sequence of business functions (or trading interactions) that are carried out by one or more parties to accomplish an explicitly shared business objective, such as ordering and delivering raw materials, and processing and paying an insurance claim [1]. The business protocol captures the information and exchange requirements, identifying the timing, sequence, and purpose of each business transaction and information exchange (interaction).

A trading party is a role-player, which carries out the abstract business functions defined by one or more roles. The contracts define the commitments of the contract parties in terms of roles. For example, the special carrier may play two roles: material transporter and product deliverer. The contract between the carrier and the manufacturer defines the commitments of the first role, and the contract between the carrier and the supplier defines the commitments of the second role.

Requesting and providing business functions involve the interactions between parties. The terms in the contracts between the parties govern such interactions. There are two main types of terms: interaction terms and general terms. The interaction terms are clauses that specify what business functions one party can request from the other party. Together, the terms express the mutual commitments of the contract parties to each other. The general terms are concerned with managing the life cycle of a contract, for example, commencement, continuation, and termination of a contract. The contract may also include the provisions for monitoring and assessing the performance of the contract parties with respect to the business functions they perform, and define the resolutions if a clause is violated or any conflict between parties arise.

The commitments expressed by contract terms can be categorized into four types: rights, prohibitions, obligations, and dispensations [15]. Rights and prohibitions are positive and negative authorizations that the contract parties have, respectively. They decide whether a party can perform an action (requesting or providing a business function) or not. Obligations express the actions that a party must perform, while the dispensations express the actions that a party is no longer required to perform. For example, the manufacturer has the right to reject an order if the calculated demands are higher than a given threshold. It has obligations to deliver the accepted order within the agreed delivery date, and to accept the returned products from the buyer.

The terms can be expressed as a set of event-condition-action rules. The condition of a rule is a set of business events (e.g., *ProductOrdered*, *MaterialsProduced*, or

ProductDelivered). The actions of a rule generally related to the business functions, for example, place a product order, and respond to a product order. The actions generate events and read, create, and manipulate business objects (e.g., order documents, and material specifications). For this purpose, the rules should be able to intercept and process the information (message) exchanges between the parties. For example, the interaction *OrderProduct* needs to be processed to identify the event *ProductOrdered* and to create a product order document business object.

A blockchain network consists of a set of (peer-to-peer) nodes, which can prove, validate, execute, and store blockchain transactions.

The blockchain transactions can be used to exchange money (in cryptocurrencies), to execute the coded functions on the blockchain network, and in general to update the data stored in the blockchain network. An immutable record of a completed transaction is stored in a block, and a combination of linked blocks are called a chain. The blocks are linked and secured using the public-key cryptography. The consensus protocol used by the nodes to validate and process transactions ensure the transactions are stored orderly across the blockchain network while guaranteeing the integrity and consistency.

The end-user of a blockchain system is an actor that owns one or more wallets and accounts (analogous to personal back accounts and wallets, but for cryptocurrencies). An account includes an address and private key/address pairs, and can store cryptocurrencies. The private key is used to sign the messages sending to the blockchain network. A wallet is to manage cryptocurrencies, that is, receive, store and spend them. A wallet can have multiple accounts. The user needs an account to perform blockchain transactions.

Business processes can use the blockchain as *shared, trusted, privacy preserving, non-repudiable data repositories* [3]. To achieve the accountability, traceability, and transparency of the partner actions and interactions in business collaborations, the contract terms can be realized using the coded functions that are stored and executed in a blockchain environment. The business events and objects, and the transactions involving creating, querying, updating, and deleting them can be stored in the blockchain in an immutable, transparent, and auditable manner.

4.4 LIFECYCLE OF SMART CONTRACT-DRIVEN BUSINESS TRANSACTIONS

Figure 4.3 depicts the life cycle of a business process running on top of the blockchain. It consists of three main phases: (1) negotiation and commitment, (2) design and implementation, and (3) deployment, execution, monitoring, and adaptation. The first phase considers the business related aspects, and the latter two phases consider the system related aspects.

In the negotiation and commitment phase, the participating business entities need to negotiate and agree upon the services provided and required, the terms and conditions of service provisioning and requesting, and QoS (quality of service) requirements. Next,

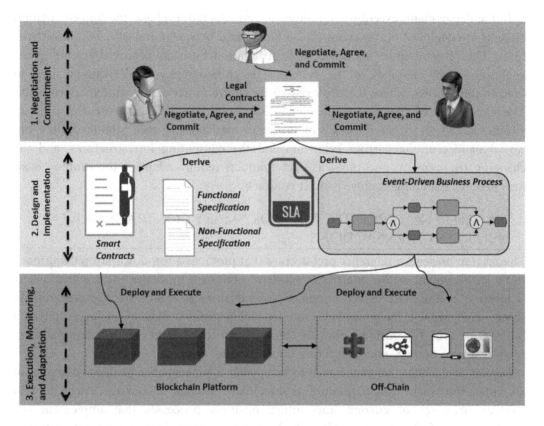

FIGURE 4.3 Life cycle of Smart Contract-Driven Business Transactions

the legal contracts (documents) are created based on the mutual agreements, and the created contracts are signed by the relevant partners. The contracts generally express the rights and obligations of the contract parties to each other, and also outlines the guidelines for handling contract violations, and the conditions of commencement, continuation, and termination of the contract.

In the design and implementation phase, the required system-level artifacts are created and/or (partially) generated based on the legal contracts and the information about the technical capabilities (e.g., service interfaces, data format and message exchange standards used) of the participants. The key artifacts include the functional and not-functional requirements for the overall business process and the partners, service level agreements (SLAs) between partners, executable smart contracts (in the contract programming language of the target blockchain platform), and business process models. The requirements and SLAs drive the design of the business process models. The business partners offer their business capabilities as business services, and the process models express the coordination of these services to realize the desired requirements while respecting the service level objectives of all the involved parties. These coordination logics in the process models can also be implemented with the smart contracts [2].

In the deployment, execution, monitoring, and adaptation phase, the implementation artifacts are deployed on on-chain (i.e., a blockchain network) and off-chain infrastructures. The relevant users should be able to enact a business process by sending the application-level messages to the system. The choreography model can be used to execute the process, where the deployed smart contracts act as the trusted coordinator. The enactment of the process instances is monitored to detect potential contract violations, and to trigger the relevant processes for handling each identified violation. The dynamics of the partner behaviors and the computing infrastructures, and the changing requirements and physical legal contracts require adapting the running business process, including deployed smart contracts.

4.5 A REFERENCE ARCHITECTURE FOR SMART CONTRACT-DRIVEN BUSINESS TRANSACTIONS

This section presents a reference architecture that provides a top-down layered approach to the development of the smart contract-driven business processes and transactions. It is inspired by the SOA (Service-oriented Architecture) reference architecture [20]. As shown in Figure 4.4, the proposed reference architecture consists of six layers: physical business network (or business domain), business process, business transaction, business service, smart contract, and computing infrastructure.

Similar to the SOA reference architecture, layer 1 presents the business domains in an enterprise such as production, finance, and human resources. Each domain consists of a set of current and future business processes that implement the requirements of the domain. Multiple business partners bound by legal contracts collaborate to realize these business processes, forming a business network. Layer 2, the business process layer, in our reference architecture is also similar to the business process layer in the SOA model. It captures the core business processes in a business domain, such as order management, production scheduling, shipping, and inventory management in the production domain.

Typically, the business processes need to integrate and coordinate business functions from multiple partners across the business network into multi-step business transactions. For example, in the production business process, purchasing raw materials is a business transaction between the manufacturer, the supplier, and the special carrier. This transaction consists of steps such as place orders, produce materials, delivery materials, pay materials, and pay delivery. It may only be considered as successful once all raw materials are delivered to the manufacturer, and the relevant payments have been issued. Such business transactions can take days or even weeks. The legal contracts between the involved participants regulate these business transactions. Layer 3 in our reference architecture is to decompose a business process into a set of composable business transactions (reflecting the business semantics).

In service-oriented business environments, the participants expose their real world business capabilities as business (IT) services. Internally, a participant may realize its

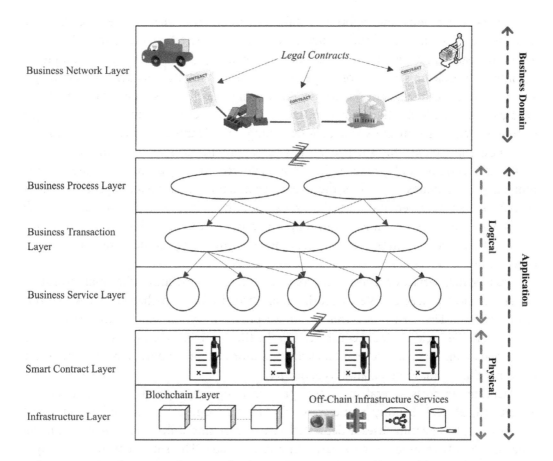

FIGURE 4.4 A Reference Architecture for Smart Contract-Driven Business Transactions

service as a complex business process that automates and coordinates its internal business tasks. For example, the manufacturer can provide a service that can be used by the bulk buyer to place orders, pay orders, cancel orders, and track delivery. Generally, the business services provide well-defined interfaces to hide their internal implementation details from other services (and thus other partners in the business network). A business transaction coordinates multiple business services into a logical atomic unit of work. The services interact will each other by requesting and providing service capabilities (business conversations). A transaction puts business constraints and invariants over these business conversations, for example, timing and ordering constraints on individual interactions. Layer 4 in our reference architecture includes the business services that can be coordinated to realize end-to-end business processes. Note that, in addition to the business services, utility (or commodity) services such as services implementing calculations and data processing algorithms are also necessary to implement business processes.

Business collaborations among untrusted parties require incorporating transparency and accountability into the relevant business processes. The participants expect the contractual obligations and rights are duly enforced. They need to be able to share a trusted representation of the contract enforcement including the transactions and assets of each participant, and the decision-making processes (e.g., handling of a contract breach or selection of a specific partner). With the blockchain technology, smart contracts can regulate the transactions using the business rules that the parties have agreed on. Ideally, the smart contracts should be derived from the relevant legal contracts. When the business interactions among participants are processed (as part of a business transaction), the smart contracts can apply the rules to check the compliance of the interactions, and produce the immutable records, reflecting the states of the individual interactions as well as the overall transactions and business processes. This shared trusted representation of the transaction data can give transparency to all relevant stakeholders if conflicts arise. Layer 5 in our reference architecture is to define the smart contracts for monitoring, regulating, and governing business transactions and processes.

Infrastructure services are necessary for automating and executing the smart contract-driven business processes. We categorize them broadly into on-chain services and off-chain services. The former services are those provided by the blockchain platform to manage the life cycle of smart contracts, invoke the contract functions, store and access data, and so on. There are several blockchain platforms that support smart contracts, for example, Ethereum, Kadena, and Hyperledger.

Ethereum supports several high-level programming languages as Serpent, LLL, and Solidity [8, 21, 22]. Solidity is the most popular language to use for Ethereum smart contracts [23]. Ethereum uses a dedicated virtual machine called the *Ethereum Virtual Machine* (EVM) to execute the smart contract bytecode. The smart contract languages offered by Ethereum are Turing complete and deterministic, they are also compiled languages; Once the smart contract is written in these high-level languages, it is compiled into bytecode that can be executed in the EVM environment [22].

The Kadena smart contracts platform offers a smart contract programming language called *PACT* [24]. Contrary to Solidity, PACT is not a compiled programming language but an *interpreter language*. Because the language is not compiled, it can be directly executed on the blockchain and verified by human eyes interactively, whereas that would be impossible for the bytecode of Ethereum. Furthermore, PACT is *non-Turing complete* and uses a declarative approach. Kadena smart contracts are stored in blocks similar to that of Ethereum. Kadena uses a *table based model* for smart contracts, while Ethereum uses an account based model.

The smart contracts in Hyperledger are called *Chaincode* [25]. Chaincode can be written in Go and Java programming languages. Chaincode program can only access its private storage that is isolated from one another. Because Hyperledger opts for portability of smart contracts and their execution, and therefore allows smart contracts to be executed in Docker containers [5]. Docker containers have as an additional advantage contrary to the EVM, that there are less coding restrictions.

The off-chain infrastructure services constitute the infrastructure services in the SOA reference architecture. Among them, technical services can provide the technical infrastructure enabling the development, delivery, maintenance, and provisioning of business services. They also offer capabilities to provide and maintain QoS such as security and performance. In this article, we assume that the choreography model is employed to coordinate the business services into business transactions and processes. Some of these coordination logics may also be realized by the smart contracts [26]. Infrastructure services also include monitoring and management services for monitoring the health and state of the business processes and resources, for detecting the potential contractual violations and trigger resolution policies, and so on. As the contract enforcement process should also be transparent to all parties, the smart contracts can also be used to realize it.

A smart contract can only access information that is stored on the ledger. However, some smart contracts operate in a wider ecosystem, and it might, therefore, be needed to acquire information about the outside world state and events. Moreover, the business services of the partners should be able to be triggered by the smart contracts, and vice versa [2]. This requires blockchain adapters/connectors that can receive messages or events from smart contracts and call external services, or receive service calls and send messages to smart contracts accordingly [2]. In the blockchain terminology, the trusted external data feeds are called *oracles*. Two current examples of oracles are Town Crier [27] and Oraclize [28].

4.6 MOTIVATING EXAMPLE WITH SMART CONTRACTS

In this section, we present the realization of our motivating example using smart contracts. We first provide an overview of the case study design, and then describe some of the smart contracts used.

4.6.1 Case Study Design

Figure 4.5 shows the high-level architecture of the system. Each partner exposes its internal business processes as SOA services. For example, the service of the manufacturer offers the capabilities to ordering the products, canceling and revising an order, paying for the products, and tracking the statues of an order. The implementations of these capabilities are internal to the manufacturer, and potentially use heterogeneous resources such as human workers, robots, software systems, and utility services. The blockchain-based smart contracts provide a trusted communication and coordination infrastructure for the business collaborations. The smart contracts between parties aim to implement the terms in the corresponding legal contracts. All the interactions (service requesting or transaction initiating interactions, and responding interactions) pass through the relevant smart contracts. A valid record of each interaction is recorded in the blockchain as a blockchain transaction. The processing of an interaction by a contract rule may generate events and business objects. The services use a blockchain connector (e.g., the trigger component in [2] or a Web3.js based connector (https:// github.com/ethereum/web3.js/)) to send interaction messages to the contracts, to read the business objects from the ledger, and to listen to the events generated. The detection

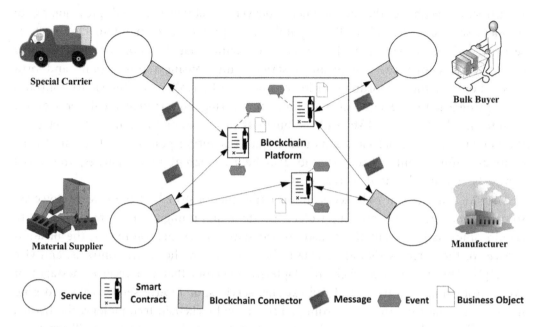

FIGURE 4.5   Motivating Example with Smart Contracts

of the event patterns can trigger the execution of the service operations (as in event-driven process chains).

Figure 4.6 illustrates the progress of a business transaction. The bulk buyer sends the product order request via a blockchain connector (client), which triggers the relevant

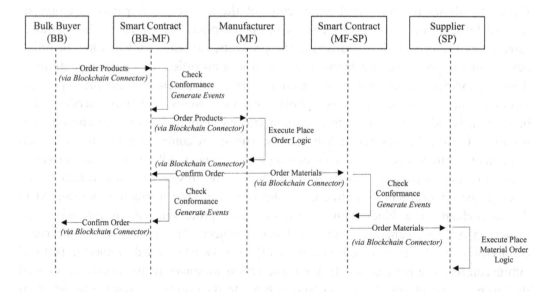

FIGURE 4.6   Sequence Diagram Illustrating Part of a Business Transaction

coded function of the smart contract to process the interaction, and to record the state of the interaction (a transaction in Ethereum). The processing may generate events indicating the state of the interaction, e.g., *ProductOrderReq* event. The blockchain connector associated with the service of the manufacturer listens to this event type (or an event pattern), and execute the place order operation of the service. This service operation may trigger internal business processes for processing the order and deciding the next actions, for example, acceptance or rejection of the order, estimating the production demands, and ordering raw materials if necessary. Upon the completion of the place order operation, the manufacturer may interact with one or more partners, for example, notifying the order acceptance to the buyer, and placing a raw material

```solidity
pragma solidity >=0.4.22 <0.7.0;
contract BB_MF {
    //addresses of the parties
    address payable public mfAddr;
    address public bbAddr;
    /// The Order business object
    struct Order {
        string goods;
        uint quantity;
        uint number;
        bool init;
    }
    mapping (uint => Order) orders;  /// The mapping to store orders business objects
    uint orderseq; /// The sequence number of orders
    /// Event triggered for every new order from the bulk buyer
    event OrderProductReqd(address buyer, string goods, uint quantity, uint orderno);
    /// Event triggered when the manufacturer sends the order acceptance notification
    event OrderConformed(address manufacturer, uint orderno, uint delivery_date);
    constructor (address _buyerAddr) public payable {
        mfAddr = msg.sender;
        bbAddr = _buyerAddr;
    }
    function sendOrder(string memory goods, uint quantity) payable public {
        require(msg.sender == bbAddr);  /// Accept orders just from buyer
        orderseq++;  /// Increment the order sequence
        /// Store the Order Business Object
        orders[orderseq] = Order(goods, quantity, orderseq, true);
        /// Trigger the event
        emit OrderProductReqd(msg.sender, goods, quantity, orderseq);
    }
    function confirmOrder(uint orderno, uint delivery_date) payable public {
        require(orders[orderno].init);  /// Validate the order number
        /// Just the manufacturer can confirm the order
        require(mfAddr == msg.sender);
        /// Trigger the event
        emit OrderConformed(msg.sender, orderno, delivery_date);
    }
}
```

FIGURE 4.7   Solidity Smart Contract between the Manufacturer and a Buyer (BB-MF)

order with the supplier. These interactions are also passed through the relevant smart contracts (BB-MF and MF-SP). The smart contracts process and regulate interactions, and create a shared, trusted complete record of the transaction data, events, and assets, enabling the validation of the past transactions and the enforcement of the legal contracts.

4.6.2 Ethereum Solidity Smart Contracts

Let us consider some of the Ethereum solidity smart contracts used in the case study. All events, business objects, and the state of the contract function executions are recorded in the blockchain.

Figure 4.7 shows a fragment of the contract BB-MF. It includes the addresses of the bulk buyer and the manufacturer. It also defines the business object *Order* and the events *OrderProductReq* and *Order Conformed*. The two functions *sendOrder* and *confirmOrder* are to intercept and validate the relevant service interactions. Figure 4.8 shows a fragment of the contract MF-SP. It binds the manufacturer and the raw materials supplier. The contract defines the business object *MaterialOrder*, the event *OrderMaterialReq*, and the function *placeMaterialOrder*. Each function generates events and populates business objects as necessary.

```
pragma solidity >=0.4.22 <0.7.0;
contract MF_SP {
    //addresses of the parties
    address payable public spAddr;
    address public mfAddr;
    /// The Material Order business object
    struct MaterialOrder {
        string materials;
        uint quantity;
        uint orderNumber;
        bool init;
    }
    mapping (uint => MaterialOrder) mOrders;  /// to store material orders business objects
    uint orderseq; /// The sequence number of material orders
    /// Event triggered for every new order from the manufacturer
    event OrderMaterialReqd (address manufacturer, string materials, uint quantity, uint ordemo);
    constructor (address payable _supplierAddr) public payable {
        mfAddr = msg.sender;
        spAddr = _supplierAddr;
    }
    function placeMaterialOrder (string memory materials, uint quantity) payable public {
        require (msg.sender == mfAddr);  /// Accept orders just from the manufacturer
        orderseq++;  /// Increment the order sequence
        /// Store the Order Business Object
        mOrders[orderseq] = MaterialOrder(materials, quantity, orderseq, true);
        /// Trigger the event
        emit OrderMaterialReqd (msg.sender, materials, quantity, orderseq);
    }
}
```

FIGURE 4.8   Solidity Smart Contract Between the Manufacturer and the Supplier (MF-SP)

4.7 SUMMARY

Blockchain, in particular, its distributed ledger system and smart contracts provide a trusted environment to share data among untrusted parties, and to execute computer programs to regulate interactions among the parties in a decentralized manner without a central trusted party. These characteristics of the blockchain enable to mitigate the lack of trust issues in the business processes that span across multiple potentially untrusted business entities. This chapter focused on smart contract-driven business transactions and processes. We presented a meta-model to capture the key abstractions and constructs in them. We also discussed their life cycle, and provided a reference architecture for aiding their development.

FURTHER READING

Wang, Shuai, et al. Blockchain-Enabled Smart Contracts: Architecture, Applications, and Future Trends. IEEE Transactions on Systems, Man, and Cybernetics: Systems (2019).

Mendling, Jan, et al. Blockchains for business process management-challenges and opportunities. ACM Transactions on Management Information Systems (TMIS) 9.1 (2018): 4.

Kosba, A., Miller, A., Shi, E., Wen, Z., and Papamanthou, C. (2016). Hawk: The blockchain model of cryptography and privacy-preserving smart contracts. In *2016 IEEE symposium on security and privacy (SP)*, 839–858. IEEE.

Delmolino, K., Arnett, M., Kosba, A., Miller, A., and Shi, E. (2016). Step by step towards creating a safe smart contract: Lessons and insights from a cryptocurrency lab. In *International Conference on Financial Cryptography and Data Security*, 79–94. Springer, Berlin, Heidelberg.

Hildenbrandt, E., Saxena, M., Rodrigues, N., Zhu, X., Daian, P., Guth, D., ... Rosu, G. (2018). Kevm: A complete formal semantics of the ethereum virtual machine. In *2018 IEEE 31st Computer Security Foundations Symposium (CSF)*, 204–217. IEEE.

Bartoletti, M. and Zunino, R. (2017). Constant-deposit multiparty lotteries on Bitcoin. In *International Conference on Financial Cryptography and Data Security*, 231–247. Springer, Cham.

REFERENCES

[1] Mike P. Papazoglou and Benedikt Kratz. A business-aware web services transaction model. In Asit Dan and Winfried Lamersdorf, editors, *Service-Oriented Computing -ICSOC 2006*, pp. 352–364. Springer, Berlin and Heidelberg, 2006.

[2] Ingo Weber, Xiwei Xu, Régis Riveret, Guido Governatori, Alexander Ponomarev, and Jan Mendling. Untrusted business process monitoring and execution using blockchain. In *International Conference on Business Process Management*, pp. 329–347. Springer, Rio de Janeiro, 2016.

[3] Richard Hull, Vishal S. Batra, Yi-Min Chen, Alin Deutsch, Fenno F. Terry Heath III, and Victor Vianu. Towards a shared ledger business collaboration language based on data-aware processes. In Quan Z. Sheng, Eleni Stroulia, Samir Tata, and Sami Bhiri, editors, *Service-Oriented Computing*, pp. 18–36. Springer International Publishing, Cham, 2016.

[4] Rishav Chatterjee and Rajdeep Chatterjee. An overview of the emerging technology: Blockchain. In *2017 3rd International Conference on Computational Intelligence and Networks (CINE)*, pp. 126–127. IEEE, Catalkoy, 2017.

[5] Tien Tuan Anh Dinh, Rui Liu, Meihui Zhang, Gang Chen, Beng Chin Ooi, and Ji Wang. Untangling blockchain: A data processing view of blockchain systems. *IEEE Transactions on Knowledge and Data Engineering*, 30(7): 1366–1385, 2018.

[6] Satoshi Nakamoto. *Bitcoin: A Peer-to-Peer Electronic Cash System*, 2008.

[7] Jan Mendling, Ingo Weber, Wil Van Der Aalst, Jan Vom Brocke, Cristina Cabanillas, Florian Daniel, Søren Debois, Claudio Di Ciccio, Marlon Dumas, Schahram Dustdar, et al. Blockchains for business process management-challenges and opportunities. *ACM Transactions on Management Information Systems (TMIS)*, 9(1): 4, 2018.

[8] Ric Shreves. *A Revolution in Trust: Distributed Ledger Technology in Relief and Development*. Technical report, Mercy Corps, Portland, OR, 2017.

[9] S. Wang, L. Ouyang, Y. Yuan, X. Ni, X. Han, and F. Wang. Blockchain-enabled smart contracts: Architecture, applications, and future trends. *IEEE Transactions on Systems, Man, and Cybernetics: Systems*: 1–12, IEEE, 2019.

[10] X. Xu, I. Weber, M. Staples, L. Zhu, J. Bosch, L. Bass ... P. Rimba. A taxonomy of blockchain-based systems for architecture design. In *2017 IEEE International Conference on Software Architecture (ICSA)* (pp. 243-252). IEEE, 2017, April.

[11] Xiwei Xu, Ingo Weber, and Mark Staples. *Introduction*, pp. 3–25. Springer International Publishing, Cham, 2019.

[12] Z. Zheng, S. Xie, H. Dai, X. Chen, and H. Wang. An overview of blockchain technology: Architecture, consensus, and future trends. In *2017 IEEE International Congress on Big Data (BigData Congress)*, pp. 557–564,. IEEE, Honolulu, 2017.

[13] Dylan Yaga, Peter Mell, Nik Roby, and Karen Scarfone. *Blockchain Technology Overview*. Technical report, National Institute of Standards and Technology, Gaithersburg, MD, 2018.

[14] Will Martino and Steward Popejoy. The kadena public blockchain, project summary whitepaper. 2017.

[15] L. Kagal and T. Finin. A policy language for a pervasive computing environment. In *Proceedings POLICY 2003. IEEE 4th International Workshop on Policies for Distributed Systems and Networks*, pp. 63–74. IEEE, Lake Como, June 2003.

[16] Alan Colman and Jun Han. Using role-based coordination to achieve software adaptability. *Science of Computer Programming*, 64(2): 223–245, 2007. Special Issue on Coordination Models and Languages (COORDINATION 2005).

[17] C. Molina-Jimenez, S. Shrivastava, and M. Strano. A model for checking contractual compliance of business interactions. *IEEE Transactions on Services Computing*, 5(2): 276–289, April 2012.

[18] Joost de Kruijff and Hans Weigand. Ontologies for commitment-based smart contracts. In *OTM Confederated International Conferences "On the Move to Meaningful Internet Systems"*, pp. 383–398. Springer, Rhodes, 2017.

[19] Joost de Kruijff and Hans Weigand. Understanding the blockchain using enterprise ontology. In Eric Dubois and Klaus Pohl, editors, *Advanced Information Systems Engineering*, pp. 29–43. Springer International Publishing, Cham, 2017.

[20] Michael Papazoglou. *Web Services: Principles and Technology*. Pearson Education, 2008.

[21] Loi Luu, Duc-Hiep Chu, Hrishi Olickel, Prateek Saxena, and Aquinas Hobor. Making smart contracts smarter. In *Proceedings of the 2016 ACM SIGSAC Conference on Computer and Communications Security*, pp. 254–269. ACM, Vienna, 2016.

[22] The Ethereum Community. Ethereum homestead documentation, release 01. 2017.

[23] Thomas Dickerson, Paul Gazzillo, Maurice Herlihy, and Eric Koskinen. Adding concurrency to smart contracts. In *Proceedings of the ACM Symposium on Principles of Distributed Computing*, pp. 303–312. ACM, Toronto, 2017.

[24] Steward Popejoy. The pact smart-contract language. 2017.

[25] Elli Androulaki, Artem Barger, Vita Bortnikov, Christian Cachin, Konstantinos Christidis, Angelo De Caro, David Enyeart, Christopher Ferris, Gennady Laventman, Yacov Manevich, et al. Hyperledger fabric: a distributed operating system for permissioned blockchains. In *Proceedings of the Thirteenth EuroSys Conference*, p. 30. ACM, Porto, 2018.

[26] G. Ciatto, S. Mariani, and A. Omicini. Blockchain for trustworthy coordination: A first study with linda and ethereum. In *2018 IEEE/WIC/ACM International Conference on Web Intelligence (WI)*, pp. 696–703, IEEE, Santiago, December 2018.

[27] Fan Zhang, Ethan Cecchetti, Kyle Croman, Ari Juels, and Elaine Shi. Town crier: An authenticated data feed for smart contracts. In *Proceedings of the 2016 ACM SIGSAC Conference on Computer and Communications Security*, pp. 270–282. ACM, Vienna, 2016.

[28] A scalable architecture for on-demand, untrusted delivery of entropyr, 2018.

CHAPTER 5

Towards Preserving Privacy and Security in Blockchain

Mohammad Mustafa Helal and Muhammad Rizwan Asghar

The University of Auckland, New Zealand

CONTENTS

Blockchain is at present one of the most disruptive technologies that have the potential to radically change today's business models. Blockchain is a decentralised database distributed across several systems. One of the key aspects of the blockchain is it does not require any dependence on a central trusted authority. Besides, no entity can tamper with data stored in a blockchain without the agreement among the majority, if not all, of the participating nodes. Blockchain is also used for smart contracts. A smart contract is a self-executed contract used to automate the verification process, execute a transaction, or exchange anything of value as per a predefined set of rules and conditions. Smart contracts do not rely on a central trusted authority.

Unfortunately, the protection of private information in the blockchain framework is still an open challenge. On the one hand, building applications on top of blockchain is growing, and expected to be used across different sectors, such as finance, government, and healthcare domains. On the other hand, protecting sensitive information is becoming very imperative as revealing such information could lead to revealing confidential business information or privacy loss. Moreover, storing smart contracts on blockchain nodes can be at risk of Man-at-the-End (MatE) attacks because the implementation of a smart contract is accessible to the curious blockchain nodes.

Bitcoin is the first blockchain application that uses the anonymity principle to tackle privacy issues. Many applications were developed afterwards for ensuring privacy in blockchain using different techniques, such as Zerocash, Coinparty, Mixcoin, and Monero. However, none of the available solutions addresses privacy in smart contracts.

In this chapter, we aim at presenting a privacy-preserving model for ensuring privacy in blockchain. Our proposed approach is based on White-Box Cryptography (WBC) to ensure privacy in smart contracts. We propose to transform the smart contract into an obfuscated smart contract, shipped to the blockchain node along with the private assets hidden within the contract implementation. In this way, we introduce a system that can protect sensitive data. First, the new system is resistant to the most serious attacks including MatE and the white-box attacks, which enable the attacker to gain full control of the execution environment. Furthermore, storing sensitive data in an encrypted form within the obfuscated smart contract prevents information leakage.

5.1 INTRODUCTION

Blockchain is currently one of the most emerging technologies that have a great potential to significantly impact industry and business models. Blockchain technology is expected to be used by different sectors, such as finance, government, and healthcare domains. Blockchain is basically a peer-to-peer cryptographic-based mechanism where each peer holds a digital database known as a ledger in some applications. Blockchain transactions are stored chronologically with timestamps in blocks. Each block is chained with the previous block. Once the blocks are created in the blockchain, the transactions cannot be tampered or removed. This provides a tamper-proof data storage that makes it computationally impossible to reverse the transactions.

A smart contract is used in the blockchain framework in order to execute some actions when certain predefined conditions in the contract are met. A smart contract is a piece of programme code stored in blockchain network. A blockchain network includes all the participants' systems, and since a smart contract is managed by those systems, it is important to find a way to hide its implementation from any observer who can have access to a system in the blockchain network.

Problem Statement. The decentralised nature of blockchain can ensure availability; however, it also raises privacy concerns. Bitcoin is the first application built on top of the blockchain where the transactions are stored in plaintext by Bitcoin nodes. In terms of privacy, Bitcoin uses anonymous public addresses in order to hide the real identity involved in the transaction. However, the transaction itself is made publicly available to all the participants in the Bitcoin network so that they can do the verification. Unfortunately, linking these transactions could reveal real identities.

Some applications deal with personal information, such as medical data. In general, protecting sensitive information is quite important as revealing such information could lead to serious consequences, such as privacy loss. Therefore, using traditional block-chain is not an option due to potential privacy issues. A smart contract has a vital role in such applications, as it is executed and running automatically on a blockchain node based on predefined rules and instructions. However, storing smart contracts on blockchain nodes at the peer's level can be at risk of a Man-at-the-End (MatE) attack because the implementation of a smart contract is accessible to the curious blockchain nodes. To address this issue, a naive approach could be to encrypt before storing the contract in the blockchain network. This simple approach introduces some new challenges when it comes to storing and executing the contract. There are several other problems, such as losing cryptographic keys could cost the users their personal information, or even worst, stolen keys could be misused. For data sharing, public keys could be used, which are typically managed by a Certificate Authority (CA). Nevertheless, public keys also come with its issues such as the single point of failure, where the Public Key Infrastructure (PKI) is highly dependent on the CA. Moreover, ineffective revocation mechanisms in the current PKI open doors for Man-in-the-Middle (MitM) attacks.

There are different techniques implemented by different blockchain applications, all of which aim to improve privacy in a blockchain network. For example, Bitcoin is one of the first applications in blockchain [1] that uses the anonymity idea to hide the real identity of the sender and the receiver. This is achieved by letting a Bitcoin user generate a new anonymous public address on each Bitcoin transaction. Another application [2] creates a separate anonymous currency called Zerocoin [3] on top of a non-anonymous currency referred to as basecoin (let us say, Bitcoin). Users then can start to deal with the new anonymous currency. It also uses the Zero-Knowledge Proof (ZKP) concept in the verification process. Coinparty [4] enables users to transfer funds that are controlled by multiple mixing peers not only one peer, and this is achieved by using the multi-signature technique. Moreover, some applications combined more than one methodology to improve the privacy such as Monero [5], which uses ring signature, ring confidential transaction, kovri, and stealth addresses to obfuscate transaction details.

Solution Statement. We propose a preserving-privacy framework for blockchain technology. Our solution is to use WBC to obfuscate the implementation of a digital smart contract. Furthermore, we hide the most valuable asset, which is the private key within the smart contract itself. In this way, blockchain nodes will be able to process the smart contract without learning sensitive information. Moreover, if a MatE attacker gets full access to the smart contract implementation, she will not be able to recover its implementation since the smart contract is obfuscated.

To the best of our knowledge, we are the first to leverage WBC to secure private data in a blockchain system. We aim at proposing a privacy-preserving framework for blockchain using the concept of WBC techniques to ensure the privacy of smart contracts, where our solution is inspired by [6], which discusses obfuscating smart contracts in blockchain.

Chapter Organisation. The rest of this chapter is organised as follows. Section 5.2 briefly discusses an overview of the privacy concept in blockchain, and then we shed lights on different types of attacks on blockchain applications. In Section 5.3, we summarise general solutions that use the blockchain framework, then review certain solutions for improving privacy in blockchain, in addition to existing frameworks including Hyperledger and Ethereum. In Section 5.4, we describe our contributions, and our proposed framework to overcome the privacy issue in blockchain. In Section 5.5, we conclude the chapter and discuss the blockchain challenges and future directions.

5.2 OVERVIEW AND ATTACKS ON BLOCKCHAIN

This section consists of two subsections. In Section 5.2.1, we provide an overview of different concepts of blockchain privacy and explain different types of blockchain. In Section 5.2.2, we discuss various attacks on systems built on top of the blockchain framework.

5.2.1 Overview of Privacy in Blockchain

In this subsection, we briefly discuss several types of blockchain and illustrate different methods and concepts used in current applications to preserve privacy.

5.2.1.1 Blockchain Types

There are multiple types of blockchain: public, private, and permission-based blockchains. Public blockchain means that everyone can join and contribute to the network. All the transaction data is recorded in a shared ledger. Bitcoin and Ethereum are examples of this type of blockchain. Public blockchain comes with a few disadvantages; the main disadvantage that we focus in this chapter is it does not address privacy issues. The second type is called private blockchain; it allows only selected entry of verified participants. The main difference between public and private blockchain is that the private blockchain controls who is allowed to join and who can be part of the network. The owner has the right to override or amend the necessary entries as required. Finally, the third type is permission-based blockchain, which allows a mixture of both public and private blockchains with customisation of features. This permission-based blockchain is built to grant special permissions to each participant on specific functions, for example, read, write, and access operations.

5.2.1.2 Anonymity

Anonymity is the idea of performing an action without revealing who has done the action. To address the privacy issue, *Bitcoin* [1] uses the anonymity concept by which the sender commits a transaction with a new and anonymous public address, which is not used in previous transactions by the user. This way, it becomes harder for an attacker to link an anonymous address to a given user. However, Meiklejohn *et al.* [7] were successful in identifying addresses belonging to online wallets, merchants, and other service providers by interacting with them and learning at least one address associated with such entities.

5.2.1.3 Mixing Protocol

In mixing protocols, the main idea is to build anonymity set for a specific transaction. For example, in a cryptocurrency transaction, a set of cryptocurrency holders can create a series of transactions, hence, making each participant anonymous within this set. This process may be repeated between different users to increase the anonymity set. CoinJoin [8] and CoinShuffle [9] have implemented this kind of protocol in their cryptocurrencies' models.

5.2.1.4 Altcoins

Altcoins are using a base currency, such as Bitcoin, to derive a new anonymous currency. Transactions are made through the new derived currency instead of the base currency to anonymise the transactions. Zerocoin and Zerocash [2] are examples of this type of currencies. Users can do a transaction in the base currency. However, users can cycle the base currency into and out of the anonymous derived currency to make the transaction anonymously.

5.2.2 Attacks on Blockchain

In this subsection, we describe major attacks on blockchain and provide a brief overview of each attack. This motivates us to explore our options towards a privacy-preserving framework.

5.2.2.1 Double-Spending Attack

In general terms, if a single transaction is executed twice in a system using the same asset, then it is considered a double-spending attack. For example, in Bitcoin, an attacker uses the same Bitcoin in (at least) two different transactions triggered simultaneously with an aim to deceive the system to spend the same Bitcoin twice. [8]

Finney attack [10] is a variation of double-spending attack where a dishonest miner broadcasts a pre-mined block for double-spending as soon as it receives products from a merchant.

5.2.2.2 Sybil Attack

Sybil attack [11] occurs when an entity tries to control multiple nodes in a network. At the same time, the network does not know that these nodes are controlled by the attacker. When the adversary maximises the control over a network, then there are chances that a victim might be connected to a node under the attacker's control.

Typically, decentralised applications are more subject to Sybil attacks than centralised applications. The existence of a trusted central authority eliminates Sybil attacks in centralised applications because the central authority is responsible for the user registration and activities. In a decentralised application, Sybil attacks can be avoided in different ways. For example, Bitcoin application avoids Sybil attacks through the proof-of-work mechanism. Bitcoin acquires the miner to consume computational power to generate a Bitcoin block. Hence, the attacker is limited on how to control more nodes in the Bitcoin blockchain.

5.2.2.3 Denial-of-Service (DoS)

An attacker aims at flooding the system with the data more than the system can handle, thus resulting in unavailability of the system. By exploiting this opportunity, an attacker can perform malicious operations. In blockchain, an attacker may try to send fake data to the nodes. For example, the Bitcoin Satoshi client version 7.0 [12] has built a system that would prevent such attacks. The signature verification process is one of the most computationally heavy processes run by the client that could lead to DoS attacks. Bitcoin Satoshi client version 7.0 introduced a signature-caching as a new feature to mitigate DoS attacks. Using this feature, developers create a cache allowing peers to store previously validated signatures and avoid redundant work. Furthermore, it does not allow transaction duplication to prevent unwanted overloading of the system.

5.2.2.4 Eclipse Attack

The target of this attack is the peer-to-peer network [13]. The Eclipse attack grants the attacker a huge advantage to take several IP addresses and manipulate the connections from/to the victim's node. Thus, the attacker controls the information flow, isolates the victim in the network from its peers, and leads the victim to communicate with malicious nodes instead of legitimate peers in the blockchain network.

5.2.2.5 Identity Lost

Users can easily lose their private assets, even without potential theft. However, losing a private key would compromise the valuable users' data in any system including blockchain applications. For example, in a cryptocurrency application, a user owns wallets to manage her assets. One possible way to secure access to the wallet is through a user-chosen password. If the user loses the password, then the entire assets that a user owns would vanish.

5.2.2.6 Identity Theft

Since the attacker knows that guessing any user's keys is practically a very complicated process and time-consuming, she may shift her focus towards stealing them instead of guessing or cracking. The attacker can increase the chances of getting the keys by attacking the weakest point in the system, which could be the users' mobile devices or their personal computers.

5.2.2.7 System Hacking

One of the key advantages of blockchain technology is it is hard to revert, amend, or alter the stored data in the blockchain network. Particularly, the attacker must have control of more than half of the nodes in order to manipulate data, and this is quite hard to achieve, if not impossible. However, programming codes, scripts, and systems that are used to implement the blockchain can be more vulnerable. For example, in 2014, some outdated codes gave attackers the ability to double spend Bitcoin transactions worth 700 million dollars [14]. A similar incident happened in 2016, where the attacker exploited a code vulnerability and was able to steal 50 million of Ethereum [15].

5.3 LITERATURE REVIEW AND EXISTING FRAMEWORKS

In this section, we mention general solutions that use blockchain to run their businesses. Then, we focus on certain solutions designed to ensure privacy in the blockchain network. Last, but not least, we explain some of blockchain frameworks including Hyperledger and Ethereum.

5.3.1 General Solutions

We summarise general solutions that use the blockchain framework. These solutions use blockchain as part of their business model. We can see different sectors that blockchain can be utilised.

5.3.1.1 Central Bank Digital Currency

Sun et al. [16] propose a model for central bank digital currency called MBDC, which is based on the permissioned-based blockchain technology. MBDC utilises the multi-blockchain to fulfil the bank's business prerequisite. The permissioned-based blockchain is utilised to guarantee that each unit of the currency is made by the central bank. The central bank maintains a blockchain with all of the business banks and different agencies. Blockchain holds the total value of daily exchanges. The central bank can examine the enormous information that is stored in the blockchain. Business banks put their nodes in the blockchain with the goal that the banks could transfer the daily exchanges. Each bank is responsible for approving the client's identity when the client is enrolled, at the same time, the client's public and private keys are created by the client's data. Clients save their particular private key, and the bank keeps a record of their public key.

5.3.1.2 Energy Trading through Multi-signatures

Aitzhan *et al.* [17] address the issue of providing transaction's security in decentralised smart grid energy trading. The proposed solution does not depend on any trusted third party. It uses multi-signatures and anonymous encrypted messaging to secure nodes communication. Multi-signature provides a way to form contracts without trusting any other party in the blockchain. Anonymous messaging streams provide two types of communication. First is sending a private peer-to-peer and second is message broadcasting. The system secures the participants through hiding the content, for example, masking identities by assigning unique strings of 36 alphanumeric characters.

5.3.1.3 Personal Data Protection

Zyskind *et al.* [18] introduce a convention that transforms a blockchain into an automated access control management that does not require trust in an external entity. This model aims to protect personal data on a blockchain. The framework consists of three elements. The first element is the users who are inspired by downloading and utilising applications. The second element is services to handle user's information and perform business operations. The third element is nodes that are substances depended on keeping up the blockchain and a disseminated private key-value data store. The blockchain acknowledges two new kinds of exchanges: Taccess, utilised to control access; and Tdata, for information storage and retrieval. A user introduces an application that uses the framework for safeguarding her security. As the user agrees to accept the first run through, a shared identity is produced and sent, alongside the associated permissions, to the blockchain in a Taccess exchange. Information gathered from the phone (*e.g.*, information from sensors, such as location) is encrypted using a shared encryption key and then is sent to the blockchain in a Tdata exchange. Tdata exchange sends the shared key to a key-value store and holds it as a link to the data on the public ledger. The link is used by the users and services to retrieve the data.

5.3.1.4 MedRec

MedRec [19] is a prototype, which gives users the ability to access their electronic medical records across multiple providers. It addresses privacy concerns in a blockchain where medical records are considered sensitive data that should not be publicly available. MedRec utilises smart contracts on an Ethereum blockchain. Contracts are used to store data pointers instead of the data itself. Data pointers are references to where the actual medical records are stored outside the blockchain. The blockchain stores the contracts data structures, references to the medical records, and permissions for ownership and viewership of the records. However, the raw data is stored separately in provider's data storage.

MedRec incentivises medical researchers and healthcare stakeholders to be part of the blockchain network by giving them the ability to access the data in a single and common interface where patients can grant the permissions to share their data. Moreover, it provides immutable audit logs, data sharing authorisation, and custom Application Programming Interfaces (APIs), which are used, for instance, for posting to the Ethereum blockchain.

5.3.1.5 Model Chain

Model Chain [20] is a decentralised framework to preserve the privacy of the Protected Healthcare Information (PHI) in a private blockchain network. The system is cross-institutional healthcare to generate and exchange models instead of exchanging the private data of patients. The exchange happens among the connected healthcare sites. These models are partially trained by machine learning algorithms. Model chain applies machine proof-of-information to decide the order of learning in the process of generating the model to be transferred. The site that contains fewer patients' data implies to have less accurate models; hence, contains more information to improve the model, the protocol will choose it as the next model to update the site. The process is repeated to update the model until a site cannot find any other site with higher error to update the model.

5.3.1.6 File Storage

Kopp *et al.* [21] designed a decentralised file storage system. It addresses the problem of a privacy-preserving payment mechanism based on ring signatures and one-time addresses. Instead of simply referencing the recipient by its public key, the sender obtains a new temporary public key using both a random nonce and the recipient's public key. The derived one-time public key, called destination key, and the original long-term public key of the recipient are unlinkable without knowledge of the recipient's private key. Ring signatures are used to prove membership in a group without explicitly revealing the identity. The signer needs its private key, as well as the set of public keys of the other members in the group to create a ring signature. The user can store their files in a storage provider by creating a contract. Storage providers publish the proof of retrieving the file using the ring signature to prove their compliance with storage contracts.

5.3.1.7 CryptoNote

CryptoNote [22] provides mainly untraceable transaction. CryptoNote scheme is based on a cryptography primitive called a group signature. It implements the ring signature technology, which allows the user to sign a message on behalf of a group. The signature is used to prove that the transaction is created by someone from the group such that all the signers are indistinguishable from each other. This protocol has better performance but weaker anonymity compared to Zerocoin or Zerocash [8].

CryptoNote solution enables a user to distribute a single address and receive unlinkable transactions. By default, the destination of each CryptoNote output is a public key, derived from the recipient's address and sender's random data. The main advantage over Bitcoin is that every destination key is unique by default. Thus, there is no external party can link two addresses together. This is based on the assumption that a sender does not use the same random data for the transactions delivered to the same recipient.

CryptoNote uses Diffie-Hellman exchange method to obtain a shared secret from the user's data and half of the recipient's address. The user then computes a one-time destination key, using the shared secret and the second half of the address. Two different keys are required from the recipient for these two steps, so a standard CryptoNote address length is nearly double as of Bitcoin wallet address. Nevertheless, the receiver conducts a Diffie-Hellman exchange to recover the corresponding secret key.

5.3.1.8 Hawk

Kosba *et al.* [23] developed a programming framework called HAWK. The framework is used for building a decentralised smart contract system. HAWK is intended to compile the program—with no implementation of cryptography—into an efficient cryptography protocol. HAWK is built on top of ZKP. The main idea of ZKP is to prove statements about a particular value without exchanging any information about that value between the prover and the verifier. HAWK protocol consists of users, a manager, and the blockchain program. Users must generate ZKP parameters and store them in the blockchain in three phases. The first phase is the freeze phase in which the data is stored in the contract. The second phase is the compute phase in which users send encrypted data with the public key of the manager. There is a finalise phase in which the manager decrypts the data with their private key, runs the functions, and creates the encrypted output, which is sent to the parties based on the previously agreed policy.

HAWK provided a sealed auction example to illustrate how HAWK can be implemented. In the sealed auction, the highest bidder wins; besides, the second highest price is rewarded as well in order to incentivise a truthful auction. Most important is that bidders submit their bids without knowing the bid of others. Hawk can compile such programs into two portions. First is the private portion that determines the winner and the price. Second is the public portion, which relies on public deposits to protect users from a quitting manager. Hawk program declares three timeouts where T1 < T2 < T3. T1 is the time of collecting the bids; no more bid can be submitted after T1. T2 is the time when all users must open their bids to the manager, if a user fails to open their bid then the bid would be dropped out the auction. T3 is to control if the manager aborts, users can reclaim their private bids.

5.3.1.9 Zerocash

Ben-Sasson *et al.* [2] constructed a decentralised cryptocurrency protocol called Zerocash. It aims not to revealing any transaction's information such as the origin address, the destination address, and the amount. Zerocash creates a separate anonymous currency called Zerocoin on top of a non-anonymous currency known as basecoin.

Users then start dealing with the new anonymous currency. Zerocash's functionality involves mint transactions and pour transactions. A mint transaction is the process of transforming the basecoins into Zerocoins. It includes a hash value of a unique serial number, coin's value, and the owner's address. A pour transaction gives the ability to the user to make a private payment through a ZKP. Pour transactions consist of up to two input coins, and up to two output coins. It uses ZKP to prove three things. First, a user has the two input coins. Second, the input coins exist in a previous mint transaction. Third, the value of the input coins is equal to the value of the output coins.

5.3.2 Solutions for Improving Privacy

In this section, we review existing solutions that address the privacy issue in blockchain applications. For each solution, we describe distinct features, advantages, and disadvantages. Recall anonymity concept to address the privacy; each solution brings in new features towards a preserving-privacy framework.

5.3.2.1 MixCoin

MixCoin [24] provides anonymity to Bitcoin transactions by allowing users to send their transactions to third-party mix peers and receive back the same amount of the transaction submitted by other users. In this case, mixing is done with the help of a trusted third-party mixing server called the mix. Each user sends a new encrypted address and transfers the funds to the mix. Afterwards, the mix decrypts the new addresses, randomly shuffles them, and sends the funds back to each participant. Moreover, MixCoin provides an accountability mechanism to expose any theft. The mix entity issues signed warranties to participants to state that if a user sends me a certain amount of coins by a specific time T1, then I will send the same amount to the user later by T2. In this way, the user can send funds to the mix with confidence that she can publish this warrant to degrade the mix's reputation if misbehaves.

This provides anonymity across external participants. Users outside the mix cannot learn about links between users in the mix. However, the primary drawback of this model is that the participants deal with a third party and need to trust the mix. In this scenario, the mix can learn which output address belongs to which input address. Therefore, the privacy is based on the assumption of a trusted third party, which can lead to de-anonymisation or exposing user's identities.

5.3.2.2 CoinJoin

CoinJoin [8] addresses the main drawback of MixCoin, where the mix can learn and link users' input and output. Coinjoin provides anonymity using multi-signature transactions. Multi-signature requires more than one party to be involved in the transaction. In order to let the participants mix their coins, they generate one single mixed transaction. The transaction with multiple inputs is considered valid only if it has been signed with all keys related to the input addresses. Hence, each user verifies the generated mix and refuses to sign the transaction in order to stop or proceed with the exchange. CoinJoin also provides external unlinkability; to this end, a set of users contributes to each transaction such that no external party can determine which input corresponds to which user. In this way, CoinJoin hides the ownership of Bitcoins by joining them with others in a single mixed transaction.

One of the possible disadvantages of CoinJoin is that one of the involved parties can learn how to link transactions between inputs and outputs.

5.3.2.3 CoinShuffle

CoinShuffle [9] is a decentralised protocol for coordinating CoinJoin transactions using a mixing protocol. Unlike CoinJoin, CoinShuffle provides anonymity even among the involved participants. It preserves the privacy of the transaction by allowing the users to mix their coins with other interested users in the network. CoinShuffle prevents any of the involved parties to link between inputs and outputs in the transaction. The recipient addresses are not known by the senders.

There are some advantages of CoinShuffle. One of the advantages is it requires only standard cryptography primitives such as signature and public key encryption. One more advantage is that it is executed only by the Bitcoin users and does not require any trusted third party. Besides, CoinShuffle does not require any change in the Bitcoin protocol; it is fully compatible with the Bitcoin network. Last, but not least, it does not charge any extra fees for additional mix transactions. Despite the aforementioned advantages, CoinShuffle increases an additional overhead for the rest of the Bitcoin network.

CoinShuffle protocol consists of three phases. First is the announcement phase, where each user generates a new ephemeral encryption–decryption key pair. Second is the shuffling phase, where each user creates a new Bitcoin address as her output address in the mixed transaction. Then, the users shuffle the newly created output addresses using the encryption keys of all users. The last is the transaction verification phase, where each user can verify if the output address belongs to her is on the list. Each user signs the transaction and sends the signature. On receiving signatures from all users, each user is then able to create a fully signed version of the mixed transaction. Then, the transaction is considered valid and pushed to the Bitcoin network. In each phase, every user checks that all other users follow the protocol or not. If this validation fails, then the user can report this misbehaviour, refuses to sign the transaction, and prevents the funds from being stolen.

5.3.2.4 Monero

Monero [25,26] is a version of CryptoNote. It hides the sender, amount, transaction, and receiver using ring signatures, Ring Confidential Transactions (RingCT), kovri, and stealth addresses, respectively. Monero provides two features unlinkability and untraceability. Unlinkability means that an inability to find a relation between two transactions sent to the same user. Untraceability means that no one can identify where the transaction is originated from.

Unlike Bitcoin, the funds are not associated with the public address. When users send funds, they actually send funds to a random newly created one-time destination address. Hence, neither public records of the sender nor the receiver will appear in a public record. Instead, Monero uses a stealth address concept to hide the recipient address. To generate a stealth address, a Monero user is associated with two key pairs. One is a secret key pair (secret viewing key as skv and secret spending key as sks) known only by the user and a second public key pair is publicly shared (public viewing key as pkv and public spending key as pks). A stealth address is a new address derived from a one-time public key generated by the sender on behalf of their intended receiver. Hence, any transaction is always marked by a unique destination address. A sender generates a stealth address by two species of information: first is a random number used to generate a shared secret known only by both parties, while second is the public key pair of the receiver. The shared secret is generated through a Diffie-Hellman exchange. On the receiver end, Monero user actively scans the network to listen to every transaction, detects if the transaction is intended for their recipient's address, and then recovers the private key associated with this one-time public key in order to spend the funds.

Monero uses ring signatures to hide the sender address and provide the untraceability feature. A user receives several inputs linked together as a ring. Any input is linked to more than one transaction, thus making it hard to track the origin of a transaction. In this way, Monero hides where the transaction is coming from because it is linked with several random other transactions and signed using the ring signature. A digital signature contains more than one element. One element is a key image created from all these selected transactions. The network scans for this key image. If the key image is found in the blockchain in any prior transaction, then the system will refuse the transaction to prevent the double spending issue.

Pedersen commitment is used to hide the actual amount that is being spent, so a user commits to spending a certain amount defined in this commitment. However, other users never know the exact amount to be spent. This Pedersen commitment is part of RingCT. It obfuscates the transaction amount by adding a random number. The commitment is then calculated using a certain formula for the set of inputs and outputs of the transaction, and then it is broadcast to the network. Hence, the actual amount is never published in the network in the plain.

Finally, Monero adopts kovri project to obfuscate the Internet traffic in a way such that any passive traffic monitoring can neither reveal the sender's geographical location nor the IP addresses. The Kovri project is based on the Invisible Internet Project (I2P) routing service. All the traffic is encrypted and then routed through the I2P nodes. Passive listeners can detect that one is using the I2P service. However, they cannot determine what are you using it for, nor the destinations set up by users.

Despite all of the aforementioned advantages, Monero transaction is significantly larger than other cryptocurrencies such as Bitcoin. For example, to construct a stealth address, the generated one-time destination address size is at least twice as Bitcoin recipient public address.

Miller et al. [27] mention the impact of some weaknesses of Monero. For example, many Monero transaction inputs contain deducible mixins and can be linked to prior transactions via chain-reaction analysis. However, Monero addressed this weakness by setting a minimum limit of mixins. This is one of the reasons why Monero had some implementation issues. However, the past discovered issues were addressed by Monero team, but there is no guarantee of having uncovered issues.

5.3.2.5 AEON

Anonymous Electronic On-line Coin (AEON) [5] is a fork of Monero. It is also a privacy-focused coin. AEON is meant to be simple enough to be used by anyone. AEON has started as an experiment but then found its vendors and now AEON is fully functional CryptoNote currency.

There are several advantages of AEON. First, AEON is considered to be mobile-friendly. It performs well on mobile devices as well as regular laptops and desktops. Second, AEON has a different proof-of-work known as CryptoNote-Lite, which is a lightweight version from CryptoNote protocol to speed up the verification process of the blockchain. Third, blockchain scalability—AEON allows the blockchain not to grow fast—it is meant to be a good match in devices with limited storage. Last, but not least, AEON gives users the ability to have a traceable transfer for non-sensitive transactions, it reduces the cost of operation and improves the performance of viewable transactions. Despite all of its advantages, having a lighter version of cryptography to run on any device can limit the usage of advanced cryptographic algorithms.

Table 5.1 provides a comparative analysis of existing solutions for improving privacy in blockchain. We present the main features besides disadvantages of each solution.

5.3.3 Existing Frameworks

We survey existing frameworks including Hyperledger [28] and Ethereum. [29]

5.3.3.1 Hyperledger

Hyperledger is a set of open-source blockchain frameworks and platforms, created to improve blockchain technologies. [30] It is a global collaboration established as a project of the Linux Foundation in early 2016. Hyperledger has a wide list of well-known industry members. The list includes huge corporates such as Airbus, IT companies like IBM, Fujitsu, SAP, Huawei, Nokia, Intel, and Samsung, besides financial companies like American Express.

TABLE 5.1 Comparative analysis of existing solutions for improving privacy in blockchain.

Solution	Main Features	Disadvantages
Mixcoin (Section 5.3.2.1)	Increase anonymity and provide accountability	Require to trust a third party mixing server
Coinjoin (Section 5.3.2.2)	Utilising anonymity using multi-signature transactions	One of the involved parties can learn to map transactions between inputs and outputs
Coinshuffle (Section 5.3.2.3)	Expand anonymity even among the involved participants	Add an additional overhead for the rest of the Bitcoin network
Monero (Section 5.3.2.4)	Hide the sender, amount, transaction, and receiver	Transaction size is doubled and experienced some implementation issues
AEON (Section 5.3.2.5)	A lighter version of Monero, suits storage-constraint devices	Limiting advanced security features because of having a lighter version of cryptography

Hyperledger Fabric Hyperledger Fabric [31,32] is an implementation of Hyperledger project. It was developed by IBM corporate. The primary consideration was to develop a blockchain framework that runs a real-world business scenario.

Hyperledger Fabric supports distributed ledger on permissioned networks for a wide range of industries. It is designed in a way to maximise the confidentiality, resilience, and flexibility of blockchain solutions.

Permissioned Membership. In a permissioned network, all participants must be known and can be identified by their unique identifiers. This kind of network is best used in a business case where the business needs to fulfil certain data regulations. For example, financial and healthcare industries are subject to data protection laws.

Performance. The Hyperledger Fabric architecture separates transaction processing into three phases. The first phase is distributed logic processing and agreement known as chaincode. The second phase is transaction ordering. The last one is transaction validation and commitment phase. This separation assists to optimise the Hyperledger performance and reduce the number of levels of trusts and verification.

We describe the transaction flow in Hyeperledger Fabric. (1) An application submits a proposal to an endorsing peer. (2) Endorsement policy determines how many endorsing peers are needed to sign the proposal and then the endorsing peers execute chaincode such as a smart contract. (3) Then, the endorsing peers send the signed proposal back to the application. (4) The application then sends the transactions and signatures to the ordering service. (5) The ordering service generates a block of transactions and delivers them to committing peers. (6) Finally, the committing peer receives the blocks of transactions and validates that the endorsement policy was met or not. Then, a block is committed to the ledger. The performance is optimised as a result that only the signatures are sent around the network.

Data on a Need-to-Know Basis. Hyperledger Fabric allows for data to go only to the parties that need to know. This is similar to the principle of least privilege, where each part must have access only to the data that it needs to know.

Protection of Digital Keys and Sensitive Data. Hyperledger Fabric supports the use of Hardware Security Module (HSM). This helps in safeguarding digital keys and managing them for strong authentication.

5.3.3.2 Ethereum

Ethereum [33] is an open-source blockchain platform. It allows developers to build decentralised applications and create many different services using the smart contracts concept. Ethereum's most innovative part is the Ethereum Virtual Machine (EVM). It allows running any program written in any language. EVM facilitates the creation of blockchain applications. For example, instead of creating a different blockchain for each new application, new applications can be created and managed on one platform. Contracts written in a smart contract are compiled into bytecode, each node in the blockchain executes this contract using its EVM. A smart contract gets executed when rules and conditions the developer initially programmed are met.

The Ethereum blockchain is a transaction-based state system. The system accepts a series of inputs and, based on those inputs, will be transitioned to a new state. In

Ethereum's state machine, it starts with a blank state called a genesis state; this is before any transactions are on the blockchain. When transactions are executed, the state transits into a final state. A state has millions of transactions grouped into blocks. Each block is chained with its previous block to form the blockchain.

Ethereum applications have several advantages inherited from all the blockchain properties. First is immutability, *i.e.,* data is considered immutable and no third party can make any changes to it. Second, there is zero downtime.

5.4 OUR PROPOSED FRAMEWORK

In this section, we first define the system and threat models, which explain the new entities in the proposed framework, the relation between them, and the adversary we consider. Then, we present our proposed approach for a privacy-preserving framework in blockchain. Finally, we discuss some benefits and limitations of our approach.

5.4.1 System Model

In this section, we define the entities of the proposed framework and their relations with each other. The system model consists of three entities: User Transaction, WBC-Smart-Contract, and Storage.

User Transaction. User transaction is the actual operation a user needs to perform on the blockchain. A transaction can be either send a request to the blockchain or get data request to receive the user's related data on the blockchain. Each user has a pair of cryptographically linked keys: private and public keys. A user uses the public key to encrypt requests before submitting a transaction to the blockchain network.

WBC-Smart-Contract. WBC-Smart-Contract is a digital contract designed by a WBC implementation. The contract hides a private key within its implementation and accepts instructions encrypted with the corresponding public key. The contract stores the user data in storage in an encrypted form. When the contract needs to read the storage, it decrypts it internally and when the contract needs to write to storage, it encrypts the desired result before writing it back to the storage. The WBC-Smart-Contract code checks the signature on the transaction sent by the user to see if that user is entitled to read the data, and only if they are entitled to read, it returns the data. If the used signature is invalid, then the contract code returns an error, and the user will not be able to extract the requested information.

Storage. Storage is an internal element in the WBC-Smart-Contract, it is used to store the data in an encrypted form. It implements two interfaces, read and write, both of which are used by the contract. The contract encrypts the data before writing it to the storage and decrypts the data after reading it before the actual processing.

Figure 5.1 is a flow diagram to illustrate the entities and operations involved in the proposed framework. First, a user encrypts the request before sending it to the WBC-Smart-Contract. The WBC-Smart-Contract validates the user request to check if the given user is entitled to the given request or not. A request can be any user-related operation data, for example, getting user balance or medical records. While processing the user request, the WBC-Smart-Contract decrypts data when reads it from the storage, processes it, and then encrypts the data back to the storage.

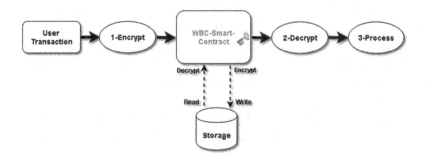

FIGURE 5.1   Flow diagram of a single user transaction in the proposed framework.

5.4.2 Threat Model

In the proposed framework, we define our threat model with the assumption that a Man-at-the-End (MatE) attacker has full access to the execution environment. Thinking of what will happen if the environment where the smart contract resides is untrusted and can be controlled by an attacker. In the context of this threat model, if an attacker managed to control a normal smart contract, they will be able to decompose the implementation to find a more compact representation that can be used in a way to control how the smart contract works effectively. Unlike the WBC-Smart-Contract, using a WBC implementation obfuscates the implementation of the smart control in a way that even if adversaries gain access to the environment, they will not be able to recover the smart contract in plaintext.

5.4.3 Proposed Approach

We propose a novel framework to address security and privacy issues in blockchain. The framework is based on WBC concept and smart contract. A smart contract is normally pushed into a blockchain node to be automatically executed as per pre-defined rules and conditions. Imagine that we have a MatE attacker who has limitless privileges and authorised access to the blockchain node. In order to minimise the loss that can be occurred, our approach is to obfuscate the contract before pushing it into a blockchain node. Moreover, we propose to embed cryptographic keys within the smart contract implementation through WBC techniques. In this way, we aim to exchange only encrypted data between a user and a blockchain node. This enables the contract to decrypt the transaction while processing it, then to encrypt the transaction to maintain it in the storage.

To obfuscate the smart contract, we propose using WBC mechanisms. The transformation process can be done either using a commercial tool, which converts a given program code into a white-box implementation such as [34], or a solution called SPNbox proposed by Bogdanov et al. [35] We denote the output of the transformation process as a WBC-Smart-Contract. The role of WBC-Smart-Contract is explained in details in Section 5.4.1.

Currently, there are two dedicated designs handling WBC implementations. The first one is ASASA by Birykov et al. [36], which suffers from key extraction and decomposition attacks. The second one is SPACE by Bogdanove and Isobe [37], where SPACE reduces the risks of ASASA but introduces new performance overhead challenges. Whilst Bogdanov *et al.* [35] propose SPNbox Ciphers to overcome the challenges of the aforementioned solutions. SPNbox is designed with consideration of software efficiency and execution time. It also relies on the black-box cipher security for resisting against key extraction attacks.

Figure 5.2 provides an overview of the proposed framework. Here, WBC-Smart-Contract holds the private key. Note that the exchange messages between the entities are encrypted messages.

WBC is the concept of protecting the cryptographic keys, whilst the implementation is subject to the white-box attack model. The white-box attack model is considered the strongest attack model, based on the assumption that the attacker has full access to the source code and the environment, the attacker is able to see and manipulate the internal implementation steps and fully control the execution environment.

The first WBC implementation was introduced by Chow *et al.* in 2002 [38], which illustrated that it is possible to transform a given implementation to a white-box secure execution. They implemented a white-box Advanced Encryption Standard (AES). White-box secure execution hides the keys without exposing them in the implementation. Chow *et al.*'s WBC transformation is based on finding a representation of the algorithm as a network of lookups in randomised and key-dependent tables.

One of the primary WBC applications is Digital Right Management (DRM) systems. The end user subscribes to get a service such as Netflix or any other on-demand videos. The digital content arrives at the user end in an encrypted form, then the software runs on the device decrypts it to stream the content to the user. The main goal in such

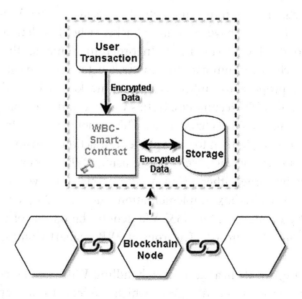

FIGURE 5.2   Overview of the proposed framework.

TABLE 5.2 Comparative analysis of our approach and previous ones.

Approach	Depends on Third Party	Cryptographic Technique	Supports Smart Contract	Resistant to White-Box Attack
Mixcoin (Section 5.3.2.1)	Yes	Encrypts Addresses	No	No
Coinjoin (Section 5.3.2.2)	Yes	Multi-signature Transactions	No	No
Coinshuffle (Section 5.3.2.3)	No	Public Key Encryption	No	No
Monero (Section 5.3.2.4)	No	Ring Signature to hide the Sender	No	No
Our Approach	No	White-Box Cryptography	Yes	Yes

a system is to prevent the user from being able to use her own stream for redistributing the digital content outside the DRM. WBC is used to hide the keys from the sight of the user or whoever can get access to the device.

Table 5.2 provides a comparative analysis of our approach and existing solutions mentioned earlier. We highlight the main two core key aspects of our proposed approach. The first aspect is we support smart contract privacy, and the other one is we have a model that is more resistant to white-box attacks.

5.4.4 Discussion

There is no entire framework that is completely secure. [39] However, a framework is considered secure relatively to a security model. By defining the threat model in Section 5.4.2, and with the assumption that there is a MatE attacker. The attacker's goal can vary. For example, revealing some sensitive data on the blockchain. Another example is learning what rules and conditions are defined in the smart contract.

In the context of WBC, it is much more difficult to extract the keys from an obfuscated smart contract than revealing them from an un-obfuscated contract.

There are several advantages of using WBC within smart contract in a blockchain. The primary advantage is, the smart contract is given the ability to store encrypted instructions along with the keys. This means smart contracts can use these keys to decrypt the instructions, verifies whether the conditions are met or not, then encrypts the content back to the storage. In these operations, only the smart contract can get access to these keys when it needs to process a transaction. Another advantage of using WBC is if an attacker can get access to the blockchain node, WBC makes revealing the keys a very difficult process and time-consuming. This is with the consideration that the keys are hidden in the smart contract and the smart contract's implementation is obfuscated.

Despite the advantages of WBC, there are few disadvantages raise with WBC implementations in general. The main disadvantage is WBC acquire more resources such as memory, storage, and CPU processing. [40] Thus, WBC may not be ideal for resource-constrained platforms such as phones and tablets. Another disadvantage is that there is no known white-box solution available for asymmetric encryption. However, the known white-box solutions are currently available to the symmetric encryption.

5.5 BLOCKCHAIN CHALLENGES AND FUTURE DIRECTIONS

Blockchain technology has great potential to grow. However, there are some fundamental challenges, which could raise serious privacy concerns. Currently, this proposed solution is in an early development phase. More work is needed to expand on the idea, also to implement the WBC-Smart-Contract to identify potential pitfalls and areas for optimisation.

We explained various attacks can occur in blockchain applications in Section 5.2.2. However, we did not address them directly in the proposed solution (Section 5.4). A potential future work we recommend is to address and tackle each attack in the context of the proposed framework.

Expressing any program. One of the known issues of the obfuscation is there is no general obfuscation solution that can obfuscate any program without limitation. A potential future work we recommend in this area is to review different obfuscation techniques and provides distinct features for each technique. This can assist in finding a solution that is more close to the ideal generic obfuscation solution. An ideal solution is that it can obfuscate any smart contract written in any language with no issues.

Lack of tools. The tools that are used to develop a blockchain play a vital role in providing application security. For example, using improper tools [41] can lead to compromising application's security or efficiency. The use of proper and adequate tools is essential before developing any framework or application. This includes the Integrated Development Environment (IDE) used by the developers, building tools, deployment tools, testing, logging, debugging, and security auditing tools. All of which must be secure in a way to prevent any information leakage and to prevent any vulnerability exploitation.

Performance. One of the important aspects is to test the solution efficiency. WBC consumes more resources including memory, storage, and CPU. We analysed different options to do the transformation process to transform a smart contract into an obfuscated contract with performance consideration. However, performance measurements are needed after the implementation phase to identify any possible bottleneck that can be encountered at runtime.

BIBLIOGRAPHY

[1] Satoshi Nakamoto. Bitcoin: A Peer-To-Peer Electronic Cash System, 2008.

[2] Eli Ben Sasson, Alessandro Chiesa, Christina Garman, Matthew Green, Ian Miers, Eran Tromer and Madars Virza. Zerocash: Decentralized Anonymous Payments from Bitcoin. In *2014 IEEE Symposium on Security and Privacy (SP)*, pages 459–474. IEEE, 2014.

[3] Ian Miers, Christina Garman, Matthew Green and Aviel D Rubin. Zerocoin: Anonymous Distributed E-Cash from Bitcoin. In *Security and Privacy (SP), 2013 IEEE Symposium on*, pages 397–411. IEEE, 2013.

[4] Jan Henrik Ziegeldorf, Fred Grossmann, Martin Henze, Nicolas Inden and Klaus Wehrle. Coinparty: Secure Multi-Party Mixing of Bitcoins. In *Proceedings of the 5th ACM Conference on Data and Application Security and Privacy*, pages 75–86. ACM, 2015.

[5] The Monero Project. AEON Isn't Just a Currency. It's a Lifestyle.

[6] Vitalik Buterin. Privacy on the Blockchain. https://blog.ethereum.org/2016/01/15/privacy-on-the-blockchain/, 2016. Last accessed: January 15, 2016.

[7] Sarah Meiklejohn and Claudio Orlandi. Privacy-Enhancing Overlays in Bitcoin. In *International Conference on Financial Cryptography and Data Security*, pages 127–141. Springer, 2015.

[8] Joseph Bonneau, Andrew Miller, Jeremy Clark, Arvind Narayanan, Joshua A Kroll and Edward W Felten. SoK: Research Perspectives and Challenges for Bitcoin and Cryptocurrencies. In *Security and Privacy (SP), 2015 IEEE Symposium on*, pages 104–121. IEEE, 2015.

[9] Tim Ruffing, Pedro Moreno-Sanchez and Aniket Kate. CoinShuffle: Practical Decentralized Coin Mixing for Bitcoin. In *European Symposium on Research in Computer Security*, pages 345–364. Springer, 2014.

[10] Eleftherios Kokoris Kogias, Philipp Jovanovic, Nicolas Gailly, Ismail Khoffi, Linus Gasser and Bryan Ford. Enhancing Bitcoin Security and Performance with Strong Consistency via Collective Signing. In *25th USENIX Security Symposium (USENIX Security 16)*, pages 279–296, 2016.

[11] John R Douceur. The Sybil Attack. In *International Workshop on Peer-to-Peer Systems*, pages 251–260. Springer, 2002.

[12] BitcoinCore. On-Chain Scaling - a Review of Historical Performance Optimization Made to Bitcoin's Reference Software.

[13] Ethan Heilman, Alison Kendler, Aviv Zohar and Sharon Goldberg. Eclipse Attacks on Bitcoin's Peer-To-Peer Network. In *USENIX Security Symposium*, pages 129–144, 2015.

[14] Muhammad Saad, My T Thai and Aziz Mohaisen. Poster: Deterring DDoS Attacks on Blockchain-Based Cryptocurrencies through Mempool Optimization. In *Proceedings of the 2018 on Asia Conference on Computer and Communications Security*, pages 809–811. ACM, 2018.

[15] Jennifer J Xu. Are Blockchains Immune to All Malicious Attacks? *Financial Innovation*, 2 (1):25, 2016.

[16] He Sun, Hongliang Mao, Xiaomin Bai, Zhidong Chen, Hu Kai and Yu. Wei Multi-Blockchain Model for Central Bank Digital Currency. In *Parallel and Distributed Computing, Applications and Technologies (PDCAT), 2017 18th International ConfYours Trulyerence on*, pages 360–367. IEEE, 2017.

[17] Nurzhan Zhumabekuly Aitzhan and Davor Svetinovic. Security and Privacy Indecentralized Energy Trading through Multi-Signatures, Blockchain and Anonymous Messaging Streams. In *IEEE Transactions on Dependable and Secure Computing*, 2016.

[18] Guy Zyskind and Oz Nathan. Decentralizing Privacy: Using Blockchain to Protect Personal Data. In *Security and Privacy Workshops (SPW), 2015 IEEE*, pages 180–184. IEEE, 2015.

[19] Asaph Azaria, Ariel Ekblaw, Thiago Vieira and Andrew Lippman. Medrec: Using Blockchain for Medical Data Access and Permission Management. In *Open and Big Data (OBD), International Conference on*, pages 25–30. IEEE, 2016.

[20] Tsung-Ting Kuo and Ohno-Machado. Lucila Modelchain: Decentralized Privacy-Preserving Healthcare Predictive Modeling Framework on Private Blockchain Networks. *arXiv preprint arXiv:1802.01746*, 2018.

[21] Henning Kopp, David Mödinger, Franz Hauck, Frank Kargl and Christoph Bösch. Design of a Privacy-Preserving Decentralized File Storage with Financial Incentives. In *Security and Privacy Workshops (EuroS&PW), 2017 IEEE European Symposium on*, pages 14–22. IEEE, 2017.

[22] Van Saberhagen Nicolas. CryptoNote V 2.0, 2013.

[23] Ahmed Kosba, Andrew Miller, Elaine Shi, Zikai Wen and Charalampos Papamanthou. Hawk: The Blockchain Model of Cryptography and Privacy-Preserving Smart Contracts. In *2016 IEEE Symposium on Security and Privacy (SP)*, pages 839–858. IEEE, 2016.

[24] Joseph Bonneau, Arvind Narayanan, Andrew Miller, Jeremy Clark, Joshua A Kroll and Edward W Felten. Mixcoin: Anonymity for Bitcoin with Accountable Mixes. In *International Conference on Financial Cryptography and Data Security*, pages 486–504. Springer, 2014.

[25] Kurt M Alonso. Zero to Monero.

[26] A Low-Level Explanation of the Mechanics of Monero Vs Bitcoin in Plain English. www.monero. how/how-does-monero-work-details-in-plain-english, 2017. Last accessed: November 28, 2018.

[27] Andrew Miller, Malte Möser, Kevin Lee and Arvind Narayanan. An Empirical Analysis of Linkability in the Monero Blockchain. *arXiv Preprint*, 2017. https://pdfs.semanticscholar.org/3d97/252f05d87d192eac5edad4b6643a3e6f00be.pdf

[28] Elli Androulaki, Artem Barger, Vita Bortnikov, Christian Cachin, Konstantinos Christidis, Angelo De Caro, David Enyeart, Christopher Ferris, Gennady Laventman, Yacov Manevich, et al. Hyperledger Fabric: A Distributed Operating System for Permissioned Blockchains. In *Proceedings of the Thirteenth EuroSys Conference*, page 30. ACM, 2018.

[29] Gavin Wood. Ethereum: A Secure Decentralised Generalised Transaction Ledger. *Ethereum Project Yellow Paper*, 151:1–32, 2014.

[30] The Linux foundation projects. About Hyperledger. www.hyperledger.org/about, 2018. Last accessed: November 28, 2018.

[31] IBM. Top 6 Technical Advantages of Hyperledger Fabric for Blockchain Networks. www.ibm. com/developerworks/cloud/library/cl-top-technical-advantages-of-hyperledg er-fabric-for-block chain-networks/index.html, 2018. Last accessed: November 28, 2018.

[32] Christian Cachin. Architecture of the Hyperledger Blockchain Fabric. In *Workshop on Distributed Cryptocurrencies and Consensus Ledgers*, volume 310, 2016.

[33] Iuon-Chang Lin and Tzu-Chun Liao. A Survey of Blockchain Security Issues and Challenges. *IJ Network Security*, 19(5):653–659, 2017.

[34] Inside Secure. Whitebox: Build, Control and Trust Your Own Software Crypto-Security. www. insidesecure.com/Products/Application-Protection/Software-Protection/WhiteBox#field-description, 2018. Last accessed: November 28, 2018.

[35] Andrey Bogdanov, Takanori Isobe and Elmar Tischhauser. Towards Practical Whitebox Cryptography: Optimizing Efficiency and Space Hardness. In *International Conference on the Theory and Application of Cryptology and Information Security*, pages 126–158. Springer, 2016.

[36] Alex Biryukov, Charles Bouillaguet and Dmitry Khovratovich. Cryptographic Schemes Based on the ASASA Structure: Black-Box, White-Box, and Public-Key. In *International Conference on the Theory and Application of Cryptology and Information Security*, pages 63–84. Springer, 2014.

[37] Andrey Bogdanov and Takanori Isobe. White-Box Cryptography Revisited: Space-Hard Ciphers. In *Proceedings of the 22nd ACM SIGSAC Conference on Computer and Communications Security*, pages 1058–1069. ACM, 2015.

[38] Stanley Chow, Philip Eisen, Harold Johnson, C Paul and Van Oorschot. White-Box Cryptography and an AES Implementation. In *International Workshop on Selected Areas in Cryptography*, pages 250–270. Springer, 2002.

[39] Marc Joye. On White-Box Cryptography. In *Security of Information and Networks*, pages 7–12, 2008.

[40] Terugu Chalapathi. How White-Box Cryptography Is Gradually Eliminating the Hardware Security Dependency. https://medium.com/engineering-ezetap/how-the-white-box-cryptography-gradually-eliminating-the-hardware-security-dependency-40622d516e02, 2017. Last accessed: November 03, 2017.

[41] Ardit Dika. Ethereum Smart Contracts: Security Vulnerabilities and Security Tools. Master's thesis, NTNU, 2017.

CHAPTER 6

Application of Blockchain and Smart Contract

Approaches and Challenges

Feiyang Qu[1], Hisham Haddad[1] and Hossain Shahriar[2]

[1] *Department of Computer Science, Kennesaw State University, USA*

[2] *Department of Information Technology, Kennesaw State University, USA*

CONTENTS

6.1 INTRODUCTION

Blockchain technology enables information sharing between individual computers [1]. It can control personal information for better protection against security breaches. For example, in Ethereum wallet (E-wallet), each user has an individual account ID (Address) along with private and public keys. Users who try to use E-wallet to complete transactions use the address and public keys, which does not contain actual personal information.

Ethereum is an example of a blockchain-based platform created by Vitalik Buterin, Ethereum is an open software constructed based on smart contracts [2]. Ethereum enables blockchain developers to build and deploy Decentralized Applications (*DApps*). Ethereum provides the foundation upon which many of blockchain applications are written today.

Ethereum based smart contract is one of the most successful blockchain platform. There are two kinds of accounts in Ethereum – Externally Owned Account (EOA) and Contract Account (CA) [2]. EOA is similar to a bitcoin account, which can be a wallet. User can store and send e-currency to another accounts. Contract is the other kind of account in Ethereum. In a CA, there is the data storage and code included for sending a transaction to another address. The contract can not only read code and quantity of currency in transaction, but also creates other contracts for reading codes and writing into storage.

The scripting language of Ethereum is called *Solidity*. User can create a complex smart contract in Solidity for sending transactions to other addresses or writing transactions into storage [2]. However, Ethereum must keep all smart contracts on the Ethereum blockchain, which results in Ethereum network increased storage spaces. Therefore, Ethereum created a concept, named *Gas*, to count the computational step in smart contract that an account can execute, which will be introduced in Section 6.3. By using Gas to limit the code size of smart contract, the computation pressure for running Ethereum will be smaller.

In this chapter, we focus on smart contracts and related applications. The chapter is organized as follows. We first introduce background of blockchain and smart contracts with diagram examples in Sections 6.2 and 6.3, respectively. We then compare traditional contracts and smart contracts in Section 6.4. Section 6.5 describes applications of smart contracts for E-auction while also discussing the advantages of smart contract in E-auction business. Section 6.6 highlights some applications of blockchain in healthcare, while Sections 6.7 and 6.8 provide example applications of blockchain in supply chain and Internet of Things (IoT) area. Section 6.9 elaborates blockchain for Vehicular Adhoc Network (VANET), while Section 6.10 shows some recent applications of blockchain in the Cloud and Education area. Section 6.11 discusses application of blockchain for Ponzi scheme detection. Finally, Section 6.12 concludes the chapter and discusses some challenges and opportunities.

6.2 BACKGROUND OF BLOCKCHAIN

Generally, blockchain is a distributed ledger where each block contains several transactions [3]. Blocks can be linked using cryptographic hash functions. In a public blockchain, there are two ways to find or mine next block – Proof-of-Work (PoW) and Proof-of-Authority (PoA). PoW means that the miner or the winner of new block must finish the most amount of computational works than any other participant. Based on the PoW theory, a broker must own more than fifty percent of the whole network computational ability to control the next block. Therefore, it is difficult to control a decentralized blockchain by one part when the input might be more than the outcome. The PoA is the other way to find the next block. The owner of next block should have the largest amount of resources or the highest technology than any other

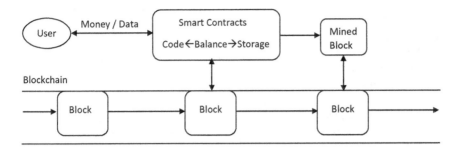

FIGURE 6.1   Blockchain and smart contract structure [4]

miner in the network. In this case, the owner who has higher technology or more resources is able to keep blockchain running in a more energy-efficient environment. The interaction between blockchain and applications is normally accomplished by smart contracts, which are agreements between two or more parties.

Figure 6.1 shows the interaction between blockchain (a collection of blocks as shown in the bottom layer) and smart contracts which result in mined block and continuously being added to the chain. Here, a contract is triggered when exchange of money or data takes place among users.

6.3 SMART CONTRACTS

A smart contract is a type of code running on the blockchain, which is executed compulsory by the consensus protocol (e.g. PoW, PoS) [5]. A smart contract can include a group of functions and rules written in Solidity programming language to process resources exchange when certain events take place in the peer-to-peer network. Therefore, smart contract can be exploited in a wide range of applications, including financial instruments and self-enforcing or autonomous governance applications. When a user creates and calls a smart contract on the blockchain, it needs to include an address (160-bit unique identifier) to send transactions. In blockchain, all miners execute smart contracts that are created and uploaded recently after the entire blockchain receives a new transaction and the recipient's address. When all participants on a network agree with a new output block, the next block will be processed using a consensus protocol (e.g. PoW, PoS). Figure 6.2 shows an example of contract for rewarding a user to solve a puzzle. Lines 2 to 6 define the variables (e.g., owner, solution, reward); Lines 8 to 13 define details of owner and reward (through the constructor method Puzzle); Lines 15 to 31 defines the event to check if a received value is equal to the reward and decides if a received message is a reward or not.

As a common cryptocurrency, Ethereum can store smart contracts on blockchain where code and value can be used multiple times [5]. Ethereum has Gas, an internal measurable unit, for keeping the fair compensation for expanded computation effort. Specifically, users need to verify the amount of gas they use to send a transaction to invoke a contract. The price of gas is announced publicly and each instruction in bytecode has a gas limit. If the gas needed in actual processing is more than the gas

```
1 contract Puzzle {
2 address public owner ;
3 bool public locked ;
4 uint public reward ;
5 bytes32 public diff ;
6 bytes public solution ;
7 function Puzzle () // constructor {
8   owner = msg.sender;
9  reward = msg.value;
10  locked = false;
11  diff = bytes32 (11111); // pre - defined difficulty
12 }
13 function () {// main code , runs at every invocation
14   if (msg.sender == owner ) {// update reward
15    if (locked)
16       throw;
17    owner.send (reward);
18    reward = msg.value ;
19   }
20   else
21    if ( msg.data.length > 0){ // submit a solution
22      if (locked) throw;
23      if (sha256 (msg .data) < diff){
24        msg.sender.send (reward); //send reward
25        solution = msg.data;
26        locked = true;
27      }
28   }
29 }
```

FIGURE 6.2   A contract that rewards users who solve a puzzle [5]

provided by users, the execution of transaction will be terminated as the state will be returned to the initial state; meanwhile, the user must pay the actual amount of gas used, which is a way to avoid resource-exhaustion attacks.

A smart contract can also be a self-execution code in blockchain. When a smart contract is created and uploaded into blockchain, it includes a contract address and some amount of Ether [5]. Users create a contract by high-level programming language, Solidity; a contract to be executed must contain a recipient address, payment for execution, and data.

Solidity is a high-level language for smart contract. Programmers write smart contracts in Solidity and compile them to bytecode of the Ethereum Virtual Machine (EVM), which is a stack-base virtual machine operating on 256-bit words [6]. A contract is executed into a transaction that contains the bytecode and initialization parameters. The smart contract is stored in one block as a transaction and each contract has a unique blockchain address. Users can interact with the specific contract by address, contained functions and arguments. The followings are several issues in Solidity when users try to develop smart contracts.

Security issue: It may be the cause of hacking a user account or contract. One preference in solidity coding is that using *send* instead of *transfer* in transaction process may cause throwing an issue [6]. In Figure 6.3, the first example suggests users not to use strict balance equality, which hackers can use definition of Gas to mandatorily send Ether from one account to another account. The second example explains that a better way for calling external codes should include a check function, which will cancel the transaction and send back Ether if the address of the receiver is not valid. The last example suggests that a conditional statement should not depend on unauthorized external call, by which external implementation may throw an exception and cause security issue.

Functional issue: This may cause the unexpected functionality problem. For example, there is no float or decimal type in Solidity [6].

Operational issue: This can normally cause run-time problems (e.g., bad performance). For example, it is better to use bytes instead of byte[] to reduce gas consumption [6]. Figure 6.4 shows an example of a costly loop structure.

```
if ( this . balance == 42 ether ) { /* ... */} // bad
if ( this . balance >= 42 ether ) { /* ... */} // good
// Balance equality
addr. send (42 ether ) ; // bad
if (!addr. send (42 ether ) ) revert ; // better
addr. transfer (42 ether ) ; // good
//Unchecked external call
function dos( address oracleAddr) public {
    badOracle = Oracle(oracleAddr);
    if (badOracle.answer() < 42) { revert ; }
    // ...
}
//DoS by external contract
```

FIGURE 6.3   Security issue examples

```
for ( uint256 i = 0; i < array. length ; i++) { costlyF(); }
It will waste Gas which exceeds the Gas limit if array. length is large enough.
```

FIGURE 6.4   Costly loop

Developmental issue: Sometimes the code may be hard to understand and improve. In Solidity, the private modifier does not make a variable invisible, which means miners can have access to all contracts' code and data [6]. Therefore, the lack of privacy is an issue in Ethereum. The following are specific code examples for different types of issues. Figure 6.5.1 shows sample code for explicit visibility declaration; while in Figure 6.5.2, a bad example that does not follow Solidity style guide for lowercase and uppercase letters will decrease readability of code.

Based on the function of smart contract included, a smart contract can call other contracts to finish transactions [6]. Costs for transactions happen when users attempt to send values to other addresses. Counting and limiting the cost during transaction is necessary to avoid spamming in smart contracts. Therefore, the Ethereum protocol defines the name of costs during transactions as gas. The gas is charged based on users expected cost of transaction for each Ethereum Virtual Machine (EVM) operation. The expected gas to send is usually more than the actual gas cost, and the computation will give partial refund back to the user's addresses. If an exception happens, which includes that actual cost is more than expected cost, all state changes are reverted, and the gas will be returned or not based on the function of the smart contract. Currently, the unit price of gas is determined by the market.

Ethereum is a "hostile execution environment", which anonymous hackers can send smart contracts containing overload function to get money [6]. Due to the feature of blockchain and smart contracts, developers cannot handle the contract which has already been deployed. "The DAO", a well-known example in June 2016, which hackers steal more than ten million dollars using flawed contracts. When people focus on a rapid growth in blockchain-based smart contracts, which can bring a lot of profit from related technology market, they should also notice the risk of crimes and similar issues. "The DAO" is an example that hackers use the outdated authorized vulnerability to attack Ethereum blockchain.

```
function foo() { /*...*/ } // bad
function foo() public { /*...*/ } // good
function bar() private { /*...*/ } // good
```

FIGURE 6.5.1   Implicit visibility level

```
function Foo(); // bad
event logFoo(); // bad
function foo(); // goodevent LogFoo(); // good
```

FIGURE 6.5.2   Style guide violation

There are some security challenges present in Ethereum [6].

- Unfamiliar execution environment – Ethereum is not a centralized environment; therefore, developers are not familiar to execute into a "profit-driven" node, which is also an anonymous environment.

- New software stack – "The Ethereum stack (the Solidity compiler, the EVM, the consensus layer, etc.) is under development, with security vulnerabilities still being discovered."

- Very limited ability to patch contracts – Based on the feature of blockchain, a contract cannot be patched or edited after been deployed. Therefore, a contract must be corrected or compiled before uploaded.

- Anonymous financially motivated attackers – As mentioned before, hackers use smart contracts to steal money that will be "safer" and gain higher profit; furthermore, they are anonymous on blockchain.

- Rapid pace of development – "Blockchain companies strive to release their products fast, often at the expense of security."

- Suboptimal high-level language – "Some argue that Solidity itself inclines programmers towards unsafe development practices".

6.4 CONTRAST BETWEEN SMART AND TRADITIONAL CONTRACTS

Compared to traditional online bidding system, blockchain-based bidding system does not need a third party to help trading [7]. It can save the cost and solve the trust problem. Therefore, people need to create a blockchain-based smart contract to finish the bidding process. The smart contract contains the address of auctioneer, date information, the current winner and highest price. Base on the feature of blockchain, the smart contract generated via Ethereum keeps the bill in secure, private and inalterability because all transactions are recorded in a decentralized ledger as the same as each node.

The traditional E-auction is currently popular [7]. It doesn't need a bidder to attend and bid together. E-auction can reduce the cost of transaction and service fee. However, E-auction is still a centralized bidding system that cannot keep customers' personal information private; meanwhile, bidders cannot make sure if the information they receive (bid price) is real. Figure 6.6 shows the flowchart of E-auction process where auctioneers

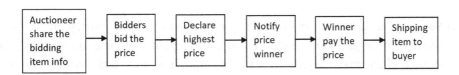

FIGURE 6.6   The flowchart of E-auction process

share bidding item information. Then bidders bid the prices, and the highest price bidder is notified as the winner. The winner pays the price and an item is sent to the buyer.

6.5 BLOCKCHAIN IN E-AUCTION

Ethereum platform has been used to execute E-auction [7]. Before creating smart contracts, there are several announcements in advance: (1) Auctioneer: the main address that records the origination contract; (2) AuctionStart: information about auction start time; (3) BiddingTime: information about bidding effective time; (4) highest bidder/highest price: record of the highest price and its owner.

There are five functions defined for an auction: (1) AuctionStart(): it is called to check if the start time of bidding is activated; (2) AuctionTime(): it is called to check if the auction started and if the effective time expired; (3) BlindAuction(): activates the contract by calling this function; (4) Bid(): a bidder can call this function to bid and send the ideal price to auction which is higher than the current highest price; (5) AuctionEnd(): checks if the bidding ended, and sends the highest price with the owner's information to the Auctioneer; (6) Withdraw(): returns the bidding price back to the bidder who is not successful in the bidding [7].

As blockchain gives organizations more privacy and maintains a complete transcript of the cost of storage and transaction execution speed (per second) become problem [8]. The Cloud can be a solution that provisioning blockchain as a service on cloud infrastructure even though organizations are looking for solution from third-party protocols on top of existing blockchain.

6.6 BLOCKCHAIN IN HEALTHCARE

Presently, healthcare organizations are trying to develop blockchain-based platforms for cross-institutional sharing of healthcare data. It has the potential to share data on blockchain instead of traditional way of requesting data from different institutions [9]. However, there are still some problems in sharing data between organizations. When organizations are concerned about privacy problems or commercial competitions, they might deny the access to share data with others. Also, blockchain technology requires several institutions in a similar technical infrastructure level, which is hard to establish in the real world. Finally, different healthcare institutions sharing data require a standard data prototype. If one organization uploads data by different data types, and the other organizations cannot understand the data, it might cause errors in blockchain.

The problems of sharing healthcare data can be divided into three parts: (i) Security (ii) Infrastructure and (iii) Interoperability [9]. These issues are discussed below.

(i) **Security**: Security is one of the major problems in data sharing. It might cause financial or legal consequences. There are two points to solve the security problem in blockchain based healthcare data sharing. First, each data sharing request must be processed between authorized addresses because an unauthorized address could expose the commercial advantage of an organization or "reveal proprietary practices". The other point is to improve data anonymity of the user/organization in blockchain. This solution requires the user's information be separated from patient records for sharing before the information is uploaded to blockchain. And, the developer can create an extra smart contract to include the user's information.

(ii) **Infrastructure**: There are some infrastructure requirements during data sharing, which can be solved by increasing technical consistency of each block miner (data's owner/organization) in the future. Data sharing between several organizations needs a centralized data source or "the transmission of bulk data to other institutions". However, a centralized data source may request the trust of a single authority, which is the risk of security; and, bulk data transmission requires organizations to monitor, control and re-edit data during transfer data, which will increase quantity of work.

(iii) **Interoperability**: In the healthcare emphasis, the data is more complex due to large number of professional data/prototypes included. Therefore, when some non-healthcare background organizations request access to data sharing, interoperability of healthcare records is hard to solve. There are two types of problem in interoperability: data structure and semantics. Due to high volume of professional knowledge included in healthcare data, data structure might be different from normal structures in organizations. Therefore, healthcare organizations need to create a standard data structure, which non-healthcare organizations can recognize and use directly. For semantics problems, healthcare organizations should create a professional digital dictionary or a smart contract for users, which can be called to translate those professional data to data that can be analyzed [9].

Blockchain-based Electronic Medical Records (EMR) information can benefit healthcare providers and physicians because of efficiency [10]. This approach gives researchers access to broad and comprehensive data sets to advance the understanding of diseases, facilitate the development of new drugs, and enhance biomedical discovery.

EMR information can be managed by blockchain-base applications as EMR information is mostly standardized [10]. With blockchain, healthcare activities, such diagnosis, blood work, and X-ray can be created as digital transactions that are then grouped into encrypted blocks with other transactions. Trusted individuals, such as administrators, physicians, and technicians, can access and validate transactions using access keys and then timestamp the transactions. Timestamps for validated blocks create sequences that show the order and procedure for every transaction. This approach improves the accuracy of patient records, as transactions cannot be irreversible.

Factom is a software company that uses blockchain technology to store data on a decentralized system [1]. As a feature of Factom's technology, healthcare organizations can create smart contracts to develop medical data. The medical data needs to be encoded with a fingerprint of the data. Blockchain uses digital fingerprints to verify processes and time-stamping. Therefore, Factom technology can help healthcare organizations to protect patient's information confidentiality.

There is decentralized record management system for Electronic Medicine Record – MedRec. MedRec uses blockchain technology [11]. The system allows patients to manage the log and access their data across providers and treatment sites. Based on the technology of blockchain, MedRec has the ability to improve authentication, confidentiality, accountability and data sharing. Those features are important for handling some sensitive information. The system encourages medical providers, researchers, and public health authorities to be the "miner". The purpose of this activity is to give "miner" access to retrieve aggregate, anonymized data as rewards of mining in return for sustaining and securing the network via Proof of Work.

In EMR environment, it is important to establish trust and continued participation in healthcare organization [11]. On the patients' side, they don't need to doubt anymore confidentiality of their records and they can totally trust the decentralized record management system for managing their records. On the researcher's side, the blockchain-based EMR system can help scientists to keep track of the accuracy of data. Meanwhile, data on blockchain will be shared more easily.

The decentralized management system MedRec records the relationship between patients and providers by smart contracts on Ethereum [11]. The system uses relationship smart contracts to check permissions and data retrieval instructions for external databases use. Under this foundation, providers can add records for patients; patients can also access the shared records between providers.

An EHR system contains three types of smart contracts: Registrar Contract, Patient–Provider Relationship Contract, Summary Contract. Registrar Contract is used to identify the address of users. [11] Patient–Provider Relationship Contract is used between two nodes on blockchain, which stores and manages medical records. Summary Contract is used for holding a list of references, which helps participants to locate their medical record histories.

6.7 BLOCKCHAIN IN SUPPLY CHAIN

Blockchain and related applications can also be developed as blockchain-enabled composites materials supply chain. [12] Raw materials, semi-finished materials, components, structures and Original Equipment Manufacturers (OEMs) can create several smart contracts based on blockchain. When one process finishes, the next process automatically starts based on the previous result. The transfer of goods can be more efficient and traceable by all owners in the blockchain. This means each owner can estimate the profit from the transaction process; meanwhile, the owners can fully stock the product before their own process. Figure 6.7 shows blockchain-enabled supply chain system.

In Figure 6.7, each stage is a node in blockchain, which contains multiple transfers of records as a distributed ledger: (1) Raw materials: provide original materials in supply chain (e.g. steel, plastic); (2) semi-finished materials: provide materials which finish the last step before producing composite materials; (3) components: provide the design and

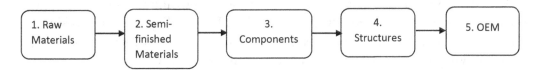

FIGURE 6.7   Blockchain-enabled composites materials supply chain

technology to develop composite materials for final productions; (4) structures: provide and collect all materials before assembled; (5) OEM: provides products for selling which is the last stage in supply chain process. [12]

Furthermore, composite material suppliers can use blockchain to keep transparency and provenance-tracking of records since it is able to monitor certificates linked to the quality of the component and true origin in the process [12].

Ethereum uses two different types of accounts (that contain an address of 20 bytes for different users): An Externally Owner Account (EOA) is an account created with a private key [13]. A CA is controlled by code that includes transactions or messages for modifying the storage, calling other contract functions, and creating new contracts.

For logistic management process, there are several smart contracts developed. [13] In Figure 6.8, the first part of the code shows the identification for EOA and CA addresses; the second part of the code shows that the address needs to be added in the function with the transaction information.

The Package contract contains the information of package and its owner's information. As a package contract being created, the information is updated and shared with each node immediately [13]. Package receiver, supplier and shipper are all parts of the nodes. One of the functions should be named as Updated function for updating personal information.

```
bytes4(keccak256("setName(strinд)")) = 0xc47f 0027 --------- (1)
EOAaddress = 0x43f c11,
CAaddress = 0xa8484f 3,
Data[name] = "Paul" ≡ 0x50 0x61 0x75 0x6c
Txdat a = 0xc47f 0027 · · · 5061756c · · · --------(2)
RPCr equest = {"jsonrpc" : "2.0",
"method" : "eth_sendT ransaction",
"params" : [{"from" : "0x43f c11",
"to" : "0xa8484f 3",
"data" : "0xc47f 0027 · · · 5061756c · · ·"}],
"id" : 1}
```

FIGURE 6.8   Smart Contract

The User contract contains public and private information. Public information includes passenger information that can be shared with all parties in tracking the shipment. Private information includes user's information for verifying proposes [13].

The Delivery contract contains information of the sender and recipient of a package. Basically, only the user in Delivery contract can control and update the package status [13].

Compared with traditional logistic management, using blockchain and smart contracts makes shipping transparent as well as timely update notifications [13]. Especially, blockchain-based smart contract can be a better substitute of logistic management for special products like medicine, chemical product, and fresh seafood.

More and more research is done on using blockchain and smart contracts in logistical domain. Under the perspective of logistics, IoT is a kind of "network of material flow objects", and some objects in the network can communicate over the Internet [14]. In the future, a blockchain-based IoT object can improve logistical processes.

A new smart contract interface has been developed onto Ethereum Github repository – Custodian-Client Contrast Standard. Smart contracts are stored on the blockchain, which is decentralized [15]. Users can store, retrieve and exchange data by smart contracts.

A two-level hierarchical architecture is created, which contains two types of smart contracts: Custodian contract and Client contract [15]. Custodian contract is high-level contract that deploys client contract based on client demand and gives feedback for different usage. Client contract is a low-level contract that collects data and sends requests to the custodian. Once the custodian contract receives the request, a new transaction is created and updated to the client contract. Several clients can share their information based on blockchain technology (see Figure 6.9).

To understand the Custodian-Client contract architecture, Figure 6.9 shows an example of a Custodian-Client contract in ticket selling system [15]. This includes the ticket seller (custodian) and the customer (client). When the customer requests a ticket, a new smart contract is created to include the customer's address. This client contract is owned by the customer and can be sold to or exchanged with another customer. The

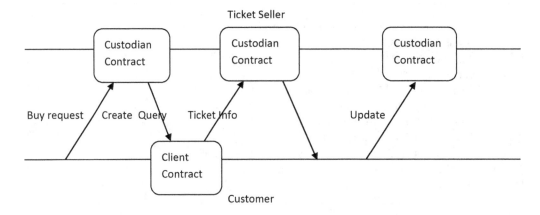

FIGURE 6.9   The process for buying a ticket based on Custodian-Client contract structure

seller can update the ticket information and track the owner of the ticket. Meanwhile, several custodian contracts are needed to create tickets, track customer's information, and update ticket information.

A custodian contract is the seller of ticket, and no other custodian contract is in experiment. The custodian contract has access to retrieve information from the client contract and only update the ticket owner by requests (for exchanging/re-selling tickets).

Compared Custodian-Client contract with another standard interfaces for Ethereum blockchain, the Custodian-Client contract standard can provide a flexible independence of client contract which is traceable by the custodian [15]. Also, the Custodian-Client standard will reduce possible losses when cyber-attacks occur, since the interaction with the client contract has been minimized and each client contract is independent of the others.

6.8 BLOCKCHAIN IN INTERNET OF THINGS (IOT)

There is an IoT data management environment to simulate the application of IoT devices in smart city initiatives. Currently, smart devices can be found everywhere, from household appliances to mobile terminals. Therefore, we can consider that all of smart devices make a system of a smart city. The experimental environment is based on the Ethereum blockchain and smart contract [16]. Specifically, it needs to explain: how to link different computing capabilities of IoT devices using blockchain technology and smart contracts; and how to store and retrieve data from different IoT devices on blockchain by smart contracts. Figure 6.10 shows an example environment of IoT simulation. Here, sensors (temperature, humidity, pressure) are connected to proxy node, which can communicate with blockchain network.

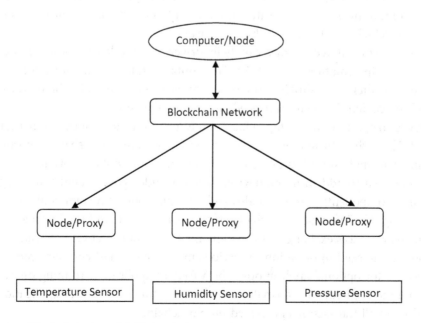

FIGURE 6.10   Blockchain-based IoT simulation structure

Currently, smart devices are widely used. As the usage of smart devices increases, the server/client storing data faces some challenges as to how to efficiently store large amounts of data and securely retrieve such data [16].

Across the technology of blockchain, data from different IoT devices can be stored and retrieved by smart contracts. Therefore, the experiment needs to build a private Ethereum blockchain, which contains a computer and several IoT devices as nodes [16]. After setting up the environment, the project needs to design smart contracts to (1) store data and retrieve data from blockchain; (2) check requests from different IoT devices for sharing information for data analytics; (3) verify the information from users for retrieving data/transaction and send notifications/alarms to users about log-in status.

Finally, there is still an issue of flexibility in using smart contracts from different types of IoT devices. In a private blockchain, IoT devices need to be connected for different proposes. Therefore, it is necessary to develop a high-level language and an operating environment that are both compatible with blockchain-based smart contracts which are for IoT devices [16].

6.9 BLOCKCHAIN IN VANET AND LOW VOLTAGE ENERGY COMMUNITY

Vehicle Ad-hoc Networks (VANETs) is the supporting structure of vehicle management and communication tool/network [17]. Main components of VANETs are On-Board-Units (OBUs), Application-Units (AUs), and Road-Side-Units (RSUs).

RSUs are normally placed on the roadside and provide a short-range communication with other devices in the same range. OBUs are used for exchanging information between OBUs and RSUs or other OBU devices in vehicles [17]. It requires communication in a short range by wireless or radio technologies. AU is an application that a driver can monitor or communicate with smart phones or other devices. It is linked to OBUs in the vehicles and managed by the drivers.

VANETs in current technology can help drivers to check the local weather, traffic jam, or speed information [17]. VANETs contain traffic regulations and rules for notification. Furthermore, OBUs can connect to each other to assist the driver's sensors to alert if an accident happens and needs to change the rout.

VANET is an application developed based on Ethereum instead of traditional centralized network [17]. Each vehicle/user has an Ethereum account and shares information in blockchain. The application has two parts – mandatory and optional. Mandatory applications are enforced to add to user's device, which includes government traffic regulations and required components. Users can also add optional applications for traffic information and platooning. The information exchange system will be built and run by smart contracts. When different services exchange information, the transaction occurs. Applications will use smart contracts to send information to services; meanwhile, smart contracts can be used to pay service fee for optional applications. The VANETs application running on blockchain will increase the accuracy of information; at the same time, the cost of application will be decreased when all transactions processed on blockchain.

Some studies suggest that the blockchain technology has the potential development in the energy sector [3]. Specifically, blockchain has an important role in energy trading, automation of processes and new business cases. There are more and more community energy pilot projects and related researches focus on electricity markets, which shows the potential of blockchain technology for "disintermediating aggregators" in energy exchanging environment.

Blockchain technology has also been applied in a local low voltage energy community [3]. In this concept, the whole energy system will be created, stored, exchanged in an internal environment, and try to avoid the external resource usage or exchange. An experiment that the control system for electrical energy storages is running on a private Ethereum blockchain and implementing smart contracts has been developed. In the experiment, households in an electricity community are represented by four computers, which can simulate electrical system. Each computer is one node on blockchain, and there is a controller on the blockchain system to manage electricity landscape of four "householders".

Based on the experiment result for testing blockchain-based energy community and controller, it is possible to accomplish a self-sufficiency energy environment; meanwhile, the efficiency of energy usage improves, and the cost of spending decreases. [3] Each "householder" has full access to store and manage the energy system. The blockchain-based energy community will not only result in a better trust environment between participants but also decreases the possibility of the extra third party cost. On the other side, the node in energy community can share resources to external users due to the feature of blockchain. During the experiment, the researcher finds that there are several factors influencing the block time and the transaction timing, which is due to the difference between "residual load" and "battery commands". The future development of the blockchain-based energy community still needs to be run in experiment process. The community system that can interact with other communities or utility organizations in a public blockchain is the next step. For example, the community can have a third party like power plant service to support the community.

6.10 BLOCKCHAIN IN THE CLOUD AND EDUCATION

The advantage of Cloud has been recognized when people talk about blockchain. Many of worldwide Cloud technology companies have already attempted to use their existing cloud investment to push market share of blockchain, which proves the potential of cloud usage in blockchain [8].

The Cloud could be the essential of blockchain system. Blockchain organizations and individual users are willing to pay a service fee to store their data instead of spending same storage and more money on storage [8]. The traditional data storage for block will not only require huge space from personal supply, but also need extra technology to manage the block for security purposes. The Cloud can solve the problem by third party, which has professional team to manage and monitor the storage of blockchain.

Blockchain technology has been introduced to education domain, especially in on-line education. On-line education provider can use blockchain to design a new information system to deliver courses, check course progress and manage students' information [8]. In this context, the blockchain-based information system in Cloud enables end users to search information, connect to course materials, and send messages through users' mobile devices.

6.11 BLOCKCHAIN IN FRAUD SCHEME DETECTION

As blockchain technology becomes more and more popular, some scams could be identified with it, particularly Ponzi schemes. In Ethereum, there are more than 400 Ponzi schemes [18].

Ponzi is the name of a notorious fraudster of almost 100 years ago. A Ponzi scheme is an illegal type of investment to attract some investments. The fraudster uses new investments to "fill/reward" the previous investor. As a result, the investor who joins in later will lose more when there is no income from investments without previous investments. Presently, some fraudsters find and try to use blockchain technology to make money. Due to the anonymous identity by using blockchain, the Ponzi scheme acts with "low risk" and higher profits; meanwhile, it is worse for government to monitor and investigate a fraud on blockchain than those happening in other environments. Unfortunately, there are more than 7 million USD worth Bitcoin, which has been stolen and gathered by scams between September 2, 2013, and September 9, 2014. [18]

Based on the investigation of Ponzi schemes [18], the Ponzi schemes on blockchain cannot be terminated or changed after it has been implemented because smart contracts are executed automatically, cannot be reversed; at the same time, the sender of a transaction is anonymous. The following message is an example of a Ponzi Scheme message sent by a smart contract:

> Hello! My name is Rubixi! I'm new & verified pyramid smart contract on the Ethereum Blockchain. When you send me 1 ether, I will multiply the amount and send it back to your address when the balance is sufficient. My multiplier factor is dynamic (min. x1.2 max. x3), thus my payouts are accelerated and guaranteed for months to come [18].

After checking the contract transaction, the researcher finds that there are 112 participants in the investment, and only 22 investors received profit. The fraud causes financial damage for most investors, and the scammers received money from those investors. As mentioned above, it is difficult to detect Ponzi scheme recently, and the most reasonable way to detect fraud is to manually check the source code. Fraud detection is hard and takes lots of time; furthermore, smart contracts can be hidden, which makes detecting fraud more difficult. Scammers need only several bytecodes to finish the transactions [18]. Based on the information from Ethereum, currently there are more than a million smart contracts. However, only about four thousand smart contracts have source code,

```
1    contract Rubixi {
2        uint private balance = 0;
3        uint private colletedFees = 0;
4        uint private feePercent = 10;
5        uint private Order = 0;
6        uint private pyramidMultiplier = 300;
7        address private creator;
8        struct Participant {
9        address etherAddress;
10       unit payout;
11       }
12       Participant [] private participants;
13
14       function Rubixi () {
15               creator = msg.sender;
16       }
17       function () { addPayout (); }
18
19       function addPayout () private {
20               unit fee = feePercent;
21               participants.push( Participant
22               (msg.sender, (mas.value x pyramidMultiplier) / 100));
23               if (participants. length == 10)
24               pyramidMultiplier = 200;
25               else if (participants. length == 25)
26               pyramidMultiplier = 150;
27               balance += (msg.value x (100 - fee)) / 100;
28               colletedfees += (msg.value x fee) / 100;
29               while (balance > participants [Order]. payout) {
30                       unit payoutToSend = participants [Order]. payout;
31                       participants [Order]. etherAddress. send(payoutToSend);
32                       balance -= participants [Order]. payout;
33                       Order += 1;
34               }
35       }
36
37       function collectAllFees () onlyowner {
38       if (collecetedFees == 0) throw;
39       creator.send(collecetedFees);
40       collecetedFees = 0;
41       }
42  }
```

FIGURE 6.11 Ponzi scheme code example

which means some Ponzi scheme are still hidden and the creators cannot be found. There are still some questions need to be answered: "How many smart Ponzi schemes exist on Ethereum? What types of smart Ponzi schemes are there? What are their characteristics? How much is the influence of smart Ponzi schemes?", and a solution is needed to detect smart Ponzi schemes without manually checking the source code.

Smart contract is written in Solidity [18]. The example of key code of smart Ponzi scheme, shown below, consists of two parts: functions and data. The function in smart contract is called during sending messages or executing transactions by any other user or smart contract; and, the data included in that contract can be covered and over written. In Figure 6.11, Lines 2 to 11 is the data definition that can measure the current state of the contract. Line 6 defines current profits (*pyramidMultiplier*) to 300. Line 12 defines all investors (*participants*) in order. Line 14 creates the constructor (*Rubixi*) that runs after the contract. Line 17 is the fallback function (*addPayout*) that runs when sending an Ether without data to a contract. Line 19 is defining the function *addPayout*, which is executed when a participant sends money. Lines 21 to 22 record the address and payment of the investor. Lines 23 to 26 reduce profits if more investors enter. Line 28 calculates the fees. Lines 29 to 34 function pays the benefits to previous investors if the balance is enough. Lines 37 to 41 collect fees by calling collectAllFees [18].

There are several reasons and benefits for criminal activities which attract people by making smart contracts [4]. First, the exchange between users can be finished without third-party intermediaries or physical communication, even between distrustful parties. Second, the interaction of criminal is too "light" to detect. Criminals only need to deploy a smart contract that the rest of transaction will automatically be done by the smart contract's functions. Third, smart contracts can use to call an external state and influence transaction through an oracle service, which will broaden the possible of crimes. Finally, each account of Ethereum only has information on address and balance; therefore, it is difficult to identify the person who owns the account.

6.12 FUTURE DIRECTIONS OF SMART CONTRACTS – ISSUES AND CHALLENGES

Bitcoin and Ethereum, two popular cryptocurrencies, have abilities to hold and manage rules or scripts of transaction during processing [5]. Cryptocurrencies process its transactions on blockchain that is a decentralized data structure. Users can create a smart contract to process transactions with other users directly; furthermore, smart contracts can call another smart contract to finish transactions.

Decentralized cryptocurrencies have been noticed as Bitcoin was introduced in 2009 [5]. More and more research show that the potential of cryptocurrencies and blockchain is not only from its new idea of digital currency but also from its decentralized characteristics that cryptocurrencies are managed by users in that network instead of a specialized management group. In other words, users on blockchain don't have to trust any third parties in transactions because the transaction will basically finish just between the sender and buyer. Users will run a "consensus protocol" to monitor and maintain the normal operation of a shared ledger of data.

There are some more features needed for the future development of blockchain related applications [14]. It is necessary to design a user-friendly IoT hardware for blockchain applications. It is also necessary to design a suitable software for block-chain applications. Current communication protocols are not enough for blockchain applications, especially IoT blockchain applications. Blockchain-based applications should be formally verified by developing a new technique because hackers can use smart contracts to attack applications, which will cause a lot of damage. Based on the previous issue in smart contracts, the role of intermediates might be considered for blockchain. The intermediate role will be able to decide the payment and other details in the transactions. It is necessary to improve the scalability of blockchain-based applications.

REFERENCES

[1] Rashi Varshney. "The Non-Financial Side of Blockchain". *Express Computer*, August 11, 2016.
[2] Karan Bharadwaj, Blockchain 2.0: Smart Contracts, www.linkdapps.com/Blockchain2.0-SmartContracts.pdf, 2016.
[3] Jonas Schlund, Lorenz Ammon and Reinhard German. ETHome: Opensource Blockchain Based Energy Community Controller. In *e-Energy '18: International Conference on Future Energy Systems*, June 12–15, 2018, Karlsruhe, Germany. ACM, New York, NY, 5 pages.
[4] Ari Juels, Ahmed Kosba and Elaine Shi. The Ring of Gyges: Investigating the Future of Criminal Smart Contracts. *CCS '16 Proceedings of the 2016 ACM SIGSAC Conference on Computer and Communications Security*, 2016, pp. 283–295. doi: 10.1145/2976749.2978362.
[5] Loi Luu, et al. "Making Smart Contracts Smarter." *Proceedings of the 2016 ACM SIGSAC Conference on Computer and Communications Security*. ACM, 2016.
[6] S. Tikhomirov, E. Voskresenskaya, I. Ivanitskiy, R. Takhaviev, E. Marchenko and Y. Alexandrov, "SmartCheck: Static Analysis of Ethereum Smart Contracts," *2018 IEEE/ACM 1st International Workshop on Emerging Trends in Software Engineering for Blockchain (WETSEB)*, Gothenburg, Sweden, 2018, pp. 9–16.
[7] Y. Chen, S. Chen and I. Lin, "Blockchain Based Smart Contract for Bidding System," *2018 IEEE International Conference on Applied System Invention (ICASI)*, Chiba, 2018, pp. 208–211. doi: 10.1109/ICASI.2018.8394569
[8] Ian Purdon and Emre Erturk. Perspectives of Blockchain Technology, Its Relation to the Cloud and Its Potential Role in Computer Science Education. *Engineering, Technology and Applied Science Research*, 7, 2340–2344, 2017.
[9] Kevin Peterson, Rammohan Deeduvanu, Pradip Kanjamala and Kelly Boles. "A Blockchain-Based Approach to Health Information Exchange Networks."
[10] D'Arcy Guerin Gue. "Why Blockchain Offers a Fresh Approach to Interoperability". *Health Data Management*, March 21, 2017.
[11] A. Azaria, A. Ekblaw, T. Vieira and A. Lippman, "MedRec: Using Blockchain for Medical Data Access and Permission Management," *2016 2nd International Conference on Open and Big Data (OBD)*, Vienna, 2016, pp. 25–30. doi: 10.1109/OBD.2016.11
[12] A. E. C. Mondragon, C. E. C. Mondragon and E. S. Coronado, "Exploring the Applicability of Blockchain Technology to Enhance Manufacturing Supply Chains in the Composite Materials Industry," 2018 IEEE International Conference on Applied System Invention (ICASI), Chiba, 2018, pp. 1300–1303.

[13] Néstor Álvarez-Díaz, Jordi Herrera-Joancomartí and Pino Caballero-Gil. Smart Contracts Based on Blockchain for Logistics Management. In *Proceedings of the 1st International Conference on Internet of Things and Machine Learning (IML '17)*. ACM, New York, NY, Article 73, 8 pages, 2017. doi: 10.1145/3109761.3158384

[14] J. Hinckeldeyn and K. Jochen, "(Short Paper) Developing a Smart Storage Container for a Blockchain-Based Supply Chain Application," *2018 Crypto Valley Conference on Blockchain Technology (CVCBT)*, Zug, Switzerland, 2018, pp. 97–100. doi: 10.1109/CVCBT.2018.00017

[15] Yao-Chieh Hu, Ting-Ting Lee, Dimitris Chatzopoulos and Pan Hui. Hierarchical Interactions between Ethereum Smart Contracts across Testnets. In *Proceedings of the 1st Workshop on Cryptocurrencies and Blockchains for Distributed Systems (Cryblock'18)*. ACM, New York, NY, 7–12, 2018. doi: 10.1145/3211933.3211935

[16] J. Lingjun Fan, Ramon Gil-Garcia, Derek Werthmuller, G. Brian Burke and Xuehai Hong. Investigating Blockchain as a Data Management Tool for IoT Devices in Smart City Initiatives. In *Proceedings of the 19th Annual International Conference on Digital Government Research: Governance in the Data Age (Dg.O '18)*, Anneke Zuiderwijk and Charles C. Hinnant (Eds.). ACM, New York, NY, Article 100, 2 pages, 2018. doi: 10.1145/3209281.3209391

[17] Benjamin Leiding, Parisa Memarmoshrefi and Dieter Hogrefe, "Self-Managed and Blockchain-Based Vehicular Ad-Hoc Networks", *UbiComp '16 Proceedings of the 2016 ACM International Joint Conference on Pervasive and Ubiquitous Computing: Adjunct*, 2016, pp. 137–140.

[18] Weili Chen, Zibin Zheng, Jiahui Cui, Edith Ngai, Peilin Zheng and Yuren. Zhou. Detecting Ponzi Schemes on Ethereum: Towards Healthier Blockchain Technology. *WWW '18 Proceedings of the 2018 World Wide Web Conference*, 2018, pp. 1409–1418. doi: 10.1145/3178876.3186046.

Blockchain Application for IoT Cybersecurity Management

Natalia Miloslavskaya[1], Alexander Tolstoy[1], Vladimir Budzko[1,2], and Maniklal Das[3]

[1] National Research Nuclear University MEPhI (Moscow Engineering Physics Institute), Moscow, Russia

[2] Institute of Informatics Problems of FRC CSC RAS, Moscow, Russia

[3] Dhirubhai Ambani Institute of Information and Communication Technology, Gandhinagar, Gujarat, India

CONTENTS

7.1 INTRODUCTION

The Internet unfolds enormous opportunities to the modern computing world where not only humans but also machines as well as any tiny sensing devices can communicate and collaborate. The Internet of Things (IoT) and Blockchain (BC) technologies can make a digital transformation of all activities around us for providing a better quality of services to the society by a sustainable and scalable infrastructure with participatory roles and responsibilities of its various stakeholders.

As history shows, all the most interesting research results are obtained at the junction of several scientific areas. The scope of the chapter covers three interdisciplinary, observable and rapidly developing areas of research, namely the IoT technologies, the BC technologies (BCT) and IoT security management. The relevance of the topic of this Chapter is underlined by Gartner in their review "Top 10 strategic technologies for 2019" (Gartner, 2018), which refers to both the BC and the IoT. In another forecast for security trends in 2019 (TopTeny, 2018), the BC is listed as prior for solving security-related problems and on the 9th place with the need to boost security everywhere.

7.2 THE IOT TECHNOLOGIES

7.2.1 The IoT Concept and Definitions

The IoT is a relatively new concept, and it is still in its early stages. Despite the fact, this term has already been used for several years definitions hasn't been agreed yet. For example, the IoT is defined in Recommendation ITU-T Y.2060 (ITU-T, 2012) as a global infrastructure for the information society which enables advanced services by interconnecting both physical and virtual things based on information and communication technologies (ICT) existing and evolving interoperable. ENISA refers to the IoT as a cyber-physical ecosystem of interconnected sensors and actuators, which enable decision-making (ENISA, 2017).

The scenarios of the IoT cover a wide range of applications starting from healthcare solutions, home appliances, wildlife monitoring, automotive technology, consumer electronics, agriculture systems, retail, industrial Internet and etc. Among the most frequently mentioned examples of IoT devices there are smartphones and home TVs, door locks and refrigerators, blood pressure meters and medicine droppers, traffic lights and connected cars, as well as smart sensors and actuators, smart homes and smart cities, smarts robots and grids, countless industrial control systems and so on. All of these things are interconnected in a unified IoT network, and they send or receive data from various mobile applications and cloud services. In the IoT network framework, different IoT devices, buildings, services supporting city life and other items embedded with electronics, software, and network connectivity collect and exchange sensitive data.

Therefore the IoT requires integration of several complementary technologies as an innovative Internet-based distributed ecosystem where information of both real and virtual worlds will be retrieved, identified, processed, combined, analyzed and distributed in a pervasive way as well as it provides new and existing applications, challenges and opportunities (European Commission, 2008). Generally, it is imperative the IoT infrastructure handles heterogeneous systems of hardware, software, and services that enable various objects to connect each other using public and private wired and wireless networks. In this case, technologies lead to an exponential increase in the creation and consumption of large volumes of data linked to individuals (consumers), as well as society (enterprises and industries) in addition to the conventional "web of the world", the convergence of mobile communication, cross-sensing platforms, and social networks.

Managing and securing data against a potential adversary is of prime concern in order to provide intended services to users in due course when creating, storing, updating, sharing, disseminating and deleting large volumes of data in IoT applications. Due to multiple vulnerabilities in the communication protocols, which manage connections of IoT devices between each other and the global networks the physical, and management, web and application interfaces, which are used for transmitting data to cloud-based resources and from it, IoT devices firmware and IoT software, many targeted attacks such as malicious modification, buffer overflow, brute force password cracking, Distributed Denial-of-Service (DDoS), Main-in-the-Middle (MitM) and many others are continuing to evolve for the IoT (Miloslavskaya and Tolstoy, 2019). Undoubtedly IoT infrastructure security and privacy as a whole, sensitive data circulating in it and continuous delivery of services become a real challenge to its providers and customers. The accountability of all operations with IoT devices, data, applications and services and the ownership of data while millions of things are exchanging their information in a collaborative and cross-sensing platform are other important issues. Besides IoT devices often store their users' personally identifiable information (PII) (e.g., name, date of birth, gender, social media accounts, email and home addresses, phone numbers, etc.) which can be of great value for malefactors. Certainly, this is not the complete list of all security issues which require security and privacy solutions.

From this point of view, the entire IoT ecosystem requires two complementary kinds of ensuring its security as "information lies at the heart of IoT, feeding into a continuous cycle of sensing, decision making, and actions" (ENISA, 2017). Specific security capabilities are closely connected with IoT-specific requirements while generic security capabilities are independent of the IoT and include traditional protection approaches such as access control via authentication and authorization, anti-virus and anti-malware systems, launching with minimal privileges, installing updates and others.

7.2.2 Generalized IoT Architecture and Reference Model

There has been not a single view on IoT architecture during the entire period since its advent. The objective has not been achieved yet despite long-standing efforts of different research groups to achieve a unified IoT architecture. The reason is in the diversity and complexity of the IoT application cases. The most interesting topic models are briefly analyzed further.

The following communication IoT models with some variations analyzed in (Zhong, Zhu, and Huang, 2017) (Belkeziz and Jarir, 2017) (Khan et al., 2012) (Al-Fuqaha et al., 2015), (Singh, Tripathi, and Jara, 2015) are the most common:

1) Three layers: perception, network, application

2) Four layers: perception, network transmission, network access, application or perception, network, cloud computing, application

3) Five layers: perception, network transmission, network access, application support, application presentation

4) Seven layers: existed application system, edge technology, access, backbone network, coordination, middleware, application.

Two service-oriented architectures (SOA) are mentioned more often among the functional IoT models (e.g., in Al-Fuqaha et al., 2015; Mishra, Lin, and Chang, 2014; Weigong et al., 2017; Yang et al., 2011):

1) Five layers: objects, object abstraction, service management, service composition, application or objects, object abstraction, service management, application, business or objects, network, middleware, tools, applications

2) Seven layers: sensing and act device; intelligent device; physical information; logical information; IoT basic service; service middle, application.

These architectures traditionally combine a few elements (min 3, max 7) from the following list of all possible layers with the difference in the way they are represented. In this list, we try to allocate them closely to each other to show some correspondence between these layers.

The perception layer unites various types of sensors, cameras, microphones, human body sensors and medical devices (like blood pressure cuffs, glucose meters, insulin pumps), actuators, Radio Frequency Identification (FRID) devices, Near Field Communication (NFC) devices, automatic recognition devices, surface acoustic wave devices, timing and positioning systems, laser scanners, remote controls, connected vehicle systems, executive devices and many others. The sensing and act device layer is presented by different types of sensors, sensing instruments and sensor networks and it is directly connected with the intelligent device layer to transform the external physical signal/data into the signal/digit information that can be recognized by intelligent devices. Act devices receive control signals from intelligent devices and control IoT things' behaviors based on these signals. The intelligent device layer via intelligent devices (such as IoT terminals with intelligent chips, general-purpose computers, industrial computers, personal mobile devices, LAN, etc.) collects information of things and directs it to the Internet.

The object layer describes all the objects (including IoT devices) as the objects of service management. The object abstraction layer focuses on the abstraction of different heterogeneous objects related to the IoT for unifying access to them.

The backbone network layer interconnects different sub-networks and provides an exchange of information between them. The network transmission layer transmits the data retrieved at the perception layer and consists of sensor networks, special-line networks, the Internet, Wi-Fi networks, ad-hoc networks, mobile communications, satellite communications, wireless personal area networks, industrial bus, etc.

The physical information layer contains the raw data of things. The logical information layer describes virtual things and is intended to simplify the use of raw data by converting it to customary information formats and adding basic descriptions (such as logical names of things and data, usage permissions, type of data, etc.).

The network access layer supports data collecting, preliminary processing and network accessing based on a wired or wireless communication network.

The cloud computing layer supports virtualization to enhance the IoT flexibility in addition to storage, networking, and computation.

The coordination layer supports interoperability by unifying the structure of packages from different applications to simplify their processing by applications.

The service management layer is responsible for managing each IoT object by supporting function like dynamic discovery, monitoring, service configuration, coordination, Quality of Service (QoS), scalability, interoperability, reliability, etc. The service composition layer deals with failures that may occur. The basic service layer provides things access to the Internet with appropriate monitoring and control. The service middle layer makes use of corresponding services to form a service hierarchy that application layer needs.

The middleware layer processes data for handling the objects abstraction for non-experts.

The tools layer is composed of tools for knowledge processing.

The application support layer provides storing, sharing and processing of all data circulating in the IoT and contains a variety of applications which are specific for a concrete IoT case such as smart home, smart city, smart traffic, smart manufacturing, smart logistics and many other areas of human activities, as well as more traditional applications for data processing, middleware, cloud platforms, databases, expert systems, security monitoring systems and so on for this purpose. The application presentation layer uses visualization tools, human–computer interfaces, multimedia, virtual reality and other technologies to build the interface between the IoT and all the categories of its users for realizing various intelligent information presentations.

The business layer includes management of the whole IoT architecture and allows decision-making based on applicable business models, big data analytics, charts, etc.

The most detailed functional model with nine components was represented in (Bassi et al., 2013). Different IoT devices are traditionally located at its bottom while IoT applications are at the top. These devices are connected to service organization (including service composition, orchestration, and choreography), IoT process management (both process modeling and execution), a virtual entity (with their resolution, service and service monitoring) and IoT services (with their resolution) via end-to-end, network and hop-to-hop communications. Applications and devices interact with a management block based on configuration, fault, member, state and reporting management as well as a security block formed by identity management, authentication, authorization, key and exchange management, trust, and reputation. The model proposed is largely relied on this as the most complete model.

IoT applications are used by intelligent transportation, smart grids, home appliances, and various utility services. It is imperative that IoT applications require heterogeneous systems of hardware, software, and services which can enable objects to connect each other using public and private networks. The usage of a mobile phone in applications ranging from home appliances to consumer electronics has increased many folds by the backbone connectivity of the Internet. This not only connected applications of service providers and consumers but also enabled a virtual human-chain through social networks and by other means across the globe. Intelligent transportation allows the integration of vehicles into the IoT that could establish smart communication between heterogeneous networks like vehicle-to-vehicle, vehicle-to-roadside, vehicle-to-human, vehicle-to-home, and vehicle-to-everything. Many objects in this landscape are going to be tiny, pervasive, resource-constrained (e.g., sensors and RFID tags) and connected to the conventional web-of-the-world with the IoT functional layers.

Generalizing all this research, adding (ISO/IEC 30141, 2018) and (ITU-T Y.2068, 2015) and updating our own view (Miloslavskaya and Tolstoy, 2019), we worked out the six-layer architecture which is best suited for further application of the blockchain technology to the IoT. It is represented on the left side of Fig. 7.1 with some examples of entities and process occurring on the corresponding layers. The IoT reference model

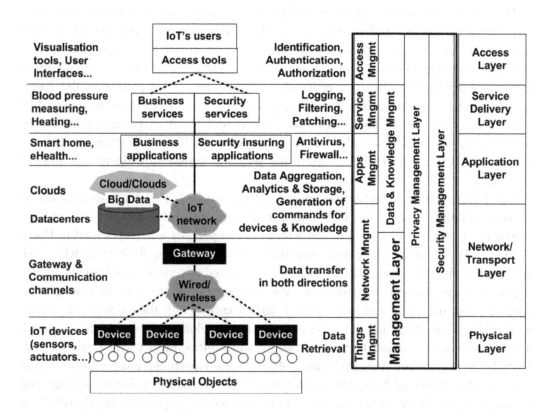

FIGURE 7.1   Generalized six-layer IoT architecture

is shown on the right side of Fig. 7.1 with the layer content given above. The main advantage of this representation is that it logically combines communication, functional, and security models in one.

The physical (perceptual) layer provides a set of resilient building blocks for the IoT. It makes IoT services "smart" with the ability for environment-sensing and intelligence for monitoring and controlling the IoT devices. Sensors, actuators, RFID tags, readers, Supervisory Control And Data Acquisition (e.g., SCADA) and related IoT technologies (e.g., GPS) play central roles in this layer. The transportation layer is governed by hundreds of network nodes connected by different communication protocols. IoT smart physical devices and sensor-equipped edge devices as well as embedded systems are linked to sensor networks and further to the IoT network using Ethernet, 802.15.4, Bluetooth, Wi-Fi, ZigBee, 6LoWPAN, RPL, WiMax, 3/4/5G, etc. Wired access is supported by a cable while wireless communications are provided by Wi-Fi, Bluetooth, infrared, radio frequency and other types of communications.

Communication sessions manage how numerous applications connect to the IoT. The information exchange methods include point-to-point or single-point-to-multi-points information transmissions. Big data sent to applications and from them are usually stored in data centers and clouds. Various applications support all IoT business cases and use appropriate application services. The application layer makes the intended service request pertaining to the application, for which the application data need to be exchanged with other participating nodes.

The service delivery layer delivers those service management activities that require input and interaction with the IoT business and service owners. The components are not only responsible for that interaction but also the translation of IoT business requirement into technology and operational capabilities (such as service optimization, service lifecycle, catalog and level management, demand management, etc.). This layer represents the IoT business perspective.

The access layer is connected to the service delivery and management layers. The IoT services end users connect to the IoT at this layer as a single point. It allows to manage and maintain access to the IoT using the combination of multiple services and solves the large-capacity, high-performance and high-reliability access problems in IoT devices, network channels, applications, etc. (e.g., via performing load balancing).

The management layer provides management services and a set of capabilities to all the IoT layers via a suite of management tools to support IoT service delivery layer and operational processes carried in the IoT (like service, network, change, capacity, configuration, monitoring, reporting, systems administration, data protection, incident, problem, availability, knowledge, etc. management), as well as to support staff. Our key idea for this layer is to separate data streams and management streams that will ensure the entire IoT management being free of the interference from other data in real time and being protected against many attacks.

All these layers are managed by specific protocols based on the rules that govern each layer and should reliably ensure that the data passing through them get to where it is going while remaining intact. By exploiting identification, data retrieval, a full cycle of data processing to new knowledge acquisition, generation of adequate to the current environmental status commands for execution by actuators, communication capabilities and much more, the IoT makes full use of things to offer services to all kinds of applications, whilst fulfilling strict security and privacy requirements. And vice versa; all these layers with corresponding things on them (called security objects) can be considered as the targets of attacks against the IoT. Therefore the layers and interconnections between them should be protected by the appropriate security measures and tools, managed in the framework of the security management layer. For example, at the physical layer access control, device integrity validation and data confidentiality and integrity protection should be implemented; at the network layer signaling data confidentiality and signaling integrity protection as well as channel availability should be provided; and at the application layer anti-virus and anti-malware, application data integrity and confidentiality protection, privacy protection, application availability should be supported.

After the IoT reference model was split into a reasonable number of layers, it can make each layer relative independent, more flexible and more easy to implement and maintain for configuration and more suitable to promote the standardization of the IoT.

7.2.3 The IoT Standardization Issues

Standards provide people and organizations with a basis for a mutual understanding of the IoT. The strongest contributors to IoT standardization and ensuring its security are the International Standardization Organization (ISO), the International Electrotechnical Commission (IEC), the International Telecommunication Union (ITU) and the IEEE Standards Association (IEEE-SA).

A variety of issues of IoT creation and use from different viewpoints are presented in the adopted in 2012–2018 standards such as ITU Y.4000/Y.2060 (Overview of the IoT, 2012), Y.4050/Y.2069 (Terms and definitions for the IoT), Y.4100/Y.2066 (Common requirements of the IoT), Y.4111/Y.2076 (Semantics-based requirements and framework of the IoT), Y.4113 (Requirements of the network for the IoT), Y.4103/F.748.0 (Common requirements for IoT applications), Y.4552/Y.2078 (Application support models of the IoT), Y.4453 (Adaptive software framework for IoT devices), Y.4101/Y.2067 (Common requirements and capabilities of a gateway for IoT applications), Y.4112/Y.2077 (Requirements of the plug and play capability of the IoT), Y.4401/Y.2068 (Functional framework and capabilities of the IoT, 2015), Y.4416 (Architecture of the IoT based on next-generation network evolution) and Y.4114 (Specific requirements and capabilities of the IoT for big data), ISO/IEC 22417:2017 (IoT use cases), 29161:2016 (Unique identification for the IoT), 29181-9:2017 (Future Network – Problem statement and requirements, Part 9: Networking of everything) and 30141:2018 (IoT reference architecture, 2018), IEEE P2413 (Architectural framework for the IoT), P1451-99 (Harmonization of IoT devices and systems), P1931.1 (Architectural framework for real-time onsite operations facilitation for the IoT) and P2668 (Maturity index of IoT: evaluation, grading and ranking) and many others. The Open Group IoT Work Group has produced two Open Group IoT standards: the Open Data Format (O-DF) and the Open Messaging Interface (O-MI) and is working on a standard for open IoT lifecycle management now. The following very expected standards are still under development: ISO/IEC 20924 (IoT definition and vocabulary), 21823-1 (Interoperability for IoT systems – Part 1: Framework) and 23093 (Internet of media things – Part 1: Architecture).

There are far fewer standards for IoT security or security-related issues. There is an almost complete list of them: ISO/IEC 29181-5:2014 (Future Network – Problem statement and requirements – Part 5: Security), ITU Y.4806 (Security capabilities supporting safety of the IoT), X.1362 (Simple encryption procedure for IoT environments), Y.4102/Y.2074 (Requirements for IoT devices and operation of IoT applications during disasters), Y.4455 (Reference architecture for IoT network service capability exposure), Y.4118 (IoT requirements and technical capabilities for support of accounting and charging), Q.3952 (The architecture and facilities of a model network for IoT testing), Y.4702 (Common requirements and capabilities of device management in the IoT) and Q.3913 (Set of parameters for monitoring IoT devices). Three very important projects under development must be added to this list: ISO/IEC 27030 (Guidelines for security and privacy in IoT), 30149 (IoT Trustworthiness framework) and 30147 (Methodology for trustworthiness of IoT system/service).

In 2017, the European Union Agency For Network And Information Security (ENISA) has published the "Baseline Security Recommendations for IoT in the context of Critical Information Infrastructures" to map critical assets and relevant threats, assess possible attacks and identify potential good practices and security measures for protecting the IoT systems (ENISA, 2017).

And at that moment (March 2019) the National Institute of Standards and Technology (NIST) has no special publications for the IoT with only two draft internal reports (NISTIR) 8222 (IoT Trust Concerns) and 8228 (Considerations for IoT cybersecurity and privacy risks). Therefore ensuring IoT's IS remains an active research area.

7.3 THE BLOCKCHAIN TECHNOLOGIES AND THEIR APPLICATION AREAS

There are countless articles and videos describing the "magic" of blockchain (BC) (Yaga et al., 2018) starting in 2009 with Bitcoin and a high level of "hype" around its use. But there is no single agreed definition of this technology and, in general, it is not well understood. The Draft NISTIR 8202 "Blockchain Technology Overview" (Yaga et al., 2018) is the first high-level technical document attempting to do this.

In recent times the BCT as technologies for creating verifiable digital records have shown notable success not only in digital currencies but also in financial application domains (such as payments, currency exchanges, money services and transfers, soft and hard wallets, trade finance, different markets, microtransactions, investments, brokerage, insurance, compliance, etc.) as well in non-financial domains (such as digital identity management, authentication and authorization, digital content/documents storage and delivery systems, smart contracts, certification validation systems, application development, real estate, election voting, patient medical records management, distributing the workload for communication system, computer systems that must comply with legal agreements without human intervention, the IoT, etc.). One can found they have great potential which can reshape IoT applications with respect to security, privacy, transparency, and fault-resistance.

In addition to conventional security solutions, IoT applications demand lightweight, resource-efficient security and privacy solutions. All the entities involved in various systems such as sensors, actuators, mobile phones, data owners, service consumers, service providers require strong security ensuring (e.g., in respect to authentication and integrity), in-network data processing and secure data aggregation, accountability, delegation and managing essential trust relationships. Furthermore, when transmitting data among many intermediate entities data ownership and accountability are also important factors that must be addressed by both service providers and service consumers. In such a context, we perceive the BCT can provide practical solutions that can address the above-stated features for IoT applications.

The description of specific applications of the BCT in such an important area as network security has not been found in open sources yet by authors at the time of writing the Chapter. There are only brief remarks (without any explanations on how to implement them) that the BCT could monitor the state and integrity of the software, data transmitted from various IoT systems and so on for illicit changes and thus ensure that the operating system (OS) and firmware used, data streams and so forth have not been forged.

7.3.1 Blockchain Basics and Glossary

To begin with, we would like to quote most interesting from our viewpoint BCT definitions from different sources:

- (UK Government, 2016): "A distributed ledger technology".

- (PriceWaterhouseCoopers, 2016): "A decentralized ledger of all transactions across a peer-to-peer network, where participants can confirm transactions without the need for a certifying authority".

- (Nielson, 2017): "A distributed file system that keeps files copies of the participants who agree on the changes by mutual consensus, where the file consists of blocks and every block has a cryptographic signature of the last block, making an immutable record".

- (Wilson, 2017): "It is not a 'trust machine'. By the blockchain protocol, it only reaches consensus about one specific technicality – the order of entries in the ledger, free of bias".

- (OpenBlockchain, 2017): "A technology that enables the secure and resilient management of distributed data in combination with data analytics techniques that add scale and flexibility".

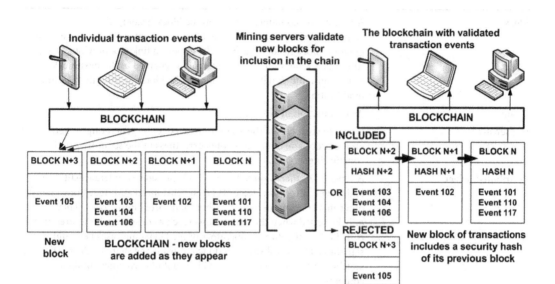

FIGURE 7.2   Inclusion of a new block into the BC

- (Primechaintech, 2018): "A peer-to-peer network which timestamps records by hashing them into an ongoing chain of hash-based proof-of-work, forming a record that cannot be changed without redoing the proof-of-work".

We define a BC as *a secure distributed data structure (database, DB) that maintains without centralized administration and data storage (repository) a constantly expanding list of non-editable time-stamped blocks/records and sets rules about transactions which are tied to these blocks* (in contrast to a conventional DB in which rules are set at the DB level or in the application) (Miloslavskaya, 2018b). This DB is shared by a group of participants with the right to submit new blocks for inclusion in it. For the IoT transactions reflect events happening in it gathered from data sources. All the transactions in a block are grouped together along with a cryptographic hash of the previous block. Any block will be included in the BC only after the consensus of a majority of participants who will agree that any transaction from the block under consideration looks valid (Fig. 7.2). This block cannot be removed or changed after published. All the blocks are linked to each other (like a chain) in a proper linear, chronological order. The public history of all blocks' inclusion is securely stored in the BC. It can be shared, immutable and verifiable for recording the history of transactions relying on different protocols.

The BC uses four protocols for its operations as a distributed networked system: for transactions, peer-to-peer communications for the equally privileged peers, the consensus for negotiation and reaching an agreement on the relevant issues and data storage for extracting and sending data to the DB.

Generalizing the basic terms from (Bluemix, 2017; Kruijff and Weigand, 2017; Medici, 2017; UK Government, 2016, etc.), the following glossary was worked out:

Block	A transaction container with a unique block header, which cryptographically commits to the block's content, a timestamp, and the previous block header. Each block contains a link to a previous block (through a series of hash pointers) and is chained to the next block, using a cryptographic signature. This makes the blocks inherently resistant to modification.
Chain	A combination of blocks.
Consensus	Serves to corroborate the accuracy of a ledger by generating an agreement on the order and confirming the correctness of the set of transactions constituting a block.
Distributed ledger	A type of DB that is spread across multiple sites/countries/institutions and is typically public. Records are synchronized and stored one after the other in a continuous ledger, rather than sorted into blocks. They can only be added when the participants reach a consensus. It requires greater trust in the validators or operators of the ledger and uses keys and signatures to control who can do what inside the shared ledger. They are scalable, fast and secure and provide proof of correctness of their contents.
Ledger	Keeps the log of ordered transaction batches. Can be programmed to record anything/everything of value. The peer ledger contains all batched transactions coming out of the ordering service (a defined collective of nodes that orders transactions into a block), some of which may, in fact, be invalid. The validated ledger contains fully validated transaction blocks. The ledger is distributed to all network nodes through replication. Can be shared and corroborated by anyone with the appropriate permissions.
Main chain	Contains the block headers of all blocks that are digitally signed and containing validated records of ownership that are irreversible, depleting the necessity for the reconciliation of data.
Miner	An anonymous node (e.g. server) that cryptographically proves a transaction to be valid using a proving mechanism like Proof-of-Work/Resource/State/Activity, etc.
Node	An entity in the BC network that accepts and processes the transaction and shares information about the candidate transaction. It either proves (public BC) or validates (hybrid/private BC) transactions and subsequently adds it to a block with a unique hash.
Peer	A network entity, which maintains a ledger and performs read/write operations to it.
Permissioned (dedicated, private) ledger	When participants for corroborating the accuracy of a ledger are preselected. It may have one/many owners and only they can add records and verify the ledger's integrity and contents. It is usually faster than an unpermissioned ledger. The consensus process used is simpler than in permissioned ledgers.
Sidechain	Allows for the transfer of assets to the main chain and vice versa. It can store assets and data that cannot be saved (or it is too expensive to save) on the main chain and may increase the transaction speed significantly by using pre-mined main chain addresses. Like the parallel BC, it improves scalability using alternative, completely independent BC.

(Continued)

(Cont.)

Shared ledger	Any DB and application that is shared by a private consortium or open to the public. It may use a distributed ledger or BC as its underlying DB, but will often have permissions for different types of users, interacting with the BC. It represents a spectrum of possible ledgers or DB designs that are permissioned at some level. It may have a limited number of fixed validators who are trusted to maintain the ledger.
Transaction	An invoke or instantiate operation between accounts, sending/receiving value to/from a transaction. Invokes are the atomic requests to the BC nodes to read/write data from the ledger and they contain an input and output (the BC) or custom data like code (altchain). All transactions made are authorized by miners, which makes the transactions immutable.
Unpermissioned (permission-less, public) ledger	When corroborating the accuracy of a ledger is open to everyone. It is open to everyone to contribute data to the ledger and cannot be owned.

Later in the Chapter, we will use these terms as they are presented in the table above but giving them a concrete meaning for BC-based IoT and its security management.

7.3.2 Blockchain Standardization Issues

In 2016, the specialized technical committee ISO/TC 307 "Blockchain and distributed ledger technologies" has been created. Its scope was defined as standardization of the BCT and distributed ledger technologies (DLT). ISO/TC 307 combines several specialized and working groups namely "Blockchain and distributed ledger technologies and IT Security techniques", "Foundations", "Use cases", "Security, privacy and identity", "Smart contracts and their applications", "Governance of blockchain and distributed ledger technology system" and "Interoperability of blockchain and distributed ledger technology systems". At present (March 2019) they are working at the following 10 standards devoted to the BCT and DLT: ISO 22739 (Terminology); ISO 23244 (Overview of privacy and personally identifiable information (PII) protection); ISO 23245 (Security risks and vulnerabilities); ISO 23246 (Overview of identity management using BCT and DLT); ISO 23257 (Reference architecture); ISO 23258 (Taxonomy and Ontology); ISO 23259 (Legally binding smart contracts); ISO 23455 (Overview of and interactions between smart contracts in BCT and DLT systems); ISO 23576 (Security of digital asset custodians) and ISO 23578 (Discovery issues related to interoperability). The majority of these standards are at the preparatory stage, and only two of them (22739 and 23455) have the first drafts registered. Therefore discussing their content is premature.

The NISTIR 8202 "Blockchain Technology Overview" (Yaga et al., 2018) discusses how the BCT work especially when applying to electronic currency. It also shows the BCT's broader applications (banking, supply chain, insurance and healthcare, trusted time stamping, energy industry) and highlights some of their limitations related to the BC control, malicious users, no trust, resource usage, transfer of burden of credential storage to users, and Private/Public Key Infrastructure and identity. This document defines the high-level components of a BC system architecture like transactions, blocks, hashes, forks, etc. It describes how new blocks are added to the BC and how consensus models resolve conflicts among miners. Different BC permission models and their use case examples are introduced. The document also covers smart contracts and BC platforms in use today. In this Chapter, we rely on the NISTIR 8202 as the only one which is currently publicly available.

In the conclusion of this section, we would like to mention the development of the new IEEE standard, the scope of which exactly coincides with the topic of this chapter. It is IEEE P2418.1 standard for the framework of blockchain use, implementation, and interaction in IoT applications which was started in June 2017 with June 2019 as the expected date of draft submission to the IEEE-SA. The developing framework will include blockchain tokens, smart contracts, transactions, assets, a credentialed network, and the permissioned and permissionless IoT blockchains. It enables decentralized, autonomous peer-to-peer, consumer-to-machine and machine-to-machine communications without the need for a trusted intermediary and addresses scalability, interoperability, security and privacy challenges with regard to blockchain in the IoT.

7.4 TWO MAIN DIRECTIONS OF APPLYING THE BLOCKCHAIN TECHNOLOGY TO THE IOT SECURITY

The new reality of more frequent and sophisticated attacks and "hacking as a service" makes the IoT break-in more professional, accessible and dangerously effective. With the availability of more and smarter gadgets in the market and using the power of ICT, more and more physical objects in our societies are getting connected to the "web of the world", which make the IoT in its desired shape. The entire IoT ecosystem poses many security challenges that need to be addressed for the IoT to reach its full potential via the appropriately designed process for managing it. To operate securely and legally and to achieve its objectives, the IoT networked infrastructure need to match a lot of internal and external requirements called compliance regulations. They require conformity to many rules like laws, standards, guidelines, policies, specifications, procedures, etc. The IoT infrastructures need to ensure the security of all its valuable assets (all entities related to the IoT), uninterrupted processes and differentiated QoS to various groups of users, as well as its operational resilience. Effective security ensuring is a need for modern a world as well as the IoT scenarios and applications.

An integrated system, being able to manage security for the IoT infrastructure in real-time while processing tremendous amounts of security-related data coming in various formats from all IoT things, is required as never before. For any security incident in the IoT, its source should be found, the type should be considered, consequences should be weighted, all affected systems should be detected, countermeasures should be prioritized, and mitigation solutions should be offered with weighted impact relevance. Thus a problem of managing IoT's security based on the structured, consolidated and visual data presentation and secure dynamical processing raises very sharply, as well as designing the secure IoT infrastructure from the beginning of a design project. From our perspective, the BCT can be applied to the IoT for achieving this goal in two complementary areas – for designing BC-based secure IoT infrastructure and BC-based management of IoT's security.

In the former part, a secure IoT infrastructure will be suggested using BC technology, which ensures secure data sharing among heterogeneous IoT objects participating in cross-sensing platforms. The framework can support authenticated key exchange, delegation based in-network authorization and BC-based service accountability and data ownership management.

In the later part, the discussion on the IoT vulnerabilities and exploiting them security threats will be followed by the demonstration how to use the BCT for constructing a BC-based Security Information and Event Management (SIEM) system as one of the essential tools for monitoring security in the IoT network infrastructure.

7.5 SECURE BC-BASED IOT INFRASTRUCTURE

As most of IoT devices are resource-constrained, the conventional security solutions with public key settings may not be suitable for practical applications. On the other hand, sensing data, as well as services need protection from malicious intention, whether accidental or intentional. DoS attacks, along with other threats pertaining to communication protocols (like sinkhole, wormhole and misbehaving nodes), are potential threats in the transportation layer. Service availability, data confidentiality, message integrity, and authentication of the communication entities per application requirement need to be addressed with proper context and adversarial assumptions. In addition, various attacks (like impersonation, MitM, and so on) are major concerns to protect data in this layer.

In addition to the above-listed threats, privacy-protection, controlling access to data, trust relationships and ownership of data, as well as services are the keys to convincing data owners, service provider and service consumers in enabling and availing services in the desired IoT infrastructure. All entities involved in various applications such as sensors and actuators, mobile phones, data owners, application providers require strong measures for in-network data processing security (e.g., authentication, authorization, availability, and integrity). Secure data aggregation, accountability and delegation of services while managing essential trust relationships are of great importance in such scenarios and applications. Furthermore, assurance of services to users in time and effective systems and services risk management are an integral part of the service providers and data owners.

We have already shown (Fig. 7.1) the distributed nature of the IoT's physical layer with its smart physical devices and sensor-equipped edge devices, which are linked to the distributed sensor network and further to the IoT network. The BCT usage in the IoT is very promising for making IoT devices secure. The distributed allocation of IoT applications also complies with the BCT. These applications support specific IoT processes with numerous transactions and interactions, which form the basis for creating the blocks for inclusion in the BC.

Adding a data layer to IoT functional layers between the transport and application layers (on the left part of Fig. 7.1) makes the service not only smart but also could address security and privacy issues efficiently. A data-centric distributed framework for managing security and privacy solutions for IoT applications involve trusted data cells structured in the data layer for different servicing units (e.g., web, proxy, application, DB, network, security) engage themselves for managing their respective activities. These services' layer must be routed through various edges which are capable of managing resource intelligently with a cloud powered by a distributed cloud architecture that is supported by software-defined networks, edge intelligence, and pervasive computing. It is commonly known that the BC foundation lies on distributed DBs; therefore having a BC-powered IoT infrastructure could make IoT operational layers transparent, accountable and auditable. It is proposed to have multiple data nodes powered by data cells for managing service logs amongst various IoT applications (Fig. 7.3).

Data nodes possess entity's data can interact with other entities, share and disseminate the application data, provide security services and so on. The IoT application running on each data node can be organized based on a distributed ledger which can help in maintaining data access as well as services offered to various IoT nodes which in turn interrogates both the application and transport layers.

Securing interactions between data nodes and delegation services could make "things" collaborate with each other through these nodes to provide services in a cooperative-collaborative framework. However, the framework may require providing immutability, transparency, traceability and availability features for the applications pertaining to the IoT infrastructure. For handling such applications' context, a BC-based framework for IoT data is proposed (Fig. 7.4). It can also address two important features, namely ownership, and accountability required for IoT scenarios and applications in the context of data privacy laws applicable in different countries. Blocks in the proposed framework fetch the transactions and have fields for specifying proof of ownership and endorser. By having these two fields in each transaction, one can address the ownership of data, as well as services, and the accountability of services can also come into the context at the same time. Another important participatory agent in this framework is an analyst, who could analyze services offered and/or access from the ledger maintained by this

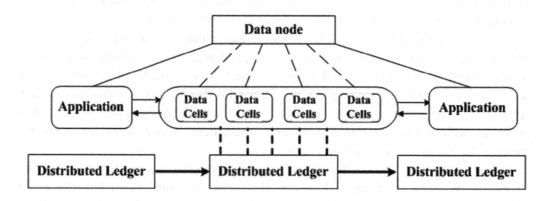

FIGURE 7.3 A distributed ledger of data nodes

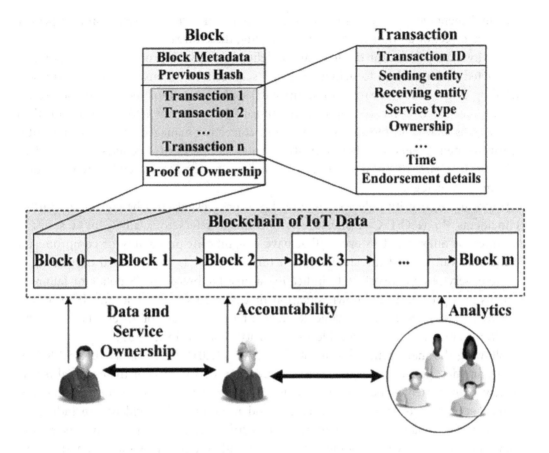

FIGURE 7.4   BC-based framework for IoT data

framework. One of the analysts could play the role of a security analyst, which should check security risk assessment and perform actions based appropriately on the application's security objectives.

7.6 BC-BASED SYSTEM FOR MANAGING SECURITY IN THE IOT

Managing security in the IoT means to manage security in IoT devices, networks, services and applications as the basic elements of the IoT. Here security means a property (quality) of all the IoT's assets (including various types of information being processed in the IoT) to preserve their availability, integrity, authenticity, confidentiality, accountability, non-repudiation, and reliability. For example, the IoT's network security is a secure (protected) state of the IoT network integrally and all its particular connections and assets, which is provided by means of security controls in the presence of emerging threats and vulnerabilities not eliminated in time. A security threat (short from a threat of security violation) for the IoT can be described as a set of conditions and factors, which create a real or potential opportunity for violating its security. Vulnerabilities are the IoT's properties, including information protection tools (IPTs), which are exploited by threats' sources for their implementation in the form of attacks. A source of security threats can be a person, a material object or a physical event, implementing these threats.

Security management for the IoT can be defined as a cyclic process consisting of a set of targeted actions taken to achieve the IoT's objectives by ensuring its security and including continuous assessment of security risks, planning, implementation and evaluation of the effectiveness of appropriate information security (IS) controls for their treatment as well as immediate response and corrective managed actions to unwanted security-related events (further security events) and security policies' or practices' violation. It is vital to know what IS threats exist at the moment and how they could grow into an incident.

According to security policies, some of the security events will be considered further as incidents. In (ISO/IEC 27000:2018), IS incident refers to a single or a series of unwanted or unexpected IS events that have a significant probability of compromising business operations and threatening IS. In turn, IS event is an identified occurrence of a system, service or network state indicating a possible breach of IS policy or failure of controls or a previously unknown situation that may be security relevant. IS event can be a part of one IS incident, while IS incident can be a set of IS events. The same definitions are completely applicable to a security violation in the IoT.

Following the main principles of ISO/IEC 27035-1:2016 (2016) and NIST SP 800-61 (2012), an effective security incident management process in place is the essential part of security management processes for the IoT. It should be based on a structured and planned approach to detect, report, assess, and respond to IS incidents, including the activation of adequate IS controls to prevent, reduce, and recover from impacts, on one hand, and to report vulnerabilities for dealing with them appropriately on the other hand and, at least, to learn from these incidents and vulnerabilities, set institute preventive controls, and make improvements to the process.

Initial data for the security incident management process can be collected during different security checks, supervision or critical observation called together monitoring. It is intended for continuous control over the normal functioning mode in the dynamic and constantly changing IoT and determining the state of IoT devices, network channels, systems, services, applications, information assets, processes, activity, and so on, on the basis of elicitation of events to be registered, as well as the collection analysis and generalization of the monitoring results in the form of pre-defined metrics of IoT and its environment's operation. The events indicate non-compliance with some requirements from internal policies and appointed external regulations.

All incidents require mandatory registration, investigation of their causes, detailed study of what has happened, activation of an appropriate response and elimination of their consequences. Timely provisioning of the authorized parties with complete and reliable information for justified security decision-making is one of the main objectives of monitoring the IoT's security. The detection of events, partly classified further as incidents; recognition of anomalies and vulnerabilities in assets, processes, etc.; collecting of logs; providing evidence in case of computer crime and for compliance purposes, etc. are among other tasks. These complicated and time-consuming activities require automation of all routine operation. So-called SIEM systems (introduced by Gartner in 2005) are used to solve the problem of real-time flow control over large volumes of security-related data to computerize security incident management process, in particular, to find specific data, characterizing attacks' phases and their typical consequence.

There are two generations of SIEM systems (Miloslavskaya, 2018a). SIEM 1.0 systems of the late 1990s were log-centric. They detected IS events through preset rules and data correlation techniques mostly for IP addresses and used relational DBs with lack of processing, little semantic richness and no support for recursion and inheritance, etc. They could not detect non-standard network traffic, protocol anomalies, malicious client's or malware's activity, unauthorized connections and tools (like Tor), SSL usage over unusual ports, etc. From the late 2000's, SIEM 2.0 systems perform behavioral and contextual analysis and implement real-time detection and centralized collection of data on IS events from all distributed heterogeneous sources, correlation of ports, protocols and users, information processing in a particular context, accumulation of statistics on previous and current users' and applications' activity, tracking the entire lifecycle of each IS event, automated generation of reports and recommendations to handle these events, use big data technologies for analytics, etc.

Modern challenges dictate the need to modify these systems for the IoT by using advanced technologies such as the BC technology. From the other side, all SIEM systems' data and its subsystems should be protected as they are vital for collecting and analyzing sensitive data, for example, for digital forensics.

It was concluded after exploring the possibilities of the BCT that they are well applicable for designing a new BC-based SIEM 3.0 system and can provide the following significant benefits:

- Interoperability on the basis of applicable international standards, interoperability of data from all sources, presented in a structural format ready for further processing, and policy interoperability

- Obligatory proof of data source's identity and authenticity prohibiting any anonymity (only authorized and verified sources can transmit collected data), resulting in trust of the parties (e.g., analytical modules, IS administrators) to it

- Ensuring data integrity for transmissions to, from and within the BC, as well as the whole BC (by using a variety of messaging and consensus techniques and by preventing valid data from being deleted or modified secretly), rather than keeping it confidential

- Real-time event recording (including, for example, security-related data access attempts, affecting the BC's security) with time-stamping and complete event history, supporting traceability and transparency

- An opportunity to investigate the consequence of events that lead to an incident. By recording every security event, they allow to use in-depth analysis and check for patterns (indicators of the IoT's components compromise) across thousands of events in real-time

- Automatic updates every time a new event occurs: new blocks with information about new events are sent to the BC in a chronological order one by one strictly according to the time of their occurrence

- The possibility of inserting additional attributes to all data coming to the BC (e.g., purpose, repeated event, composed of other events, affected asset's location) to "colorize" events according to their seriousness for further mandatory tracking

- Independence of the BC from the type and number of data sources – if they are replaced by new ones or their number increases, the BC continues to operate

- A sufficient capability to register, validate, process and transmit to the BC billions of events per second in hard real-time without any delays

- Hard to attack because of the multiple shared copies of the same BC.

In the BC-based SIEM 3.0, the BC is streamlining all events taking place in the IoT. Thus it can be considered as a unidirectional (without feedback) chain with a linked by hash pointers blocks, each one referring back to the one that went before (Fig. 7.2). Blocks have unique identifiers (IDs) and hashes (cryptographic links to previous valid blocks, confirming their relationship) and contain data on security events collected by preselected data sources. Rules are set for the events tied to a specific incident. Security events, belonging to the same incident as its consequent steps, will be combined in one block. Creating a block with content similar to one of the preceding blocks (so-called repeated block) but with a larger ID means that some repeated events appear in the IoT that characterize, for example, a DoS attack.

The SIEM 3.0 system should be agent-based. Agents will be deployed on each IoT asset to be monitored. They offer more functionality and preprocess the collected events to reduce their volume before transmitting to the BC by discarding events not affecting the IoT's security.

From our viewpoint, the SIEM 3.0 system should utilize a permissioned ledger. Firstly, the IoT is used in a closed community – one IoT. Secondly, all preselected and trusted data sources (IPTs) collect raw events, discard those not related to IoT's security and send all remaining events (suspicious and pure events, violating IoT's security) to a single centralized DB (ledger) of pending events (PEL) shared by all data sources. The sources should be able to view in the PEL only their collected data. Events from the PEL are used for insertion into blocks, which will then be transmitted for inclusion in the BC (Fig. 7.2).

Some node (called "a miner") vacant at that time takes a pending event from the PEL, validates it (e.g., its data source and time of occurrence), creates a new block from one or several events and orders events in the block. After the block has been created, all events in it became confirmed. Using events' timestamps, the miner decides on this block to become the next block in the BC and creates its unique hash. Then the block is distributed around the BC (i.e., replicated to all its nodes). The trusted nodes have permission to add blocks to the BC after their verification and confirmation. They are able to write anytime to the BC without a coordinating node. All these nodes check that the block is correct (e.g., from the viewpoint of the presence of obvious traces of any known incident in it) and add it to their copy of the BC. The significant benefit of this approach is that if only one node is compromised by intruders, a shared ledger has a high degree of transparency for the in-depth analysis of incidents if later required.

A special additional type of nodes called "peers" is proposed to reduce the workload of miners in this dynamic BC. They do peer exchange and share information on other nodes (e.g., they can tell them that "block N+1 has parent N, has event 102, its hash is HASH N+1, etc.") and their status (e.g., out-of-service because of compromise) as well as perform read/write operations to the ledger.

Data sources collecting raw events store them in the place where they were collected. All preprocessed results characterizing security events are transmitted to the PEL. After the initial preprocessing these events can be considered later as the steps of one incident.

According to the IoT's security policy, an event can be classified as a non-security event, suspicious event or security event/incident. For example, log in to start a service with the right credentials is only an event. Any login attempt with wrong credentials is a security event, and it can be either a user's error or the beginning of an attack against the IoT. In the latter case, an actual unauthorized activity, leading to a security incident in the future, may be detected after this event.

Instead of the logs of data sources, where the raw events were fixed, it is proposed to write suspicious events and pure security events into a single PEL, data to which comes from different trusted data sources. The creation of a unified distributed DB containing only security events falls well in the BCT. It is useful to take into account typical attacks against IoT targets, which were described partially in (Miloslavskaya and Tolstoy, 2019), to formulate the events. One block will contain one single (atomic) suspicious event, atomic security event or compound from several atomic security events (Table 7.1).

It is reasonable that each block going to the BC should include references to all initial raw events for the cases if an additional analysis of the given event will be required in the future. All data sources transmitting event data to PEL should be synchronized through a reconciliation process to guarantee that the same incident is documented from different perspectives. Any incident can be described simultaneously in real-time from different viewpoints in one BC shared by them instead of storing data sources' separate records with the same events in their privately managed logs. Blocks with "pure" events will come to the main chain. Blocks with suspicious events will come to the side chain for additional analysis or wait for the arrival of blocks with events into both chains that will confirm their "pure" security events status. These blocks will be transferred to the main chain if so.

TABLE 7.1 Examples of security-related events for the IoT

Event type	Events	Data sources	Further actions
Suspicious event 1	Single (atomic) event: to access one of the IoT's services the authorized user enters his credentials three times, first two times with errors	Access Control System (ACS) of the IoT service	The block is formed for transmission to the sidechain; the event is stored in the individual DB of the ACS; the reference to the initial event is inserted in the block.
Suspicious event 2	Compound event: • To access one of the IoT services the authorized user quickly and without any mistakes types his/her credentials • The user initializes an update of a firmware of a few IoT devices (maybe to fix bugs and security vulnerabilities) • The user checks that the updates were installed successfully	• ACS of the IoT service • Task manager, user's actions recording tool (UART) • Task manager, UART, logs of the IoT devices	The block is formed for transmission to the sidechain; the separate events are stored in the individual DBs of ACS, UART and IoT devices' logs; the references to the initial events are inserted in the block.
Pure security event 1	Single (atomic) security event: In the absence of the owner, one of the sensors was replaced by a fake product	• Video Surveillance System (VSS), visual inspection of the sensor	The block is formed for transmission to the main chain; the event is stored in the DB of VSS; the reference to the initial event is inserted in the block.
Pure security event 2	Single (atomic) security event: The ping request to the remote sensor without its reply (maybe because of a DoS attack)	• No reply from the sensor on the screen in Windows Command prompt	The block is formed for transmission to the main chain; the event is stored in the special DB (as a screenshot, for example); the reference to the initial event is inserted in the block.
Pure security event 3	Compound security event: • In the absence of the owner, one of the sensors was replaced by a fake product	• Video Surveillance System (VSS) • Automated and visual checks of applications' outputs • Antivirus software on this and other	The block is formed for transmission to the main chain; the separate events are stored in the individual DBs of VSS, antivirus software, sensor's ACS, etc.; the references to the initial events are inserted in the block.

(Continued)

TABLE 7.1 (Cont.)

Event type	Events	Data sources	Further actions
	• The fake sensor generates incorrect measurement results • The fake sensor sends a virus (attaches malicious payloads) to other sensors • Somebody enters remotely the fake sensor without any authentication because it allows unauthorized access • and so on	sensors, task manager • Sensor's ACS, sensor's stack buffer overflow or changed default configurations found	

To illustrate how to form a block, let us look at the compound security event 3 from Table 7.1. In the absence of the owner, somebody replaced one of the sensors not properly controlled by a fake product for physical access to it (e.g., during non-working hours). This sensor was located in a zone being in sight of one Video Surveillance System (VSS), which recorded this action. After that, the fake sensor has begun to generate incorrect results of some measurements and to send viruses and malware. The day after somebody logged remotely in it without any authentication. No other actions have been recorded yet. A new block will contain all these events one by one excluding cases of a repeated description of the same event by different data sources (event 4 was fixed on three infected sensors) and the references to all sources with initial raw data on these events and timestamps of their occurrence or detection (Fig. 7.5). Events 6, 7 and 8 are good examples showing that one atomic security events characterize it from different sides and help to find vulnerabilities exploited by them.

One important note for the implementation of the BC-based SIEM 3.0 system: the typical atomic security events for the whole IoT can be inserted in it in the form of reusable patterns.

7.7 DISCUSSION AND CONCLUSION

It has been already noted that the BC will be updated every time a new block will come. Its size will grow very quickly. As a result, the SIEM 3.0 system will run slower over time. Therefore a technique to support its flexibility and scalability is very much required. The idea of a convolution (other terms are pruning, truncation, curtailment) can be applied for this purpose in two ways: automatic meaning the deletion of all blocks older than a pre-set lifetime for example three or six months (to have a possibility

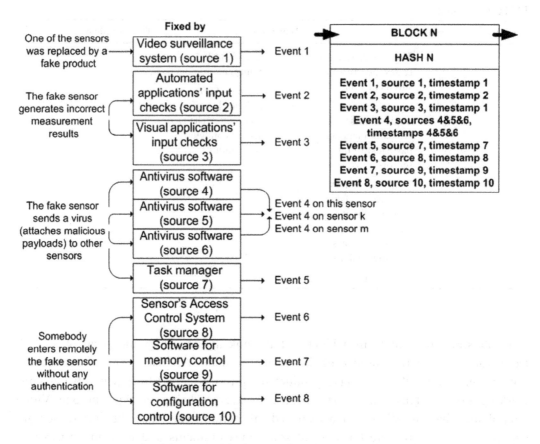

FIGURE 7.5   One example of forming a block in BC-based SIEM 3.0 system for the IoT

to gather more statistics on security incidents and to conduct its correlated analysis) or selective when a designated operator/administrator with access to the entire BC scans (manually or using a specialized application) the BC to find and remove any "expired" blocks (recall that our BC is permissioned by design). An expire block is a block with obsolete security events or suspicious events not resulted in any security incident or not being its part for a long time period, for example, one year. In other words, suspicion of this event was not justified. The main reasons why BC should be convoluted are the following:

- The obsolescence of events recorded (e.g., the related asset was withdrawn)

- Changes in the IoT's security policies and corresponding update of the incidents' registry

- An erroneous assignment of an event which has never appeared before to the category of security-related events

- The presence of a block created by mistake.

The time period before the next automatic BC convolution depends mainly on the duration of typical attacks against the IoT which varies from several seconds for short-lived (like DDoS and quick scans) to several months for long-lived (e.g., Advanced Persistent Threats) attacks.

The sidechain, where the blocks with suspicious events, are included requires more frequent convolutions to be carried out.

The selective convolution can be fulfilled by one or several authorized peers in the BC notation. First of all, the DELETE operation should be applied only to those blocks that need to be removed. This will prevent any unauthorized action for hiding attack traces and will provide storage of blocks for computer forensics.

The main issue is what to do with its cryptographic links to the previous and following blocks, which should be linked together when removing a block. The convoluted BC's integrity can be restored due to the usage of the references to the initial events from data sources which are fixed in the previous block. The timestamp fixing the time of the event occurrence or detection added to the block can also help to do this. At present, the convolution technique for BC has not yet reached maturity. It deserves separate detailed consideration, which is beyond the scope of this chapter.

As it was found later, the idea of removing blocks from the BC has been developing by us in parallel to Dr. G. Ateniese and the Accenture Company. They propose so-called "redactable BC" (Ateniese et al., 2017) with modified chameleon hashes (Krawchyk and Rabin, 1997) that allow designated authorities to edit and remove previous blocks without breaking the BC by means of building a virtual padlock on the link connecting the block to be changed and its successor. After that, the chameleon hash key is used to unlock this link and to substitute the block with a new one without breaking the hash chain.

Then the resulting BC-based SIEM 3.0 system should be tested for satisfying the requirements for the SIEM systems. A methodology should be chosen in advance for proving that it is realizable, complete, consistent, unambiguous, and verifiable although the system is not yet implemented. The Z notation (ISO/IEC 13568, 2002) is one of the possible solutions having a standard status. It can be used for modeling by means of mathematical notation various computing and among other security systems such as communication and transaction processing systems to which a SIEM system can be attributed. Specifying the BC-based SIEM 3.0 system in such a way aids the under-standing of its functioning and assists its development and maintenance. Another possibility is to apply a tool-supported B method, which is the most popular in industry projects and safety-critical system applications (Lano, 1996). The B method allows for highly accurate expressions of the properties required by specifications and models systems in their environment. It solves some limitations of Z, for example, supports consistency checking (ensures the operations conducted by the abstract machine do not invalidate the invariant) and refinement checking (ensures each machine is a valid refinement of a previous machine), which is crucial for the BCT's application and real-time software. After comparison, we chose the B method. We understand that its application will reveal the limitations of the results obtained that should be addressed in our future work.

For the evaluation of BC-based SIEM 3.0 system's efficiency (performance) from goal-centered and system resources views, the main indicators are typical for this kind of systems: downtime, idle time, response time, work in case of temporary limited resources, operating modes and frequency of need for maintenance and modification, data loss, unreliable system outputs in form of false positives/negatives, the ability to interface with various types of IPTs and to update incident classifications, SIEM administrator's and operators' satisfaction with output format, content or timeliness and so on, as well it SIEM's self-protection against typical attacks (like DoS attacks, blocking of data transmission channels from the IPTs, attempts of erasure data on events, etc.).

The BC-based SIEM 3.0 system should be run on a secure dedicated network of servers protected by traditional network security controls and should support BC's copies with offline back-ups. Its main security advantages are robustness (more in terms of integrity) and operational resilience as the ability to adjust its functioning to sustain operations during expected conditions and in the face of escalating demands, disturbances and unforeseen circumstances (Nemeth, Hollnagel, and Dekker, 2009). Thus the private BC-based SIEM 3.0 system provides highly-verifiable data sets with a high degree of trust in integrity and security of the BC as a whole as well as all its separate blocks and their sequence for security management for the IoT. This SIEM system will serve as a single window into the IoT's security health when integrated with IPTs as data sources.

To sum up, it can be concluded that the Chapter shows the full applicability of the BC concept to the creation of secure BC-based IoT and the next-generation SIEM 3.0 systems designed to detect security incidents in a modern fully interconnected network environment like the IoT. The most important area of future work is to bring to life the ideas proposed. The implementation, deployment, and testing onto a real-world IoT will show their viability or a need to work out more sophisticated models as very many open questions still remain. How to arrange streaming and correlation analytics of blocks' content containing events taking place in the IoT? How to visualize the results obtained after deep analysis to find insights and patterns in historical BC data for better incident management in the IoT? The list of questions can be continued indefinitely for a full-fledged design of the SIEM 3.0 system proposed.

Recently, there is a huge amount of investment from the industries, as well as significant interest from academia, to solve major BCT's research challenges. For example, the consensus protocols as its major building blocks are targets for different attacks. At the same time, the BC's forks, as well as the maintenance of several BCS requiring a significant amount of power consumption, become the significant research issues.

ACKNOWLEDGEMENT

This work was supported by the MEPhI Academic Excellence Project (agreement with the Ministry of Education and Science of the Russian Federation of August 27, 2013, project no. 02.a03.21.0005) and possibly the Russian Foundation of Basic Research (its decision on funding as of 03.03.2019 has not announced).

REFERENCES

Al-Fuqaha, A., Guizani, M., Mohammadi, M., Aledhari, M., and Ayyash, M. 2015. Internet of Things: A Survey on Enabling Technologies, Protocols, and Applications. *IEEE Communication Surveys and Tutorials*, 17(4), pp. 2347–2376.

Ateniese, G., Magri, B., Venturi, D., and Andrade, E. 2017. Redactable Blockchain – Or – Rewriting History in Bitcoin and Friends. https://eprint.iacr.org/2016/757.pdf (accessed March 3, 2019).

Bassi, A., Bauer, M., Fiedler, M., Kramp, T., van Kranenburg, R., Lange, S., and Meissner, S. 2013. *Enabling Things to Talk*. Heibelberg New York Dordrecht, London: Springer. 349 p.

Belkeziz, R., and Jarir, Z. 2017. IoT Coordination: Designing a Context-Driven Architecture. *Proceedings of the 2017 13th International Conference on Signal-Image Technology & Internet-Based Systems (SITIS)*. DOI: 10.1109/SITIS.2017.70.

Bluemix. 2017. Blockchain Basics. https://console.bluemix.net/docs/services/blockchain/ibmblockchain_overview.html (accessed March 3, 2019).

European Commission. 2008. Internet of Things in 2020. A Roadmap for the Future. https://docbox.etsi.org/erm/Open/CERP%2020080609-10/Internet-of-Things_in_2020_EC-EPoSS_Workshop_Report_2008_v1-1.pdf (accessed March 3, 2019).

European Union Agency For Network And Information Security (ENISA). 2017. Baseline Security Recommendations for IoT in the Context of Critical Information Infrastructures. www.enisa.europa.eu/publications/baseline-security-recommendations-for-iot (accessed March 3, 2019).

Gartner Top 10 Strategic Technology Trends for 2019. 2018. www.gartner.com/smarterwithgartner/gartner-top-10-strategic-technology-trends-for-2019/ (accessed March 3, 2019).

ISO/IEC 13568:2002/Cor 1:2007 Information Technology – Z Formal Specification Notation – Syntax, Type System and Semantics.

ISO/IEC 27000:2018 Information Technology – Security Techniques – Information Security Management Systems – Overview and Vocabulary.

ISO/IEC 27035-1:2016 Information Technology – Security Techniques – Information Security Incident Management – Part 1: Principles of Incident Management.

ISO/IEC 30141:2018 Internet of Things (Iot) – Reference Architecture.

ITU-T Y.2068 Functional framework and capabilities of the Internet of things. 2015.

Khan, R., Khan, S. U., Zaheer, R., and Khan, S. 2012. Future Internet: The Internet of Things Architecture, Possible Applications and Key Challenges. *Proceedings of the 10th International Conference on Frontiers of Information Technology (FIT 2012)*. Pp. 257–260.

Krawchyk, H., and Rabin, T. 1997. Chameleon Hashing and Signatures. https://eprint.iacr.org/1998/010.ps (accessed March 3, 2019).

Kruijff, J., and Weigand, H. 2017. Understanding the Blockchain Using Enterprise Ontology. In *The Proceedings of CAISE2017*. www.researchgate.net/publication/316636055_Understanding_the_Blockchain_Using_Enterprise_Ontology (accessed March 3, 2019).

Lano, K. 1996. *The B Language and Method: A Guide to Practical Formal Development*. Secaucus, NJ: Springer-Verlag New York, Inc.

Medici. 2017. Know More about Blockchain: Overview, Technology, Application Areas and Use Cases. https://gomedici.com/an-overview-of-blockchain-technology/ (accessed March 3, 2019).

Miloslavskaya, N. 2018a. Analysis of SIEM Systems and Their Usage in Security Operations and Security Intelligence Centers. In: Samsonovich, A., and Klimov, V. (eds) *Biologically Inspired Cognitive Architectures (BICA) for Young Scientists. BICA 2017. Advances in Intelligent Systems and Computing*. Springer, Cham, Vol. 636, pp. 282–288. DOI: 10.1007/978-3-319-63940-6_40.

Miloslavskaya, N. 2018b. Designing Blockchain-Based SIEM 3.0 System. *Information and Computer Security (UK)*, 26(4). DOI: 10.1108/ics-10-2017-0075.

Miloslavskaya, N., and Tolstoy, A. 2019. Internet of Things: Information Security Challenges and Solutions. *Cluster Computing*, 22, pp. 103–119. DOI: 10.1007/s10586-018-2823-6.

Mishra, N., Lin, C. C., and Chang, H. T. 2014. A Cognitive Oriented Framework for IoT Big-Data Management Prospective. *Proceedings of the 2014 IEEE International Conference on Communication Problem-Solving*. DOI: 10.1109/ICCPS.2014.7062233.

Nemeth, C.P., Hollnagel, E., and Dekker, S. 2009. *Resilience Engineering Perspectives, Volume 2: Preparation and Restoration*. CRC Press, Taylor & Francis. 288 p

Nielson, B. 2017. Blockchain Solutions for Cyber & Data Security. https://richtopia.com/emerging-technologies/blockchain-solutions-for-cyber-data-security (accessed March 3, 2019).

NIST SP 800-61 Rev. 2. Computer Security Incident Handling Guide. 2012.

OpenBlockchain. 2017. Researching the Potential of Blockchains. http://blockchain.open.ac.uk/ (accessed March 3, 2019).

PriceWaterhouseCoopers. 2016. Making Sense of Bitcoin, Cryptocurrency, and Blockchain. www.pwc.com/us/en/financial-services/fintech/bitcoin-blockchain-cryptocurrency.html (accessed March 3, 2019).

Primechaintech. 2018. Blockchain Security Controls. www.primechaintech.com/docs/blockchain_security_controls.pdf (accessed March 3, 2019).

Recommendation ITU-T Y.2060. 06/2012. *Next Generation Networks – Frameworks and Functional Architecture Models – Overview of the Internet of Things*. International Telecommunication Union. www.itu.int/rec/T-REC-Y.2060-201206-I

Singh, D., Tripathi, G., and Jara, A. 2015. Secure Layers Based Architecture for Internet of Things. *2015 IEEE 2nd World Forum on Internet of Things (WF-IoT)*. DOI: 10.1109/WF-IoT.2015.7389074.

TopTeny. 2018. Top 10 Cyber Security Trends to Look for in 2019. www.topteny.com/top-10-cyber-security-trends-to-look-for-in-2019/ (accessed March 3, 2019).

UK Government, Office for Science. 2016. Distributed Ledger Technology: Beyond Block Chain (Report). https://assets.publishing.service.gov.uk/government/uploads/system/uploads/attachment_data/file/492972/gs-16-1-distributed-ledger-technology.pdf (accessed March 3, 2019).

Weigong, L. V., Fanchao, M., Ce, Z., Yuefei, L. V., Ning, C., and Jianan, J. 2017. Research on Unified Architecture of IoT System. *Proceedings of the 2017 IEEE International Conference on Computational Science and Engineering (CSE) and IEEE International Conference on Embedded and Ubiquitous Computing (EUC)*. DOI: 10.1109/CSE-EUC.2017.249.

Wilson, S. 2017. How It Works: Blockchain Explained in 500 Words. www.zdnet.com/article/blockchain-explained-in-500-words/ (accessed March 3, 2019).

Yaga, D., Mell, P., Roby, N., and Scarfone, K. October 2018. NISTIR 8202 Blockchain Technology Overview. https://nvlpubs.nist.gov/nistpubs/ir/2018/NIST.IR.8202.pdf (accessed March 3, 2019).

Yang, A., Peng, Y., Yue, Y., Wang, X., Yang, Y., and Liu, W. 2011. Study and Application on the Architecture and Key Technologies for IOT. *Proceedings of the 2011 International Conference On in Multimedia Technology (ICMT 2011)*. Pp. 747–751.

Zhong, C., Zhu, Z., and Huang, R.2017. Study on the IOT Architecture and Access Technology. *Proceedings of the 2017 16th International Symposium on Distributed Computing and Applications to Business, Engineering and Science*. DOI: 10.1109/DCABES.2017.32.

CHAPTER 8

IoT Security using Blockchain

Hanif Ullah[1], Mamun Abu-Tair[1], Aftab Ali[1], Kashif Rabbani[1], Joshua Daniel[2], Joe Rafferty[1], Zhiwei Lin[1], Philip Morrow[1], and Gery Ducatel[2]

[1] *Ulster University, UK*

[2] *British Telecom, UK*

CONTENTS

This chapter addresses security issues with respect to the Internet of Things (IoT) and in particular investigates the use of blockchain technology to address these issues. Some foundational concepts, related to the topic are highlighted, including smart contracts, verifiable claims, self-sovereign identity, along with General Data Protection Regulation (GDPR) and Network and Information Security (NIS) principles. Beyond the block chain-based solution, a secure IoT architecture based on blockchain technology is also presented.

8.1 INTRODUCTION

Analysts and researchers have predicted that the emergence of the IoT is creating an ecosystem where hundreds of thousands of IoT services will connect billions of IoT devices by the year 2026. It is also suggested that with such rapid growth in smart devices and high-speed networks providing a variety of IoT services, the entire ecosystem could be exposed to fraud and security attacks. An example of one such attack is the famous Mirai attack which affected millions of internet-connected devices and temporarily crippled the servers of some well-known services such as Twitter, Netflix, and PayPal [1]. In order to cope with such attacks, not only the IoT devices themselves but the overall deployment architecture needs to be secured from attacks to protect privacy, integrity, and data confidentiality [2].

Recently, tremendous efforts have been made to address these security issues in the context of IoT, for example Sicari, Rizzardi, et al. [3] discussed security and privacy requirements in terms of data confidentiality and authentication. The authors also discussed access control within the IoT network, privacy and trust among users and things, and middleware security along with the enforcement of security and privacy policies. This was a very good effort to draw the attention of academia and industry towards the security and privacy issues of IoT infrastructure.

Similarly, Zhou, Cao, et al. [4] introduced an architecture with some unique security and privacy requirements for the next generation of mobile technologies and cloud-based IoT. The authors identified issues in existing works, and proposed a new efficient, privacy preserving, data aggregation mechanism. This mechanism addressed these deficiencies by being able to operate without public key, homomorphic encryption. Historically reliance on homomorphic encryption has had several limitations such as the performance is entirely infeasible at worst, while extremely bad at best. Also, the key size, encryption operation, and key generation exponentially grows with the increase in security which in turn degrades the overall performance of the system [5]. The developed novel mechanism addressed the deficiencies and enabled more efficient secure packet forwarding and privacy preserving authentication. Future directions in terms of enhancing the proposed technique for smart grid IoT applications to protect individual's real-time power usage data from exposure while judging the peak/off-peak status of the total power consumption for all consumers in a specific region were also highlighted.

Despite all of the efforts made to secure the IoT through conventional security and privacy approaches IoT is still experiencing privacy and security vulnerabilities issues. The main reason for these issues is the decentralised topology and the resource-constraints of many devices in the context of conventional security and privacy techniques.

In 2008, a technology with the name of Bitcoin [6] was launched where the technology incorporated a changeable public key that was used as a user identity to provide anonymity and privacy [7]. The main technology behind Bitcoin is blockchain, a distributed ledger database that is shared, replicated, and synchronised among the members of a decentralised network. The transactions in terms of assets (cars, homes, patents, certificates etc.) or data that is shared or exchanged among the participants in the network can be stored in distributed ledger database. Blockchain has also characteristics such as:

- Tamper evident: This means that an asset or data cannot be changed, without this being noticed by all members of the network. Blockchain is not only tamper-evident, but also tamper-proof (the data or asset cannot be tampered with). Both these properties enable the blockchain to be immutable.

- Distributed to all members of the network: This means that the database is shared among all the participants of the network, and no transaction can be approved without the consensus of all members of that network.

- Records the transactions in a public or private peer-to-peer network in a sequential chain of cryptographic hash-linked blocks: All the transactions are stored in hash-linked blocks in a sequential order. Each block is linked to the previous block through cryptographic hashes that ensure the authenticity and integrity of transactions.

All the confirmed and validated transaction blocks are part of these hash-linked chains starting from the beginning till the most recent one, and only the members of a blockchain network can view those transactions that are relevant to them [8].

Similarly, Nick Szabo, a cryptographer and legal scholar introduced Smart Contracts (SC) in 1994, which helps to exchange money, property, shares, or anything of value in a transparent, conflict-free way while avoiding the services of any third-party/middleman [9]. Smart contracts are essentially blocks of pre-written computer code that are stored and replicated on a distributed storage platform, potentially executed by a network of computers that can result in ledger updates [10]. Just like traditional contracts, smart contracts not only define the rules and penalties related to an agreement, but also automatically enforce those obligations. SCs can be assured by Verifiable Claims (VC), which is a qualification, achievement, quality, or piece of information about an entity background such as name, government ID, payment provider, or University degree [11].

Verifiable claims enable SC parties and other entities to have control over the data associated with identities in terms of sharing and providing access to other bodies specifying what data they can access and under what circumstances. In order to strengthen the concept of smart contracts and verifiable claims, the idea of Self Sovereign Identity (SSI) was introduced. SSI in general means that the individual has ownership over his/her personal data and control over how, when, and to whom their personal data should be revealed [12]. SSI is basically a digital equivalent to our paper-based identities such as driving license, passport, birth certificate etc. that are digitally stored in a wallet created by the owner with a unique self-generated identification number based on a public and private key combination. The owner then uses this identification number along with identity claims to verify and attest his/her claims from the concerned authorities. These attested claims can be presented as a proof of identity information or document. For example, if the identity owner wants to hire a car, the car renting authority will ask for a proof of identity document (e.g. driving license). The owner will present an attested claim verified by the licensing authority instead of revealing the actual driving license information. In this manner, SSI will address the issues of massive data breach, will increase the efficiency of different companies to get the identity assurances in their identity verification process, and will allow the individuals to decide how their personal data can be shared and monetised without the involvement of any third-party identity providers such as Google and Facebook [13].

8.1.1 IoT Security Overview

With the rapid growth of smart devices and high-speed networks, the IoT has gained huge popularity through providing an integration of various sensors and objects that can communicate directly without the involvement of any human being. It is expected that by 2022, the number of connected IoT devices will number approximately 29 billion [14]. This large base of devices will exacerbate the issues discussed previously by providing a large and diverse attack area. These issues will need to be addressed with proper techniques and mechanisms.

Sicari, Rizzardi, et al. [3] analysed the available approaches with respect to confidentiality and access control in terms of IoT. They also highlighted the security and trust issues to ensure policy enforcement in IoT applications along with middleware security and security of mobile IoT devices. Sha, Wei, et al. [15] analysed the security challenges which arise from new topographies of IoT applications and along with some potential solutions that could help to address the issues. The authors also considered the inadequacies of the existing security solutions in the context of three main IoT application areas: smart home, smart grid, and smart connected health. A comparative study of the three architectural security designs/layers (including things layer, cloud layer, and edge layer) with some implemented examples was also carried out to highlight the security concerns in respect to each architecture layer. The authors concluded their work by identifying some open issues at each layer of the IoT architecture. For example, building a secure and efficient edge layer to securely connect edge devices and to organise them in a way to perform complicated security tasks efficiently. Intrusion detection and threat analysis at the edge layer is also of great interest. Similarly, distributing the security tasks to each layer, minimising the complexity of security solutions and preserving privacy in situations when all three layers are involved in a specific solution, and implementing distributed security analysis across multiple layers are the issues that needs to be addressed in the future.

Similarly, a threat model for IoT security is presented here. For example, In [16], the authors provide an extensive survey of vulnerabilities along with countermeasures with respect to the edge-side layer of IoT. The authors investigated three distinct IoT reference models, identified different threats and attacks along with possible solutions. Vulnerabilities and threats were mainly addressed at edge nodes, communication, and the edge computing level of the edge-side layer of the IoT. At the edge nodes level, the authors explored the vulnerabilities with respect to hardware Trojans, non-network side-channel attacks, Denial of Service (DoS) attacks (battery draining, sleep deprivation, and outage attacks), tampering, node replication, and malicious nodes etc. Similarly, at the communication level, attacks such as eavesdropping, side-channel attacks, DoS (continuous jamming and intermittent jamming), routing, injecting fraudulent packets, and unauthorised conversation were addressed. While at the edge computing level, malicious injection, integrity attacks against machine learning, side-channel attacks, inadequate testing, and insufficient logging were explored. The authors also proposed potential solutions for each of these attacks at different levels.

8.1.2 Blockchain Overview

Before exploring blockchain, the underlying technology of the distributed ledger should be understood. A distributed ledger is a type of database that records transactions among the participants of the network and is shared, replicated, and synchronised across the decentralised network. This decentralisation property offers the facility of multiple copies of the identical data across multiple computers. Participants of the network govern and authenticate/agree any updates to the records in the ledger by consensus and without the involvement of any third-party mediator. Also, the data is publically verifiable based on integrity and transparency. Integrity assures that the retrieved data is uncorrupted and unaltered since its last update, while transparency assures how and by whom the data was changed over time. In contrast, the current conventional business ledgers are:

- Expensive: In a centralised network infrastructure, data exchanges are usually authorised by third-party mediators, which incurs cost. Also, the performance can be compromised [14].

- Subject to misuse and tampering: As the data is administered by a third-party, if the security of the responsible authority is compromised, the data can be misused, or even deleted without the knowledge of the data owner.

- Exposure to corruption and fraud with lack of transparency: Any hacker who obtained access to the data can corrupt it, can steal the data and can provide it to any third party.

In order to cope with all these deficiencies, blockchain was introduced. Blockchain is a distributed digital ledger that records the transactions in a sequential chain of cryptographic hash-linked blocks in a public or private peer-to-peer network that is distributed in nature to all member nodes and is tamper-evident [8]. Each block has two main parts i.e. a header and a body. The header part carries the hash value (identifier) along with some other meta information, while the body part carries/stores the transactions. The identifier is calculated based on the cryptographic hash and keeps the blocks linked with each other just like a chain. If by any means a hacker obtained access to any block and changed its contents, the identifier for that particular block will no longer be valid. This will also affect the identifiers of all the subsequent blocks [14].

The driving technology behind blockchain is Bitcoin which is a unit of the Bitcoin digital currency (BTC). In order to store and track the transactions performed in blockchain using the bitcoin, a ledger file is used, which is distributed across the world by a network of private computers represented by nodes. These nodes are responsible for both storing data and executing network related computation, such as transactions.

To explain the proper working of the blockchain, let us take an example where Alice wants to send some bitcoins to Bob. Alice will broadcast the message to the network mentioning that the amount of bitcoins in her account should be debited (let say 10 BTC), and the same should be credited to Bobs account [17]. Figure 8.1 shows a typical transaction broadcast message across the network where both the ledger files are updated after the validation process by the network nodes. A debit of 10 BTC can be seen in Bob's ledger with respect to Alice's account, while a credit of same amount can be seen in Bob's account. This means that all the transactions in blockchain are transparent and any kind of change or variation can easily be detected and traced.

Blockchain is not only restricted to Bitcoins but can also be used for a number of other applications. Tama, Kweka, et al. [18] reviewed state-of-the-art blockchain applications including financial services, healthcare, business and industry, and IoT security etc. Fernández-Caramés and Fraga-Lamas [19] presented an approach on how to adapt blockchain to accommodate the specific needs of IoT and to develop blockchain-based IoT (BIoT)

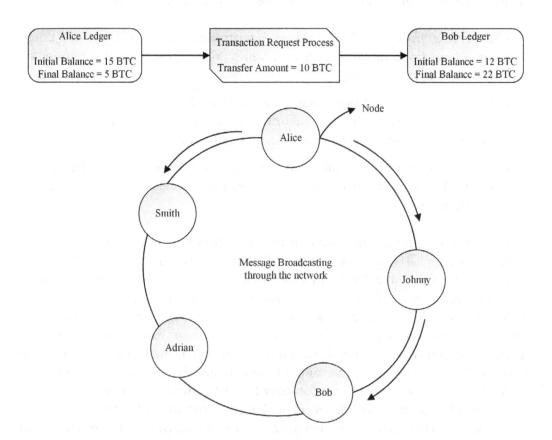

FIGURE 8.1 Transaction request and message broadcasting over the network

applications. The authors also explored the current challenges that may affect the design, development, and deployment of BIoT applications. BIoT applications such as energy, transportation, smart objects, fleet monitoring and management, industry (logistics), personal sensing (smart living and healthcare), smart cities, defence and public safety, telecommunication and information system were mainly considered. Challenges with respect to BIoT applications in terms of privacy, security (confidentiality, availability, integrity), energy efficiency, throughput and latency, blockchain size, bandwidth, and infrastructure along with some other issues were also addressed. Finally, the authors highlighted some of the future challenges and provide recommendations in order to cope with those challenges.

Lee [20] utilised blockchain technology to create a new blockchain based ID as a service (BIDaaS) for authentication and identity management between a BIDaaS provider and its partners. Three different identities (BIDaaS provider, partner, and user) were involved to implement the proposed idea through a practical example for mobile users of a telecommunication company. The authentication phase of the proposed system is carried by establishing a mutual authentication between the user and the partner without creating any ID and sharing any prior information. The BIDaaS provider basically maintains the BIDaaS private blockchain, while the partner can access the BIDaaS blockchain with certain permissions (read only). Initially, by using the digital signature, the user's virtual ID and public key along with some other information will be stored on the BIDaaS blockchain by the BIDaaS provider. Upon a receipt for accessing any service from the user, the partner will verify the user's virtual ID by accessing the BIDaaS blockchain, and if the ID matches, the partner will permit the user to access the particular service. In this case, mutual authentication has successfully occurred without any prior information from the user to the partner [20].

8.1.3 Smart Contracts

Smart contracts were first introduced by Nick Szabo in 1994. According to Szabo [21], a smart contract is basically a computerised transaction protocol that mainly implements the terms and conditions of a contract. The main purpose of smart contract is to minimise the involvement of any trusted third-party mediators between participating parties, diminish any malicious and unintended exceptions, and satisfy the communal contractual conditions in terms of payments, confidentiality, and implementation. Smart contracts in the context of blockchain are the scripts that reside inside a chain with a unique address that are stored on the blockchain. It a particular transaction, the smart contract will be executed independently and automatically on every node over the network based on the information included in the triggering transaction [22]. Similarly, in terms of IoT networks, smart contracts are an astonishing asset that offers higher degree of coordination and authority and guarantees proper cohesion with respect to managing transactions and interactions between the participating bodies. Incorporating blockchain in an IoT ecosystem is a twofold process, where on one side blockchain distributes the nature of a ledger, while on the other side smart contracts extend the functionality of the ledger by introducing the terms and conditions of the agreement [23].

8.1.4 Verifiable Claims

Despite the tremendous enhancements in internet technology over the last few decades, digital identities, also known as claims, are quite hard to trust due to their verification over the internet. Instead, physical credentials such as a passport, driving license etc. for renting a car, or hotel booking are quite easy to validate by the verifier. The question arises as to how these physical credentials can be transferred to digital identities that can act as claims for registration, login etc. purposes over the internet [24]. The World Wide Web Consortium (W3C) for the first time started an initiative to standardise digital credentials in April 2017 in order to solve the problem of digital credential verification. According to W3C, a verifiable claim is a claim that is efficiently fiddle-proof and the authorship can be authenticated/verified cryptographically [25].

Verifiable claims consist of three basic terminologies i.e. entity, subject, and claim. An entity is an object/thing with discrete and autonomous presence, for instance a device, person, concept, or organisation. A subject is the object about which the claim will be made, while a claim is a declaration/statement about the subject initiated by an entity. A verifiable claim works in a way such that the issuer (individual, government, corporation etc.) creates a claim with respect to a specific subject that is then transferred to a particular holder (student, employee, customer etc.). The holder then presents this claim to the verifier (employer, security personnel, website etc.) for verification process, while the verifier validates the authenticity of the claim through the registry (distributed ledger, government ID database, employee database etc.) [25].

8.1.5 Self-Sovereign Identity

Verifiable claims have solved the problem of digital credential verification but finding a way to standardise the procedure of how to verify the digital signatures of issuers is challenging. A simple solution to this problem is the public key infrastructure (PKI), but PKI is costly (in terms of individuals) and is centralised. Also, the involvement of a third party (middleman) itself is a vulnerability that can lead to a security lapse, censorship, or single point of failure. To resolve these issues, again W3C introduced a new idea called a decentralised identifier (DID) that enables true self-sovereign identity [24]. With self-sovereign identity, every person will be able to create and manage his/her own digital credentials without the involvement of any third party (independent of identity administration), and with the characteristics of being self-controlled, persistent, portable, interoperable, along with full access to his/her own data with protected rights [26,27].

8.1.6 NIS Directive and GDPR Principles for IoT Security

Services, data and the network are the most vital elements that reside at the heart of any IoT Ecosystem. To safeguard services, data, network and enhance cyber security levels we needed trust. This was achieved through Article 11, Chapter III [28] and GDPR under bullet point 7 [29] which would also lead to digital single market. These directives on security of Network and Information systems (NIS directive) and the

General Data Protection Regulation (GDPR) was assimilated by the European Commission on 6 July 2016 and 27 April 2016 respectively.

The NIS directives were formulated with the intention of protecting the network and information systems which would elevate security across the European Union. In particular guidance is provided mainly for service providers and data controllers as to how they should operate as described under Article 1 of the NIS directives [30]. Conversely GDPR protects the interest of a person as to how his/her personal data would be processed and the migration and repealing of such data through a data controller or a data processor intending to give the data subject total control over their personal data as described under Article 5 [31]. NIS not only considers personal data produced from an IoT device that resides in the network and information systems but also other data that resides in such network and information system. The NIS directives and the GDPR combined intend to protect the two sections of the society in the digital world. On one hand, there are the operators of essential services and digital service providers for a particular IoT service for any use case scenario whose security constraints are derived from the NIS directives. While on the other hand there are individual data subjects of a particular IoT device whose security liability is protected by the GDPR.

In a specific scenario where if an IoT device produces data safeguarded by GDPR and the data travels through the network of any organisation or service provider working under the strict regulations and directives of GDPR and NIS, then during this process if a security incident occurs both the GDPR and the NIS will be triggered. An organisation can be fined, and further actions can be taken against this organisation under both laws.

Under the NIS directives Article 16 [30] the digital service provider for the IoT service shall notify all entities of a security breach or disruption to a competent authority in accordance with the law supervised by the member states in the European Union. After consultation the public would be notified either by a designated authority or by the digital service provider themselves. However, under GDPR if any data breach occurs in accordance with Article 33 and Article 34 [31], it has to be categorised as "High risk", "Medium Risk" and "Low Risk" and then the data controller has to inform the regulatory authority in all cases but inform the data subject in the case of a data breach tagged under "High Risk".

Article 9 [31] under the GDPR categorises personal data for processing to safeguard the rights and freedom of data subjects using a particular IoT device, but no such categorisation of personal data has been outlined by the NIS under Article 2 [30].

8.2 IOT SECURITY ARCHITECTURE USING BLOCKCHAIN

In this section we will provide a brief overview of the state of the art IoT security architectures along with the existing solutions for IoT security using blockchain. Also, an IoT architecture based on blockchain technology will also be proposed.

8.2.1 State of the Art IoT Security Architecture

IoT infrastructure provided a new shape to future internet communications by enabling imbedded computing devices to communicate with one another using internet communication protocols [32], such as HTTP. A comparative analysis of different IoT frameworks has been presented in [33]. The authors analyzed the frameworks in terms of methodologies used, supported protocols, hardware requirements, and applications development. The protocols used in IoT are standardised and made available in the Institute of Electrical and Electronics Engineers (IEEE) and Internet Engineering Task Force (IETF) protocol stack [34]. The protocol stack defines the mechanisms for communicating between these resource constrained devices by keeping in mind the low-energy requirements, applicability and reusability of the IoT applications. Due to the involvement of different communication devices and protocols in an IoT architecture, the associated security risks may also vary i.e., wireless sensor network (WSN) and machine to machine (M2M) security risks and requirements are different. Moreover, the requirements at each layer of the protocol stack needs to be understood in order to reach an optimal solution. An illustration of a protocol stack for IoT is given in Figure 8.2.

The following subsections will briefly discuss the security requirements, challenges and possible solutions for an IoT environment at each layer of the Open Systems

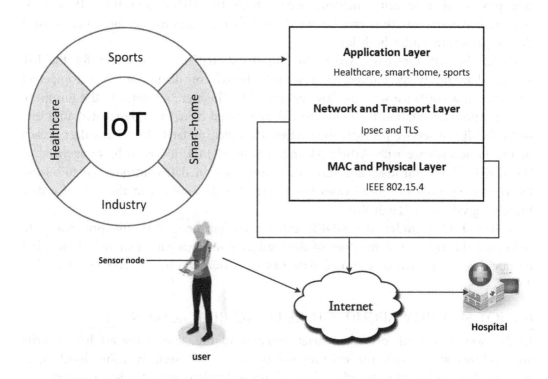

FIGURE 8.2   A layered approach to IoT communication

Interconnection (OSI) model. In particular, the subsections will cover the application layer, network and transport layer, and data link and physical layer threats and solutions.

8.2.1.1 Application Layer Security

IoT incorporates a vast variety of applications such as, healthcare technologies and smart environments. Therefore, it inherits different application specific attacks and risks. IoT provides a candidate environment where malware can easily create and control botnets. A good example is the Mirai [1] Linux-based malware, that caused the 2016 internet outage in the US by utilising a distributed denial of service (DDOS) attack. Mirai scanned the internet for open telnet and ssh ports with the default passwords. In this way Mirai was successful in creating a botnet of never before seen proportions. Another similar attack was IRCTelnet which targeted Linux-based insecure IoT devices to recruit them and subsequently participate in attacks, such as DDOS.

In [35] the authors provided a comprehensive review of continuous authentication mechanisms. The authors developed a wearable plantar bio-feature extractor by employing a commercial pressure sensor and a Raspberry PI platform. These features are then utilised to construct a continues authentication mechanism. The scheme uses Support Vector Machine with Gaussian Radial Basis Function (SVM-GRBF) learning technique to accurately extract the user's plantar pressure patterns as major data analysis features for the classifiers.

8.2.1.2 Network and Transport Layer Security

In [36] a Software Defined Network (SDN) gateway-based solution for IoT traffic analysis is presented. All the traffic must pass through the gateway which subsequently then detects abnormal behavior in traffic flows by pattern analysis. The solution will raise an alarm if a traffic pattern falls outside of historically derived expected traffic patterns.

FlowFence [37] is a denial of service (DoS) attack detection and mitigation mechanism. FlowFence runs as a daemon on a router to detect congestion by using SDN to administrate the bandwidth assignment of controlled links. FlowFence ensures a fair bandwidth allocation for each user and prevents any unexpected traffic from abusing the whole communication system.

The authors in [38] provided an overview of cyber-attacks in fog-to-thing computing environments. The authors discussed the limitation of existing cryptographic solutions which originate from the original design goals of the solutions. Namely, these solutions were developed to tackle security issues of traditional internet communication. The authors found that the previous machine-learning-based attack detection mechanisms are not suitable for IoT infrastructure for several reasons including the following:

- System development flaws.
- Increased number of susceptible points.
- Improved hacking skills.

These issues can leave some potential loopholes in the system which can cause serious security attacks. To tackle these issues a distributed deep learning-based attack detection scheme for fog-to-things computing is used. The authors concluded that by using a deep learning-based solution accuracy and efficiency of cyber-attack detection could be improved in fog-to-things environments.

Wireless channels are considered to be one of the most commonly used communication mediums of IoT devices/things. In [39] the authors provided a comprehensive review of the most relevant wireless communication standards used in IoT environment. They addressed wireless communication security challenges in IoT environments such as the increasing number of IoT devices will increase the chances for eavesdropping, covert channels and malicious nodes, and information leakage.

8.2.1.3 Data Link and Physical Layer Communications

In recent years a lot of research effort has been made in designing a secure architecture for IoT communications. The international protocol standard 802.15.4 [40] defines the security requirements for data link layer communication in low-rate wireless personal area networks. In this regard, Chakrabarty et al. in [41] describe a Software Defined Network (SDN) architecture for secure communication in IoT using IEEE 802.15.4. The scheme secures meta-data and the payload within 802.15.4 link layer communications by considering a SDN centralised controller as a trusted third party for secure routing and optimised system performance management. The authors in [42] analyzed the tradeoff between link layer security and energy consumption for IoT devices communication. The analysis shows that security in IoT infrastructure will come at a cost of higher energy consumption.

8.2.2 Existing IoT Security with Blockchain

In 2008, the first blockchain platform was introduced by Satoshi Nakamoto [6] for cryptocurrency systems. A blockchain is a publicly shared back-ordered list of hash functions in a peer-to-peer environment. The popularity of blockchain-based cryptocurrencies during the last five years has increased enormously. It is evident from the applications of blockchain in most of the aspects of communication, that blockchain based solutions are more secure and reliable compared to ordinary solutions. This is because, the blockchain works in a synchronised and regularly updated decentralised peer-to-peer network. Hence, there is no single point of failure and a massive amount of computing power would be required to access every instance [43]. A basic IoT architecture using blockchain is depicted in Figure 8.3, where the transaction of every IoT entity is authenticated and recorded in a blockchain. A brief description of some blockchain-based security architectures for IoT environments follows.

In a blockchain, every member (i.e. the owner and the device) is addressable by the hash value of a public key. Upon a new transaction, the owner of the transaction encrypts the hash value of the block by using their private key. All other members of the blockchain will have to decrypt the hash value with their private keys. In this manner, only authorised members can access the blockchain and the transactions within.

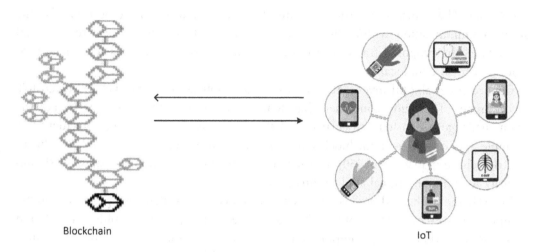

Blockchain   IoT

FIGURE 8.3   IoT using Blockchain

Currently most of the IoT architectures are centralised and depend upon some centralised security servers. To improve the performance of the IoT in terms of security, blockchain-based security mechanisms will potentially provide an optimal security and privacy option. Moreover, as discussed earlier the use of blockchain will bring decentralisation to IoT architectures, which will eventually solve many inherited problems coming from centralised IoT architectures [44].

Huang et al. in [45] propose a decentralised trusted data exchange solution using blockchain for IoT environments. The solution is a layered approach consisting of Data, Network, Protocol and Interaction Layers. The data layer is responsible for storing and exchanging data using a blockchain network. The role of the Network layer is granting access to, and transmission of data. IoT data management is done by the application layer (management layer), while mobile and web interfaces are used to facilitate communication between network peers. In the interaction layer user interfacing is provided by web or mobile applications. Similarly, the network layer defines the network topology (e.g. peer-to-peer), access methods and storage (e.g. cloud-based storage).

Another decentralised approach for secure data exchange is provided in [46], where the authors guaranteed secure economic transactions by incorporating a blockchain-based solution. The authors developed a blockchain-based prototype to replace a conventional trust-based coffee shop payment solution (i.e. shifting from a trust-based to a trust-free solution).

In [47] the authors proposed a decentralised blockchain-based solution to provide security and privacy for smart home environments. The solution is a three-tier framework incorporating cloud storage, overlay, and smart home tiers. The scheme stores the data in a first-in-first-out (FIFO) method. The overlay is used to solve the problem of an individual belonging to more than one smart home. The smart home tier consists of IoT devices, local storage and a device with sufficient computation resources (transaction processor). The transaction processor runs the blockchain and is responsible for the secure communication within the smart home and outside. In addition to the local blockchain, the proposed framework has a local backup drive that is used by devices to store their own data locally.

Conoscenti et al. [48] investigated use cases and applications of blockchain for an IoT environment. The study concluded that adaptability, anonymity, and integrity are the main challenges of an IoT infrastructure that can be solved using blockchain. Identified example application areas for blockchain are user identity management [49], intelligent electric vehicle management [50], privacy and security for automotive systems [28], and security for mission critical applications [29].

In [51], the authors described a blockchain-based IoT system using homomorphic computation to secure data storage. The advantage of using homomorphic computation is that it supports arbitrary computation (i.e. unlimited number of addition and multiplication operations) and is therefore more powerful. By leveraging the abilities of homomorphic computation, the proposed system can process users' data without gathering/storing any information about the data. There are several steps involved in the process as described below:

- Initially all IoT devices record transactions to the blockchain. The leaders (i.e. users) then can generate and send a query transaction to get the desired information.

- The servers process the query using the related transactions from the blockchain and generate responses for the blockchain. The leader collects and verifies the respond transactions.

The authors in [52] provide a description for IoT service models and propose a service based on a collaborative architecture for cloud service entities, i.e. JointCloud using blockchain to provide privacy and data fusion. The proposed platform provides a secure environment for resource exchange among the clouds using a blockchain to record the transactions.

Novo [53] proposed a distributed access control system for IoT devices using blockchain technology. The scalability of the architecture is analyzed using a proof of concept implementation in a realistic environment. The following are the main constituents of this architecture:

- Wireless Sensor Network which acts as a communication medium.For communication among the devices a wireless sensor network is utilised, while for access control management, there is a component which performs the task to provide access control permissions to IoT devices.

- Agent Nodes responsible for smart contract deployment.Similarly, an agent node is responsible for deploying a smart contract in the proposed architecture. The smart contract defines the rules and operations to run the access control system.

- Blockchain based protocol responsible for network stability and transaction approval.The whole system is made secure by using a blockchain network which approves the transactions and keeps copies.

- Management hubs which act as a translator.This is an interface that translates the information originating from the IoT devices into understandable messages for the blockchain nodes.

8.3 PROPOSED IOT SECURITY ARCHITECTURE USING BLOCKCHAIN

In order to provide a blockchain based solution for an IoT environment, we need to consider it within the context of an IoT architecture. Figure 8.4 shows our proposed reference IoT architecture, the main common components of which are as follows:

- Agnostic integration for IoT devices including sensors and actuators. This will be facilitated though a schema-less/schema on a read data storage model.

- Cloud Edge devices which act as a gateway between the IoT devices and the backend service. Edge devices have limited computation power and will perform basic operations, such as data encryption, local device management, pre-processing raw sensor data or running a small knowledge base intelligent system.

- A backend service which will be deployed across a number of virtualised servers and/or containerised services such as Docker. This service will be built to scale up and will incorporate a clustered, cloud hosted, design to achieve this. Specifically, the service will support a scalable data storage backend which is coupled with scalable stateless end-points.

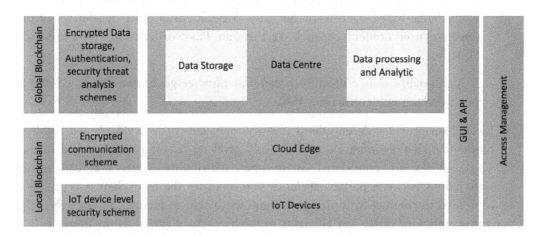

FIGURE 8.4   A conceptual overview of the proposed IoT architecture

- Comprehensive security – this framework will deploy several different levels of security, including:

  o IoT device level: As the IoT devices have limited computational power, a hardware accelerated security protocol embedded within the transmission layer is necessary to secure the short-range communication between the devices and the edge node/gateway. This would incorporate hardware accelerated encryption of a reasonable strength, such as AES-256-CBC.

  o Edge Nodes level: Strong, proven, encryption will be applied to all communications between Edge Nodes and the backend service. This will initially be in the form of AES, in Chained Block Cipher mode using 256-bit keys. Future stronger and proven encryption will be adopted and incorporated as needs evolve. Symmetric encryption keys will be enrolled onto edge devices at a factory initialisation stage. In cases where pre-shared keys cannot be facilitated a strong key exchange mechanism incorporating public-private keys will be adopted.

  o Ecliptic Curve Cryptography (ECC) will be incorporated where necessary to provide high cryptographic strength with relatively low computational complexity. Given the historical precedent of compromised curves being published by state actors, a combination of curves, from trusted sources, will be adopted. In addition, the prospect of applying a combination of Elliptic Curve Diffie–Hellman and Elliptic Curve Digital Signature Algorithm processes should be facilitated to enable strong hybrid security. In 2005, National Security Agency (NSA) of the United States government deployed the ECC mechanism in the key exchange algorithm and digital signature in their suite B standard instead of legacy RSA.

  o Data Centre level: data at rest in a data centre which hosts the backend service will be encrypted using strong encryption. Keys for these will be stored in a challenge-based Hardware Security Module or would be derived from sensitive user credentials such as through Password-Based Key Derivation Function 2.

  o A high-quality source of entropy/random number generator will be employed in all cryptographic processes [54].

- Blockchain provides decentralised identity management by a distributed database blockchain that maintains a continuously growing list of records, called blocks. Those blocks are considered as an open distributed ledger that can record transactions between parties efficiently. To build up the blockchain a transaction id needed to conduct by a user/device and the blocks to record and store the valid transaction. One of the key elements in the blockchain system is the miner who is responsible for mining/adding new blocks to the blockchain. The proposed blockchain solution is a hybrid blockchain in which local and global blockchains are considered as follows:

○ The local blockchain: In the proposed solution all IoT devices should be only accessed through APIs and any access to a device should be recorded as a transaction on the local storage. The local blockchain is generated by all local IoT devices and keeps track of all valid transactions done by the IoT devices. In addition to its functionality the edge node should act as a miner to authenticate, authorise and audit the IoT devices' transactions.

○ The global blockchain: Additionally, a global blockchain is managed by the datacentre which keeps track of all valid transactions between the local domain of the IoT environment and any another third party from different domains including other data-centres.

• A suite of comprehensive API modules will be incorporated to facilitate consumption of data via several IoT-compatible communication strategies. These include MQTT, Web-sockets, protocol buffers and HTTP-based REST.

• User interfaces/GUIs will be developed through modular, scalable and responsive technologies such as AngularJS. Careful selection of this implementation technology will enable code sharing between web interfaces and mobile applications. A specific example would be incorporation of AngularJS and its mobile application companion, Ionic.

• Data storage will be facilitated though real-time capable storage engines. Specifically, a scalable time series database will store sensor data – akin to the IoT solution offered by Kx or OpenTSDB.

• Access management will rely on a combination of user rights profiles coupled with API Keys generated from secure 512-bit nonce values, use of strong salted password hashes, challenge-based handshakes incorporating strong hashes and secure nonce values and certificate-based authentication. A hardware security module will be used to securely store sensitive material, where possible.

8.4 CONCLUSION

In this chapter, we provide an overview of IoT security along with some of the key issues with respect to blockchain-based IoT. We then explain the basic working of blockchain and also investigated that how blockchain technology could be used to cope with IoT security issues. Moreover, we have covered some of the basic ideas such as smart contracts, verifiable claims, self-sovereign identity, NIS and GDPR principles for data protection and sharing etc. We also explain the basic working of each of these concepts and investigated that how they can be integrated with blockchain in order to address the security issues of IoT. A comprehensive review of State of the art IoT security architectures along with the existing IoT security using blockchain is then presented to inform the reader about the existing work. Finally, a secure IoT architecture based on blockchain technology is proposed.

REFERENCES

[1] M. De Donno, N. Dragoni, A. Giaretta, et al., DDoS-Capable IoT Malwares: Comparative Analysis and Mirai Investigation. Security and Communication Networks, 2018. 2018: pp. 30.

[2] M. A. Khan and K. Salah, IoT security: Review, blockchain solutions, and open challenges. Future Generation Computer Systems, 2018. 82: pp. 395–411.

[3] S. Sicari, A. Rizzardi, L. A. Grieco, et al., Security, privacy and trust in Internet of Things: The road ahead. Computer Networks, 2015. 76: pp. 146–164.

[4] J. Zhou, Z. Cao, X. Dong, et al., Security and Privacy for Cloud-Based IoT: Challenges, Countermeasures, and Future Directions. IEEE Communications Magazine, 2017. 55(1): pp. 26–33.

[5] L. Morris, Analysis of partially and fully homomorphic encryption. Rochester Institute of Technology, Rochester, New York, 2013. pp. 1–5. Available from: https://pdfs .semanticscholar.org/0303/6b989a3f838a9e130563357492fcc4d76402.pdf?_ga=2 .250465541.246612487.1563274044–470432912.1553512172.

[6] S. Nakamoto. Bitcoin: A peer-to-peer electronic cash system. 2008. Available from: https:// bitcoin.org/bitcoin.pdf.

[7] A. Dorri, S. S. Kanhere, and R. Jurdak, Blockchain in internet of things: challenges and solutions. arXiv preprint arXiv:1608.05187, 2016.

[8] S. Brakeville and B. Perepa. Blockchain basics: Introduction to distributed ledgers. Accessed Online: [20 May, 2018]; Available from: https://www.ibm.com/developerworks/cloud/library/ cl-blockchain-basics-intro-bluemix-trs/index.html.

[9] Blockgeeks. Smart Contracts: The Blockchain Technology That Will Replace Lawyers. A Beginner's Guide to Smart Contracts, Accessed Online: [25 May, 2018]; Available from: https://blockgeeks.com/guides/smart-contracts/.

[10] A. Lewis. A gentle introduction to smart contracts. Accessed Online: [25 May, 2018]; Available from: https://bitsonblocks.net/2016/02/01/a-gentle-introduction-to-smart-contracts/.

[11] S. Lee and N. Otto. W3C Verifiable Claims Task Force Use Cases Specification, Credentials Community Group. Accessed Online: [25 May, 2018]; Available from: https://opencreds.org/ specs/source/use-cases/#references.

[12] K. H. Duffy and N. Smolenski. The Time for Self-Sovereign Identity is Now: Blockcerts, Decentralized Identifiers, and Verifiable Claims. Accessed Online: [25 May, 2018]; Available from: https://medium.com/learning-machine-blog/the-time-for-self-sovereign-identity-is-now-222aab97041b.

[13] A. Preukschat. Self-Sovereign Identity—a guide to privacy for your digital identity with Blockchain. Accessed Online: [25 May, 2018]; Available from: https://medium.com/@Alex Preukschat/self-sovereign-identity-a-guide-to-privacy-for-your-digital-identity-5b9e95677778.

[14] M. S. Ali, M. Vecchio, M. Pincheira, et al., Applications of Blockchains in the Internet of Things: A Comprehensive Survey. IEEE Communications Surveys & Tutorials, 2018. 21(2): pp. 1676–1717.

[15] K. Sha, W. Wei, T. Andrew Yang, et al., On security challenges and open issues in Internet of Things. Future Generation Computer Systems, 2018. 83: pp. 326–337.

[16] A. Mosenia and N. K. Jha, A Comprehensive Study of Security of Internet-of-Things. IEEE Transactions on Emerging Topics in Computing, 2017. 5(4): pp. 586–602.

[17] M. D'Aliessi. How Does the Blockchain Work? Blockchain technology explained in simple words. Accessed Online: [26 May, 2018]; Available from: https://medium.com/s/story/how-does-the-blockchain-work-98c8cd01d2ae.

[18] B. A. Tama, B. J. Kweka, Y. Park, et al. A critical review of blockchain and its current applications. In 2017 International Conference on Electrical Engineering and Computer Science (ICECOS). 2017.

[19] T. M. Fernández-Caramés and P. Fraga-Lamas, A Review on the Use of Blockchain for the Internet of Things. IEEE Access, 2018. 6: pp. 32979–33001.

[20] J. Lee, BIDaaS: Blockchain Based ID as a Service. IEEE Access, 2018. 6: pp. 2274–2278.

[21] N. Szabo, Smart Contracts. Accessed Online: [20 October, 2018]; Available from: http://www.fon.hum.uva.nl/rob/Courses/InformationInSpeech/CDROM/Literature/LOTwinterschool2006/szabo.best.vwh.net/smart.contracts.html.

[22] K. Christidis and M. Devetsikiotis, Blockchains and Smart Contracts for the Internet of Things. IEEE Access, 2016. 4: pp. 2292–2303.

[23] Smartz. How Blockchain and Smart Contracts Can Impact IoT. Accessed Online: [20 October, 2018]; Available from: https://medium.com/smartz-blog/how-blockchain-and-smart-contracts-can-impact-iot-f9e77ebe02ab.

[24] S. Foundation. Sovrin™: A Protocol and Token for Self-Sovereign Identity and Decentralized Trust. Accessed Online: [21 October, 2018]; Available from: https://sovrin.org/library/sovrin-protocol-and-token-white-paper/.

[25] M. Sporny, D. Bazaar, D. Longley, et al. Verifiable Claims Data Model and Representations. Accessed Online: [25th October, 2018]; Available from: https://www.w3.org/TR/2017/WD-verifiable-claims-data-model-20170803/.

[26] U. Der, S. Jähnichen, and J. Sürmeli, Self-sovereign Identity-Opportunities and Challenges for the Digital Revolution. arXiv preprint arXiv:1712.01767, 2017.

[27] C. Allen. The Path to Self-Sovereign Identity. Accessed Online: [31 October, 2018]; Available from: http://www.lifewithalacrity.com/2016/04/the-path-to-self-soverereign-identity.html.

[28] N. Directive, Directive (EU) 2016/1148 of the European Parliament and of the Council of 6 July 2016 concerning measures for a high common level of security of network and information systems across the Union. Google Scholar, 2016.

[29] P. Regulation, Regulation (EU) 2016/679 of the European Parliament and of the Council. REGULATION (EU), 2016: pp. 679.

[30] J. Granjal, E. Monteiro, and J. S. Silva, Security for the Internet of Things: A Survey of Existing Protocols and Open Research Issues. IEEE Communications Surveys & Tutorials, 2015. 17(3): pp. 1294–1312.

[31] H. Derhamy, J. Eliasson, J. Delsing, et al. Translation error handling for multi-protocol SOA systems. In 2015 IEEE 20th Conference on Emerging Technologies & Factory Automation (ETFA). 2015.

[32] M. R. Palattella, N. Accettura, X. Vilajosana, et al., Standardized Protocol Stack for the Internet of (Important) Things. IEEE Communications Surveys & Tutorials, 2013. 15(3): pp. 1389–1406.

[33] K. Yeh, C. Su, W. Chiu, et al., I Walk, Therefore I Am: Continuous User Authentication with Plantar Biometrics. IEEE Communications Magazine, 2018. 56(2): pp. 150–157.

[34] P. Bull, R. Austin, E. Popov, et al. Flow Based Security for IoT Devices Using an SDN Gateway. In 2016 IEEE 4th International Conference on Future Internet of Things and Cloud (FiCloud). 2016.

[35] A. F. M. Piedrahita, S. Rueda, D. M. F. Mattos, et al. Flowfence: a denial of service defense system for software defined networking. In 2015 Global Information Infrastructure and Networking Symposium (GIIS). 2015.

[36] A. Abeshu and N. Chilamkurti, Deep Learning: The Frontier for Distributed Attack Detection in Fog-to-Things Computing. IEEE Communications Magazine, 2018. 56(2): pp. 169–175.

[37] A. Burg, A. Chattopadhyay, and K. Lam, Wireless Communication and Security Issues for Cyber–Physical Systems and the Internet-of-Things. Proceedings of the IEEE, 2018. 106(1): pp. 38–60.

[38] IEEE Standard for Information Technology - Telecommunications and Information Exchange Between Systems - Local and Metropolitan Area Networks - Specific Requirement Part 15.4: Wireless Medium Access Control (MAC) and Physical Layer (PHY) Specifications for Low-Rate Wireless Personal Area Networks (WPANs). IEEE Std 802.15.4a-2007 (Amendment to IEEE Std 802.15.4-2006), 2007: pp. 1–203.

[39] S. Chakrabarty, D. W. Engels, and S. Thathapudi. Black SDN for the Internet of Things. In 2015 IEEE 12th International Conference on Mobile Ad Hoc and Sensor Systems. 2015.

[40] S. Alharby, A. Weddell, J. Reeve, et al., The Cost of Link Layer Security in IoT Embedded Devices **I wish to present my special thanks to Majmaah University in Saudi Arabia for their care and funding. IFAC-PapersOnLine, 2018. 51(6): pp. 72–77.

[41] C. Miles, Blockchain security: What keeps your transaction data safe? IBM, 2017.

[42] A. Banafa. IoT and Blockchain Convergence: Benefits and Challenges. IEEE News Letter. Accessed Online: [25th Oct, 2018]; Available from: https://iot.ieee.org/newsletter/january-2017/iot-andblockchain-convergence-benefits-and-challenges.html.

[43] Z. Huang, X. Su, Y. Zhang, et al. A decentralized solution for IoT data trusted exchange based-on blockchain. In 2017 3rd IEEE International Conference on Computer and Communications (ICCC). 2017.

[44] R. Beck, S. C. Jacob, N. Lollike, et al., Blockchain – The Gateway to Trust-Free Cryptographic Transactions. In Twenty-Fourth European Conference on Information Systems. 2016.

[45] A. Dorri, S. S. Kanhere, R. Jurdak, et al. Blockchain for IoT security and privacy: The case study of a smart home. In 2017 IEEE International Conference on Pervasive Computing and Communications Workshops (PerCom Workshops). 2017.

[46] M. Conoscenti, A. Vetrò, and J. C. D. Martin. Blockchain for the Internet of Things: A systematic literature review. In 2016 IEEE/ACS 13th International Conference of Computer Systems and Applications (AICCSA). 2016.

[47] D. Wilson and G. Ateniese. From pretty good to great: Enhancing PGP using bitcoin and the blockchain. In International Conference on Network and System Security, pp. 368–375. Springer, Cham2015.

[48] X. Huang, C. Xu, P. Wang, et al., LNSC: A Security Model for Electric Vehicle and Charging Pile Management Based on Blockchain Ecosystem. IEEE Access, 2018. 6: pp. 13565–13574.

[49] A. Dorri, M. Steger, S. S. Kanhere, et al., BlockChain: A Distributed Solution to Automotive Security and Privacy. IEEE Communications Magazine, 2017. 55(12): pp. 119–125.

[50] N. Kshetri, Blockchain's roles in strengthening cybersecurity and protecting privacy. Telecommunications Policy, 2017. 41(10): pp. 1027–1038.

[51] L. Zhou, L. Wang, Y. Sun, et al., BeeKeeper: A Blockchain-Based IoT System with Secure Storage and Homomorphic Computation. IEEE Access, 2018. 6: pp. 43472–43488.

[52] W. Chen, M. Ma, Y. Ye, et al. IoT Service Based on JointCloud Blockchain: The Case Study of Smart Traveling. In 2018 IEEE Symposium on Service-Oriented System Engineering (SOSE). 2018.

[53] O. Novo, Blockchain Meets IoT: An Architecture for Scalable Access Management in IoT. IEEE Internet of Things Journal, 2018. 5(2): pp. 1184–1195.

[54] W. Stallings, Cryptography and network security: principles and practice. Upper Saddle River: Pearson; 2017.

CHAPTER 9

Blockchain in Global Health

An Appraisal of Current and Future Applications

Chandana Unnithan, Alexander Houghton, Aranka Anema, and
Victoria Lemieux

CONTENTS

9.1 GLOBAL HEALTH SYSTEMS AND STAKEHOLDERS

In 2015, the United Nations General Assembly including 194 signatory Member States agreed to work towards a set of 17 Sustainable Development Goals (SDGs) by 2030.[1] Whilst SDG Goal #3 is specifically focused on improving health, there are numerous health-related targets integrated within other SDGs. The WHO's Global Acton Plan recognizes data and digital health as important 'accelerators' that will speed progress towards reaching the health-related SDGs. In 2018, the World Health Assembly (WHA) released the first ever Resolution on Digital Health which urges all 194 Member States of the United Nations to adopt and scale digital solutions as a pathway to achieving the SDGs[2] and calls upon countries to both assess their use of digital technologies for health and integrate them into existing health systems infrastructures.

To begin with, the WHO and International Telecommunication Union (ITU) recommend that all countries have a national eHealth strategy that describes how electronic transfer of information will support the delivery of health services and the management of health systems.[3] According to the WHO, eHealth is 'cost-effective and secure use of information communication technologies (ICT) in support of health and health-related fields, such as health-care services, health surveillance, health literature, and health education, knowledge and research.'

9.2 BLOCKCHAIN IN HEALTH – THE CONDUITS

There are a few channels through which blockchain has been envisioned as applying to the digital health acceleration, as described in this section.

9.2.1 Digital Health

A 2016 eHealth survey by the WHO among United Nations member states ($n = 125$) found that 58 percent had an eHealth strategy and 66 percent had a national Health Information System.[4] The sharing and exchange of electronic patient data are essential to collaborative decision-making – between patient and provider, inter-professional care teams and across healthcare institutions. However, electronic health systems and data within healthcare are plagued by issues of hacking, fraud and counterfeit drugs. Additionally, hospitals, clinics and clinical practices have disparate IT systems, with different methods for storing and retrieving data. These systems are not interoperable and typically not designed for the efficient as well as secure sharing of data. Blockchain technology promises to alleviate some of these issues (see for example[5]).

The issue of data security could be addressed when the encrypted distributed ledger blockchain technology can be used for the safe and immutable transmission of electronic health record data. While issues of hacking and ransomware attacks are prevalent within the health sector (see Section 9.3.2), suitably implemented blockchain technology could potentially enable patient health data to be shared while preserving data security and integrity.

Technically, unauthorized blockchain data manipulation or falsification is nearly impossible, because the integrity of the data is mathematically provable by the encryption and block hashing process. The feature that distinguishes blockchain security from existing approaches to health data sharing (such as Health Information Exchanges) is the ability for all parties on the blockchain network to *validate* the stored data. Such validation is also completely automated. In addition to the security of built-in hashing encryption used in blockchains, security is further guaranteed by the fact that every node on the network will ultimately have a copy of the blockchain. If hacking or fraud is attempted, the node sending the block that contains the fraudulent data will be rejected by the wider network.

Data provenance is enhanced where blockchain can help track the origin and subsequent changes to patient data such as medical records, imaging data, treatment plans, test results, etc. Conversely, blockchain technology decentralizes the data, which means that delays in treatments that result from issues of data interoperability with exchanging health records could be minimized. Jurisdictional issues surrounding access to medical data could also be accommodated automatically as blockchain software could approve or deny access to data depending on the state or country in which it is being used. Even if one node on the network goes down due to a power failure, the rest of the network will be able to continue to function.

If patient data can be securely and appropriately accessed by authorized parties at any point on the network, any relevant changes to associated information would be immediately visible. This has important implications for insurers, providers, regulators, auditors and healthcare workers as there would be a significant decrease in transaction fees and other overheads. The use of blockchain technology could help to substantially eliminate costs as middlemen, brokers and intermediaries become redundant. As a result, there is reduced transaction costs and automated billing using smart contracts that automate the billing cycle.

Another area of high relevance is pharmaceutical supply chain integrity where block chain technology can help ensure the concomitant supply chain issues. Common systems can be implemented by manufacturers, distributors and wholesalers to prevent and detect the global problem of counterfeit drugs. The issue of counterfeit medicine is a critical global issue. According to the World Health Organization, globally, ten percent of drugs are counterfeit while in developing countries, the number upsurges to 30 percent.[6] Counterfeit drugs not only impact lifestyle drugs but also medicines for the treatment of cardiovascular disorders, cancer, antibiotics, painkillers, contraceptives and prescription drugs. Forged drugs do not have the active substance expected to treat humans, which can result in fatalities.

Hyperledger is a research network project[7] which includes Accenture, Cisco, Intel, IBM, Block Stream and Bloomberg, focusing on the drug counterfeit issue and applying blockchain technology. Each drug produced, as part of this project, is marked with a timestamp so that it is possible to determine the place of origin and time when the drug was produced, enabled by blockchain application. Any transfer of ownership is transparent to all the stakeholders so that any forged, low quality or even filched drugs can be tracked and identified.

In 2016, $3.3 billion was recaptured by the US government, according to The Department of Health and Human Services and The Department of Justice as part of their Health Care Fraud and Abuse Control Program.[8] 300 people were charged as a result of nation-wide fraud sweeps in in the same year, and those involved include healthcare providers, doctors, nurses, patients, vendors and pharmacists included in fraudulent activities. Medicare and Medicaid programs are particularly at risk as healthcare records are seen as highly valuable by filchers as these can be used to obtain prescriptions for drugs. While Medicare spending is expected to expand significantly until 2024, the amount of associated fraudulent activity is expected to increase proportionally and is currently estimated to be between 3 percent and 10 percent of spending. Conversely, according to the Cost of a Data Breach Study by IBM and the Ponemon Institute[9] in 2018, the average total cost of a data breach is $3.86M. Of all the industries investigated, the healthcare industry had the highest costs, due to data breaches at $408 per lost or stolen record.

Billions of dollars have been lost to insurance and billing fraud, but the greater data transparency that results from easily accessible records by authorized parties with the application of blockchain would result in the reduction of fraud. The use of crypto-graphic verification of data makes an attempt at fraudulent alteration or deletion of data very easy to recognize and almost immediately. The result would be that not only would that block and all blocks after it be invalidated, but those blocks would not match the recorded data on the rest of the network meaning that it would be regarded as an invalid blockchain. The changed data would then be erased and replaced with the original, uncorrupted data on the next network update. By acting as a single data source for providing secured, permissioned healthcare data access only to approved parties, regulatory oversight and compliance can be made considerably cheaper and more efficient as all the required data will already be stored on the blockchain. In summary, that results in improved regulatory compliance and audit.

9.2.2 Electronic Health Records

Transmission of electronic health data enables collaborative decision-making between patient and provider, and between healthcare providers and institutions. The WHO recommends that all countries globally should work towards administrating national electronic health records (EHRs) for its citizens giving proven efficiencies in quality, safety and cost. EHRs are typically administrated by national governments and are a prospective repository of individual patient medical data including – medical history, pharmaceutical prescription profile, diagnostic imaging, clinical, emergency and clinical visits. EHRs are considered to be a cornerstone of 'integrated care[10]', which enables pulling together fragmented patient and health system information into a more stream-lined and comprehensive view of healthcare access, delivery and outcomes.

The type and extent of EHR adoption vary globally between countries, with notable disparities between high- and low-income settings. A WHO 2016 survey found that EHRs are found in over 50 percent of high-income countries, 35 percent in middle-income countries and 15 percent in low-income countries.[11]

The universal adoption of EHRs globally is limited by several concerns around data management. The electronic transmission of confidential patient data remains vulnerable to breaches without highly secure infrastructure in place, placing patient, payer and provider at risk of unintentional and malicious data breaches, including identity theft.[12] Lack of trust between healthcare institutions limits data sharing between hospital and ambulatory care settings.[13] The share of large-scale datasets may be limited by restrictions in institutional firewall settings or bandwidth, the latter of which is notable in rural or remote settings.[14] Finally, data sharing is impeded by the lack of enforcement of interoperability standards, making the integration and interpretation of data from disparate systems difficult.[15]

Blockchain presents several advantages for medical records management, which were summarized by Kuo et al.[16] in Table 9.1.

Over recent years, case studies and pilots have explored the use of blockchain to support EHR adoption in different jurisdictional and country-wide settings. One of these initiatives is in Estonia, where the national government led the world's first national pilot of blockchain for secure protection of the integrity of EHRs. Estonia has been experimenting with the use of blockchain for management of national data repositories since 2008.[17] Estonia partnered with Estonian private sector technology vendors to link eHealth capabilities in electronic prescriptions, hospital information systems, emergency systems, patient portals and medical data exchanges.[18] Estonia's health information is integrated through a centralized system, which allows for seamless access and data

TABLE 9.1 Blockchain benefits to Medical Records Management, by application feature

Core Blockchain Feature	Benefit to Medical Records Management
Decentralized Management	Patient owns and controls access to their health care data – facilitates transfer to other providers
Immutable Audit Trail	Medical data cannot be changed
Data Provenance	Medical records are source verifiable
Robustness/ Availability	Lowered risk of patient recordkeeping and distributed network means that no single institution can be attacked to obtain medical records
Security/Privacy	Data are encrypted and can only be decrypted with the patient's private key

sharing across health systems and providers, whilst giving patients the ability to control/ hide to their health data through an 'opt-out' model.[19]

Partnerships between public and private sector have proven essential to accelerate the scale-out of blockchain solutions in healthcare. In 2016, the US Office of the National Coordinating Office for Health Information Technology opened a competition for private sector firms to propose blockchain-enabled solutions for the transfer of electronic health information.[20] Among the winners of the competition, professional services firms and third-party technology vendors proposed varying solutions and prototypes. For example, Deloitte Consulting suggested an implementation framework and business case for using blockchain as part of health information exchange[21]; Accenture LLP proposed that blockchain's most valuable contribution to national health information systems include the creation of secure records, linkage of identities and recording of consent.[22] The Massachusetts Institute of Technology (MIT) presented a prototype and case study blockchain-enabled health information exchanges, including a peer-to-peer network for joint storage and analysis of data[23] and decentralized record management system to handle EHR authentication, confidentiality, accountability and data sharing.[24]

The Mayo Clinic has proposed an approach that trades a single centralized source of trust for a network consensus, founded on proof of structural and semantic interoperability[25]; The VA has prototyped *ModelChain*, a framework to increase interoperability between institutions and real-world predictive modelling.[26] Zhang *et al.* developed 'FHIRChain' a blockchain-based architecture designed to meet the US Office of the National Coordinating Office for Health Information Technology requirements, HL7 Fast Healthcare Interoperability Resources (FHIR) standard, for shared clinical data. They demonstrated how the FHIR Chain-based decentralized application effectively used digital health identities to authenticate participants in decision-making for remote cancer care.[27]

Similar partnerships between public and private sector have been noted in other countries for the secure and immutable transmission of health data. In Canada, the Ontario Public Health Department has partnered with a company to enable public health inspectors to transmit inspection reports through an Ethereum-based blockchain.[28] These reports from around the world point toward a growing ecosystem of blockchain solutions for electronic transmission of patient data. A 2016 survey by IBM and The Economist Intelligence United report involving 200 healthcare executives across 16 countries found that 16 percent of private sector institutions planned to have a commercial blockchain application brought to scale in 2017.[29] Blockchain-based solutions to inter-operability in the U.S. have typically focused on addressing institutional silos between healthcare businesses. However, one of the major opportunities of blockchain technology is the potential to move data ownership from institutions and corporations into the hands of citizens. A recent trend towards patient-driven and patient-mediated access to health data is now stimulating new approaches to the retrieval, sharing and access to health data using blockchain. Gordon *et al.* have explored how blockchain technology can facilitate patient-driven and patient-mediated health data exchanges through new mechanisms of digital access, data aggregation, data liquidity, patient identity and data immutability.[30] One of the challenges for blockchain implementation is to secure patient data in a way that still maintains the open nature of blockchain. Solutions such as OnmiPHR have aimed to be a hybrid model.[31]

9.2.3 Biomedical Research

Blockchain technology is being piloted for use in the context of biomedical research using primary and secondary data sources. The Australian Ministry of Health has run a pilot to use blockchain or medical research records.[32] The Ministry partnered with a secure cloud and blockchain start up company[33] to provide an immutable record for tracking health data search queries and downloads – allowing the researcher to protect his/her intellectual property associated with their proven hypotheses, whilst protecting highly sensitive data in alignment with the government's Data Access and Release Policy.[34] The power of this technology is that it can enable the government to make de-identified and confidential patient health records available to the research community in a way that fosters traceability and reproducibility of research results. This 'democratization' of access to data will open massive new opportunities for innovation and solutions for patient and population health. As academics and contract research organizations seek to rigorously synthesize data in the form of systematic literature reviews and meta-analyses they need to both justify and ensure the reproducibility of their search queries and results. This includes articulating their search methodology in a way that ensures data integrity (query and retrieved data are not modified) and non-repudiation (proof that data was acquired at specific time based on query).

Blockchains have the potential to instil an even higher level of rigor in biomedical knowledge synthesis by providing immutable proof of what data was accessed, from which database, at what time. This functionality becomes all the more relevant in the context of Big Data, where biomedical researchers are accessing data from 'dynamic' databases, which may involve informal data from online sources, patient clinical data, pharmaceutical data and various forms of 'omics' data. Several examples of blockchain applications have been cited in peer-reviewed biomedical journals. For example, Kleinaki *et al.* report on findings from a blockchain-based notarization pilot solution that purports to address this very issue of data integrity and non-repudiation in biomedical research.[35] The 'Smart Digital Contract' tool has been tested on the

Ethereum blockchain platform and shown to effectively query and retrieve data using a third-party notary service on two major biomedical databases PubMed MEDLINE and CARRE risk factor reference repository. Kleinaki *et al.* team suggests that the current method for ensuring data integrity and non-repudiation (e.g., digital signatures) can be combined with blockchain features to enhance their traceability, robustness and cost-effectiveness.

9.3 EFFECTIVENESS – A CRITICAL APPRAISAL

The opportunities offered by blockchain technology is certainly being noticed by governments and private sector, and some of these have been scaled up nationally.

9.3.1 Block Chain Pilots in Health – Key Learning

In the health care industry, a decentralized up-to-date database has distinctive advantages, as there are many different stakeholders requiring the same access[36], including general practitioners, specialists, therapists and hospitals. In addition, there are multiple medical records, varied communication media and interoperable IT interfaces. The combination can lead to resource intensive, onerous processes of authentication and information flow. Matthias cites the US based venture Gem Health Network[37] – based on the Ethereum Blockchain technology which has, through shared network infrastructure, enabled different stakeholders access to the same information.

Gem is an example of a healthcare ecosystem that combines businesses, individuals and experts while improving patient-centered care and operational efficiency. All relevant stakeholders get access to transparent and clear access to the latest treatment information. And this can minimize medical negligence due to outdated information and also prevent escalation of health issues at an early stage, which in turn reduces the costs. On the other hand, it allows medical experts involved to track the interactions between the patient and all medical practitioners in the past. The treatment of any patient becomes transparent, with informed consent and raised confidence levels. This example is not only for direct patient-physician relationships; rather, it can be scaled up to national infrastructure as demonstrated by countries such as Estonia.

Australia has now completed the implementation of a national electronic health record as of January 31st, 2019.[38] Similar to Estonia, Australians had the opportunity to 'opt-out,' and subsequently, the electronic health records are now in the process of being created, which in turn enables every citizen to manage information and preferences through their relevant e-government account. Healthcare providers will also simultaneously be able to view the records with real-time updated information, while patients can track, share and manage their information. It would only be a matter of time before all the citizens are able to utilize this facility, enabled and secured by blockchain technologies.

The private sector has also been part of blockchain solutions that enable health. Medicalchain from Groves Medical Group is planning to use Medical chain so that records can be shared by patients and doctors, while patients can pay for health services using cryptocurrency.[39] Illinois Blockchain Initiative, Hashed Health[40] is exploring opportunities to improve the efficiency and accuracy of the medical credentialing process in Illinois, USA. The Nokia Healthcare Blockchain Pilot in Finland is sharing personal health data via a wearable smart watch.[41] DNAtix[42] is a Blockchain ecosystem for anonymous genetic testing bringing in a new revolution in preventative medicine. Delaware Blockchain Pilot (Medscient)[43] is aiming at streamlining Medicaid Preauthorization. These are some examples of the many pilots that are being initiated from private–public partnerships.

9.3.2 Challenges and Opportunities

To be able to adopt and scale blockchain technology in health, trust and transparency in the coordinated healthcare chain is a primary factor. The potential of hacking attacks on blockchain platforms needs to be considered closely. We examine the challenges and suggest solutions as follows.

In a regular public, permission-less blockchain environment, such as Bitcoin or Ethereum, the following attacks are often cited:

- Double spending attacks where one entity controls just over half of the hashing power of the network, enabling the attack. However, these are only applicable to Proof of Work blockchains. Longer transaction confirmations deter these attacks, and bigger networks make these networks more secure.

- Sybil attack, where one computer falsely assumes the identity of one or more computers on the blockchain network, enabling the attacker to be able to steal information, disrupt communications, or influence operation of the consensus mechanism on the network. Sybil attacks are theoretical and have never occurred in the blockchain world as most cryptocurrencies are fundamentally designed to prevent these attacks.

- A routing attack where an Internet Service Provider could partition a blockchain network into two or more separate networks, exposing either side of the partition to double spending attacks. The peer-to-peer nature of blockchain networks could enable prevention of such attacks by making peers aware of routing behavior and monitoring for anomalous routing behavior and acting accordingly

- **Direct Denial of Service** is when bad actors attempt to cripple a blockchain network node. Networks such as Bitcoin are designed to mitigate this risk.

Unauthorized blockchain data manipulation or falsification is impossible because the integrity of data is mathematically proven by the encryption and block hashing process. In theory, the integrity of data stored in a blockchain is never compromised with the use of distributed ledger technology.

The cryptographic proof of work that can be designed into blockchain systems may be able to verify the integrity of data pertaining to patient records, clinical trials, genomics and academic research. For example, in each of these areas it may become possible to find (1) who recorded the data, (2) when and (3) where, as well as exactly (4) how and (5) why it has changed. The ability to securely share data may eventually lead to increased efficiencies. These properties of blockchain technology are dependent on the design of the system; that is, whether it is a public, a private or a consortium blockchain, whether nodes and users must be authorized to participate in the network, and which consensus mechanism is used. The security risks of each blockchain solution must be identified and understood.

It is certain that in the coming years, numerous healthcare applications featuring blockchain technology will be created. Common data format standards and agreed protocols for the transfer and consumption of such data in health care could directly influence intermediaries by either significantly increasing operational throughput of such entities or completely removing the need for such intermediaries. In fact, disintermediation using blockchain has already had a profound impact on banking, travel, music, real-estate and publishing industries. This process is very likely in the healthcare sector, where coordination is enhanced with trust and associated implications for insurers, patients, doctors and drug companies, to name a few.

The introduction of common data standards in a blockchain solution would allow greater interoperability between different health systems. In many countries and spaces where digital health records exist, they tend to be highly specialized, resulting in 'data siloes'. This makes data sharing difficult and expensive. Lack of interoperability results in a health consumer or patient having to repeatedly provide similar information to multiple providers. If a consumer has to give access to their medical data to a new provider, they need to seek permission as there is no ownership of their own record. This results in healthcare providers becoming custodians of bigger data seta. Having to process voluminous, ever expanding information is increasingly difficult as data is added from not just patient treatment histories, but also from lab tests, imaging studies and moreover, data from Internet of Medical Things (IoMT) devices.

Verifying the origin and tracking changes being made to this data is challenging as the data passes through many institutions and stakeholders, as well as systems. The data is also stored in multiple formats that are not compatible with each other, which further adds to the challenge when attempting to establish alteration points in the data stream. As a result, there is a fragmented or incomplete picture of individual medical histories. There are also additional problems with detecting incorrect or outdated information as well as how to correct such errors and establishing where the corrected data should reside. If an unauthorized or untrusted entity tampers with healthcare data, a patient's safety can be seriously compromised.

Globally, health consumers are now being encouraged to contribute their health data in electronic formats to their health care providers, and this data is provided by a multitude of different devices, apps and software. Shifting the focus of managing this data from healthcare providers to the patients would help to improve the quality of information recorded and exchanged as individuals will own and trust their own information, taking responsibility. On the other hand, a shared responsibility of managing this data is enabled by blockchain applications as it enhances trust.

Giving individuals full or shared responsibility for managing their health data using blockchain technology assumes that individuals wish to and are capable of taking on this level of responsibility. Currently, access to data recorded using blockchains is dependent on controlling a private cryptographic key. When such keys are lost or inaccessible (e.g., because an individual becomes incapacitated), data cannot be accessed, since there are no inherent means of key recovery in typical blockchain systems. Loss of individual private keys could cause disruptions in the accessibility of health data that could cost lives. In addition, such solutions assume that all individuals are capable of taking on personal responsibility; thought must be given, however, to individuals without the cognitive capacity to take on this level of responsibility (e.g., those suffering from brain injuries or Alzheimer's as examples). Even for the fully cognitively capable individual, blockchain user interfaces and the complexity of managing private keys are currently challenging. Current user interfaces are overly complicated and require more technical knowledge about the inner mechanisms and functionality of the blockchain. This is even more true for anyone attempting to send a transaction or use, let alone construct, a smart contract.

The existing medical records systems are highly fragmented with each having its own set of standards and processes for sharing data. A decentralized database such as blockchain can be used to securely store all patient data in an encrypted format on a database that is almost tamper proof. Patients could stake control of how their medical data is accessed and grant or deny permission for its uses as they see best. This is also the logic and perception behind the blockchain-enabled electronic health records to scale up at national levels (e.g., Estonia).

All patient medical data could be stored, including treatment plans, procedures, IoMT data, lab results and imaging data; securely and then referenced by health professionals, where appropriate. In this manner, blockchain can be used to securely streamline access to longitudinal patient records without the involvement of a trusted third party and avoiding hurdles in performance. Over time, the blockchain data would represent a complete medical history of a patient that would be accurate in real-time, consistent and accessible on numerous digital platforms, in a manner that facilitates enhanced security in data sharing throughout the public health sector.

Though the idea of securely storing integrated medical data on the blockchain is attractive, there are challenges and concerns. Current cryptographic hashing algorithms have not been broken, so as long as any data recorded on the blockchain is encrypted using these algorithms, its confidentiality is protected. The introduction of quantum computing could allow these secure cryptographic algorithms to be broken, thereby exposing previously confidential private medical information. In addition, solution designs sometimes have incorporated the recording of metadata about transactions onto the blockchain. This has resulted in cases of encrypted personally identifiable information being entered into the immutable blockchain record in contravention with such privacy regulations as the EUs General Data Protection Regulations. Once recorded on the ledger, such information cannot be erased, making impossible to honor individuals' 'right to be forgotten'. Historically, there are many lessons regarding negative 'unintended' consequences of keeping large databases of personal information. Creative design of blockchain data architectures can potentially avoid such eventualities.

The use of blockchain technology could help to substantially eliminate costs, as middlemen, brokers and intermediaries become redundant. If patient data can be securely and appropriately accessed by authorized parties at any point on the network, any relevant changes to associated information would be immediately visible. This has important implications for insurers, providers, regulators, auditors and healthcare workers as there would be a significant decrease in transaction fees and other overheads. On the other hand, billions of dollars have been lost to insurance and billing frauds in the health sector. Greater data transparency that results from easy access by authorized parties would result in the reduction of fraud. This is essentially due to the use of cryptographic verification of data whereby any attempt at fraudulent alteration or deletion of data is easily detectable. In the blockchain, if one block is altered, and all the other blocks would become invalidated. The result is that there would be a mismatch of blocks that have recorded data, and this 'mismatch' would invalidate the blockchain records that followed. The changed data could then be identified and replaced with the original, uncorrupted data on the next network update. Thus, blockchain applications can become very useful in preventing fraud.

There are some processing efficiency limitations to blockchain applications. In a centralized database, a piece of data is written quickly and efficiently and typically only once, excluding matters of backups and database replication. In a blockchain, a given transaction will have to be stored by many nodes, and each one does exactly the same amount of work, by design. While this is one of the features that gives blockchain technology its security, it results in a much longer time for data to be stored. There may be creative solutions developed to address this as technologies progress.

It is perceived widely (or misconstrued) that transactions have to be processed by every node in the network before they become spendable. In reality, transactions are spendable after a minimum amount of confirmations. Since each transaction stored on a blockchain has to be confirmed, it can take a little while before data can be considered to be reliably stored. This reduced transaction speed is due to the wait for a minimum amount of confirmations (six for example), and is due to the time taken for a given node to receive a transaction, validate it and add it to its own local copy of the ledger, and then rebroadcast it out to nodes in its local network. Newer blockchains are in development with faster confirmation times. Litecoin, for example, is technically nearly identical to Bitcoin but features faster transaction confirmation times and improved storage efficiency thanks to reduction of the block generation time and a proof of work consensus which is based on scrypt, a memory intensive password-based key derivation function.

Another challenge in the application of blockchain technology is consensus algorithms. Every node on a blockchain network stores its own local copy of the blockchain, which then raises the question of which node's blockchain propagate the 'official' record of transactions. Consensus algorithms are used for this purpose, for example, Proof of Work (or mining), Proof of Stake, Byzantine Fault Tolerance, etc. In blockchains using the Proof of Work consensus mechanism, transactions are first verified as being valid by miners through a complex series of checks, or else they are discarded outright. Once transactions have been validated, they are aggregated into 'candidate' blocks which are not then considered valid until the miner solves a Proof of Work algorithm, which is essentially a complex mathematical puzzle. Whichever node solves this mathematical puzzle first claims a small amount of Bitcoin (or similar) as a reward, as well as any fees from transactions in the block that was just mined.

The mathematical puzzle is of sufficient difficulty that the chances of any two given nodes solving the puzzle at exactly the same time are very small. Once a miner has solved the puzzle for a block, the block gets broadcast back out as a valid block, and each receiving node then adds the block to its own local blockchain. Any miners currently attempting to mine the same block abandon their attempt and accept the new block and then validate it through a series of tests. The process makes it computationally infeasible for a dishonest actor to try and fake a new transaction or block while rewarding honest miners with a reward. This helps to guarantee that only legitimate transactions are stored on the network. However, this comes at the cost of duplicated work, complexity and wasted energy. The Proof of Work mining process is extremely energy intensive, with thousands of computers running exactly the same calculations to achieve the same result. All these calculations are discarded if a miner receives a valid block. In 2017, Bitcoin mining was estimated to use 30 terawatt hours, more than the whole of Ireland for that year.[44] There has been a considerable drive towards using alternative consensus algorithms, such as Proof of Stake, to reduce energy consumption.

Blockchain will never achieve mass adoption if existing problems unless scalability can be addressed. These problems stem from the fact that there is a limited amount of transactions stored per block and a limit to how many transactions can be processed in a given amount of time. This results in a delay for transactions that cannot be immediately processed into a block, reducing the overall transaction throughput for the network. Mass adoption will also be severely hampered unless there are significant improvements in the usability of blockchain systems.

Bitcoin has had a negative perception in the public mind resulting in an image problem as it is widely used by criminals, for example, to sell drugs on the black market. This has raised public concerns about using blockchain applications, such as worry about becoming victims of scams, fraud, or unknowingly taking part in some other illegal activity. This is even more relevant in the health realm. Such perceptions will fade eventually, but serious efforts will be required to win public support to trust their health care data to a blockchain system.

Integrated to this perception is regulation. The global regulatory environment has yet to catch up with the speed of innovation in the blockchain space, and regulators have become increasingly uncomfortable with blockchain-related concepts such as ICOs and smart contracts. Given the clear improvements for auditability and transparency that blockchain can introduce, changes will have to be made to regulations that cover the storage, retrieval of and consent to use of information in highly regulated industries such as health, that adopt and scale this technology in the sector.

9.4 CONCLUSIONS AND OUTLOOK

As the many developments and pilot projects continue, scaling up blockchain solutions also continues, suggesting that blockchain applications will continue to proliferate in the health sector. The role of blockchain is more apparent in the realm of public health. As the ageing population rises across the globe, and as the millennials age, there is a growing need to manage big data generated through smart devices, including Fitbits. Millennials are increasingly demanding access to manage their own health data, and many governments such as Australia are placing the management of health in the hands of every citizen. The shared responsibility of managing health together with health practitioners enabled by blockchain applications has high potential – whether it is using electronic heath records or sharing data securely for biomedical research.

Reyna et al. summarized some salient features of the integration of IoT with blockchain.[45] They suggest that IoT is transforming and optimizing manual processes and managing big data generated, improving the quality of life through digitization of public health services. This concept is often known as development towards smart, healthier cities. In this context, the integration of IoT with blockchain offers some benefits:

- Decentralization and scalability: Moving to a peer-to-peer decentralized architecture will improve fault tolerance, system scalability and limit powerful stakeholders controlling the processing and storage of information.

- Identity: using a common blockchain system stakeholders can be identified for every single device, data inputs and changes. In addition, blockchain can provide trusted distributed authentication and authorization of devices for IoT applications.

- Autonomy: With blockchain technology, devices are capable of interacting with each other without the association of any servers. This function benefits IoT applications as it enables device-agnostic and decoupled-applications.

- Reliability: IoT information can remain irreversible and distributed over time in blockchain. Participants of the system (in this context, public health systems) are capable of verifying the authenticity of the data. Moreover, the technology allows sensor data trace-ability and accountability.

- Security: Blockchain can treat device message exchanges as transactions, and this is validated by smart contracts. Current secure standard-protocols used in IoT can be optimized with the application of blockchain.

Blockchain applications in health and integration with IoT is expected to revolutionize public health systems and interactions between citizens, governments and public health. Many of the challenges in blockchain and its integration with IoT are being addressed by government-enabled infrastructures and public–private partnerships, ushering in a transparent, secure era of empowered citizens in healthy smart cities.

NOTES

1   Resolution A/RES/70/1. Transforming Our World: The 2030 Agenda for Sustainable Development. In: *Seventieth United Nations General Assembly, New York*, September 25, 2015. New York: United Nations, 2015. Available at: www.un.org/ga/search/view_doc.asp?symbol=A/RES/70/1&Lang=E. Accessed on: November 27, 2018.

2   Seventy-first World Health Assembly (WHA). Digital Health. May 26, 2018. WHA 71.7 Agenda Item 12.4.

3   World Health Organization (WHO) and International Telecommunication Union (ITU). 2012. National eHealth Strategy Toolkit: Overview. Available at: www.who.int/ehealth/publications/overview.pdf. Accessed on: November 26, 2018.

4   World Health Organization (WHO). 2016. *Global Diffusion of eHealth: Making Universal Health Coverage Achievable*. Report of the third global survey on eHealth Global Observatory for eHealth.

5   Juan M. Roman-Belmonte, Hortensia De la Corte-Rodriguez & E. Carlos Rodriguez-Merchan. How Blockchain Technology Can Change Medicine, *Postgraduate Medicine* 2018;130(4):420–427.

6   World Health Organization. Growing Threat from Counterfeit Medicines. *Bulletin of the World Health Organization* 2010;88(4):241–320.

7   Taylor P. 2016, April. *Applying Blockchain Technology to Medicine Traceability*, [Online]. Available: www.securingindustry.com/pharmaceuticals/applying-blockchain-technology-to-medicine-traceability/s40/a2766/#.V5mxL_mLTIV

8   https://oig.hhs.gov/publications/docs/hcfac/FY2016-hcfac.pdf

9   https://newsroom.ibm.com/2018-07-11-IBM-Study-Hidden-Costs-of-Data-Breaches-Increase-Expenses-for-Businesses

10 World Health Organization (WHO). October 2016. *Health Services Delivery Programme Division of Health Systems and Public Health*. Available at: www.euro.who.int/__data/assets/pdf_file/0005/322475/Integrated-care-models-overview.pdf.

11 World Health Organization (WHO). *Global Diffusion of eHealth: Making Universal Health Coverage Achievable*. Report of the third global survey on eHealth Global Observatory for eHealth. 2016. Available at: www.who.int/goe/publications/global_diffusion/en/. Accessed on: November 27, 2018.

12 Terry M. Medical Identity Theft and Telemedicine Security. *Telemedicine and e-Health* 2009;15:1–5.

13 Hripcsak G, Bloomrosen M, Flatelybrennan P, Chute CG, Cimino J, Detmer DE, et al. Health Data Use, Stewardship, and Governance: Ongoing Gaps and Challenges: A Report from Amia's 2012 Health Policy Meeting. *Journal of the American Medical Informatics Association* 2014;21:204–211.

14 Larose R, Strover S, Gregg JL, Straubhaar J. The Impact of Rural Broadband Development: Lessons from a Natural Field Experiment. *Government Information Quarterly* 2011;28:91–100.

15 Richesson RL, Krischer J. Data Standards in Clinical Research: Gaps, Overlaps, Challenges and Future Directions. *Journal of the American Medical Informatics Association* 2007;14:687–696.

16 Kuo T, Kim H, Ohno-Machado L. Blockchain Distributed Ledger Technologies for Biomedical and Health Care Applications. *Journal of the American Medical Informatics Association* 2017;24(6):1211–1220.

17 Available at: https://e-estonia.com/wp-content/uploads/faq-a4-v02-blockchain.pdf. Accessed on: November 27, 2018.

18   Available at: https://e-estonia.com/solutions/healthcare/e-health-record/. Accessed on: November 27, 2018.

19   Novek A. *Blockchain in Estonian National Health Information System*. Health and Welfare Information Systems Centre. Available at: https://cdn.ymaws.com/echalliance.com/resource/resmgr/images/DHW_2018_Profiles_/2018_Presentations_/Artur_Novek.pdf. Accessed on: November 27, 2018.

20   United States Office of the National Coordinating Office for Health Information Technology (ONC). CCC Innovation Center. Winners Announced! Papers Suggest New Uses for Blockchain to Protect and Exchange Electronic Health Records. www.cccinnovationcenter.com/challenges/block-chain-challenge/view-winners/. Accessed 06/11/18.

21   Krawiec RJ, Barr D, Killmeyer K, Filipova M, Nesbit A, Israel A, Quarre F, Fedosva K, Tsai L. August 2016. *Blockchain:Opportunities for Health Care*. Available at: www.healthit.gov/sites/default/files/4-37-hhs_blockchain_challenge_deloitte_consulting_llp.pdf. Accessed on: November 27, 2018.

22   Brodersen C, Kalis B, Leong C, Mitchell E, Pupo E, Truscott A./Accenture LLP. Aug 2016. Blockchain: Securing a New Health Interoperability Experience. Available at: www.healthit.gov/sites/default/files/2-49-accenture_onc_blockchain_challenge_response_august8_final.pdf. Accessed on: November 27, 2018.

23   Ackerman Shrier A, Chang A, Diakun-thibalt N, Forni L, Landa F, Mayo J, van Riezen R, Hardjono, T. Blockchain and Health IT: Algorithms, Privacy, and Data. Project PharmOrchard of MIT's Experimental Learning 'MIT FinTech: Future Commerce.' Available at: www.healthit.gov/sites/default/files/1-78-blockchainandhealthitalgorithmsprivacydata_whitepaper.pdf. Accessed on: November 27, 2018.

24   Ekblaw A, Azaria A, Halamka J, Lippman A. August 2016. *A Case Study for Blockchain in Healthcare: 'MedRec' Prototype for Electronic Health Records and Medical Research Data*. MIT Media Lab, Beth Israel Deaconess Medical Center. Available at: www.healthit.gov/sites/default/files/5-56-onc_blockchainchallenge_mitwhitepaper.pdf. Accessed on: November 27, 2018.

25   Peterson K, Deedvanu R, Kanjamala P, Boles K. *The Mayo Clinic. A Blockchain-Based Approach to Health Information Exchange Networks*. Available at: www.healthit.gov/sites/default/files/12-55-blockchain-based-approach-final.pdf. Accessed on: November 27, 2018.

26   Kuo T, Hsu C, Ohno-Machado L. *ModelChain: Decentralized Privacy-Preserving Healthcare Predictive Modeling Framework on Private Blockchain Networks*. Available at: www.healthit.gov/sites/default/files/10-30-ucsd-dbmi-onc-blockchain-challenge.pdf. Accessed on: November 27, 2018.

27   Zhang P, White J, Schmidt D, Lenz G, Rosenbloom S.T. FHIRChain: Applying Blockchain to Securely and Scalably Share Clinical Data. *Computational and Structural Biotechnology Journal* 2018;16:267–278.

28   HealthSpace Data. HealthSpace Announces Peterborough Public Health to Participate in the Alpha Phase of Its Blockchain Initiative – the VI Marketplace API. Available at: www.newswire.ca/news-releases/healthspace-announces-peterborough-public-health-to-participate-in-the-alpha-phase-of-its-blockchain-initiative—the-via-marketplace-api-681593361.html. Accessed on: November 27, 2018.

29   IBM. Healthcare Rallies for Blockchains: Keeping Patients at the Center. Available at: www-01.ibm.com/common/ssi/cgi-bin/ssialias?htmlfid=GBE03790USEN/ Accessed on: November 27, 2018.

30   Gordon WJ, Catalini C. Blockchain Technology for Healthcare: Facilitating the Transition to Patient-Driven Interoperability. *Computational and Structural Biotechnology Journal* 2018;16:224–230.

31   Roehrs A, Da Costa CA, Da Rosa R.R. OmniPHR: A Distributed Architecture Model to Integrate Personal Health Records. *Journal of Biomedical Informatics* 2017;71:70–81. https://doi.org/10.1016/j.jbi.2017.05.012.

32   www.zdnet.com/article/australian-department-of-health-using-blockchain-for-medical-research-records/

33   Agile Digital. Available at: https://agiledigital.com.au/clients/department-of-health/. Accessed on: November 8, 2018.

34   Australian Government. Department of Health. Data Access and Release Policy. Available at: www.health.gov.au/internet/main/publishing.nsf/Content/Data-Access-Release-Policy. Accessed on November 8, 2018.

35   Kleinaki AS, Mytis-Gkometh P, Drosatos G, Efraimidis PS, Kaldoudi E. A Blockchain-Based Notarization Service for Biomedical Knowledge Retrieval. *Computational and Structural Biotechnology Journal* 2018;16:288–297. doi:10.1016/j.csbj.2018.08.002. eCollection 2018.

36   Matthias Mettler, Blockchain Technology in Health Care, 2016 IEEE 18th International Conference on e-Health Networking, Applications and Services (Healthcom), Boydak Strategy Consulting AG, Freienbach, Switzerland.

37   https://enterprise.gem.co/gemology/

38   www.myhealthrecord.gov.au/for-you-your-family/howtos/record-creation

39   https://medicalchain.com/en/

40   www.hashedhealth.com

41   https://hitconsultant.net/2017/12/08/nokia-healthcare-blockchain-pilot/#.XFpMJC0ZNo4

42   www.the-blockchain.com/2018/06/28/dnatix-introduce-pilot-using-blockchain-for-preventative-healthcare/

43   www.scsuntimes.com/news/20170807/medical-society-of-delaware-partners-with-medscient

44   www.theguardian.com/technology/2017/nov/27/bitcoin-mining-consumes-electricity-ireland

45   Reyna A, Martin C, Chen J, Soler E, Diaz M. On Blockchain and Its Integration with IoT. *Challenges and Opportunities, Future Generation Computer Systems* 2018;88:173–190.

CHAPTER 10

A Blockchain Use Case for Car Registration

Tiago Rosado, André Vasconcelos, and Miguel Correia

Instituto Superior Técnico, Universidade de Lisboa, Portugal

INESC-ID, Instituto Superior Técnico, Universidade de Lisboa, Portugal

CONTENTS

B lockchain enables the development of decentralized business models with enhanced security for critical data. In this chapter, we present a car registration system based on the Hyperledger Fabric blockchain technology. This system considers several government entities in a single country, but might be extended to a cross-border scenario, possibly supporting car data sharing at the level of the EU.

The system – BCar – handles the processes related to car registration management, e.g., registering a vehicle, changing ownership status, and registering a leasing contract between a lessor and a lessee. This system can simplify the information exchange among multiple states as the car registration information is distributed to each government entity in a single decentralized system. We analyse the benefits and implications of the blockchain technology application and present an evaluation of the system's performance.

10.1 INTRODUCTION

Blockchain technology has reached the mainstream because it is the basis for many cryptocurrencies, which have been shaking the notion of currency in recent years. Bitcoin, as the first and best-known application of blockchain technology, is a digital currency that does not rely on a central authority to be managed [1]. The decentralization provided by blockchain technology can be considered a direct competitor to organizations relying on a centralized business model, such as banks and governments. In a utopian scenario, blockchain technology could present a decentralized collection of services competing with government's services such as property registration, citizen registration and even a financial system replacement that could render most of the government's work useless.

Nevertheless, organizations can also look at blockchain technology as an innovation that is an opportunity for them to improve their efficiency. Currently, many organizations are investigating and implementing blockchain technology to the benefit of business efficiency and government transparency. One example comes from the Estonian government that has been implementing services using this technology since 2012 [2].

Considering the potential of blockchain technology, the main objective of this chapter is to present a car registration infrastructure based on blockchain. A car registration system based on blockchain can decentralize this kind of registries and, in consequence, improve data availability and resilience to faults. As a set of entities, ranging from leasing companies to government offices, rely on the car registration system, a decentralized system based on blockchain can improve performance and security when compared with a centralized solution.

Given the decentralization inherent to blockchain, it is crucial to understand the role of an entity such as the national car registry. As will be discussed, a blockchain application for car registration can still take into consideration the authority of the national registry entity. With this requirement, a blockchain-based car registration system can benefit from decentralization but still maintain a centralized authority to partially manage and control the system.

One may consider that blockchain technology has a limited set of use cases, however, the case for a car registration system based on blockchain may provide a starting point to research and implement further government services and information systems based on this technology. Regarding car-related services, the proposed solution could provide a starting point for a single system to manage registration, tax and vehicle's characteristics and requirements for a car to be legal to drive. Regarding government registration services, blockchain may also be considered for civil, commercial and criminal registration systems, driving innovation of government services.

This technology can also represent an effort to improve government efficiency and transparency [2]. As blockchain technology tends to decentralize data storage, it is also necessary to weigh the effort needed to implement the system in a full scale and identify possible struggles over this approach, ranging from the initial setup of the system to the maintenance effort towards the needed hardware and possible software updates. Therefore, we propose an implementation of blockchain technology for car registration using smart contracts and analyse its impact on car registration business processes.

10.2 BACKGROUND

In this section, we go over background that is relevant for our work. First, we present an overview of how car registration works today, including its main components. Then, we introduce the notion of smart contract, which is at the core of most applications based on blockchain. Next, the notion of consensus is presented, and the two major alternative approaches are discussed, as this is a major design decision that we had to make. These two approaches are tightly related to the two main families of blockchains, permissioned and permissionless, which are discussed next. Then Hyperledger Fabric, the blockchain technology that we selected is presented. Finally, we mention some applications currently using blockchain technology, their configuration and how businesses benefit from them.

10.2.1 Current Car Registration System

A car registration system, as implemented by most government entities around the world, is usually a centralized information system. This is the case of Portugal, which is the country's car registration system that we studied in more detail. This information system handles every information related to car registration and is managed by a national registry entity, although other governmental and non-governmental entities have access to services handling car registration information.

Citizens are able to request information related to vehicles, as most of the information stored in the car registration system is available for the public. Government entities responsible for controlling motorized vehicles are able to interact with the system to issue and cancel registration plates and to change the official characteristics of a vehicle.

Regarding seizure orders, lawyers, courts and solicitors are allowed to interact with the car registration system to issue or consult those orders. External entities, such as leasing companies, are also allowed to consult car records on the car registration system.

A car registration system may be composed of several servers responsible for different operations, such as having servers responsible for providing web services to external entities relying on car registration information, as tax authorities, vehicle regulation authorities or even some companies directly related to vehicle registrations, such as leasing companies. Another component of such a system is a client interface for employees handling car registry data, which can be presented in a client side application or a website providing a mean to execute operations over a car registry.

All of the system components described interact with the core of the information system, which in most of the cases is a relational database hosted on a different server, responsible for managing and storing the information required to handle car registries. Each of the components described might vary on its complexity by having backup servers to tolerate system fault or attacks from malicious parties, preventing data losses and system failures on each of the components constituting the car registration system.

Within the EU, there is cooperation among member states to exchange car registration information, to issue transit violations or simply consult registry information regarding a vehicle in a different EU country. Thus, some of the described system components are exposed to cross-border access to provide vehicle information to different member states. However, as opposed to using blockchain technology, member states rely on the availability of each other's car registration systems to read cross-border vehicle's information.

10.2.2 Smart Contracts

Smart Contracts are programs written to form agreements between users in the blockchain [3]. Using smart contracts, it is possible to ensure that the clauses of a contract are accomplished automatically and that breaching the contract is expensive or even prohibitive [4].

Blockchain establishes a consensus based on minimal trust between network nodes to execute smart contracts. When a node receives a transaction, contract functions are run to ensure the validity of the transaction and the conditions stated in the contract are met. In case of failure, the transaction is discarded by the network nodes.

By extending the capabilities of smart contracts, it is possible to run decentralized applications based on blockchain technology. Therefore, we can create applications such as car registry platform completely based on smart contracts.

10.2.3 Consensus

A blockchain is a distributed replicated sequence of blocks of data. To guarantee that all nodes have the same sequence of blocks, the nodes have to reach consensus on which are the blocks and their order. There are basically two approaches to do that.

10.2.3.1 Proof-of-work

The first approach is proof-of-work (PoW), first implemented in Bitcoin [1]. The idea is that in order for nodes to agree on the next block to add to the blockchain, there is a need to decide who should be the author of the block. In Bitcoin, Ethereum and other blockchains, PoW is used to decide that, i.e., who is the author of the block. A PoW must be hard to produce and easy to verify. This implies the need for a computationally intensive problem to be solved. The node responsible for solving the problem is the potential author of the next block to be added to the blockchain [5]. In the case of Bitcoin, a node needs to scan for a nonce value for a block so that the hash of the block starts with a defined number of zero bits.

This form of consensus has the side effect of slowing down the transaction processing within the network, as major computational work is wasted to create a block instead of processing transactions. The approach used by PoW increases the difficulty of successful attacks, given the need for a great computational power to create a PoW and use it to tamper blockchain data.

Given the concurrency between nodes, it is possible for two nodes to broadcast different versions of the next block with a valid PoW at approximately the same time. In this situation, other nodes start working over the first block they receive but still save the other branch, which represents a fork. A fork is removed once the next PoW is found. As the new block is added to one of the branches, the branch becomes longer, and the shorter branch is removed [1].

There are a set of other approaches related to PoW, e.g., Proof-of-Stake, but they are still not much adopted.

10.2.3.2 BFT Approach

We designate the second consensus approach Byzantine fault-tolerant (BFT), as it follows a long line of distributed algorithms (e.g., [6,7,8]) that started with the work of Lamport et al. on agreement among a set of "Byzantine generals" [9]. These algorithms are known not to scale well, as they involve several steps of communication involving all nodes, on the contrary of the PoW approach that involves one node flooding the network with its block and PoW. However, for a small number of nodes, the BFT approach allows fast transaction processing (e.g., tens of thousands per second).

Regarding consensus conflicts, such as the creation of temporary forks in the blockchain, BFT algorithms do not suffer from this problem. BFT algorithms grant the property of consensus finality, as in Definition 1 [10]. Considering this property, block addition to the blockchain is immediately confirmed.

Definition 1 *(Consensus Finality) If a correct node p appends block b to its copy of the blockchain before appending block b, then no correct node q appends block b' before b to its copy of the blockchain.*

Resilience to attacks is also a matter of analysis, as one of the key advantages of blockchain is the assurance of immutable data, once the data is stored in the blockchain. The PoW approach arguably supports up to 50% of faulty nodes in the network, however, regarding Bitcoin's approach to fault mitigation, tolerance drops to 25% [11], contrasting with BFT algorithms that support up to $\lfloor \frac{n-1}{3} \rfloor$ faulty nodes, where n is the number of nodes. Given the possibility of forks, in Bitcoin, it is a good practice to take a block as final only when six or more blocks have been appended to the blockchain after that block. On the other hand, this approach can be circumvented by timestamp manipulation [10]. BFT algorithms, as complying with Definition 2.3.2, support long asynchronous periods and global outages. Latency in BFT algorithms usually matches network latency, contrary to PoW approach where rising block size translates in higher throughput with the downside of higher latency. As latency of the system increases, the number of possible blockchain forks increases as well, resulting in more opportunities to perform double spending attacks and successfully executing them.

10.2.4 Permissionless versus Permissioned Blockchains

Public blockchains rely on public nodes; thus any node can contribute to the network by running a client designed to keep a local blockchain copy, contribute to network consensus, contribute to process transactions and create blocks. Public blockchains rely on public nodes without restricting their access and actions in the blockchain. Considering public blockchains, the requirement of making public any data stored in the blockchain has the advantage of increasing data transparency, but it sacrifices privacy [2].

Permissioned blockchains emerged as a necessity to restrict blockchain network participants to identifiable and explicitly authorized nodes with specific permissions [12]. Therefore, private blockchains provide mechanisms to restrict the nodes accessing and contributing to the blockchain. As a result, private blockchains increase the confidentiality of the data they store. However, a restricted number of nodes with access to the blockchain may provide less resilience and sturdiness.

10.2.5 Hyperledger Fabric

Hyperledger Fabric is a blockchain software sponsored by the Linux Foundation and IBM. Hyperledger Fabric, as a private blockchain, restricts the nodes participating in the system to trusted and identifiable nodes. This enables for performance improvements over consensus mechanisms and can reduce the power consumption of such system. Permissioned blockchains may be used by a group of entities who may not completely trust each other [13].

Hyperledger Fabric uses an execute-order-validate architecture [12,13] based on a modular consensus mechanism that can be adjusted to the specific need of smart contracts running on the blockchain. Through execute-order-validate, a transaction entails three different phases. During the execution phase, each transaction is executed and its correctness verified by a restricted set of peers called "endorsement peers." During this phase, it is possible for transactions to be executed in parallel. The second phase is assigned to an ordering service, responsible for establishing signed transactions' total order, using the consensus mechanism defined and fabricating blocks accordingly. Ordering service nodes are also responsible for updating the blockchain's state to all peers using atomic broadcast. For any of the operations, ordering service nodes do not need to execute smart contracts, know about the current application state, or validate the smart contracts. In validate phase, transactions are validated by the remaining peers of the network, checking against the trust assumptions considered for each specific application, and endorsement policies are verified. If there is no issue in this last step, the block is appended to the blockchain on each peer's local copy.

Regarding ordering services' operations related to consensus mechanisms, Hyperledger Fabric currently has three consensus mechanisms implemented [13]: a one-node consensus, requiring a single node to establish total order of transactions, a method normally used to speed up the development environment of smart contracts, a crash fault-tolerant (CFT)-based ordering service run on cluster, and a BFT-SMaRt [14] consensus mechanism tolerating almost one-third of faults. The Ordering Service creates a block as one of the following conditions occurs: (1) the maximum number of transactions per block is reached, (2) the maximum block size is reached or (3) a certain time has passed since the first transaction was added to the block.

10.2.6 Applications

Although cryptocurrencies, like Bitcoin, are the most popular application of blockchain technology, there is a large set of applications based on blockchain backed by governments, banks and private companies. The use of blockchain and smart contracts may improve the government relationship with citizens and help government initiatives to take part in the digital world. As stated [2], this technology improves the privacy of citizens and transparency of government work.

Applying blockchain technology to a business may lower operations costs and coordination efforts, as the system automatically handles possible conflicts [2]. Distributed ledgers can be used to better secure data itself contained in the blockchain, easily share citizen's data between government entities and secure critical infrastructures [2], such as a country's electrical grid.

The Estonian government implemented a blockchain solution in 2012 applied to registries of the national health system (e-Health Records[1]), judicial and citizen registry system. A concrete application of the blockchain technology by the Estonian government is e-Residence.[2] Through this application, digital identities are issued (together with a digital ID smart card) for people and organizations around the world who want to develop a location independent business. Using this application, e-Residents can start a company, access business banking, sign and securely send documents and declare taxes online. The Estonian government takes advantage of blockchain technology in order to keep track of all changes performed to the system, ensuring data integrity [15].

10.3 BUSINESS PROCESSES OF CAR REGISTRATION

In this section, we present an overview of the business processes involved in the operation of a centralized car registration system. A new car registration system, based on blockchain technology, may bring innovation over a centralized car registration system and change some of the business processes currently in place. An analysis of the current business processes of the Portuguese national registry entity will be conducted, and a set of changes over the current business processes will be suggested as a way to improve those processes. The information to model the presented business processes was obtained through public domain information. Finally, we will go over a scenario using a blockchain-based car registration system and model some of the business processes associated with this new system.

10.3.1 Current Business Processes

Analysing the current car registration system, a user can interact with the car registration system by going to a national registry office and requiring information regarding a vehicle or requiring to change a vehicle's registry. Then a national registry employee consults the car registration system and provides the information to the user or updates the vehicle's registry. Information changes, for registered vehicles, mostly require the owner or an authorized party to fill in a form.[3]

On the other hand, a vehicle owner can have a narrower but more direct access to the car registration system by using an online platform, although most of the information updates still require approval from a registry employee. In both methods described, most of the operations available require some sort of payment to be executed. A simplified version of the required actions to interact with the current car registration system is shown as a business process model diagram in Figures 10.1 and 10.2.

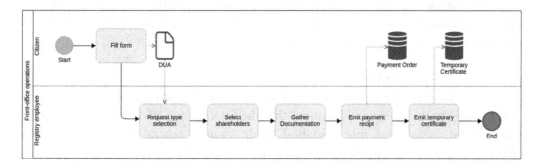

FIGURE 10.1   Over-the-counter (or front-office) operations

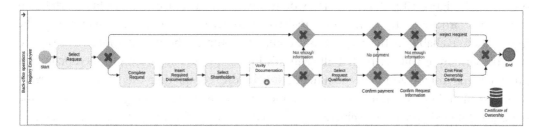

FIGURE 10.2   Back-office operations

10.3.2 National Registry Office Operations

A back-office process, as modelled in Figure 10.2, is needed to fully process the citizen's request. The back-office process starts when a registry employee looks for the list of pending requests in the car registration system. As a registry employee selects a pending request, he or she may reject the request or complete a pending request. When completing a request, the necessary documentation may be introduced. After this step, the list of shareholders to the processing request is inserted, and document verification is executed by the registry employee.

Finally, the request result is issued, and the process is finished. A request result may vary with the type of request specified in the form by the citizen. In case of a vehicle ownership change, this process results in a final ownership certificate being issued to the new owner.

10.3.3 Business Processes on a Blockchain-Based System

Given the properties of a blockchain-based car registration system, the business processes presented in the previous sections can be modified to benefit from blockchain properties. A blockchain-based car registration system should work following the principle that information updates over vehicle's data are correct unless this information is latter proven to be wrong. Thus, we propose a blockchain-based car registration system on which change requests over vehicle information can be firstly registered to the system, as soon as the request is issued by the respective participant and the request's payment is confirmed. This approach takes advantage of blockchain technology and its immutability to simplify business processes.

10.3.3.1 Register a New Vehicle

Taking into account the registration of a newly fabricated vehicle into a blockchain-based car registration system, we assume that the intervention of a registry employee is recommended, given that this operation might require several authorizations from authorities, such as the Department of Motor Vehicles. On the other hand, registering a vehicle implies creating a new registry, thus allowing user's requests to directly create entities in the system can lead to a system bloated with malformed asset registries.

We propose a registration process for a new vehicle in the car registration system, as presented in Figure 10.3. A request is made through a front-office or an online portal, and it is latter processed by a national registry employee. The employee will verify the information available in the request and complete some of the information. As a second step, the employee will verify that all request's information is according to the documents provided and might add new documentation before completing the process. As every information and documentation is correct and verified by a national registry employee, the request is fulfilled and a new vehicle is registered in the blockchain registration system.

10.3.3.2 Request a Change of Ownership

Regarding ownership change process, we propose a two-phase process. The current owner of a vehicle wishing to pass his ownership position to another entity is required to fill an online form with all the necessary information and documentation. Once this form is submitted, a pending ownership change is submitted to the blockchain-based car registration system, as modelled in Figure 10.4, which is latter confirmed by the prospect owner.

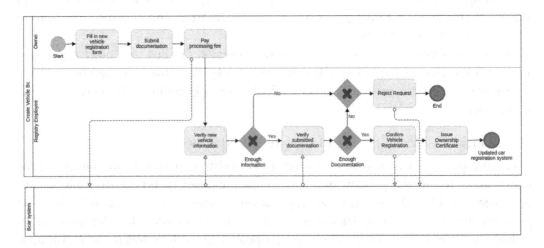

FIGURE 10.3 Proposed process for creating a vehicle in a blockchain-based system

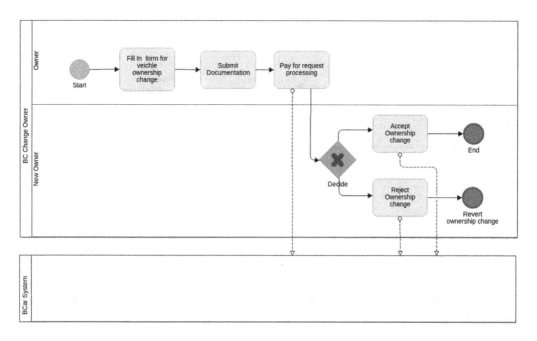

FIGURE 10.4 Proposed process for changing ownership information of a vehicle in a blockchain-based system

As the vehicle's owner issues a change of ownership request, with information about the new owner and its share of ownership, the vehicle ownership is registered as a pending ownership, and the prospect new owner is required to take action. The prospect owner is then able to accept or reject the ownership change (Figure 10.4). Only after the prospect owner confirms the ownership change, the new owner is effectively registered as the owner of the vehicle in the blockchain, and the old owner is removed as owner. Considering the prospect owner of the vehicle rejects the ownership change, the vehicle ownership information in the blockchain is updated so that the old ownership settings remain valid and the prospect owner is no longer tied to the vehicle.

The proposed process aims to simplify the ownership change using blockchain technology to improve the overall efficiency of the process, considering a national registry employee is only required to intervene when the process is incorrectly executed.

10.3.3.3 Register as Guarantee

When registering a vehicle as a loan guarantee, the process can be modified as modelled in Figure 10.5. Thus, when a vehicle owner wants to register a vehicle as a guarantee for a loan, he issues a request with the intended documentation. In the request, the vehicle owner is required to specify who is the creditor entitled for this guarantee, the total value to which the vehicle is given as guarantee and the penalty for missing payments. Once the payment for the request is confirmed, the blockchain is updated with new information regarding the guarantee tied to the vehicle.

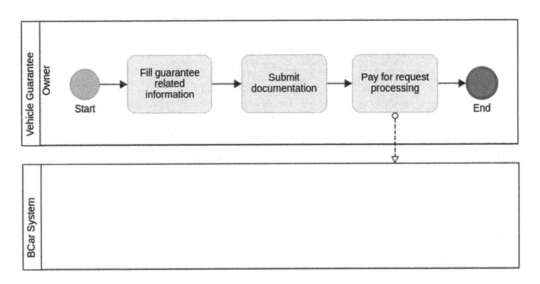

FIGURE 10.5 Proposed process for registering a vehicle as a guarantee for a loan in a blockchain-based system.

10.3.3.4 Associate Lease Contract

When owning a vehicle, the owner is able to issue a lease contract signed by the owner, as a lessor and a third party, as a lessee, with a specific duration. A lease contract expects the lessee to make regular payments for a specified number of months. In exchange, the lessor gives permissions for the lessee to use the vehicle for the duration specified on the contract.

A lease contract association in a blockchain-based car registration system is divided into two phases. The lease registration process is started by a vehicle owner, submitting lease information, as well as a copy of the lease contract in digital form, as shown in Figure 10.6. Once the request's payment is completed, the lease details are associated with the vehicle's information in the blockchain-based system. As this operation hands over responsibility to the lessee, the lease information remains in a waiting state. Then the lessee is required to confirm or deny his involvement in the contract. If the lessee accepts the lease contract, the contract is validated in the system. Otherwise, the lease operation is reverted once the prospect lessee rejects the pending proposal.

10.3.3.5 Execute a Vehicle Seizure

A vehicle seizure occurs when, by judicial order, the ownership of an asset, in this case, a vehicle, is forcibly changed in order to liquidate owner's debt. A vehicle seizure request is currently made by a judicial officer and latter executed by national registry employees. On a blockchain-based car registration system, we propose the process to be executed by a judicial order, providing the supervision role to a registry employee.

Once a vehicle's seizure order is emitted, a judicial officer must fill in a seizure request with the required information and documentation, as the judicial order number issuing

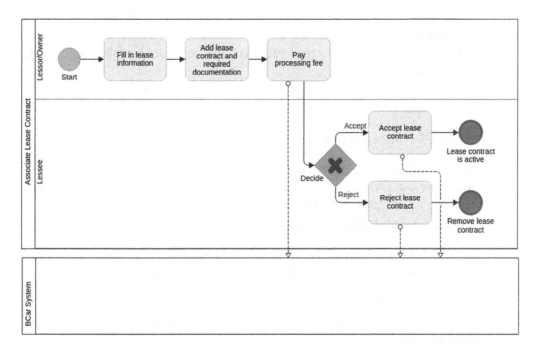

FIGURE 10.6   Proposed process for registering a lease in a blockchain-based system

the seizure. As soon as a judicial officer submits the required information for seizure of the vehicle, the action is submitted to the blockchain, and the ownership of the vehicle is changed. On the other hand, the entity specified in the seizure order becomes the new owner of the vehicle.

10.4 BCAR SYSTEM

In this section, we describe the proposed car registration system. At first, we consider the requirements of a car registration system, starting from the currently centralized system and its properties. We then propose to implement a blockchain-based information system with granular access control. A set of use cases is defined, as part of the requirements for the proposed system and a light consideration on the permissions of each participant is presented. Considering vehicle information required by the European law, a data model is presented.

10.4.1 Requirements

Car registration systems in Europe are controlled and maintained by each member state. As blockchain technology relies on distributed nodes, the control detained by government entities should be adapted. Therefore, a car registration system based on blockchain technology can distribute most of the maintenance effort and some of the system's control by network nodes. However, the government entities of each European member state could still detain control over the registered cars in that state. The European member states or even the European Commission should also be able to have the role of a supervising authority.

As part of a car registration system's requirements, at least the following use case scenarios were identified:

A. Main use cases:

1. A car seller wishes to transfer car ownership to a car buyer.

2. A leasing company provides a contract to a client with the clauses of the client using the car for a defined period of time on which the leasing company is responsible for paying maintenance and insurance expenses in exchange for a defined monthly payment by the client.

3. A car owner submits a request to give the car ownership as a guarantee to a creditor in case the car owner does not fulfil the contract.

B. Secondary use cases:

1. A car manufacturer submits a request to create a car registry entry for a newly produced car.

2. Given a judicial order and in order to liquidate a car owner debt, the car ownership is transferred to the entity responsible for collecting the debt payments.

10.4.2 Solution

Considering the granular access control required for a government service, such as the car registration system, it was necessary to select a permissioned blockchain. As we intend to provide most of the blockchain control to a set of entities such as the national registry institution of each European member state.

This configuration ensures the safety and confidentiality of data. As a private blockchain, only authorized nodes detained by the government entities or by trusted external entities join the network.

10.4.2.1 Participant Definition

As the car registration system requires access control to registry information, a set of participants were defined along with their specific permissions. Considering main and secondary use cases specified in Section 10.4.1, five concrete participants were defined. A class diagram as an overview of the information stored for each participant of the car registration system can be consulted in Figure 10.7.

10.4.2.2 Citizen

A citizen-type participant encompasses the simplest entity able to take ownership of a vehicle. As other entities are represented in the system, a citizen inherits from an abstract Natural Person participant. A Natural Person participant type is defined by

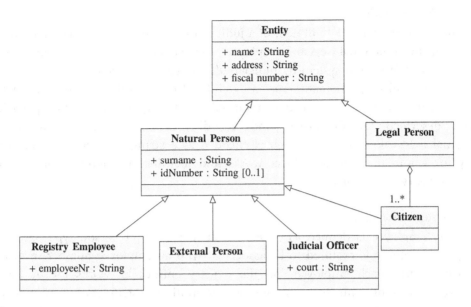

FIGURE 10.7 Proposed car registry system's participant types

a name, an address (which represents the official residence of the entity) and its fiscal number. Optionally, the personal identification document number can be stored with the remaining information, although only a fiscal number is required to identify a citizen in the car registration system. A citizen is able to execute the following operations when owning a vehicle: Start a change of ownership of a vehicle; start a lease contract; accept or reject a lease contract; request a lease contract cancellation; accept or reject a lease contract cancellation; add the vehicle as guarantee for a loan; request for a vehicle guarantee to be cancelled.

10.4.2.3 Legal Person

A legal entity is represented as a Legal Person type participant on the proposed car registration system. Similarly, to a Citizen type participant, it is identified by a name, an official fiscal address and a fiscal number, which are all encoded as strings on the data model. A fiscal number is the primary identifier of a legal person in this car registration system. A Legal Person type participant also requires a list of entities which are Citizen type participants. These entities are the Legal Person's owners or the entities responsible for this Legal Person's actions on the car registration system.

As a Legal Person may not represent a singular entity, car registry operations cannot be performed by a Citizen type participant. Car registry operations on behalf of a Legal Person participant are required to be performed by the Citizen identified as owner or Citizen participants in charge of the Legal Person's actions on the car registration system.

10.4.2.4 Judicial Officer

Operations executed as the fulfilment of a judicial order can only be executed by judicial entities or by a national registry employee. Judicial entities are represented in the proposed car registration system by Judicial Officer type participants.

A Judicial Officer participant type is extended from a Natural Person participant type, thus it includes the same data required to identify a Citizen type participant already described. On the other hand, a Judicial Officer is required to have an additional field called "court," which is encoded as a string and registers the judicial entity for whom the Judicial Officer works and identifies the judicial entity issuing the car registry operations.

10.4.2.5 Registry Employee

A registry employee is defined as an extension to a Natural Person type participant. A registry employee is required to be associated with an employee number in order to uniquely identify each employee and the registry entities he works for. A Registry Employee type represents users of the car registration system working for national registry entities. When compared to the other participant types, registry employees have unrestricted permissions to car registries in the information system. Registry Employee participants are able to solve conflicts on the system and are still accountable for their actions, given the nature and architecture of the blockchain technology.

10.4.2.6 External Person

An additional participant was required to be defined in order to include operation's permissions within the car registration system which were executed by external entities to the national registry and were not included in the above mentioned participant types. For example, consider the use case described in Section 10.4.1; an authority needs to verify the ownership of a car. Thus, employees working for an external entity allowed to read car registry information are registered as an External Person type participant.

10.4.3 Data Model

Based on the European regulations [16] and the vehicle registration modification form,[4] a simplified data model was built. The resulting data model was also based on the use cases specified in Section 10.4.1.

A vehicle is registered in the car registration system with the following information: a registration number, a make, a vehicle identification number (VIN) and a category. Vehicle owners are identified, and their shares are registered in an Ownership object. An Ownership object for each owner is associated with the vehicle, as presented in Figure 10.8.

Considering vehicle category's classification [17], a vehicle can be categorized as able to carry passengers (M), able to carry goods (N), two- or three-wheel vehicle or a quadricycle (L) and agricultural and forestry tractors and their trailers (T). In case of vehicles carrying passengers (M) or goods (N), they are also categorized in classes by their weight as light-duty vehicles when under 3500 kg and heavy-duty vehicles when

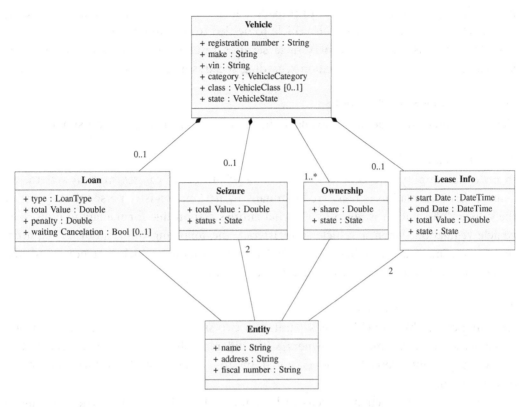

FIGURE 10.8   Proposed vehicle data model

equal or above 3500 kg. A vehicle can be registered in the car registration system in several conditions; this information is stored as a Vehicle State type. The different available states that a vehicle can belong to are presented in Table 10.1.

Analysing the special conditions of a vehicle, information regarding leases, loans or seizures are also stored in the car registration system. Lease information related to a certain vehicle is stored in the LeaseInfo object associated with the vehicle, as shown in Figure 10.8.

A vehicle can be submitted as collateral for loans; therefore, the entity responsible for the loan and possible penalties are registered, along with the total value of the loan and its

TABLE 10.1   Vehicle State object possible states.

State	Description
Active	Vehicle in circulation
Inactive	Vehicle no longer in circulation (e.g. exported vehicle)
Destructed	Vehicle with a destruction order issued
Suspended	Vehicle reported as not proper for circulation
Stolen	Vehicle reported as stolen by authorities

type. A loan guarantee is intended to provide a guarantee for loan payment, in this case, the vehicle. Thus, we consider each vehicle to be tied to maximum one loan at a time.

Lastly, we consider the case of vehicle seizures resulted from court orders or other judicial entity's decisions. Information regarding seizures is stored in a SeizureInfo object.

10.4.4 Car Registry Operations

Next, we present the operations available in the proposed car registration system.

10.4.4.1 Create a Vehicle

In order to simplify interactions over the blockchain-based car registration system, we assume this information is registered manually by national registry personal. As most of the vehicle information is given by external entities responsible for managing motorized vehicle regulation, when a vehicle is registered, the following information is required: registration number (number plate), VIN, make, model, vehicle category and the owners' information along with their respective shares.

10.4.4.2 Change Ownership

Changing ownership of vehicles is separated in two steps and is specific for each owner, as vehicles can have multiple owners with different shares each. As expected, this operation is only allowed to be executed by the owners of the vehicle subject to ownership change.

Thus, an ownership change needs to be initialized by the current owner wishing to give up his position on a certain vehicle, as proposed in Section 10.3.3.2. This step requires the owner to issue a *Change Owner* transaction, specifying the VIN, the registration number and the make of the vehicle, as well as the list of the new owners to which the current owner will give his share of the vehicle and the share percentage that he wants to transfer to the new owners.

Once the first step is completed, the vehicle ownership changes to the new owner. However, the new ownership is still required to be approved by the new owners. This state is represented in Figure 10.9 as *Waiting Ownership Change* state. In order to complete the ownership change, only the new owner registered in the initial *Change Owner* transaction is able to confirm this operation issuing a *Confirm Ownership* transaction specifying the vehicle's VIN, the registration number, the make, and the ownership share. Only after this step the ownership information is considered valid; for judicial obligations the new owner is considered as the legitimate owner.

10.4.4.3 Lease

As proposed in the business process presented in Section 10.3.3.4, the process for registering a lease contract is separated into a two-step operation. The owner is proposed to issue a *Create Lease* transaction that can be cancelled through a *Cancel Lease* transaction by the lessor, the lessee or by a registry employee. On the other hand, the lease registration can be accepted either by a registry employee or by the prospect lessee issuing a *Confirm Lease* transaction.

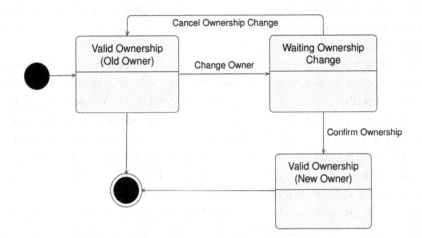

FIGURE 10.9   Change ownership transaction flow

As part of the *Create Lease* transaction, the VIN, the registration number, the make of the vehicle, the start and end dates of the contract, the expected total value of the lease, and the third party tied to the lease contract are required.

Once the *Create Lease* transaction is correctly executed, the vehicle enters a *Waiting lease confirmation* state. In order to successfully register a lease contract, the lessee registered in the initial *Create Lease* transaction is required to issue a *Confirm Lease* transaction containing the VIN, the vehicle's make and the registration number, as well as the total value of the lease contract. In case the transaction issued by the lessee matches with the information passed by the lessor, in the *Create Lease* transaction, the system registers the lease as associated with the vehicle and the vehicle enters the *Active lease* state.

For a lease contract termination to happen, it is necessary to issue a *Cancel Lease* transaction. Considering the *Cancel Lease* operation is issued by a judicial officer, this action takes into effect immediately; thus the lease contract is revoked.

In case the *Cancel Lease* transaction is issued by a lessee or a lessor, and the vehicle is in *Active lease* state, the process takes two steps, as both parties need to agree on cancelling the contract. To this extent, the first transaction to be issued will be the *Cancel Lease* transaction; thus the lease contract state is changed to *Waiting lease cancellation*. At this stage, any of the parties can revert the cancellation process by issuing a *Cancel Lease Termination*, specifying the VIN, the vehicle's make and the registration number. For the lease contract to be actually terminated after a *Cancel Lease Termination* transaction, it is necessary for the other party to issue a *Confirm Lease Termination* transaction with the same arguments as *Cancel Lease* transaction. It is possible to reject or cancel the lease termination process by issuing *Cancel Lease Termination* transaction.

10.4.4.4 Seize Vehicle

Given a process on which a vehicle owner is subject to a court to liquidate his debts, judicial officers can seize a vehicle or issue a pending seizure. Thus, if a pending seizure is in place, the asset cannot be sold or the ownership changed until the process is solved. Later, the same process can also result in a seizure, and the ownership of the asset can only be changed according to a court order.

In order to issue a pending seizure for a vehicle, a judicial officer is required to submit an *Issue Pending Seizure* transaction. An *Issue Pending Seizure* transaction should contain information about the owner of the vehicle, the total value of debt, the creditor and information about the vehicle in the form of VIN, the registration number and the make.

Considering a case on which the *Pending seizure* state needs to be changed back, a *Cancel Seizure* transaction should be emitted, containing the same information required for the *Issue Pending Seizure* transaction. The *Cancel Seizure* transaction can be issued only by a judicial officer.

In order to effectively seize the asset, an *Issue Seizure* transaction is required to be issued. An *Issue Seizure* transaction requires the same information used by *Issue Pending Seizure* transaction but also requires to refer to the date on which the seizure order was emitted and the court order number supporting this decision. When a vehicle is in its initial state with neither seizure nor pending seizure associated, it is possible for the judicial officer to directly emit an *Issue Seizure* transaction.

During *Issue Seizure* transaction execution, the ownership of the vehicle is changed by removing the owner implied in the seizure. The creditor specified in the *Issue Seizure* transaction is then assigned as an owner of the vehicle.

10.4.4.5 Register as Guarantee

In order to register a vehicle as guarantee, the vehicle's owner is required to order a *Register Guarantee* transaction mentioning the creditor, the type of loan (collateral or mortgage), the total value of the loan given to the vehicle owner and the penalty which the debtor needs to pay in case the loan is paid ahead of time. Vehicle information is also registered on the *Register Guarantee* transaction, such as the registration number, the make and the VIN. During the *Register Guarantee* transaction execution, a set of rules is verified in order for the transaction to be successful. The transaction can be issued by only the owner, and it is not possible to register a vehicle as a guarantee to a loan if the vehicle is already tied as a guarantee to a previously issued loan. The *Register Guarantee* transaction will not succeed if the vehicle is subject to a seizure or a pending seizure by a judicial order.

It is possible to cancel the guarantee by issuing a *Cancel Guarantee* transaction. A creditor can issue a *Cancel Guarantee* transaction with immediate effect, requiring to identify the vehicle through the VIN, registration number and the make.

On the other hand, if *Cancel Guarantee* transaction is issued by the vehicle owner, it requires the creditor to confirm or deny the operation accordingly using the transactions *Confirm Guarantee Cancellation* or *Reject Guarantee Cancellation*. Both transactions are required to include the VIN, the registration number and the make.

A *Confirm Cancellation* transaction is required to be issued by the creditor associated with the loan guarantee or by a national registry employee, for the vehicle to enter *No loan guarantee* state. On the other hand, as a *Reject Guarantee Cancellation* transaction is issued by the creditor or by a registry employee, the guarantee remains valid.

10.4.4.6 Change Vehicle State

As presented in vehicle data model of Figure 10.8 and explained in Section 10.4.3, a vehicle can be registered in the proposed car registration system according to different states. A change in a registered vehicle's state is usually presented by an external entity such as the Department of Motor Vehicles; however, as simplification, the national registry employee is in charge of this update on the car registration system. Thus, when a national registry employee receives a request for updating the state of a vehicle in the system, he issues a *Change State* transaction.

A *Change State* transaction is required to specify the vehicle's make and the registration number to which the state update is necessary. This transaction is also required to include the new state to which the vehicle will transit to and the VIN. The vehicle states which a vehicle can have were already described in Section 10.4.3.

10.5 IMPLEMENTATION

Based on the data model described in Section 10.4.3, a similar data model was created using a domain-specific language of Hyperledger Composer,[5] which later was deployed to a Hyperledger Fabric version 1.1-based network. Hyperledger Composer Modeling Language is an object-oriented modelling language designed to define the domain model for a business network defined for the Hyperledger Fabric.

Each transaction described throughout Section 10.4.4 was also modelled in Hyperledger Composer Modeling Language. Every information regarding the created data model was stored on the Hyperledger Fabric's blockchain with no off-chain database handling car registry records. Furthermore, the entire developed smart contract functions were developed using JavaScript and Hyperledger Composer API version 0.19.7. Hyperledger Composer provides an interface adaptable to any language to interact with Hyperledger Fabric blockchain.

Specific access control rules were defined using Hyperledger Composer access control language. Hyperledger Composer access control is defined through a set of rules that can detail CRUD access control considering the participant executing the transaction or reading asset information. Access control is fine-grained with the ability to restrict access to certain participants only through specific pieces of data of an asset and through specific transactions. Therefore, a set of rules were created to enforce permissions for each participant and each transaction.

10.5.1 Implemented Access Control Rules

Regarding the vehicle creation, as presented in Sections 10.3.3.1 and 10.4.4, this operation can be executed only by a Registry Employee participant type. Thus, a rule allowing Registry Employee type participants to issue *Create Vehicle* transactions was created.

Considering *Change Ownership* transactions, all participants of the system are entitled to issue this transaction. However, the verification of these rules is done through the smart contract's code, as verifying these rules through the access control mechanism leads to performance issues. Specific rules verifying that only the owner or owner of the

Legal Person owning the vehicle or a registry employee have permissions to issue *Confirm Ownership* and *Cancel Ownership* transactions were defined.

In the process of creating a lease, such as issuing a *Create Lease* transaction, only the Registry Employee participants and vehicle owners are entitled to execute this transaction. As presented earlier in this section, given the performance issues, the access control verification when issuing a *Create Lease* transaction is provided through the smart contract. Regarding lease transaction flow, the same rules as described for *Create Lease* transaction are defined for *Confirm Lease, Cancel Lease, Confirm Lease Termination* and *Cancel Lease Termination* transactions.

All transactions regarding seizure flow, such as *Issue Pending Seizure, Issue Seizure* and *Cancel Seizure* transactions, have the same rules as follows. Hyperledger Composer access control mechanism has a rule allowing Judicial Officer and Registry Employee participant types to create each of the vehicle seizure flow transactions.

Registering a vehicle as guarantee (*Register as Guarantee* and *Cancel Guarantee* transactions) requires that only vehicle owners or registry employees are allowed to execute the transaction. Thus, the verification of ownership and verifying that the transaction issuer is a registry employee is made through the smart contract's code for *Cancel Guarantee, Confirm Cancelation* and *Reject Cancelation* transactions. Finally, Hyperledger Composer access control mechanism allows only Registry Employee participant types to create *Change Vehicle State* transaction.

10.5.2 Hyperledger Fabric Configuration

In this section, we go over each system's components, explaining their contribution in the Hyperledger Fabric infrastructure. Then we present how a client is able to interact with the Hyperledger Fabric's blockchain and describe each step required to execute a transaction.

10.5.2.1 System Components

As part of the Hyperledger Fabric infrastructure, a network peer can be an endorsement peer, an anchor peer or a normal peer. As each peer type is not mutually exclusive, it is possible for a peer to be both an endorsement peer and an anchor peer, as shown in Figure 10.10.

Smart contracts' data is stored as key-value pairs in this database. Thus, when executing a transaction, the state database is used to make chaincode execution more efficient. As an alternative, CouchDB[6] can be used as an external state database, providing additional query support and richer queries when compared with the default state database.

An endorsement peer is responsible for validating transactions by executing transactions' chaincode (functions of the smart contract required by the transaction). An anchor peer is responsible for communicating with the Hyperledger Fabric network exterior to the organization on which it belongs. Finally, a normal peer is responsible for receiving a block of transactions issued by the ordering service and updating its local blockchain with the corresponding block.

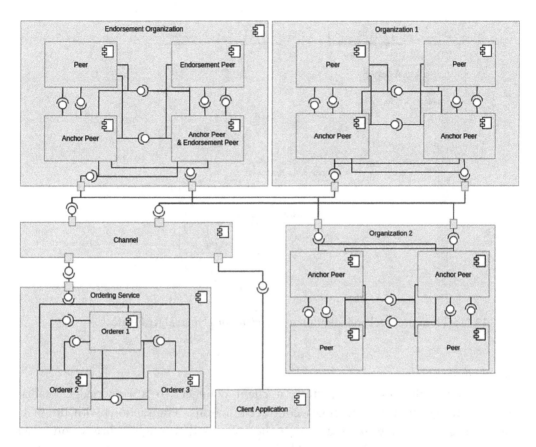

FIGURE 10.10   Component diagram of Hyperledger Fabric infrastructure

The ordering service is a core component of any Hyperledger Fabric infrastructure. The service is composed by ordering nodes (see Figure 10.10), responsible for reaching a consensus on building a block of signed and verified transactions to update the blockchain. The endorsement policies in place may vary according to the configuration setup defined by network's administrators.

As in Figure 10.10, three organizations are presented, and each of them comprises four peers. An endorsement organization (which can be a National Registry Entity) is responsible for endorsing transactions and comprises two endorsement peers and two normal peers. In addition, an endorsement peer and a normal peer also act as anchor peers. The remaining organizations are composed of four peers each and two of those peers act as anchor peers for the organizations.

An ordering service is presented, composed of three orderers, in order for the infrastructure to be fault tolerant. Finally, we consider a client application which is responsible for providing a platform for the end-users to use the BCar system proposed.

In order for the different components to interact and to maintain access control to information stored in the blockchain, Hyperledger Fabric provides channels. In case of the BCar system, a unique channel is used in the Hyperledger Fabric infrastructure.

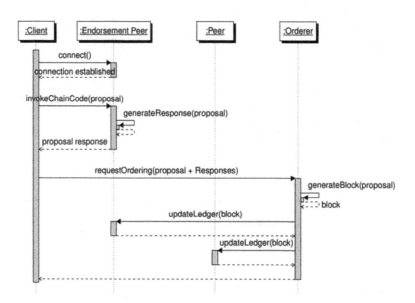

FIGURE 10.11 Block proposal and addition mechanism for Hyperledger Fabric.

10.5.2.2 System Behavior

In order to use the proposed system, a client connects to a Hyperledger Fabric network running the described smart contract functions. Transactions with intent to update blockchain's state are required to be submitted through Fabric's consensus mechanism, as shown in Figure 10.11. Then he submits the blockchain's update proposal to endorsement peers responsible for verifying and signing transaction proposals. According to a customizable policy, a specific number of valid proposal signatures are required in order for the transaction proposal to be accepted as valid by the network peers.

As the client collects the required proposal signatures, the list of signatures along with the proposal are sent to an ordering service, responsible for grouping signed transactions into a block, ordering them. Once transactions are ordered into a block, the block is sent to every peer on the network, and the blockchain is updated with the newly proposed block.

10.6 RESULTS

To assess the performance of the blockchain-based car registration system proposed we had at our disposal a single Virtual Machine (VM) with 8vCPU, 32 GB of RAM and 40 GB of HDD space, running Ubuntu Xenial (16.04.5 LTS). Regarding the software setup, tests were performed on top of Docker containers running over Docker v18.06.0-ce. Each peer, certified authority node and orderer was running on the base image of Hyperledger Fabric x86 64 v1.1.0. As state database, instances of Hyperledger Fabric CouchDB image version x86 64 v0.4.6 were used.

In order to measure system's performance, Hyperledger Caliper[7] software was used. Given the Hyperledger Caliper is still in the development phase, a version based on commit *c37860b042*[8] was adapted for the BCar registration system to be tested.

Hyperledger Caliper is a blockchain benchmark tool developed within the Hyperledger projects. Caliper allows measuring the performance of multiple blockchain implementations; one of them is Hyperledger Fabric, given a set of use cases. This tool can produce reports containing various performance indicators, such as transactions per second, transaction latency and resource utilization.

Considering Hyperledger Fabric nodes setup, we configured the system with a total of nine containers two Hyperledger Fabric peers. The system was configured using solo consensus mechanism, thus a single orderer container was set up for the experiments. A total of two organizations were configured, requiring a certified authority running on a separate container for each organization.

Organization's peers used in the experimental setup were configured as endorsement peers. Thus, an additional container (Chaincode Peer) is used to execute the transaction's required chaincode. This ensures process isolation from endorsement peer process. Hyperledger Fabric infrastructure was set up to ensure a single transaction signature from an endorsement peer was enough for the ordering service to accept the operation.

10.6.1 Methodology

A set of functions was selected to sample the system's overall performance based on the principal transaction flows described in Chapter 1.4. Thus, we evaluated the performance of *Create Vehicle, Change Vehicle State, Change Ownership, Issue Seizure* and *Register as Guarantee* functions.

Each function was tested three times with a varying number of fixed throughput issued by the testing software, for each block size configuration. First, a set of 100 vehicles was created and a set of 100 transactions were issued against the BCar registration system with a fixed send rate of 50 transactions per second (TPS). Then, a set of 200 vehicles was created, and a set of 200 transactions was issued with a fixed send rate of 100 TPS. Finally, a set of 400 vehicles was created, and 400 transactions were issued with a fixed send rate of 200 TPS against the BCar registration system. As each set of transactions was sent, the time taken for the system to fulfil the requests was measured, then the throughput was calculated dividing the number of transactions successfully executed by the time taken to execute such transactions.

As each component of the Hyperledger Fabric system is running on a single Virtual Machine, we took advantage of Hyperledger Caliper functionalities by tracking the RAM and CPU usage of each Docker container.

Regarding block size and maximum time for block formation, three experiments were conducted. Each function's throughput and latency information was measured against a block size of 1 MB, with 250 ms timeout configuration, 2 MB block size with 500 ms timeout and a 4 MB block size with a 1 s timeout.

10.6.2 Evaluation

Considering the four functions selected to evaluate the system, we averaged the throughput of each function given a certain block size, based on the information of Table 10.2. As we analysed in Section 10.2, a higher block size is expected to provide a higher throughput to a blockchain-based system, as shown in Figures 10.12 and 10.13.

The maximum throughput achieved was around 7.67 TPS, with a 4 MB block size and a 1 s timeout, when issuing an *Issue Seizure* transaction. However, these same transactions presented a latency of 23.53 s. By analysing the graphics (Figures 10.12 and 10.13), we can conclude the best compromise to optimize both throughput performance and lower latency achieved using a 2 MB block size.

10.6.3 System Bottlenecks

In this section, we go over the system resources statistics, collected throughout the system's evaluation, in order to understand the obtained results. In Table 10.3, we notice that across all tested block sizes, the latency suffers a major increase when comparing a 100 TPS send rate with the 200 TPS send rate. The overall latency is roughly doubled when the send rate is around 200 TPS, with no major increase in throughput. Raising

TABLE 10.2 Throughput in TPS considering the variation of block size.

	1MB			2MB			4MB		
Send Rate (TPS)	**50**	**100**	**200**	**50**	**100**	**200**	**50**	**100**	**200**
Create Vehicle	5	6	timeout	6	6	5	6	6	5
Change Ownership	6	7	7	7	7	7	7	8	7
Issue Seizure	6	8	8	7	8	7	8	8	7
Register as Guarantee	6	7	6	7	8	6	7	8	6
Change State	7	7	8	6	8	8	7	8	8

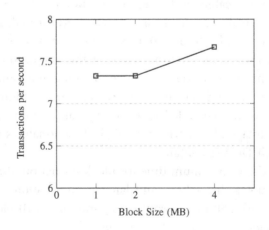

FIGURE 10.12   Throughput of Issue Seizure function

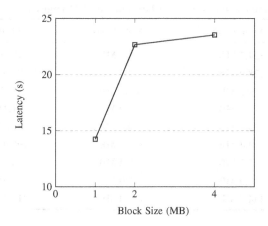

FIGURE 10.13   Latency of Issue Seizure function

TABLE 10.3 Latency (seconds) considering the variation of block size

	1MB			2MB			4MB		
Send Rate (TPS)	**50**	**100**	**200**	**50**	**100**	**200**	**50**	**100**	**200**
Create Vehicle	13.74	25.68	timeout	12.68	25.62	57.87	11.65	24.15	64.25
Change Ownership	12.28	21.04	40.37	11.43	21.29	42.24	10.05	19.26	47.03
Issue Seizure	12.05	11.09	19.61	11.35	19.82	36.82	9.15	18.9	42.54
Register as Guarantee	39.73	11.75	20.74	9.75	18.66	46.85	10.05	20.63	45.36
Change State	10.79	20.29	35.38	11.56	18.32	36.85	11.18	19.73	36.39

the thesis that such performance is due to the single orderer setup used for the system tests, we expect an overload of CPU usage or RAM consumption. However, analysing the system statistics for 1 MB block size during a 100 TPS send rate test, as in Table 10.4, it is clear that the ordering peer (orderer) is not requiring above average CPU or memory usage. Furthermore, the ordering peer presents low memory and CPU usage during the test. Regarding all components used in the test, CouchDB instances reveal to be the most resource-hungry containers.

On the other hand, the use of Hyperledger Composer framework might have a significant impact on Hyperledger Fabric overall performance. It is possible that the use of native Hyperledger Fabric chaincode to develop the car registration system's smart contracts might lead to performance improvements. Considering the complexity of a car registration system, it is plausible that the quantity of information stored in the blockchain and the complexity of available operations might provide a reason for such latency and throughput results. Even though access control rules embedded in the smart contract improved these results, it is still noticeable that the access control mechanisms used in BCar system contribute to lower performance regarding throughput and latency.

TABLE 10.4 Register Guarantee function (100.0 TPS send rate/1 MB block size)

Name	Memory (max.)	Memory (avg.)	CPU (max.)	CPU (avg.)
dev-peer0.org2	124.7 MB	116.8 MB	90.68%	25.30%
dev-peer0.org1	128.9 MB	120.9 MB	82.95%	25.42%
peer0.org2	77.5 MB	65.9 MB	96.47%	38.99%
peer0.org1	74.1 MB	62.9 MB	91.21%	40.05%
orderer	23.2 MB	19.1 MB	22.63%	3.91%
couchdb.org2	134.4 MB	124.7 MB	195.93%	82.82%
ca.org1	7.2 MB	7.2 MB	0.00%	0.00%
ca.org2	7.0 MB	7.0 MB	0.01%	0.00%
couchdb.org1	144.9 MB	127.0 MB	211.25%	83.66%

10.7 CONCLUSION

Throughout this chapter, a use case for blockchain technology in public registries was presented. Blockchain technology, as of its decentralized nature, can provide a different approach to registry storage. In fact, a blockchain-based car registration system was proposed (BCar), taking advantage of decentralization capabilities of the technology.

Based on the car registration business processes and public information about the systems currently in place, a set of requirements for a car registration system was defined. A data model was built considering the operations identified for a car registration system as well as the participants of the system. The set of available operations for the BCar registration system was then described.

Considering BCar system roles, five participant types were defined with different permissions over the vehicle registration operations. A Citizen type participant was defined as a singular entity able to own a vehicle. A Legal Person type participant was defined as a collective of citizens owning a vehicle. A judicial officer participant was entitled to execute judicial orders in the system. Then, a registry employee participant presented as a supervisor of the system able to perform operations to maintain a correct car registration system. Finally, an External Person type was presented to allow employees of external entities, as tax authorities, to read vehicle registry information.

Regarding vehicle registry's operations, we presented a set of operations, such as the initial vehicle's registration transaction and two-step transaction flows as *Change Ownership* transaction flow, taking advantage of a blockchain-based car registration system. Those operations enabled registry employees to lower their intervention in those transaction flow.

Finally, we conducted a set of performance tests over a simple configuration of the Hyperledger Fabric system and conducted an analysis of the data collected from those tests. In the test results, we analysed the throughput and latency results over a set of system's functions varying the block size of the system.

As the BCar registration system was designed, it encompasses most of the operations over car registries. However, the system focuses only on car registry data. Considering such a system, blockchain technology could be used to join the car registry systems of the EU member states into a distributed system. Furthermore, blockchain technology could be applied to every other government registry domains, as the civil registry system, the land registry or the business registry.

NOTES

1 e-Health – https://e-estonia.com/solutions/healthcare/e-health-record
2 e-Residency – https://e-resident.gov.ee/
3 Documento Único Automóvel – www.irn.mj.pt/sections/irn/a_registral/servicos-externos-docs/impressos/automovel/requerimento-de-registo/downloadFile/file/DUA_modelo_unico.pdf
4 Documento Único Automóvel – www.irn.mj.pt/sections/irn/a_registral/servicos-externos-docs/impressos/automovel/requerimento-de-registo/downloadFile/file/DUA_modelo_unico.pdf
5 Hyperledger Composer – https://hyperledger.github.io/composer/latest/
6 CouchDB – http://couchdb.apache.org
7 Hyperledger Caliper – www.hyperledger.org/projects/caliper
8 Hyperledger Caliper Repository – https://github.com/hyperledger/caliper/tree/c37860b042

REFERENCES

[1] Satoshi Nakamoto. *Bitcoin: A Peer-to-Peer Electronic Cash System. www.bitcoin.org*, page 9, 2008.
[2] Mark Walport. *Distributed Ledger Technology: Beyond Block Chain.* Government Office for Science, pages 1–88, London, UK, 2015.
[3] Vitalik Buterin. Ethereum: A next-generation cryptocurrency and decentralized application platform, 2014.
[4] Nick Szabo. The Idea of Smart Contracts. *Nick Szabo's Papers and Concise Tutorials*, 1997.
[5] Xiwei Xu, Cesare Pautasso, Liming Zhu, Vincent Gramoli, Alexander Ponomarev, An Binh Tran and Shiping Chen. The blockchain as a software connector. In *Proceedings of the 13th Working IEEE/IFIP Conference on Software Architecture*, pages 182–191, 2016.
[6] Miguel Castro and Barbara Liskov. Practical Byzantine fault tolerance. In *Proceedings of the 3rd USENIX Symposium on Operating Systems Design and Implementation*, pages 173–186, February 1999.
[7] Miguel Correia, Giuliana Santos Veronese, Nuno Ferreira Neves and Paulo Verissimo. Byzantine consensus in asynchronous message-passing systems: A survey. *International Journal of Critical Computer-Based Systems*, 2(2): 141–161, 2011.
[8] Giuliana Santos Veronese, Miguel Correia, Alysson Neves Bessani, Lau Cheuk Lung and Paulo Verissimo. Efficient Byzantine fault tolerance. *IEEE Transactions on Computers*, 62(1): 16–30, 2013.
[9] Leslie Lamport, Robert Shostak and Marshall Pease. The Byzantine generals problem. *ACM Transactions on Programming Languages and Systems*, 4(3): 382–401, July 1982.
[10] Vukolić. Marko. The quest for scalable blockchain fabric: proof-of-work vs. BFT replication. *Lecture Notes in Computer Science*, 9591: 112–125, 2016.
[11] Ittay Eyal and Emin Gün Sirer. Majority is not enough: Bitcoin mining is vulnerable. *Lecture Notes in Computer Science*, 8437: 436–454, 2014.
[12] Vukolić Marko. Rethinking permissioned blockchains. In *Proceedings of the ACM Workshop on Blockchain, Cryptocurrencies and Contracts*, pages 3–7, 2017.
[13] Elli Androulaki, Artem Barger, Vita Bortnikov, Christian Cachin, Konstantinos Christidis, Angelo De Caro, David Enyeart, Christopher Ferris, Gennady Laventman, Yacov Manevich,

et al. Hyperledger fabric: A distributed operating system for permissioned blockchains. In *Proceedings of the 13th ACM EuroSys Conference*, 2018.

[14] João Sousa, Alysson Bessani and Marko Vukolic. A Byzantine fault-tolerant ordering service for hyperledger fabric. In *Proceedings of the 48th Annual IEEE/IFIP International Conference on Dependable Systems and Networks*, 2018.

[15] Sarah Underwood. Blockchain beyond bitcoin. *Communications of the ACM*, 59(11): 15–17, 2016.

[16] Council of European Union. Council directive 1999/37/ec of 29 April 1999 on the registration documents for vehicles. *OJ, L*, 138: 57–65, 1999-06-01.

[17] UN-ECE. Consolidated resolution on the construction of vehicles (r.e.3), ece/trans/wp.29/78/rev.6, July 2017.

CHAPTER 11

Advancing the Cybersecurity of Electronic Voting Machines Using Blockchain Technology

Nitin Sukhija and John-George Sample

Slippery Rock University of Pennsylvania, Slippery Rock, USA

Elizabeth Bautista

Lawrence Berkeley National Laboratory, Berkeley, USA

CONTENTS

Cybersecurity has become central for empowering national and international progress in diverse scientific and non-scientific domains. With the advent of myriad different technologies in the post peta-scale computing era, the future of computing involves a significantly greater degree of cyber incidents than we are observing currently. The rapid advancement and introduction of new processing technologies for computing has facilitated the convergence of Artificial Intelligence (AI) and Machine Learning (ML), Data Analytics and Big Data and the High Performance Computing (HPC) domains platforms to solve complex large-scale real-time analytics and scientific applications pertaining to diverse scientific and non-scientific fields. As we move towards exascale future and beyond, the new convergent computing platforms along with a paradigm shift in programming applications leveraging these platforms provide both challenges and opportunities for cyberinfrastructure facilitators, researchers and administrators to develop, deliver, support, and prepare a diverse set of solutions utilizing emerging technologies to mitigate cyber-attacks and achieve cyber resilience in real time. Blockchain is one of the powerful emerging technology that is diverse, dynamic, and promises substantial resiliency against malicious adversaries when employed in the advanced, unpredictable, and heterogeneous computing ecosystems, such as financial services industry, national cyberinfrastructures, and more. One of the most significant benefit of the blockchain technology is its inherent resiliency to cyber-attacks. While blockchain is not immune to all forms of cyber threats, its exceptional configuration facilitates cybersecurity features that are not currently present in the traditional ledgers and other legacy technologies. Consequently, a comprehensive study of how blockchains may fit within broader cybersecurity objectives is of paramount importance, especially for researchers from both academic and industrial domains dealing with facilitating innovative solutions for enabling cybersecurity in their respective domains. This chapter presents an implementation of the electronic voting machine (EVM) illustrating the applicability of emerging blockchain technology-based solutions to address current and emerging cybersecurity threats.

11.1 INTRODUCTION

Today's computing technology has enabled new opportunities for diverse industrial ecosystems and their users to save time and money along with the computing power by facilitating processes and interactions to execute on remote and virtualized servers as opposed to local machines. With ubiquitous computing gaining traction, the concern for cybersecurity is becoming increasingly important. For instance, when a consumer is interacting with the application service hosted on the cloud, they are generally without knowledge about where or how their data is being stored. They could be sharing a single server with large number of other users, and if these servers are not properly setup to section off use to individual users, it could be problematic for the security of other users. Moreover, any data manipulation or subversion attempts can have lethal impact on business operations of the users interacting with a compromised server. Thus, in the shared computing ecosystems the cybersecurity solutions should also focus on the integrity aspect of the classic security CIA triad rather than just highlighting only the confidentiality and availability aspects. Furthermore, data integrity concern is even more pertinent for the government and the military establishments where manipulation of data can negatively impact decision-making at critical times. In recent years, both academia and industrial community are increasingly interested in blockchain technology because of its potential to be tailored to accommodate various types of data, and to facilitate trust between counterparties based on the technology's integrity. Blockchain technology can help in facilitating digital trust by building tamper-proof digital vaults to protect connected users/devices, define their access control permissions and provide redundancy in the systems, such as, EVMs. [1, 2].

EVMs were first implemented in the mid-1990s. Since their introduction, their legitimacy has been called into question numerous times over the years [3, 4]. A catch-22 that exists with voting machines is how they normally operate. A closed-source voting machine that does not disclose how it operates is known as black box voting machine. This concept makes interfering with votes more difficult but leads to the general public lacking the trust that votes are being counted genuinely. The inverse of this is equally problematic [5]. If a voting machine is entirely open source, modifying votes is easier as malicious users have a deeper understanding of the system. An EVM that utilizes blockchain technology solves both of these problems. All records are open source but are also incredibly difficult to modify. This is a result of every node in the blockchain having a copy of the previous transactions; a discrepancy would be immediately noted. Some of the early concerns were that they could be maliciously controlled by politicians, and that they could possibly skew the results to make themselves win. There also exists the issue of accessibility for everyone who can vote. These issues of accessibility were remedied very quickly by a myriad of tools that let individuals with disabilities vote with ease. One of the earliest methods to prove that a voter's ballot was correctly submitted was to have a voter-verifiable audit trail. This consisted of a physical print-out of the candidates that were selected by the voter that they again confirm were correct, which is then stored for future reference in the event of questionable vote tallying by electronic means. The AccuVote-TS was an early electronic voting terminal that was used around 2002 and was created by Diebold Nixdorf, a financial and retail technology company [6]. In 2004, the source code for this machine was erroneously uploaded to a publicly available FTP site, which was then discovered and quickly shared around the internet for all to investigate. The voter then could initiate their vote with a smartcard that would allow the machine to start accepting input votes, thus a malicious user could easily create several fake smartcards that the system would accept with no issue and they could cast the votes as if they were real voters [7].

Many relevant implementations for EVMs exist across the world, as many countries have implemented their own EVMs, some even going as far as allowing online by issuing each voter a national ID card to make sure all voters have equal representation. The idea of having a blockchain-based EVM for enabling cybersecurity is still a relatively new concept. With the rise in cryptocurrencies taking advantage of the distributed ledger, blockchains have been examined for their use in voting machines. The advantages of a blockchain-based EVM include: no single point of failure, no single entity controlling the blockchain, and immense computing power requirement for attempting modification of a block (or a vote in our case) [8]. The voting machines are the veins of the democracy, and failure to understand the impact of these machines (and their flaws) on elections will lead to votes being compromised, leading to an inevitable illegitimate victory. This topic of research will continue to grow in importance as EVMs become more ubiquitous [9, 10].

This chapter covers the relationship between cybersecurity and blockchain technologies deployed in the EVM domain. There is considerable ongoing research into cybersecurity solutions. However, research on employing blockchain technology for reducing cyber-attacks and for enhancing data integrity of EVMs is still in early stages. This chapter especially involves investigating the applicability of the blockchain technology for advancing cybersecurity of voting systems through the following:

1. Explaining a shared understanding of some of the cybersecurity considerations and risk inherent to blockchain, and form recommendations for academia and industry to facilitate blockchain innovations.

2. Exemplifying an EVM based on a form of Byzantine fault tolerance (BFT) for determining the confirmed ledger, which requires a ledger to have 66% of validator's agreement.

3. Illustrating a workflow for integrating the replica of the awed WINVote system [11] with the blockchain technology to demonstrate how easily votes could be viewed, manipulated and secured.

11.2 BACKGROUND

11.2.1 Blockchain

The blockchain technology was first presented by Satoshi Nakamoto (a pseudonym) in 2008 [12]. He proposed the first peer-to-peer payment cryptocurrency named Bitcoin, which facilitates the cash transactions via the Internet and relieves the need of trustor required by financial institutions [13]. Blockchain technology is inherently secure, and its design is an example of a system with significantly high byzantine failure tolerance (BFT) [14]. Bitcoin, the first application of the Blockchain, relies on a decentralized public ledger along with the stochastic consensus protocol to create a chain that is tamper-proof and uses cryptography to publicly verify the currency exchange over the Internet, thus securing the currency transactions.

The blockchain is in general an append-only data structure where all blocks of transactions are chained together. The new blocks of data can only be appended to the chain with an immunity with respect to deletion of medication. Thus, each block in the chain is cryptographically linked via a hash to the previous block in the chain. The first block in the chain is termed as the foundation block of the stack and every new block of data that is being formulated gets appended on top of the previous block in chain, thus forming a final stack termed as a blockchain. Moreover, you can view blockchain as a digital book where the transactions completed in a bitcoin or another cryptocurrency are chronologically documented, publicly verifiable and assures immutability.

The blockchain is a nascent technology which can be considered as a newer kind of database which has now become a fancy solution for addressing security issues in storing digital data and information. The blockchain technology allows the digital information to be distributed not copied, thus creating the backbone of a newer internet technology. The term blockchain signifies that all the transactions occurring in a network are congregated into blocks of data and thereafter linked together using sophisticated hash functions. Therefore, it makes it impossible to alter or delete the older records which makes blockchain an attractive solution acting as an incorruptible digital book for commercial transactions to not only just record financial transactions but almost everything which is valuable. A basic understanding of the blockchain technology can envisioned by assuming a spreadsheet which is replicated many times across a computer network and the spreadsheet is regularly updated the designed network. The blockchain database is not centralized which means that the data is not stored in any single location but is distributed among the network and can be easily publicly verified, thus limits the hacking and tampering attempts of the cyber adversaries. Moreover, the chain is hosted on a network comprising millions of computers simultaneously, thus enables easy access to community via the internet. The identical data information blocks are stored across the blockchain network, thus enabling no single entity control, and no single point of failure.

The blockchain lives in a state of general agreement, that facilitates automatic checks within a designated timeframe. The blockchain eliminates the vulnerability of storing data centrally by holding the data across its whole network. Major industry players are adopting this new way of storing data, given if an industry's database is maintained by a central authority, and if that authority gets tampered by a malicious entity, or even by a natural disaster then all the data and information of the corporate clients can be either lost or compromised. However, by adopting blockchain, all the corporate users can access and rely on the distributed database that stores and update their own duplicate of the data and information.

Bitcoin, another alternative currency, utilizes blockchain technology [15]. Bitcoin and blockchain are not the same. Bitcoin is just one of the applications of blockchain. Let's imagine a sheet of paper that has 25 lines. When a sheet is filled up with 25 transactions, the block is validated by a group and comes to an agreement. Once the page has been validated, it is added to a stack of previously validated sheets. Each sheet on the stack can be assumed to be trustworthy because once the sheet has been validated it cannot be changed. At this point, all the sheets are linked together and to link our sheet together we embed information from the previous sheet of paper into the new, recently validated sheet. In blockchain, our sheet of paper is equal to a block. The act of embedding a previous block of information into the current block of information is called chaining, hence the name blockchain.

Some of the main components encompassing a blockchain ecosystem [16] are:

1. distributed P2P system

2. public shared ledger

3. decentralized consensus algorithm

4. cryptography

Distributed P2P System—In blockchain, the most recent state of the data information is not stored on a single computer. However, the blockchain is synchronized and is made accessible via millions of computers across the world. The computers in this network are called nodes, which are connected in a P2P (peer-to-peer) network [17], and each one of these nodes store the most recent updated version of the data blocks of the chain to enable security and public verification.

Public Shared Ledger—In blockchain, there is a publicly available ledger that is distributed among all the nodes across the network [18]. This data structure provides immutability to the blockchain records as any changes made to any of the blocks data or information can be viewed across the blockchain ecosystem, thus ensures the rights of the users and limits hacking attempts.

Decentralized Consensus Algorithm—The decentralized consensus algorithms, such as proof-of-work (POW), proof-of-stake (POS), delegated proof of stake (DPOS), transaction as proof of stake (TAPOS), delegated Byzantine fault tolerance (dBFT) are implemented in the nodes and facilitates the secure updating of the states according to some set transition rules [19]. The algorithm specifies the rules of the game where the state transition rules are determined and distributed among the nodes who collectively have the right to perform state transitions.

Cryptography—Cryptography is one of the main technologies that plays a vital role in blockchain and making blockchain secure and immutable. Blockchain makes use of several different types of cryptography. Among these are [20]:

- Public Key Cryptography: Pair of public and private keys used for encryption and digital signatures.

- Zero-Knowledge Proof: Prove knowledge of a secret without revealing it.

- Hash Functions: One-way pseudo-random mathematical functions and Merkle trees.

11.2.2 Electronic Voting Machines

In recent years, many countries across the globe are progressing towards testing and adopting EVM technology as their sole voting mechanism over the traditional paper-based systems. Even though EVM systems facilitates key advantages, such as convenience, agility, tally speediness, cost-effectiveness, and flexibility, the adoption of this technology has been somewhat limited because of its debatable security features, such as confidentiality, accuracy, anonymity, verifiability, and secrecy [21]. Given the significant challenges in the development of EVM systems that meet optimal design requirements, a few countries have successfully tested and adopted EVM systems, while some countries have tried and abandoned it, and some countries continue to evaluate them or plan of testing and adopting them in near future. Currently, a small number of countries have employed EVM systems as their nationwide sole voting method, while some countries are trialing the usage of EVM technology in a smaller subset of elections/constituencies (relative to nationwide voting) [22]. A global view on the adoption of EVM can be found at [23].

There are three main types of electronic voting systems that have been employed for conducting elections around the world.

1. **Optical Scan Voting**: It is the oldest and most common voting systems where paper ballots are used by the voters and then are scanned for electronic tabulation. The optical scan voting has been used in many countries across the world, such as Canada, United States, Philippines, South Korea, and many more, either for nationwide voting or for small subset of elections especially for the absentee votes. However, some countries like United Kingdom and Germany have abandoned the optical scan voting system [24, 25].

2. **Direct Recording Voting**: It is newer voting technology where no paper ballots are used. The direct recording electronic (DRE) voting machines uses touchscreen interfaces, dial controls, and pushbuttons to record and store the individuals votes electronically, with no physical ballots. However, some of the DRE machines are designed to create a paper trail which is used for the purpose of verification and recounting votes. The DRE voting has been used for nationwide elections in countries, such as Brazil, Estonia, India, and Venezuela, and for small subset of elections in countries, such as Canada, United States, Peru, and Argentina. However, countries like Belgium, France, Netherlands, Germany, Paraguay, and Japan have discontinued the DRE voting system [26, 27].

3. **Internet Voting**: Also known as remote electronic voting (REV) over internet, I-voting is the newest and most rare form of electronic voting technology. In I-voting, the voters register their votes over the internet and can do so via physical polling booths or via their own devices in their own homes. Given the flexibility of casting votes remotely, I-voting can be of extreme convenience and can significantly increase voters turnout/participation. However, cyber threats to the I-voting system is a major concern in employing these systems nationwide. Only a very few countries have employed I-voting for conducting internet elections nationwide. In 2005, small Baltic republic of Estonia was the first country in the world to introduce I-voting at local scale and continued using the I-voting system for conducting elections on a national scale since 2007 [28, 29]. Some countries like Netherlands, Austria, Germany, Kazakhstan, and Norway tried and tested I-voting but rejected it over evaluation phase. However, some countries like Canada and Switzerland are still considering adopting the internet voting system [30].

11.2.3 Surveying Recent Threats

In recent years, many reports of meddling in election processes has finally brought attention to all sorts of vulnerabilities in the election infrastructure, including in voting machines used across different nations.

1. Ukraine: In 2014, Ukraine's election infrastructure was targeted by malicious entities where attackers used distributed denial-of-service (DDoS) attacks at the internet links targeting the vote tally computerized system that is used to aggregate the election results from around the country, thus disrupting tallying process and blocking election results. Moreover, the attackers also employed a malware in the election commission computers with an attempt to discredit the election process by reporting incorrect election results [31].

2. Germany: Beginning January 2015, malicious actors continuously attacked German federal legislature (Bundestag) resulting in installing a malware infecting the Bundestag network, thus compromising thousands of computers and registered users information. This cyber-attack was reported to be most extensive and damaging cyber-attack on German government institutions to interfere in the German elections which resulted in days of shutdown of the entire Bundestag network [32, 33].

3. Montenegro: In 2016, the malicious foreign actors used denial-of-service attacks on the Montenegrin parliamentary elections, multiple media and government websites. These hacks were intended to disrupt web servers, and to make election infrastructure unavailable for certain state users [34, 35].

4. France: During 2017, the French presidential election campaign was target of phishing attacks and gigabytes of campaign data was stolen and published online. The cyber incident was geared to discredit the election process and influence the election outcome [36].

11.2.4 Cybersecurity of Voting Machines

As most of the industrial and government systems have been digitized or are in process of digitization, cybersecurity has become central for every nation's security and has been topic of discussion in most of the political debates in countries. The modern sophisticated malicious entities can easily find vulnerabilities in myriad of the locally or remotely managed systems and exploits these back doors to attack these systems to achieve specific objectives, which can be political, financial or for creating instabilities of various kinds. Some common instances of attacks which are becoming a norm than an exception, include a range of DDoS attacks to disrupt the major corporations, phishing attacks to leak confidential private information for monetary or defamation objectives, malware attacks, DNS poisoning or fraudulent websites with malicious content and many more [27]. With the evolving technological proliferation, the critical infrastructure of any nation is undoubtedly a vital target for the most advanced cyber adversaries. One of the most recently heard incidents include malicious cyber-attacks on the election infrastructure of many nations. The cyber adversaries intend to exploit the vulnerabilities in the systems comprising the existing election infrastructure to materialize the disinformation in the election campaigns, thus preventing citizens from exercising their fundamental democratic choice [4].

Securing election infrastructure is becoming increasingly important as many countries in the world have started embracing DRE voting or remote election voting (I-voting) systems. The democratic election process of most of the nations include information receiving and dissemination mechanisms influencing voters decisions and actions, and the machines/systems to cast, tabularize, and tally the votes determining the winning party. However, the most potential hacking threat to election security process stems from the easily exploitable vulnerabilities in the current EVMs that are being employed to cast votes in the states/constituencies in many nations [15]. Most of the common vulnerabilities in the electronic machines are related to their inability of the EVMs to cope up with the technological changes. Most of the EVMs are almost a decade old, which are prone to random failures and crashes, such as memory card failures, and have serious security and reliability flaws that are easily exploitable [37]. For instance, the EVMs uses significantly weaker and outdated Wi-Fi encryption standards that can be easily hacked by malicious actors to access, record and modify the legitimate voters data on the EVMs. Moreover, the operating system installed on most of these machines is not updated with the most recent security patches, thus leaving ports open to be exploited by external actors. Furthermore, the database used by these EVMs to store results also lack significant encryption, thus exposing the database to be hacked and to tamper with the election results easily. Thus, the EVMs are not only more prone to aging hardware and software failures but also are notoriously available to hack and cause election meddling. A perfect illustration of the outdated EVM is the now decommissioned Virginia WINVote machine [38].

The state of Virginia found numerous security vulnerabilities in voting machines used from 2003 to 2015. These WINVote systems had flaws involving easily broken encryption methods, insecure passwords, lack of firewalls, and numerous open ports, all of which contributed to the possibility of votes being modified for over a decade. After the Virginia Information Technologies Agency (VITA) was instructed by the Department of Elections (ELECT) to perform numerous tests on the security of the EVMs, VITA ultimately recommended the decommissioning of use of Advanced Voting Systems WINVote devices [39]. The issues involving modifying the peoples voice still plague elections to this day. Many new approaches to combat these problems are emerging daily. One of the newest methods is the use of a distributed ledger, a type of database that utilizes a peer-to-peer network without a central authority, where all nodes on the network synchronize and update every change independently. Implementing this technology in the context of voting machines would introduce a level of security that is invulnerable to flaws that were present in the WINVote systems [40]. Each change to a block, a collection of transactions, generates a unique hash that links the block to the previous block, reflecting across the whole chain of blocks. The hashes used in a distributed ledger are superior to the wired equivalent privacy (WEP) encryption. The following sections presents our methodology to create a replica of the flawed WINVote system (with modern technology) to demonstrate how easily votes could be both viewed, manipulated and secured. This is accomplished by simulating the peer-to-peer network with WEP encryption. By tracing the packets sent over the network, a network packet is created that aids in exploiting the WEP algorithm and cracking the WEP encryption key. Additionally, a voting system is created using a distributed ledger. The benefits of using a distributed ledger makes the new improved voting system not only more secure, but safe from any exploit that were used on the WINVote system. To create this improved voting system, the blockchain is employed that ensures all votes are securely transmitted with Python3 language. As each node checks against every other node, information is difficult to change. Additionally, modifying anything on a node will result in a new hash being created. This new hash will not only be identified immediately but would require an enormous amount of computing power to appear genuine due to the need to update all blocks on the chain. The following sections demonstrate the use of a distributed ledger in a small-scale environment and display the feasibility in implementing a blockchain-based voting system in an actual election.

Even though the electronic voting system insecurities has prevailing concerns, there have been some emergence of successful electronic voting systems which have been tested, adopted and has sustained to this day. This section provides a brief historical background of some of the electronic voting systems based on internet and blockchain that have been proposed to address the security flaws of the current electronic election process.

The first successful internet-based voting system was used in Estonia in 2005. The system is accessed by the citizens using internet and their identity is authenticated by their National ID cards to sign their ballot to cast their vote. The voters first download the voting client application on their electronic device and signs in using ID with PIN associated with their authentication key [29]. Once the vote is cast, the vote will be encrypted using the 2048-bit election public key and signed using the voters private key. Once vote is cast, the vote is sent to the storage server. Once the election concludes, the tabulation process takes place where storage server removes invalid votes by reverifying the signatures of the encrypted votes. To avoid intimidation the votes can vote multiple times where the last vote is only counted. However, there still exist certain tradeoffs including the need to trust the central server which still pose security concerns for the internet voting [41]. The Norwegian Voting System was also developed on the lines of electronic voting system of Estonia. The system was tested for local and national elections in 2011 and 2013. However, the system was abandoned in 2014 in lieu of safeguarding the voters confidence in the Norwegian electoral process, given there were fears of comprising secrecy of votes due to limited knowledge of security mechanisms. The largest deployment of the internet voting was seen in 2015 when 280,000 citizens castes their votes using iVote system in New

South Wales, Australia. The New South Wales iVote system was developed by a vendor named Scytl in collaboration with the New South Wales Electoral Commission (NSWEC). There are mainly four steps in casting a vote via iVote system, which are: (1) Voter registration to obtain a 8-digit iVote ID and a 6-digit PIN; (2) casting vote by logging into voting server using the 8-digit iVote ID and a 6-digit PIN and obtaining a 12-digit confirmation receipt; (3) verifying the vote via interactive voice response (IVR) system using the iVote ID, PIN and the confirmation receipt (Optional); and (4) conforming the inclusion of the voters vote in the final count using the verification service and the receipt number (optional). However, many security flaws were illustrated in the iVote system risks exposing and replacing valid votes [42]. In 2010, United States also built and tested a pilot internet voting system, D.C. Digital Vote-by-Mail Service (DVBM). This trial was conducted to oversee absentee voters to cast their votes online. However, there were critical vulnerabilities were found and the project was abandoned [43].

Regardless of being new, the blockchain technology has been identified as a useful technology to address the challenges pertaining to the electronic voting systems. Recently, few countries and corporations have proposed and have started evaluating blockchain bases solution for electronic voting on corporate, municipal, or national levels. In 2016, NASDAQ successfully tested blockchain-based solution for shareholders of an Estonian Financial group named LVH. The trial version of the electronic voting used at the LVHs annual general meeting (AGM) comprised of four web-based user interfaces in Estonia where the shareholders used Estonian digital ID to cast vote to decide on corporate decisions [44]. Similarly, blockchain-enabled vote tallying system were deployed at the annual general meeting of Banco Santander, a Spanish banking group in 2017–2018 and at the Netherlands-based Bank, Kas, in 2018 [45, 46]. In 2014, Danish Liberal Alliance used a blockchain voting system to conduct an internal party vote at the party's annual meeting [47]. In 2017, a successful government initiated blockchain enabled voting solution was tested by 9000 residents of the province of Gyeonggi-do in South Korea. The blockchain platform developed by the Korean Fintech startup Blocko was used by voters to cast both online and offline votes on community projects [44]. Moreover, blockchain technology was also employed by city of Moscow in 2017. The city piloted the move of its active citizen program onto blockchain to enhance accountability and security. This ethereum-based platform was audited and studied by the City of Moscow commissioned accounting firm PwC, which reported no vote tampering concerns in more than 300,000 votes [48]. In 2018, a partial version of the blockchain-based voting system was used by the Agora team in Sierra Leone. The Agora project founded the by Swiss Federal Institute of Technology Lausanne was used as a test case to only verify votes, where nearly 400,000 votes were entered into its distributed ledger with the permission of the Sierra Leones National Election Committee [49].

In recent years, various implementations of blockchain-based voting systems have been proposed by few U.S.-based startups, such as Votebook, Follow My Vote and VoteWatcher. The Votebook was a New York University Masters students' initiative and is based on a permissioned blockchain concept [50]. Herein the nodes in the blockchain must seek permission from a centralized authority to make changes to the ledger via the encryption keys [51]. In Votebook, the voters experience is similar to the paper voting systems but it is much secure as it uses blockchain for committing certain data which is used later for verification in the electoral process. The Follow My Vote is another initiative, which uses blockchain technology for online electronic voting without using real voting booths or paper-trail. The project is currently seeking funding and was criticized for its security concerns over the identity authentication of its remote users, thus making it an impractical solution as a governmental elective system [52]. One another open-source blockchain enabled voting system which is very similar to the Votebook is VoteWatcher, where voters interact with the system using trusted paper ballots. The VoteWatcher is so far the most mature and tested solution which its source code available for inspection by the Blockchain Technologies Corp. (BTC). The Vote-Watcher use of blockchain is a decent tamper-proof auditing system backed up by scanned paper ballots. The system uses optical mark recognition (OMR) software for extracting the voters' data from the ballots. As ballots are counted a local blockchain is created for every ballot. All the election ballot data is then uploaded to two public blockchains, Florincoin and Bitcoin. The two existing chains are merged together and then posted to the Bitcoin blockchain once more. However, the promised security of using three separate blockchains comes with a price. Moreover, VoteWatcher does not control or own the chains used for votes, thus their data is susceptible to forks. A second fork of Bitcoins blockchain like the fork resulting in Bitcoin Cash could nullify potentially thousands of votes previously cast. Our solution employs one blockchain that is strictly used for voting. Therefore, no unexpected forks can disrupt an election that employs our solution [53]. Additionally, we do not rely on Bitcoins proof-of-work to perform vote validation. This flexibility allows our solution to scale with new validation methods, such as Federated Byzantine Agreement.

As detailed above, many authors have reported on demonstrating the use of block-chain for enabling the transparency and creating tamper-proof audit trails for public verification. However, very few literature researches detail the implementation of blockchain enabled voting system. To the best of our knowledge, there are no reports on implementation details emphasizing the integration of blockchain technology with WINVote EVM with the goals of making the EVM more secure and robust. The following sections highlights implementation of the blockchain enabled WINVote internet voting system along with the discussion on potential future work and challenges.

11.3 WORKFLOW AND IMPLEMENTATION OF BLOCKCHAIN-BASED EVM

This section gives a detailed overview of the simulation workflow of the replica of the WINVote machine using blockchain technology (shown in Figure 11.1) to overcome the security threats. The basic idea is that every vote is a block in the chain (shown in Figure 11.2). These blocks are created by when a vote is cast, i.e., clicking on a candidate's name in the voting machine graphical user interface (GUI). Every block/vote is an instance of the Block object, whose attributes correspond to the

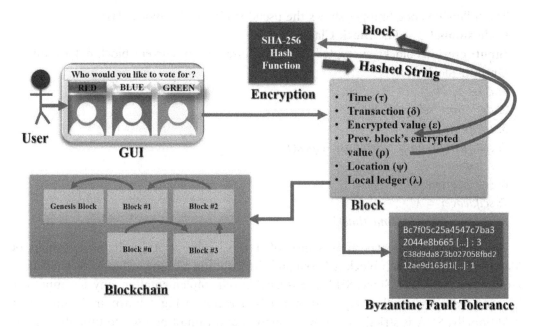

FIGURE 11.1   The workflow for the blockchain-based EVM.

FIGURE 11.2   The chain of votes.

voters selection, which are: time of vote casted, data/transaction, index in the chain, the Blocks current hash and the previous block in the chains hash. The following pseudocode illustrates how votes propagate from the EVM's GUI to becoming blocks that are added to the chain.

Code snippet 1 – From GUI to Block

```
    def vote(name):
    build–block(name)
def main():
btn1 = Button(vote("Red"))
    btn1 = Button(vote("Blue"))
    btn1 = Button(vote("Green"))
```

The following code Snippet shows the pseudocode for the Block class.

Code snippet 2 – The Block Class

Input: previous blocks encrypted value ρ, transaction of current block δ, location Ψ

Output: Block

```
1: class Block:
2: def –init–(self, ρ, δ, Ψ):
3: self.prev–hash = ρ
4: self.current–hash = self.hash–block()
5: self.data = δ
6: self.location = Ψ
7: self.ledger = λ
8: self.timestamp = time.time()
```

The above code creates an instance of a Block object. As each block should be identified uniquely, each block is hased and the resulting 64-long string is assigned as an attribute of the object. Since, SHA-256 is used in our implementation, any size input can be accepted which will always return a 64-character string (shown in Figure 11.3). Additionally, SHA is strictly a one-way function and cannot be used to unhash a string. The SHA-2 (Secure Hash Algorithm 2) is used in our machines with a digest size of 256 for hashing blocks. This was chosen to reduce the chances of encountering a collision to statistically extremely low. The SHA-256 method takes a block and returns a hashed 64-character string, which is then set as the blocks current hash upon creation. Each node has an attribute for its current hash and the previous block in the chains hash. By tracking a blocks hash in the ledger, any modification to the vote can be determined as changing the data of the block will result in a generating a new hash. Our solution made use of Python3's hashlib module which includes a method for hashing with SHA-256.

The Code Snippet 3 shows the pseudocode for using the SHA-256 hashing function.

Code snippet 3 – SHA-256

Input: Block

Output: String that is 64 characters long

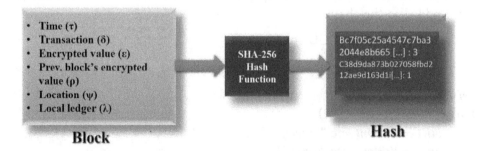

FIGURE 11.3   The basic functionality of SHA-256 hash function.

```
1. def hash–block(block):
2. return sha256((block))
```

Byzantine Fault Tolerance After the Block has been hashed, it is now ready to be added to the ledger. The ledgers validation can be performed in a number of ways, with one of the most popular being BFT. Blockchains main advantage is the lack of need for a centralized voice of authority to verify transactions. However, there must be some form of verification done to ensure Blocks are valid and unmodified. Using a predefined number of validator blocks, we can find which version of the ledger is the most prevalent amongst blocks in the chain, and presumably correct. A basic implementation is to keep track of the different ledgers in a dictionary/hashmap. After iterating through the chain and maintaining count of ledgers and their frequency, a master ledger can be decided upon. This master ledger is any singular ledger that 66% of validators agree on. Any block whose local ledger does not match will be removed as it can be considered to be invalid. This method is known as BFT. It has advantages in speed when compared to different protocols such as proof of work, but it introduces the idea of a central voice of authority with the master ledger- the very idea of which blockchain attempted to remove. The following python libraries [54] were used in implementing our blockchain enabled solution:

Module: hashlib
Description: The hashlib module provides an interface to several hash algorithms. Some of these algorithms include SHA1, SHA224, SHA256, and SHA384.
Use in project: SHA256 was used to encrypt each blocks value, where the hashlib accepts an object and returns a 64-character long string.
Module: pickle
Description: pickle is commonly used for pickling, or serializing objects. The need for pickling arises when an object needs to be converted to a byte stream.
Use in project: Our implementation used pickle for serializing objects. The hashlib's SHA-256 method only accepts serialized objects, thus there was a need to serialize the block objects.
Module: tkinter
Description: Tkinter is a popular module for creating GUIs with python. It makes use of OS assets to make buttons, images, etc. resemble a native program.
Use in project: Tkinter powered the implemented voting machines GUI.
Module: PIL
Description: PIL (Python Imaging Library) introduces an image object to Python.
Use in project: Within the GUI, the photos of the candidates were displayed below the buttons using PIL.

11.4 ANALYSIS OF RESULTS AND DISCUSSION

The WINVote machines experienced a number of security vulnerabilities that most DRE voting machines face. First, the encryption used was WEP. Cracking the encryption was trivial, proved by the FBI in 2005 in a matter of minutes. [55] Additionally, the all systems kept the votes casted in a local database. Malicious actors could easily target machines to modify the votes of since they each were a single point of failure. Lastly, DRE machines are only as secure as the operating system the run. In the case of Virginias WINVote machines, they were as secure as an unpatched 2002 version of Windows XP. Using a blockchain-based voting machines solves all of these issues. More modern encryption, such as SHA-256, cannot be easily cracked. Even if the encryption for one vote was cracked, one would need to decrypt the entire chain of votes to successfully modify votes. Operating system security is another major factor where blockchain reigns supreme. Because votes are shared amongst a network of notes and are not local to each machine, compromising a single voting machine is almost meaningless.

11.4.1 Attacks Used on WINVote

In our recreation of WINVote voting machines, we implemented a man-in-the-middle attack. The first computer attempted to send votes to a second computer which was listening to receive said votes. However, a third computer was used to intercept these votes and modify them before sending them to the second, receiving computer. This was done by sniffing packets over a LAN that all machines were on. This flaw does not exist in blockchain-based voting machines due to ledger valida-tion. In our WINVote replica, there was no validation of votes. Similarly to the actual WINVote systems used throughout Virginia, a single vote or entire collection of votes could me modified with ease. The blockchain implementation performs validation by checking ensuring local ledgers match the most popular, accepted ledger version. Votes are only accepted if they are determined to be valid, removing any fear regarding tampered votes. Our implementation was powered by a network of three devices where each machine had an Intel i7 processor and 16GB of RAM. All devices operated on a LAN.

When a vote is cast, it must be agreed upon by the validators. These validators are checking the prev-hash attribute of the block, ensuring that it matches the preceding blocks hash. In other words, each vote casted contains information about the previous vote. This allows the chain to be traversed backwards, helping to validate future votes.

In the beginning of the election when only one vote is cast the chain resembles as shown in Figure 11.4.

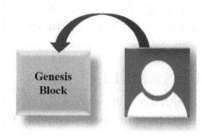

FIGURE 11.4   Initial vote chain.

Thereafter, a vote for Red candidate is cast, where now the vote also contains information about the person who voted before the second vote which was a vote for Blue candidate. Similarly, the vote for Blue candidate contains information about the Genesis Block. The Genesis block is the very first block in the chain. It is automatically generated and serves as the end of the chain. The voters vote format is illustrated in Figure 11.5.

Now, the information about the entire chain up to this point is stored in the current vote, along with every vote in the chain. As long as current blocks value for the previous vote matches the previous votes, current vote will be accepted as valid and added to the chain. At that point, the chain should look as shown in Figure 11.6.

What happens in Block?—However, a lot goes into creating the block for your vote. Just like how the first vote had a value your block had to match, your vote must also generate a unique value that the block after yours will have to match. This unique value is the result of hashing the block with SHA-256.

What happens in BFT?—Once your vote has been created, it must be validated before it gets appended to the blockchain. This validation comes in the shape of multiple validators agreeing that your votes ledger matches the most popular version of the

```
Selected Candidate..................Red
Time.......................................12:04 P.M EST
Encrypted Value.................ED03353266[...]
Prev Hash.........................A069C3027B[...]
Location of Vote...............City_X, State_Y

Local Ledger:
        Genesis Block:  4 A44DC1536[...]
        1st Block:       A069C3027B[...]
```

Vote

FIGURE 11.5   Illustration of a vote.

FIGURE 11.6   Flow of a valid vote.

ledger. Every time a vote is cast, a predefined number of validator nodes determine what version of the ledger is most prevalent. Assuming the new incoming votes ledger matches the most popular ledger, it will be accepted as valid and added to the chain. To reflect the newly added block, all blocks must then update their ledgers to show the owner block. The validator nodes who determine a blocks legitimacy are predefined and only modifiable by the owner of the chain. Our basic implementation keeps track of the frequency of a particular ledger in a hashmap. The correct ledger is whatever key in the hashmap (a hashed value that corresponds to a ledger) has a value that is greater than or equal to 66%.

An example of an invalid vote could be one where the local ledger was modified as shown in Figure 11.7. Instead of casting a legitimate vote for Red candidate, you can modify your votes local ledger to make it appear that the vote before yours was also for Red candidate instead of Blue candidate. However, when your vote reaches the validators, it would be rejected on the basis of its ledger not matching the most popular version of the ledger.

11.4.2 Benefits, Challenges and Opportunities

By moving away from a centralized database, our blockchain voting machine is more secure than the now decommissioned WINVote machines. Instead of simply compromising one machine and manipulating all the votes, one would need to modify the entire network of nodes to change a single vote. This would require an immense amount of computational power that is unavailable to the majority of individuals. Additionally, the SHA-256 encryption used in the solution implemented is far more complex than the WEP encryption used by WINVote systems.

Our solution biggest shortcoming is the use of BFT. A single, centralized voice of authority is used to determine if a block is valid or not. Only the list of validator nodes can approve or deny a votes validity.

A more complex, yet more versatile implementation of ledger validation is Federated Byzantine Agreement (shown in Figure 11.8). This was first conceptualized and implemented by Stanford professor David Mazires. An excerpt below from the Stellar Consensus Protocol white paper explains the concept.

FIGURE 11.7   Flow of an invalid vote.

Federated Byzantine Agreement

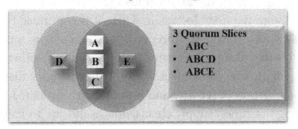

FIGURE 11.8   Federated byzantine agreement consensus protocol.

In FBA, each participant is aware of other participants that are considered to be important. Moreover, each participant waits for the vast majority of those other important participants to agree on any transaction in order to consider the transaction as settled. Furthermore, the important participants also do not agree to the transaction until the participants considered important by them also agrees, and so on. Gradually, there are enough participants of the network who accepts a transaction making it impossible for an attacker to roll it back. Only then do any participants consider the transaction settled. The FBA's consensus aids in decentralized control ensuring the integrity of a financial network. [56]

The FBA protocol removes the need for a list of validators, which is a common limitation of BFT. In FBA, each validator decides on other validators which they trust. This list of trusted validators associated with a single validator is a quorum slice. These slices can overlap, forming shapes similar to the ones seen in Figure 11.8. When several quorum slices overlap, it forms a quorum. Once groups intersect, consensus is considered to be reached within the whole set of validators. In the Figure 11.8, the two slices (green and pink) agree on nodes A, B, and C. Any person can create a new validator and participate in the consensus as long as they are added to a quorum slice by an already existing validator to their quorum slice. This is starkly different than BFT where only a set list of validators may participate in determining ledger legitimacy. The FBAs open membership makes its consensus protocol truly decentralized.

11.5 CONCLUSION

While there is no standard voting machine configuration, many share similar properties in the context of security. These machines use direct-recording, allowing the voter to interact with the machine by means of mouse, touch screen, etc. These votes are typically recorded and stored locally on the voting machine. In the case of WINVote systems used throughout the state of Virginia, votes were stored in a Microsoft Access database; storing all votes in a single, mutable point of failure made modifying votes trivial. By implementing a blockchain-based voting machine, the threat of compromising data locally is removed along with the benefit of hard encrypted data. The security features of blockchain are not exclusive for EVMs. A number of cryptographic hash functions are available, with one of the most common being SHA-256. Designed by the National Security Agency in 2001, SHA (Secure Hash Algorithm), the anonymous creator(s) of Bitcoin, Satoshi Nakamoto, implemented SHA-256 in the first blockchain where it is continued to be used for hashing. Moreover, the distributed ledgers inception was used in tandem with Bitcoin, a cryptocurrency. As the technology matures, its benefits in other areas are becoming more obvious. Many industries can benefit from the transparency that comes with utilizing blockchain. The combination of security and immutability facilitated by blockchain aids its applicability to voting machines, supply chains, and healthcare to name only a few.

REFERENCES

[1] Jesse Yli-Huumo, Deokyoon Ko, Sujin Choi, Sooyong Park, and Kari Smolander. Where is current research on blockchain technology? A systematic review. *PloS One*, 11(10): e0163477, 2016.

[2] Marc Pilkington. 11 blockchain technology: Principles and applications. In *Research Handbook on Digital Transformations*, edited by Xavier Olleros F. and Zhegup Majlinda, 225. Edward Elgar Publishing, 2016.

[3] Stephen M. Nichols and Gregory A. Strizek. Electronic voting machines and ballot roll-off. *American Politics Quarterly*, 23(3): 300–318, 1995.

[4] Jonathan Bannet, David W Price, Algis Rudys, Justin Singer, and Dan SWallach. Hack-a-vote: Security issues with electronic voting systems. *IEEE Security & Privacy*, 2(1): 32–37, 2004.

[5] Tadayoshi Kohno, Adam Stubblefield, Aviel D. Rubin, and Dan S. Wallach. Analysis of an electronic voting system. In *2004 IEEE Symposium on Security and Privacy*, pp. 27–40. IEEE *Proceedings*, Berkeley, CA, 2004.

[6] Benjamin B Bederson, Bongshin Lee, Robert M. Sherman, Paul S. Herrnson, and Richard G. Niemi. Electronic voting system usability issues. In *Proceedings of the SIGCHI Conference on Human Factors in Computing Systems*, pp. 145–152. ACM, New York, NY, 2003.

[7] Barbara B. Simons. Electronic voting systems: The good, the bad, and the stupid. *ACM Queue*, 2(7): 20–26, 2004.

[8] Melanie Swan. *Blockchain: Blueprint for a New Economy*. O'Reilly Media, Inc., Sebastopol, CA, 2015.

[9] Patrick McCorry, Siamak F Shahandashti, and Feng Hao. A smart contract for boardroom voting with maximum voter privacy. In *International Conference on Financial Cryptography and Data Security*, edited by Kiayias A., pp. 357–375. Lecture Notes in Computer Science, Vol 10322. Springer, 2017.

[10] Nir Kshetri and Je_rey Voas. Blockchain-enabled e-voting. *IEEE Software*, 35(4): 95–99, 2018.

[11] Feng Yumeng, Tian Liye, Liu Fanbao, and Gan Chong. Electronic voting: A review and taxonomy. In *2012 International Conference on Industrial Control and Electronics Engineering (ICICEE)*, pp. 912–917. IEEE, Salem, Tamilnadu, 2012.

[12] Marco Iansiti and Karim R Lakhani. The truth about blockchain. *Harvard Business Review*, 95 (1): 118–127, 2017.

[13] Zibin Zheng, Shaoan Xie, Hong-Ning Dai, Xiangping Chen, and Huaimin Wang. Blockchain challenges and opportunities: A survey. *International Journal of Web and Grid Services*, 14(4): 352–375, 2018.

[14] Marko Vukolic. The quest for scalable blockchain fabric: Proof-of-work vs. BFT replication. In *International Workshop on Open Problems in Network Security*, edited by Camenisch J. and Kesdoğan D., pp. 112–125. Lecture Notes in Computer Science, vol 9591. Springer, 2015.

[15] Donald P. Moynihan. Building secure elections: E-voting, security, and systems theory. *Public Administration Review*, 64(5): 515–528, 2004.

[16] Xiwei Xu, Ingo Weber, Mark Staples, Liming Zhu, Jan Bosch, Len Bass, Cesare Pautasso, and Paul Rimba. A taxonomy of blockchain-based systems for architecture design. In *2017 IEEE International Conference on Software Architecture (ICSA)*, pp. 243–252. IEEE, Gothenburg, 2017.

[17] Rudiger Schollmeier. A definition of peer-to-peer networking for the classification of peer-to-peer architectures and applications. In *First International Conference on Peer-to-Peer Computing, 2001*, pp. 101–102. IEEE, Linkoping, Sweden, 2001.

[18] Advait Deshpande, Katherine Stewart, Louise Lepetit, and Salil Gunashekar. *Distributed Ledger Technologies/blockchain: Challenges, Opportunities and the Prospects for Standards*. Overview report The British Standards Institution (BSI), UK, 2017.

[19] Lakshmi Siva Sankar, M. Sindhu, and M. Sethumadhavan. Survey of consensus protocols on blockchain applications. In *2017 4th International Conference on Advanced Computing and Communication Systems (ICACCS)*, pp. 1–5. IEEE, Coimbatore, 2017.

[20] Michael Nofer, Peter Gomber, Oliver Hinz, and Dirk Schiereck. Blockchain. *Business & Information Systems Engineering*, 59(3): 183–187, 2017.

[21] Sanjay Kumar and Ekta Walia. Analysis of electronic voting system in various countries. *International Journal on Computer Science and Engineering*, 3(5): 1825–1830, 2011.

[22] D. Ashok Kumar and T. Ummal Sariba Begum. A comparative study on fingerprint matching algorithms for evm. *Journal of Computer Sciences and Applications*, 1(4): 55–60, 2013.

[23] E-voting.CC GmbH competence center for electronic voting and participation. Firm Website: www.e-voting.cc/en/it-elections/world-map/.

[24] Digital technology in elections efficiency versus credibility? European Parliament: www.europarl.europa.eu/RegData/etudes/BRIE/2018/625178/EPRSBRI(2018)625178EN:pdf

[25] Melanie Volkamer. Electronic voting in Germany. In *Data Protection in a Pro_led World*, edited by Gutwirth S., Poullet Y., and De Hert P., pp. 177–189. Springer, Dordrecht, 2010.

[26] Robert A. Pastor. Improving the us electoral system: Lessons from canada and mexico. *Election Law Journal*, 3(3): 584–593, 2004.

[27] Dimitris A. Gritzalis. *Secure Electronic Voting, Volume 7*. Springer Science & Business Media, 2012.

[28] Norbert Kersting and Harald Baldersheim. *Electronic Voting and Democracy: A Comparative Analysis*. Springer, Palgrave Macmillan, London, 2004.

[29] Ulle Madise and Tarvi Martens. E-voting in estonia 2005. The first practice of country-wide binding internet voting in the world. *Electronic Voting*, 86(2006): 15-26, 2006.

[30] Nicole J. Goodman. Internet voting in a local election in Canada. In *The Internet and Democracy in Global Perspective*, edited by Grofman B., Trechsel A., Franklin M., pp. 7–24. Studies in Public Choice, vol 31, Springer, 2014.

[31] Tim Maurer and Scott Janz. The russia-ukraine conflict: Cyber and information warfare in a regional context. *The International Relations and Security Network*, 17: 277–293, 2014.

[32] Chris Tenove, Jordan Bu_e, Spencer McKay, and David Moscrop. *Digital Threats to Democratic Elections: How Foreign Actors Use Digital Techniques to Undermine Democracy*. 2018.

[33] Constanze Stelzenmuller. *The Impact of Russian Interference on Germanys 2017 Elections*. Testimony before the US Senate Select Committee on Intelligence, Brookings Institution, June 28, 2017.

[34] Christopher S. Chivvis. *Understanding Russian Hybrid Warfare*, pp. 2–4. The RAND Corporation, Santa Monica, CA, 2017.

[35] Paul Baines and Nigel Jones. Inuence and interference in foreign elections: The evolution of its practice. *The RUSI Journal*, 163(1): 12–19, 2018.

[36] John Bambenek. Nation-state attacks: The new normal. *Network Security*, 2017(10): 8–10, 2017.

[37] Lawrence D. Norden and Christopher Famighetti. *America's Voting Machines at Risk*. Brennan Center for Justice at New York University School of Law, New York, 2015.

[38] Jeremy Epstein. Weakness in depth: A voting machine's demise. *IEEE Security & Privacy*, 13 (3): 55–58, 2015.

[39] Charity King and Michael Thompson. Security of electronic voting in the United States. *The CIP Report*, Argonne National Lab.(ANL), Argonne, IL, 2016.

[40] Ryan Osgood. *The Future of Democracy: Blockchain voting'.COMP116: Information Security*, pp. 1-21. MA, 2016.

[41] Arne Ansper, Ahto Buldas, Mart Oruaas, Jaan Priisalu, Anto Vel-dre, Jan Willemson, and Kaur Virunurm. *E-voting Concept Security: Analysis and Measures*. Technical report, Technical Report EH-02-01, Estonian National Electoral Committee, Tallinn, 2003.

[42] J. Alex Halderman and Vanessa Teague. The new south wales ivote system: Security failures and verification flaws in a live online election. In *International Conference on E-voting and Identity*, pp. 35–53. Springer, Washington, DC, 2015.

[43] Scott Wolchok, Eric Wustrow, Dawn Isabel, and J. Alex Halder-man. Attacking the Washington, DC internet voting system. In *International Conference on Financial Cryptography and Data Security*, edited by Keromytis A.D., Lecture Notes in Computer Science, vol 7397, pp. 114–128. Springer, 2012.

[44] Adegboyega Ojo and Samuel Adebayo. Blockchain as a next generation government information infrastructure: A review of initiatives in d5 countries. In *Government 3.0—Next Generation Government Technology Infrastructure and Services*, edited by Adegboyega Ojo, and Millard Jeremy, pp. 283–298. Springer, 2017.

[45] Julia Kokina, Ruben Mancha, and Dessislava Pachamanova. Blockchain: Emergent industry adoption and implications for accounting. *Journal of Emerging Technologies in Accounting*, 14(2): 91–100, 2017.

[46] Anne Lafarre and Christoph Van der Elst. *Blockchain Technology for Corporate Governance and Shareholder Activism*. ECGI Working Paper Series in Law, Web publication/site, 2018.

[47] Marcella Atzori. Blockchain technology and decentralized governance: Is the State still necessary? *Journal of Governance and Regulation, Virtus Interpress*, 6(1): 45-62, 2017.

[48] MyungSan Jun. Blockchain government-a next form of infrastructure for the twenty-first century. *Journal of Open Innovation: Technology, Market, and Complexity*, 4(1): 7, 2018.

[49] Michał Pawlak, Jakub Guziur, and Aneta Poniszewska-Maranda. Towards the blockchain technology for system voting process. In *International Symposium on Cyberspace Safety and Security*, edited by Arcangelo CastiglioneFlorin PopMassimo FiccoFrancesco Palmieri, pp. 209–223. Springer, 2018.

[50] Marko Vukolic. Rethinking permissioned blockchains. In *Proceedings of the ACM Workshop on Blockchain, Cryptocurrencies and Contracts*, pp. 3–7. ACM, New York, 2017.

[51] C. K. Adiputra, R. Hjort and H. Sato. A Proposal of Blockchain-Based Electronic Voting System. In *2018 Second World Conference on Smart Trends in Systems, Security and Sustainability (WorldS4)*, pp. 22-27. London, 2018.

[52] Follow my vote: Blockchain technology in online voting. Project Website: https://followmyvote.com/online-voting-technology/blockchain-technology/.

[53] VoteWatcher-The world's most transparent voting machine. Project Website: http://votewatcher.com/

[54] Doug Hellmann. *The Python Standard Library by Example*. Addison-Wesley Professional, Boston, MA, 2011.

[55] S. Vinjosh Reddy, K. Sai Ramani, K. Rijutha, Sk Mohammad Ali, and C. H. Pradeep Reddy. Wireless hacking-a wifi hack by cracking WEP. In *2010 2nd International Conference on Education Technology and Computer (ICETC)*, Vol. 1, pp. V1–189. IEEE, Shanghai, 2010.

[56] David Mazieres. *The Stellar Consensus Protocol: A Federated Model for Internet-level Consensus*. Stellar Development Foundation, Citeseer, 2015.

CHAPTER 12

Implementing the Blockchain Technology in the Financial Services Industry

Edward Chen

University of Massachusetts Lowell

CONTENTS

12.1 INTRODUCTION

Blockchain is a decentralized and distributed ledger that can record transactions between any two parties efficiently and in a verifiable and permanent way. Distributed ledger enables data to be exchanged directly between different parties within a network without the need for third-party intermediaries. As a result, blockchain has far-reaching implications and potential for bringing radical changes in a wide range of industries, especially in the financial industry (Deshpande, Stewart, Lepetit, & Gunashekar, 2017; Radziwill, 2018).

Blockchain technology was first introduced in 2008 as the underpinning technology for the popular cryptocurrency known as Bitcoin. Since its inception, blockchain has continued to draw a considerable amount of interest, and there has been a spike in blockchain investments globally (Hughes, 2018). In the first half of 2018, over 1.3 billion funding was raised by venture capitals for projects and companies working on blockchain technology (Pollari & Ruddenklau, 2018).

While the blockchain was first invented as the technology for Bitcoin, the purpose of this chapter is to explore the many possibilities besides Bitcoin for blockchain technology in finance industry. We all know banking industry has many challenges and blockchain could be the one transformative technology that can resolve some of the issues with excessive costs, security, and efficiencies. Even with its many key enabling features, the actual implementation or applications for banking systems has neither been widespread nor easy, due to many regulatory issues that come with trustless, self-governing nature of blockchain (Batlin, Jaffrey, Murphy, Przewloka, & Williams, 2016; Michel, 2018). In this chapter, we will try to capture some likely paths of innovation financial industry can take with blockchain applications and issues that will need to be resolved for widespread acceptance of such experiments into mainstream business models.

Before we understand how Blockchain works, we should understand the history behind this technology. Blockchain was the outcome of the global financial crisis of 2008, when people lost faith in the intermediary-based systems and institutions such as banks and other financial institutions. The crisis highlighted the core vulnerabilities in trusting these intermediaries, which led to a fundamental shift toward the development of concepts and ideas that did not necessarily rely on an intermediary system and traditional flat currencies.

This was when an individual or group going by the pseudonym Satoshi Nakamoto published a paper titled, "Bitcoin: A Peer-to-Peer Electronic Cash System." This paper described a mechanism of electronic cash transfer using distributed network that would allow payments and transfer of currency to be made directly from one party/individual to another without going through an intermediary institution.

12.2 BLOCKCHAIN AND THE FINANCIAL INDUSTRY

Blockchain technology and the financial services industry can trace its beginnings to the cryptocurrency company Bitcoin.org, which started at the end of 2008 and launched its first block, named Genesis, in 2009. The principles of this technology stem from the white paper written by the developer of the initial technology Satoshi Nakamoto. In the white paper, Satoshi writes, "Internet has come to rely almost exclusively on financial institutions serving as trusted third parties to process electronic payments. While the system works well enough for most transactions, it still suffers from the inherent weaknesses of the trust based model" (Nakamoto, 2008). The thought that grew from there has become the basis of cryptocurrency and blockchain. Nakamoto further suggests that "an electronic payment system based on cryptographic proof instead of trust, allowing any two willing parties to transact directly with each other without the need for a trusted third party" (Nakamoto, 2008).

Since the initial block was established back in 2009, there have been many difficulties for the Bitcoin Company. However, what is clear is that the future is bright for blockchain technology as more companies are becoming receptive to the currency and technology. According to Deloitte, Bitcoin investment has risen from 1 deal worth 1.2 million in funding in the first quarter of 2011 to 27 deals worth 233.8 million in funding in the first quarter of 2015 (Deloitte, 2015). This is a net increase of 27 times the deals and 233 times the funding. As the costs of running an Internet-based ledger decrease and the blockchain technology advances, it would be hard for other services not to follow, with financial services being one of the larger industries to embrace the technology. According to a Morgan Stanley report, the banking industry's current proof-of-concept or testing phase completed in 2018. The report also shows blockchain adoption by financial institutions by the year 2020 (Van Steenis, Graseck, Simpson, & Faucette, 2016).

All aspects of trades, whether that is post-trade settlement, financing, or payments internationally, would be utilized with the new web-based technology. The trades would be visible to all parties within the network transacting. This will allow for shorter settlement windows, faster payments, and reduced confirmation times. Additionally, recordkeeping services would be able to use the web-based system and software to compile client-reporting needs. This would eliminate the need for large hardware systems kept by companies. Also, regulatory reporting history would be at the fingertips as the transactions are kept within the chain and would be easily accessed by regulatory bodies. Although this technology seems to be the answer to a lot of issues that are currently faced in the financial industry, it will create a new set of problems organizations will need to reign in, such as anti-money laundering, KYC regulations, regulatory reporting, and many more (Bandyopadhyay & Bandyopadhyay, 2018; Campbell-Verduyn, 2018; Dostov & Shust, 2014).

12.3 BUSINESS PROBLEM TO BE SOLVED

Financial institutions are exploring a variety of opportunities to use blockchain, including applications to improve and enhance currency exchange, supply chain management, trade execution and settlement, remittance, peer-to-peer transfers, micropayments, asset registration, correspondent banking, and regulatory reporting, including applications related to "know your customer" and anti-money-laundering rules (Petrasic, 2016). In addition to improving the operations of the financial institutions, blockchain will also allow for a decentralized structure in which transacting through a centralized third-party custodian will no longer be needed, allowing for cost savings and operations to take place in virtual teams linked to the network. The blockchain technology could cut banks' infrastructure costs for cross-border payments, securities trading and regulatory compliance by $15–$20 billion a year from 2022 (Wild, Arnold, & Stafford, 2015).

12.3.1 Currency Exchange

In the current centralized model, currency exchange and international payments can be a long and cumbersome process due to risk and regulatory reviews taking multiple days to settle out foreign transactions. In the blockchain, the process will be sped up and by operating on the encryption process and will reduce the risk of fraud or money laundering. According to SWIFT, the standard for international settlements, same-day payments are not far behind, with cross-country blockchain networks within the peer group.

12.3.2 Trade Execution and Settlement

The first problem with Trade Execution and Settlement in the current trust model and centralized structure is that each financial institution has teams of people who oversee each step in the process. This can be in the form of trade settlement departments, auditors (internal and external), regulatory teams, including but not limited to AML (anti-money laundering), KYC (know your customer), and more on a single transaction. By utilizing the blockchain, the historical information of each asset can be tracked to the initial transaction, decreasing the need for the transaction to be scrutinized in such minutia. Another issue in the current process is that the settlement period can be timely because of the communication needed between two centralized parties. Additionally, funding must also be confirmed prior to the settling of the transaction. By operating on a virtual network of peers, the settlement process itself will be shortened, and less capital will be tied to open transactions, resulting in the capital being circulated back into market more quickly. Not only will the physical settlement of an asset shorten in the decentralized virtual system, the confirmation of funding for the asset will be confirmed in a much faster and easier fashion.

12.3.3 Recordkeeping

The current business problem with recordkeeping is that it is housed on computer systems within each centralized institution. The transaction reconciliation process can be tenuous, with institutions communicating with each other in order to have accurate recordings of what transpired.

Companies can use the distributed, publicly verified, and nearly real-time ledger of transactions for bookkeeping, data mining, and records verification. This could reduce the effort spent on reconciling information among various computer systems. It could also link the systems to external information sources, such as pricing feeds (electronic vendors of trading data), in a more customizable and secure way (Plansky, O'Donnell, & Richards, 2016).

12.3.4 Regulatory Reporting

Financial institutions have recently dedicated a lot of capital to the enhancement of their regulatory reporting (including AML and KYC) infrastructure. This includes dedicating teams to oversee the process and to develop the technology for the new infrastructure. Since the housing crisis in 2008 and Dodd-Frank Wall Street Reform and Consumer Protection Act in 2010, financial institutions have been under scrutiny to provide more reporting and to be as transparent as possible. The ability of the technology to provide an unforgeable record of identity, including the history of an individual's transactions, is one area being eagerly explored. Intermeshing records could prove highly useful, insurers believe, in cross-checking an individual's actions (Wild et al., 2015). The ability to cross-check individuals could greatly reduce the risks inherited with money laundering and fraud. In addition, the use of blockchain would allow for this cross check to be performed in real time, without doing so after the transaction has been processed. No matter how much capital is put into these systems currently, there is no way to alleviate the risk all together. With the blockchain, it would enhance the process and mitigate that risk even further.

12.4 FINANCIAL MODELS WITH BLOCKCHAIN TECHNOLOGY

Banks and many other traditional financial institutions came into being with from the need to have trusted parties or intermediaries to protect people's money and make processing complex transactions easier. The traditional banking system was built on a model of centralized trust where banks and other financial institutions have served as guardians by providing assorted services such as record keeping, fraud protection, safeguarding accounts, facilitating payments, providing credit, thus offering the much-needed security, stability, and accuracy to the financial transactions and its customers. This model is complemented by regulatory bodies, government legislations to ensure the model as a whole is compliant and safe-guarding the interests of end users and customers (Hyvärinen, Risius, & Friis, 2017; Michel, 2018; Turner & Irwin, 2018).

Last few years, several new technological innovations have introduced an array of changes that have challenged the traditional models of doing business or the core concepts of those models. One such disruptive technology that has the potential to strike one of the core values of financial sector – the notion of trust, is blockchain (Radziwill, 2018). Bitcoin is a well-known cryptocurrency, also the first application of blockchain technology. This application can be extended to other complex transactions associated with trading and transfer of financial instruments such as bonds, stocks, and loans (Dostov & Shust, 2014).

Blockchain can alternate models for payment clearing process. Currently, interbank payments rely on an intermediary clearing house for book keeping, transaction and balance reconciliation, payment initiation, and settlement. Therefore, the entire process is time consuming and transaction costs are high. By implementing payment systems on blockchain technology, we can eliminate the dependency on intermediary clearing systems, and this can greatly increase the efficiency of processing fund transfer and reduce the costs associated with it.

Blockchain can also resolve some of the issues surrounding those of banking credit information systems. The primary issue with credit information is the lack of sufficient and superior quality data despite massive data being collected on the Internet, which could be valuable proof of an individual's credit situation. There are multiple reasons such as the lack of data sharing between the institutions, privacy and security laws around data, multiple/redundant copies of the data being maintained by institutions, etc. (Genkin, Papadopoulos, & Papamanthou, 2018).

12.5 CURRENT LANDSCAPE OF BLOCKCHAIN IN FINANCIAL INDUSTRY

Blockchain as a technology has the potential to change the financial sector. With all the initial hype around this disruptive technology beginning to settle down, more companies, start-ups, entrepreneurs, and investors are developing solid use cases and exploring new areas to deliver business value. According to Leising (2018), some major financial institutions such as Credit Suisse, Wells Fargo, Western Assets have already tested distributed ledger technology to standardize the data involved in securitized home loans to make it more transparent, easier and less costly to track mortgage-based securities (Deshpande et al., 2017).

Blockchain has the potential to simplifying and redefine areas of banking such as payments and KYC, at least to start with. There is much scope for streamlining the business-to-business payments, especially with large payment exclusive to businesses and across-border payments that involve foreign exchange. However, for blockchain to implement such a use case successfully, new standards and governance and regulations must be established to protect assets, banks and its customer, transacting on this emerging technology (Bandyopadhyay & Bandyopadhyay, 2018; Michel, 2018; Turner & Irwin, 2018).

At the same time, streamlining cumbersome processes such as KYC has become a major priority for institutions in the banking sector, as banks are being fined substantial amounts for sanctions and anti-money laundering breaches. BNP was forced to pay close to 8.9 billion for U.S. sanctions breaches between 2008 and 2015 (Campbell-Verduyn, 2018; Dostov & Shust, 2014). For any potential use cases to get any serious traction in financial sector, it is necessary that people such as board members, stakeholder, investors in general are educated of the difference between blockchain as a technology from its most well-known implementation Bitcoin (Radziwill, 2018).

In the next few sections of this report, we will cautiously explore the possible implementation of blockchain technology in financial services for individuals, businesses, and other services at large. Look at the challenges to the implementation and acceptance of these applications in wide scale and features that make this blockchain technology the most hyped and sought-after technology in the past few years.

12.5.1 Financial Services for Individuals

Blockchain-enabled banking system for an individual would be a very different experience. Smart wallets that blockchain users use currently to access any blockchain-enabled financial system would replace the many identification processes required by traditional systems, such as username and password. Blockchain-enabled systems can give customers control over their identities and their usage in the financial sector. All transactions on the blockchain are digitally signed using the pseudonyms based on the public key cryptography, and hence the authenticity of the participant is easily verifiable. This feature could be extended to allow customers easy access to the creation of bank accounts across institutions and access to financial products. This will greatly reduce redundancy in gathering customer data, credit checks and validation by financial institutions, and costs.

Another area that could greatly benefit is the KYC process. Currently, financial institutions spend anywhere between $60 million and $500 million to keep up with the KYC process according to a Thomas Reuters survey (Thomas Reuters, 2016). These regulations help with reducing money laundering and terrorism activities by ensuring businesses have the required data to identify and verify their clients. This data is gathered and verified independently by each institution. The outcome of such a verification process by any institution can be made available to all other institutions, thus reducing the costs associated with compliance requirements (Swan, 2017).

12.5.2 Banking Services for Business

Businesses could greatly benefit from blockchain-enabled financial systems. Blockchain could enable direct transactions between parties without the involvement of intermediaries, thus, eliminating overdue payment and costs associated with transferring of funds. With the cost of payment reduced to almost zero, most fund transfers including micropayment would be on time and free capital for other investments. One instance of this application is BitPesa, a Kenya-based start-up which has combined mobile money and bitcoin blockchain technology to support payments and transactions between African businesses and the rest of the world (Zambrano, Seward, & Sayo, 2017).

Blockchain can bring in the much-needed efficiency in business administration processes such as accounting, payroll, regulatory reporting, and compliance. Another area of potential impact is crowdfunding, by providing a platform for the entrepreneurs and investors to establish connection and trust using crypto tokens and smart contracts. Crowdfunding existed even before the exploding interest in blockchain technology emerged. But blockchain could just be the technology to propel crowding to completely new paradigm by bringing investors and those seeking funds closer. Use of smartcards could create more accessible avenues for those corporations seeking funding such as loans for small- and medium-sized enterprises and funding from capital markets (Egelund-Müller, Elsman, Henglein, & Ross, 2017; Swan, 2017).

12.6 IMPACT ON OTHER AREAS OF FINANCE

12.6.1 Digital Currency

Non-fiat digital currencies like Bitcoin and Altcoin are the cornerstones of the new digital banking and financial services era. The introduction of digital currencies in the banking and financial services brings in new challenges, and yet their development is key to creating a truly digital financial sector. The technological ability of Bitcoin to support a variety of use cases has resulted in much interest and investment in the last few years. Despite the popularity, most financial organizations have not adopted digital currency mainly due to regulatory compliance concerns such as identity management, anti-money laundering, KYC processes. By extending the existing technology to address some of these issues related to identity management, compliance and reporting, and transaction management. Mainstream financial institutions would be encouraged to accept digital currency as a legitimate currency and provide secure and compliant services on these platforms to their end users (Campbell-Verduyn, 2018; Dostov & Shust, 2014; PwC, 2017).

12.6.2 Remittances

One area of financial services that could benefit the most from blockchain applications, as proven by the implementation of Bitcoin, is remittances. The World Bank estimated global remittances at $582 billion in 2014 and rising to $608 billion the following year. Remittances to developing countries itself were expected to be around $454 billion in 2015. As the remittances continue to grow the cost of sending remittances continues to show downward trends, 7.9 percent of the value in 2014 compared to 8.4 percent the previous year. By contrast, Bitcoin transaction cost $0.0753 on average from January 2012 to June 2015 (World Bank, 2014).

Considerable investment has been made in this space, to use blockchain technology for direct fund transfers between any two individuals, across the globe in short duration and at low cost. If successfully implemented, it could bring down the cost and time of remittances considerably. The impact would likely be seen in Sub-Saharan Africa countries where the cost of remittance is still extremely high at 9.8 percent of remittance value (World Bank, 2018).

12.6.3 Real-Time Settlements

Another area that blockchain could revolutionize is the settlement model. Current settlement process is far from ideal, and the entire process requires information to be shared along a chain of system, resulting in redundancies. There is a log between when a transaction is processed and when it is settled. Between this time, one or more parties involved in the transaction could go in a situation where they are unable to make the payment. The cost of such insuring against such counterparty risk or data discrepancy which results in manually reconciliation is very high (Egelund-Müller et al., 2017).

Blockchain enables real-time settlement process by allowing direct and immutable transaction between parties and immediate fund transfer. For banking and financial institutions, this would result in a simpler, cheaper, robust infrastructure that could reduce transaction costs and fees. This would also mean a drastic reduction in the collateral deposited at banks to insure against counterparty risk. Thus, blockchain technology makes capital available for other purposes. Additionally, blockchain's ability to maintain the transaction history within every block of data will ensure there is no room for disagreement between the parties involved as to what was transacted (Egelund-Müller et al., 2017).

12.7 BLOCKCHAIN INNOVATIONS AND POTENTIALS IN FINANCIAL INDUSTRY

Regarding the innovativeness of blockchain and the potential to cause revolutionary changes in the financial industry by this technology, blockchain enables participants to receive benefits of costless verification and the reduction in networking costs at the same time. Catalini and Gans (2017) mention that value can be reliably transferred by this technology between two distant, untrusting parties without the need of a costly intermediary anonymously through the network for the first time in history. It also means that such intermediaries can be eliminated from current business processes by this technology. It significantly reduces the time of transaction. Similarly, Lakhani also mentioned in his interview that the innovativeness of blockchain is the elimination of intermediaries. The blockchain technology replaces the programmable credit verification to reduce transaction costs and confirmation time among participants while keeping transactions trustworthy at the same time (Lakhani, 2017).

Furthermore, according to the white paper issued by Federal Reserve Board, financial industry stakeholders insist that they have following common motivations to apply and implement blockchain technology to their businesses (Mills et al., 2016):

- Reduced complexity

- Improved end-to-end processing speed and availability of assets and funds

- Decreased need for reconciliation across multiple recordkeeping infrastructures

- Increased transparency and immutability in transaction recordkeeping

- Improved network resiliency through distributed data management

- Reduced operational and financial risks

Many banking companies and financial institutions are currently examining the application of blockchain conducting proof of concepts (PoC) that confirms veracity and achievability of application through prototype testing. Though the blockchain PoC has already been used in a few areas such as digital identification in Estonia (Shen, 2016), there are numerous cryptocurrencies with PoC technology listed in the Cryptocurrency Market Capitalizations website (Cryptocurrency Market Capitalizations, 2018).

The most intensifying financial services using blockchain applications can be found in the following areas.

12.7.1 Clearing and Settlement

This is one of the hottest areas of attracting financial institutions. Although stock transaction can be done instantaneously, it usually takes 3–5 days to complete stock settlement mainly because many verification intermediaries are involved in the settlement process. Australian Securities Exchange is replacing their clearing and settlement system called CHESS with the DLT technology to speed up the clearing and settlement process (Australian Securities Exchange, 2018).

12.7.2 Central Bank-Issued Digital Money

Central banks are examining and researching the possibility of application of blockchain from various points of view, including central bank-issued digital currencies as a substitute for existing physical money. There will be a great impact on monetary policy and the society when it is materialized. For instance, both the U.S. Federal Reserve Board and Bank of England are already considering issue their own digital currency as standard cryptocurrencies (Bank of England, 2019; Cox, 2017).

12.7.3 Payments

Other than central banks, commercial banks and institutions are experimenting with issuing their own digital currencies or payment methods using blockchain technology, especially, for cross-border payments. The current cross-border payment service provided through Swift's international network and overseas correspondent banks requires 3–5 days for completion. Ripple, a San Francisco-based company, develops cross-border protocol and platform as an alternative for Swift's network. Many financial institutions such as Santander, American Express, and several Japanese and South Korean banks are considering adopting Ripple (Browne, 2017; Nikkei, 2017).

12.8 CONSIDERATIONS OF IMPLEMENTING BLOCKCHAIN TECHNOLOGY

As noted in the earlier sections, blockchain technology could streamline many processes. Many institutions are experimenting and exploring this technology and are participating in proof of concept to better understand the technology and its limitations. Many companies that are forging forward with implementation of this technology as an extension of its existing IT landscape should evaluate through a holistic lens to access the impact from a technical aspect and business perspective. Some factors to consider are listed as follows.

Scalability—Most popular implementation of blockchain is on Bitcoin and Ethereum. Bitcoin takes about 10 minutes to validate a block of transaction, and it takes about six rounds to validate a block. That is approximately 60 minutes per block. Ethereum, on the other hand, is known to do the same in 16–17 seconds. While Ethereum is faster, it may not meet all the requirements of interbank fund transfers or high-volume transaction processing capabilities. Hence, it is necessary to understand and test a solution before its implementation to ensure the new application meets all business needs (Brown, 2018).

Security—It is essential to secure digital wallets when using blockchain technology. Public key cryptography commonly used in blockchain application uses private and public combination to digitally sign and authenticate users on the network. Private keys are stored in digital wallets protected by a paraphrase. Therefore, it becomes critical to have a clear strategy to manage and access these wallets. It is also important to have ways to recover lost or forgotten paraphrases, which are required to unlock the wallets (Turner & Irwin, 2018).

Operations—As is the case with any new application being deployed in production, one must look at how the blockchain technology will be set up and interact with the existing legacy systems and the overall impact on the IT landscape. Another area of consideration should be support activities. If an issue should arise in production, companies must have resources capable of understanding the existing legacy applications and those built on blockchain to debug and resolve issues successfully. Hence, staff training should be given priority.

Data Privacy—One of the key features of blockchain is immutability of data that is once verified and added to the chain. Data persists on the network for the life of the technology. With the ledger being duplicated across the network, the data is available to all participants of the network. This could result in possible data privacy issue if the data is not encrypted and can be used to identify personal information (Genkin et al., 2018).

Regulatory and Compliance—After the financial crisis of 2008, government and regulators have pushed for stronger oversight and control over financial institutions in an effort to prevent such future occurrences. Therefore, any innovation or new technology in this sector will face stringent regulatory scrutiny (Michel, 2018).

12.9 LIMITATIONS OF BLOCKCHAIN TECHNOLOGY

As is the case with any emerging technology, blockchain faces many limitations that might prevent its widespread use immediately. Considerable work is yet to be done to mitigate these risks and limitations.

Privacy—The first limitation would be the lack of privacy. Everyone in the peer-to-peer network would have the history of the blockchain once they enter into the chain. This could cause conflicts of interest for the underlying customers of the transaction. For example, a large public fund is a client of a custodial bank. This public fund hires an investment manager to manage a certain subset of assets, and the custodial bank is on the new blockchain public ledger. The manager decides to sell an equity stock, which through blockchain goes to a broker, and ultimately out to another investment manager. The recipient of the stock now knows that the stock came from the public fund via their manager. This creates multiple conflicts of interest for the end manager from knowing who contracts with the public fund client to what investments the public fund is investing in (Bachmann et al., 2011; Genkin et al., 2018).

Scalability—As it works today, blockchain can add a new transaction or a block of data to the chain every 10 or so minutes. This means the volume of data to be processed into a blockchain is considerably lower than traditional transactional networks. A financial platform that can be used by the world would be a nice thing. However, it is not conceivable in the near future. The amount of bandwidth, storage, and processing power needed to operate the system are astronomical. In order for blockchain to move forward in the financial industry, it must be more efficient than the current structure.

High Costs—Costs are a large limitation at this point to the technology. For a financial institution to adopt the blockchain technology, there must be a tangible benefit to switching. Otherwise, the money would be better spent on enhancing the current IT infrastructure. In addition, the costs of the infrastructure are being debated over who will pick up the tab. Banks will need to share infrastructure build-out costs equitably if new systems are to be truly inter-operable industry utilities. This is potentially subject to organizational disputes as users assess how much to invest (which can enable free or freer riders), or customize (which degrades interoperability/speed) and by which measure to allocate costs among participants (by revenues? market share?) (Van Steenis et al., 2016). Miners use expensive and sophisticated hardware to run proof of work algorithms. Due to the excessive cost associated with this process, proof of algorithm which includes both the hardware and electricity costs. Hence, it prevents most nodes from participating in the process (Swan, 2017).

Security and Accessibility—Blockchain's encryption process works based on a combination of keys, both private and public keys. These keys need to be securely managed by the nodes and users. Today's wallet software is highly secure for maintaining such keys. But, if the private keys are lost or stolen, it can pose a serious risk and essentially mean the user will lose access to all data and currency. If someone would be able to find a way into the chain, all of the historical information could be compromised. While there have been strides in the cryptocurrency space which are reassuring, financial institutions will not make a move to new technology without assurances behind the security and whether they would be able to protect its monies behind a cyber-attack. Investments will need to be made in the IT infrastructure around this technology, which will add to the upfront costs of entering into this space (Turner & Irwin, 2018).

Regulatory—Features that make blockchain so desirable are also the reason why it is in a bit of a grey area when it comes to regulation. Much work needs to be done in this area. Compliance can be ensured only when there is an open dialogue between the developing community, industry leaders, and regulatory body. Since the technology is in its infancy as far as the financial industry is concerned, there are currently no standards to how it will operate. In order to move forward, a standard of the market must be developed to "play" in this space. Part of the standards being developed are also who will be in charge of governing the technology? This will include who will be in charge of permitting users to the blockchain, especially when it comes to KYC and AML. In a highly regulated environment such as financial services, this becomes a very important factor that needs to be answered before the technology can move forward. Will the regulatory bodies allow the industry to move towards a decentralized and mutualized infrastructure? (Bandyopadhyay & Bandyopadhyay, 2018; Michel, 2018; Van Steenis et al., 2016).

12.10 CONCLUSION

Blockchain technology is still in its infancy. There is much to be explored, fine-tuned, and resolved in terms of the limitations mentioned earlier in this report. Nonetheless, there is a lot of interest in this technology, and much work has been done to explore possibilities and applications of this technology and to make it the next foundational technology.

Implications to the new decentralized blockchain system will be seismic in the financial services industry. First and foremost, it will change how the financial world connects. By being part of the network, the communication between organizations will be less frequent and operated in a different manner. It appears that governance will be at the forefront of managing the blockchain instead of security settlements and reconcilement between organizations. Another effect of this blockchain technology will promote virtual teams with these organizations. By being able to operate on the blockchain in a decentralized manner, virtualization will be an offshoot of adoption of this technology. It will force management to interact and review performance of individuals differently.

While all the hype around blockchain technology, the capabilities of this technology have been enhanced by the software industry and the financial industry for the past few years. We believe many new breakthroughs and features will be unfolded in the coming years. As with any new innovative technologies, blockchain has many use cases, but implementation across businesses is hit by problems with performance, oversight, and operations. Additionally, to introduce such technologies that are capable of overhauling traditional models in financial sector requires broad collaboration within the industry participants, regulatory bodies, and other impacted parties.

If some of the limitations such as cost, scalability, and regulatory issues were resolved, then the applications could be manifold. Blockchain technology is moving very quickly to assume the future versions of the technology will facilitate the financial industry. Bitcoin's cryptocurrency-based protocol, Ethereum's smart contract-based blockchain or some new yet to be discovered platform on blockchain is already addressing many of the issues and concerns. What remains to be seen is how quickly and widespread will its adoption be in the financial sector.

Blockchain technology has already demonstrated great success, especially with cryptocurrency. The underlying technology is being looked at across many industries, with financial institutions being one of the industries with the most intrigue. Blockchains, if implemented into the financial industry in the appropriate way to satisfy regulatory and governance, can enhance security around transactions, lower costs by utilizing the virtual space, increasing the speed in which transactions happen in the market, and provide greater visibility and fraud reduction. Distributed ledger and the blockchain technology has the potential to be disruptive, as it could completely change processes and systems within financial services. The technology could remove trusted third parties, decrease costs, and ultimately increase profits. The financial industry is looking for ways to move into the future with a virtually based technology and appear to be moving forward with blockchain. Blockchain will be the next successful step to reduce costs and risks, while increasing security around the industry.

REFERENCES

Australian Securities Exchange. (2018). ASX is replacing CHESS with distributed ledger technology (DLT) developed by Digital Asset. *Australian Securities Exchange CHESS Replacement.* Retrieved February 7, 2019 from www.asx.com.au/services/chess-replacement.htm

Bachmann, A., Becker, A., Buerckner, D., Hilker, M., Kock, F., Lehmann, M., Tiburtius, P., & Funk, B. (2011). Online peer-to-peer lending–a literature review. *Journal of Internet Banking and Commerce, 16*(2), 1–18.

Bandyopadhyay, S., & Bandyopadhyay, K. (2018). The European general data protection regulation and competitiveness of firms. *Competition Forum, 16*(1), 50–55.

Bank of England. (2019). Digital currencies. Retrieved February 7, 2019 from www.bankofengland.co.uk/research/digital-currencies

Batlin, A., Jaffrey, H., Murphy, C., Przewloka, A., & Williams, S. (2016). Building the trust engine. *UBS Group Technology White Paper.* Retrieved October 15, 2018 from www.ubs.com/maga zines/innovation/en/teasers/_jcr_content/mainpar/gridcontrol/col1/actionbutton.1656714339. file/bGluay9wYXRoPS9jb250ZW50L2RhbS91YnMvbWVnYXppbmVzL2lubm92YXRpb24v ZG9jdW1lbnRzL3doaXRlcGFwZXXItMTkwNTE2LnBkZg==/whitepaper-190516.pdf

Brown, R. (2018). Decentralized autonomous organization: On the blockchain, no one knows you're a fridge. *Ethereum: Start a democratic organization.* Retrieved October 10, 2018 from www.ethereum.org/dao.

Browne, R. (2017). American Express, Santander team up with Ripple for cross-border payments via blockchain. *CNBC: The Fintech Effect.* Retrieved February 7, 2019 from www.cnbc.com/ 2017/11/16/american-express-santander-team-up-with-ripple-on-blockchain-platform.html

Campbell-Verduyn, M. (2018). Bitcoin, crypto-coins, and global anti-money laundering governance. *Crime, Law and Social Change, 69*(2), 283–305.

Catalini, C., & Gans, J. S. (2017). Some simple economics of the blockchain. *Rotman School of Management Working Paper No. 2874598. MIT Sloan Research Paper No. 5191-16.* Retrieved December 17, 2018 from https://papers.ssrn.com/sol3/papers.cfm?abstract_id=2874598.

Cox, J. (2017). Federal Reserve starting to think about its own digital currency, Dudley says. *CNBC: The FED.* Retrieved December 15, 2018 from www.cnbc.com/2017/11/29/federal-reserve-starting-to-think-about-its-own-digital-currency-dudley-says.html

Cryptocurrency Market Capitalizations. (2018). All cryptocurrencies. Retrieved February 7, 2019 from Cryptocurrency Market Capitalizations: https://coinmarketcap.com/all/views/all/

Deloitte. (2015). Blockchain: Disrupting the financial services industry? Retrieved October 8, 2018 from www2.deloitte.com/content/dam/Deloitte/ie/Documents/FinancialServices/IE_Cons_Blockchain_1015.pdf.

Deshpande, A., Stewart, K., Lepetit, L., & Gunashekar, S. (2017). Distributed ledger technologies/ Blockchain: Challenges, opportunities and the prospects for standards. *British Standards Institution Overview Report,* 1–40. Retrieved October 5, 2018 from www.bsigroup.com/Local Files/zh-tw/InfoSec-newsletter/No201706/download/BSI_Blockchain_DLT_Web.pdf.

Dostov, V., & Shust, P. (2014). Cryptocurrencies: An unconventional challenge to the AML/CFT regulators? *Journal of Financial Crime, 21*(3), 249–263.

Egelund-Müller, B., Elsman, M., Henglein, F., & Ross, O. (2017). Automated execution of financial contracts on blockchains. *Business & Information Systems Engineering, 59*(6), 457–467.

Genkin, D., Papadopoulos, D., & Papamanthou, C. (2018). Privacy in decentralized cryptocurrencies. *Communications of the ACM, 61*(6), 78–88.

Hughes, T. M. (2018). The global financial services industry and the blockchain. *Journal of Structured Finance, 23*(4), 36–40.

Hyvärinen, H., Risius, M., & Friis, G. (2017). A blockchain-based approach towards overcoming financial fraud in public sector services. *Business & Information Systems Engineering*, *59*(6), 441–456.

Lakhani, K. (2017). Blockchain — what you need to know. *Harvard Business Review*. Retrieved October 10, 2018 from https://hbr.org/ideacast/2017/06/blockchain-what-you-need-to-know.html

Leising, M. (2018). Blockchain tested for making mortgage securities easier to track. *Bloomberg Markets*. Retrieved October 10, 2018 from www.bloomberg.com/news/articles/2018-01-18/blockchain-eyed-for-mortgage-bundling-that-caused-2008-crisis

Michel, N. (2018). Special interest politics could save cash or kill it. *Cato Journal*, *38*(2), 489–502.

Mills, D., Wang, K., Malone, B., Ravi, A., Marquardt, J., Chen, C., Badev, A., Brezinski, T., Fahy, L., Liao, K., Kargenian, V., Ellithorpe, M., Ng, W., & Baird, M. (2016). Distributed ledger technology in payments, clearing, and settlement. *Finance and Economic Discussion Series: Division of Research & Statistics and Monetary Affairs*, Federal Reserve Board, 1–36. Retrieved February 7, 2019 from www.federalreserve.gov/econresdata/feds/2016/files/2016095pap.pdf

Nakamoto, S. (2008). Bitcoin: A peer-to-peer electronic cash system. Retrieved May 8, 2016 from https://bitcoin.org/bitcoin.pdf.

Nikkei. (2017). Japan-South Korea blockchain payments enter trials Friday. Nikkei Asian Review. Retrieved February 7, 2019 from https://asia.nikkei.com/Business/Deals/Japan-South-Korea-blockchain-payments-enter-trials-Friday

Petrasic, K. (2016). Beyond bitcoin: The blockchain revolution in financial services. *White & Case*. Retrieved December 17, 2018 from www.whitecase.com/publications/insight/beyond-bitcoin-blockchain-revolution-financial-services

Plansky, J., O'Donnell, T., & Richards, K. (2016, January 11). A strategist's guide to blockchain. *PwC strategy+business*. Retrieved December 17, 2018 from www.strategy-business.com/article/A-Strategists-Guide-to-Blockchain

Pollari, I., & Ruddenklau, A. (2018). The pulse of fintech 2018: Biannual global analysis of investment in fintech. *KPMG International White Paper*, 1–58. Retrieved December 16, 2018 from https://assets.kpmg/content/dam/kpmg/xx/pdf/2018/07/h1-2018-pulse-of-fintech.pdf.

PwC. (2017). A non-technical summary of the proof-of-concept to enable regulatory compliant Bitcoin transactions. *Trusted Bitcoin Ecosystem White Paper*, 1–36. Retrieved October 10, 2018 from www.pwc.com/sg/en/financial-services/assets/fintech/fintech-trusted-bitcoin-ecosystem-whitepaper-201706.pdf.

Radziwill, N. (2018). Blockchain revolution: How the technology behind Bitcoin is changing money, business, and the world. *The Quality Management Journal*, *25*(1), 64–65.

Shen, J. (2016). e-Estonia: The power and potential of digital identity. *Thomson Reuters*. Retrieved February 7, 2019 from https://blogs.thomsonreuters.com/answerson/e-estonia-power-potential-digital-identity/

Swan, M. (2017). Anticipating the economic benefits of blockchain. *Technology Innovation Management Review*, *7*(10), 6–13.

Thomson Reuters. (2016). Thomson Reuters 2016 know your customer surveys reveal escalating costs and complexity. Retrieved October 10, 2018 from www.thomsonreuters.com/en/press-releases/2016/may/thomson-reuters-2016-know-your-customer-surveys.html.

Turner, A., & Irwin, A. S. M. (2018). Bitcoin transactions: A digital discovery of illicit activity on the blockchain. *Journal of Financial Crime*, *25*(1), 109–130.

Van Steenis, H., Graseck, B. L., Simpson, F., & Faucette, J. E. (2016). Global insight: Blockchain in banking: Disruptive threat or tool? *Morgan Stanley Research: Global Financials/FinTech*, 1–31. Retrieved October 10, 2018 from http://linkback.morganstanley.com/web/sendlink/webapp/f/7ts1o97g-3pg7-g000-a67d-005056012000?store=0&d=UwBSZXNlYXJjaF9NUwBhMWJjY2V

lYy1mNWMyLTExZTUtYmQyZS1hYmRhODUzZjA3NTI%3D&user=ldxp64j6odko-48&__gda__=1587331995_9d54f6d26fbc407c41db59cd77468e8e

Wild, J., Arnold, M., & Stafford, P. (2015). Technology: Banks seek the key to blockchain. *Financial Times*. Retrieved December 17, 2018 from www.ft.com/content/eb1f8256-7b4b-11e5-a1fe-567b37f80b64#axzz4CxeAR5OA

World Bank. (2014). Remittances to developing countries to grow by 5 percent this year, while conflict-related forced migration is at all-time high. World Bank Report. Retrieved October 15, 2018 from www.worldbank.org/en/news/press-release/2014/10/06/remittances-developing-countries-five-percent-conflict-related-migration-all-time-high-wb-report.

World Bank. (2018). Accelerated remittances growth to low- and middle-income countries in 2018. *World Bank Report*. Retrieved January 15, 2019 from www.worldbank.org/en/news/press-release/2018/12/08/accelerated-remittances-growth-to-low-and-middle-income-countries-in-2018.

Zambrano, R., Seward, R. K., & Sayo, P. (2017). Unpacking the disruptive potential of blockchain technology for human development. *International Development Research Center White Paper*, 1–85. Retrieved October 15, 2018 from https://idl-bnc-idrc.dspacedirect.org/bitstream/handle/10625/56662/IDL-56662.pdf?sequence=2&isAllowed=y.

CHAPTER 13

Blockchain and the Financial Industry

Giovanni Cucchiarato and Giacomo Bocale

CONTENTS

13.1 BACKGROUND OF BLOCKCHAIN IN THE FINANCIAL INDUSTRY

A blockchain is a distributed database, which is used to store data in "blocks" and is shared across a network of computers. We can imagine a blockchain as a register of digitally recorded information, the security of which is ensured through encryption, in such a way that the integrity of the system is not disrupted.

A blockchain database, from a functional perspective, consists of a series of blocks "chained" together, with each block of information containing a cryptographic reference to the previous one. Every time a new block is formed, it can be added to the existing chain only after the network of participants has reached a consensus on the validity of the information contained therein.

Although primarily identified as the technology that underpins the Bitcoin system—its first successful implementation—blockchain's unique application and development potential goes far beyond this, despite it is still being relatively unknown in the public domain. Indeed, while the public is aware of Bitcoin—thanks largely to the flow of enthusiasts and the extensive media coverage it has received, particularly between the years 2013 and 2017—far fewer people are aware of blockchain's key features and potential.

The term "blockchain" typically refers to the transparent, trustless, publicly accessible ledger that allows users to securely transfer ownership of units of value using encryption methods. The term "blockchain" can be used for each type of distributed database that stores a permanent and tamper-proof ledger of data. In fact, using blockchain architecture, it is possible to indelibly register any kind of digital data in a secure and distributed manner so that it cannot be subsequently edited. For example, it can be used on a transaction, a contract, a registration of ownership document, as well as for medical and personal data. In recent times, we have also seen potential applications for the technology within the field of finance.

The current financial system is based on reliance of certain trusted institutions, which are responsible for ensuring a comprehensive, effective, and consistent level of regulation and supervision. This translates into protecting investors and savers, as well as promoting the effectiveness, smooth functioning, and integrity of financial markets. Despite these efforts, the system has to deal daily with deep-structural problems such as growing costs and delays, increasing administrative tasks, bureaucracy and unnecessary paperwork and documentation. These issues are the direct consequences of the underlying architecture that supports the system, which is built upon decades-old, highly centralized infrastructures.

This is where blockchain, with its unique characteristics, could prove invaluable and play a key role in the years to come. If it was to apply to consensus-building processes, blockchain's potential could have a disruptive effect on the industry. It could facilitate a smooth transition from reliance on trusted third parties, towards innovative distributed consensus mechanisms.

Thanks to these features, for some years now, blockchain has gained ground in the industry and has attracted attention in the eyes of investors, financial institutions, regulators, and key market players. They have all identified potential areas where the technology is expected to play a role in the future, and noted its capacity to introduce a new and innovative approach to the way financial activities are conducted.

One possible development objective could be to facilitate and simplify the raising of capital, through funding campaigns carried out on blockchain-based platforms. These innovative operations have recently become widely known as "initial coin offerings" (ICOs).

13.2 INITIAL COIN OFFERINGS

ICOs have emerged in recent years as a new and innovative method for companies to raise capital and to start or fuel the development of projects and businesses. Through an ICO, an issuer uses blockchain-based architecture to create a certain quantity of digital tokens and sell them in exchange for capital, often in the form of Bitcoins or Ethers (two of the most popular cryptocurrencies). An ICO is a cost-effective alternative to traditional fundraising mechanisms, since it benefits from the competitive advantages of non-regulation or under-regulation. These operations experienced a large-scale expansion in 2017, following the considerable popularity gained as a result of the heightened media interest in technology issues.

In an ICO, a company promotes a fundraising campaign (similar to a crowdfunding campaign) on a blockchain-based platform, aimed at collecting funds for the development of an innovative project. In order to launch an offer, it normally first needs to draft a white paper. A white paper is a document that is modelled on the form and substance of an IPO prospectus. While it is somewhat less comprehensive than an IPO prospectus, it should contain the necessary information for investors to be able to understand the key features of the offered tokens and then to make informed investment decisions. The information routinely supplied by the issuer and included in the white paper contains details concerning the principles and basic features of the project behind the offer, the tokens distribution procedures, and guidelines regarding how the funds collected will be spent.

During an ICO, in order to submit purchase orders, investors are requested to register on the platform. Once registered, they are able to buy tokens in exchange for money or cryptocurrencies, which can be used as a means of payment and are transferred to the issuer's digital wallet. After completion of the offering, tokens are usually listed on an exchange.

The first ICO dates back to 2013, when the pioneering Mastercoin became the first project to sell digital tokens, collecting over $7 million. A year later, Ethereum launched its ICO, raising $18.4 million in capital.

A significant growth of the ICO market has been observed in recent years, and the ease of creating new tokens has led to a surge in the number of campaigns. In addition, a large number of investors have been attracted to ICOs against a backdrop of steadily increasing Bitcoin prices.

In 2018, the global amount of capital raised through ICOs reached the remarkable milestone of $7.9 billion, with 1258 offerings completed.[1] In 2017, the total amount collected through ICOs resulted in $6.2 billion.[2] This marked a significant increase in volume compared to the results for the previous year: in 2016, in fact, the capital raised totaled only $90.2 million.[3]

According to a report released by the advisory firm Satis Group LLC,[4] however, more than 80% of ICOs have been proved to be fraudulent. The research highlighted that four ICOs out of five were projects that "expressed availability of ICO investment"—for example, through a website or social media—but "had no intention of fulfilling project development duties with the funds, and/or was deemed by the community (message boards, website or other online information) to be a scam". Only 8% resulted in successful campaigns.

The relevance of these statistics has led to a change in the approach of market operators. The lack of regulatory burdens—which once constituted one of the most attractive features of these fundraising campaigns—has proved over the years to be a double-edged sword. The growing awareness that most ICOs could be fraudulent has prompted a considerable reduction in investor purchasing volumes.

Following the many cases of scandals and frauds involving savers, regulators have started taking steps to ensure investor confidence. This has resulted in an ever-growing number of regulations, issued with the common intention of increasing investors' protection, but has also had the consequence of increasing regulatory burdens for those involved in the ICO market.

In particular, authorities have posited whether these tokens were not, after all, securities, with all related regulation that this entails.

13.3 ICOS VS. STOS

The requirement to give structure to an issuing scheme compliant with securities regulations led to the creation of a new, more suitable instrument: the STOs.

STOs—which stands for "Security Token Offerings"—represent a remarkable but natural step forward in the evolution of blockchain-based funding campaigns. Chronologically, blockchain-based funding models have undergone two different phases. The emergence, growth, and confirmation of ICOs have covered a span of time that stretches approximately from 2013 until the end of 2018. After this period of considerable enthusiasm and in the wake of financial scandals and frauds that affected several campaigns, ICOs have started to be supplanted (and, according to expert opinion, will be replaced) by a more compliant model for innovative companies to raise capital: STOs.

Tokens sold through an STO, as made clear from the acronym, are considered securities for regulatory purposes. They consist of tokenized securities, digital representations of the issuer's shares, bonds, or other similar financing instruments. When they take the form of equity, their holders are considered as shareholders of the issuer.

These new financing instruments, on the one hand, allow investors to rely on a consistent level of transparency and protection and contribute to a substantial reduction of risks; on the other hand, however, they affect financing costs, since the issuer has to bear the expenses associated with an issuance of securities. While ICOs allow the issuance of coins/tokens normally intended to act as means of payment or ensure that users have access to a service or a product through the platform of the issuer, security tokens are to all intents and purposes regulated securities. As such, their issuance must be conducted in accordance with the applicable regulatory provisions. For example, the offeror will be obliged to prepare and publicize a prospectus, approved by the competent authority, for a public offering of security tokens aimed at the general public, unless certain exemptions apply. It follows that ICO platforms are generally not required (if the tokens are not deemed to be securities) to comply with standards and processes specific to the field of securities legislation, thereby avoiding added complexities and compliance costs. However, if a company decides to promote an STO, the offer of tokens will only be allowed if the related issuance meets all the conditions provided for by the applicable regulatory framework.

13.4 ICOS AND THE TOKEN LEGAL QUALIFICATION (TOKEN TAXONOMY)

What emerges from the analysis of token offerings practice is that there is not just one type of "token", but rather they may take a variety of forms. Nevertheless, at present there is no clear legislative framework, either at the international or national level, which establishes a comprehensive token classification. Therefore, it is not easy to indicate a common and widely accepted taxonomy, and is just as difficult to provide for a uniform definition of "token".

In the absence of an adequate legislative framework, reference should be made to certain approaches adopted by some financial supervisory authorities.

The categorization proposed by the Swiss Financial Market Supervisory Authority (FINMA) seems to be the most effective. In its "Guidelines for enquiries regarding the regulatory framework for initial coin offerings (ICOs)",[5] published on 16 February 2018, FINMA suggested classifying tokens on the basis of their underlying economic function. As a result of this approach, FINMA proposed categorizing tokens into three different categories: Payment Tokens, Utility Tokens, and Asset Tokens:

- Payment Tokens (or cryptocurrencies) are considered means of payment, useful in acquiring goods or services. These tokens give rise to no claims on their issuer.

- Utility Tokens are intended to provide digital access to the issuer's specific application or service, where they are intended to be spent.

- Asset Tokens are analogous to equities, bonds, or derivatives, as they promise a share in future company earnings or future capital flows.

In January 2019, the United Kingdom's Financial Conduct Authority (FCA) published a consultation paper entitled "Guidance on Cryptoassets".[6] In this document, FCA noted the need to introduce a categorization of tokens, which was still lacking in the present legislation. Tokens were grouped into three categories according to their characteristics:

- Exchange Tokens, not issued or backed by any central authority and intended to be used as a means of exchange for buying and selling goods and services without traditional intermediaries;

- Security Tokens, with specific characteristics that mean they meet the definition of a "Specified Investment" under the UK Regulated Activities Order[7] like a share or a debt instrument;

- Utility Tokens, which grant holders access to a current or prospective product or service but do not grant holders rights that are the same as those granted by the above-mentioned "Specified Investments".

13.5 A BRIEF OVERVIEW OF CERTAIN REGULATORY FRAMEWORKS

13.5.1 United States of America

The U.S. Securities and Exchange Commission (SEC) is the federal government agency responsible for protecting investors, maintaining fair, orderly and efficient markets and facilitating capital formation in the United States of America. The Congress created it in 1934 as the first federal regulator for securities market. The SEC has also been among the first US regulators whose efforts have been recognized in laying the groundwork for the establishment of a regulatory framework for ICOs. In fact, while several federal and national authorities had the opportunity to exercise jurisdiction on this matter, it has been the Security and Exchange Commission who has provided answers. The Commission has attempted to deal with the big questions around how regulators should deal with the challenges arising from ICOs' growing emergence, against a backdrop of increasing concern about the risks of potential fraudulent activities.

Considerable efforts have been concentrated on setting up a valid reference framework with regard to ICOs for the years to come. The two most important interventions on this complex issue date back to 2017, when the SEC released its first provisions after investigations conducted on two of the first token offerings. These documents have so far defined and guided the systematic approach of the SEC in addressing regulation and specific concerns regarding ICOs.

This approach has at its heart the analysis of each particular token issuing scheme, aimed at determining whether there might be a breach of the relevant U.S. federal securities laws. A similar breach may be detected where the relevant digital tokens fall within the definition of "securities", based on the specific facts and circumstances ascertained on a case-by-case basis. This conclusion may be drawn in particular when the digital token qualifies as an "investment contract", and the respective ICO as an "offer and sale of securities".

On 25 July 2017, the SEC circulated a report[8] of an investigation pursuant to Section 21(a) of the Securities Exchange Act of 1934.[9] The aim was to verify whether the offer promoted by the company involved in the investigation—The DAO—might fall within the scope of U.S. federal securities laws.

The DAO qualified as a "decentralized autonomous organization", a sort of "virtual company" operating through the combination of algorithms and computer codes executed on a blockchain (the so called "smart contracts"). The DAO was established as a for-profit entity, with the aim of creating and selling digital tokens (the "DAO Tokens") to the investment public. The amount of capital raised through the offer was to be used for the financing of future projects.

DAO Tokens gave holders the possibility to participate in the selection and approval of the operations to be funded, and granted participation in future profits. DAO Tokens could also be resold by the holders on the secondary market through a limited number of platforms.

Started in April 2016, The DAO's ICO was able to raise a significant amount of capital. Once the token offering was completed, however, some hackers exploited a flaw in the codes and stole approximately one-third of the capital.[10] This situation led to the commencement of the SEC's investigation and proceedings, which aimed at verifying whether DAO Tokens were covered or not by the definition of "securities" under the relevant U.S. legislation. A positive response would have had significant implications.

In fact, when an offer or sale falls under Section 5 of the Securities Act[11]—the relevant U.S. act on securities together with the Exchange Act—the issuer must file a registration with the SEC, which needs to be accompanied by a prospectus. A prospectus is a document that contains the information regarding the issuer and the offer, and it is necessary for prospective investors in order to make informed investment decisions. It is not possible to launch an offer without filing a registration and publishing a prospectus unless expressly permitted under a specific exemption from registration.

The Securities Act lays down a broad definition of "security".[12] The analysis conducted by the SEC revealed that, in light of their specific characteristics, DAO Tokens did fall under the qualification of "investment contract", a subcategory in the aforementioned broader definition of "security". In order to reach this conclusion, the authority relied on objective elements deriving from the application of the so-called "Howey Test".

The U.S. Supreme Court established this test for the first time in 1946 in the case SEC v. W.J. Howey Co.,[13] setting out a list of the conditions required for a product to be considered as an "investment contract". The Securities Act, in fact, did not provide a specific definition of "investment contract", thus leaving it subject to interpretation.

The SEC, in accordance with the established Supreme Court's case law and interpretation, explained that to determine if a product could be classified as an "investment contract", and therefore as a "security", a substance-over-form analysis should be adopted. "Form", in fact, "should be disregarded for substance, and the emphasis should be on economic realities underlying a transaction, and not on the name appended thereto".[14]

Under the Howey Test, an "investment contract" requires four different elements:

- an investment of money;

- a common enterprise;

- a reasonable expectation of profit;

- a profit deriving from the managerial efforts of others.

The SEC analyzed in detail the DAO Tokens offering, in order to establish whether each of the above-mentioned conditions had been fulfilled.

With reference to the "investment of money", the SEC considered that the investment in DAO Tokens fell within such a definition, even if it was made in Ethers (one of the most widespread cryptocurrency) and not in cash (i.e. in fiat money). In determining whether an investment contract exists, the SEC underlined that an "investment of money" does not need to take the form of cash, since cash is not the only form of possible contribution.

The second requirement was fulfilled since Slock.it UG—the company that had created and issued the DAO Tokens—constituted, according to the Commission, a "common enterprise".

Regarding the presence or not of "a reasonable expectation of profit", the SEC deemed the condition as met, since DAO Token holders could reasonably expect, at the time of their investment, to earn potential profits through the above-mentioned "common enterprise" when they forwarded their purchase orders.

And such profits, as clearly stated in the SEC's report, "were to be derived from the managerial efforts of others". Specifically, the "others" were Slock.it UG and its co-founders (those who had set up the project), and The DAO's Curators (people appointed by Slock.it UG with the crucial mandate to decide whether or not a proposal could be voted by DAO Token holders and then possibly funded by The DAO).

Lastly, provided the absence of any valid exemption, the investigation concluded by stating that the DAO Tokens offer was required to be registered with the Security and Exchange Commission.

On 11 December 2017—five months after the DAO Tokens investigation—the Security and Exchange Commission took a similar stance against another company, Munchee Inc., a California-based business that had created an iPhone application for clients to review restaurant meals.[15]

The SEC deemed it appropriate to open a cease-and-desist proceeding pursuant to Section 8A of the Securities Act against Munchee Inc. after the company decided to sell digital tokens to investors through an offer aimed at raising capital in order to fuel the development of a food review-related project. This offer, however, constituted to all intents and purposes a securities offer and sale, following the application of the Howey Test, and hence needed to be registered with the SEC, unless it qualified for exemption from registration. Moreover, in this case, the obligation to file a registration statement with the SEC was not fulfilled, and then the Commission had no other choice but to act.

As a result of its analysis, MUN Tokens were classified as "securities" under the Securities Act on the basis of the specific facts and circumstances and despite their designation as "tokens", as in The DAO case. It was therefore confirmed that they should be treated as an "investment contract", as per the application of the Howey Test.

Under the Howey Test—as previously pointed out—a token, in order to be considered as an "investment contract", must be examined in order to determine whether it contains the following four different elements: an investment of money; a common enterprise; a reasonable expectation of profit; a profit deriving from the managerial efforts of others.

Following its investigation, the cease-and-desist order explained the grounds for the SEC's decision to consider MUN Tokens as "securities". The substantial nature of the Commission's approach led the SEC to this conclusion, provided that:

- the investment in MUN Tokens constituted an "investment of money" since the company launched an ICO with the general aim of encouraging the investment public to contribute in the form of Ethers or Bitcoins. "Such investment"—as the Commission had already the opportunity to point out in the DAO Tokens investigation—"is the type of contribution of value that can create an investment contract"[16];

- on the existence of an effective "common enterprise", it had to be highlighted that the SEC did not evaluate this element. However, it can be stated that Munchee Inc. was in all respects a "common enterprise" since it was a company incorporated in Delaware, United States, and based in San Francisco, California;

- investors in MUN Tokens, at the time of their purchase orders, had a "reasonable expectation of profit". The funds raised through the ICO were in fact intended to fuel the Munchee's project development, aimed at building an "ecosystem" based on MUN Tokens. In its white paper, the company underlined its intention to provide incentives for users to write food reviews (by paying them in MUN Tokens) and, on the other hand, to sell advertising to restaurants in exchange for MUN Tokens. Any rise in MUN Tokens' value deriving from a positive development of this "ecosystem" could have reasonably led to potential profits for investors;

- lastly, any potential profit would have resulted from the company's "managerial efforts", and not from the investors' efforts. The only people that could have generated incremental revenues or profits, in fact, were Munchee Inc. and its agents, for example by driving MUN Tokens appreciation in value, or by developing an effective secondary market.

The SEC contacted Munchee Inc. on the second day of sales of MUN Tokens, and requested to shut down the offer and return funds to purchasers. Since the company agreed to the SEC's conditions, the Commission ordered it to cease and desist from future violations without imposing any civil penalty.

The SEC has proved to be a close observer of the ICO industry. It was the Commission that first took appropriate measures regarding the supervision of token offerings, establishing a clear regulatory framework for start-ups and companies launching an ICO and closing a legal vacuum.

This purpose could be achieved by making use of the Howey Test, an interpretative model based on the analysis of objective criteria whose coexistence makes it possible to bring tokens within the definition of "investment contract" and consequently within the definition of "securities".

13.5.2 Italy

In Italy, with regard to financial markets and investors' protection, the national legal system provides for cooperation between the two main financial supervisory authorities. The Bank of Italy is the Italian central bank, whose aim is to guarantee price stability, the efficiency of the financial system and the constitutional principle of the protection of savings. It is also the national competent authority for banking supervision and resolution.[17] Consob—the financial services supervisor—is instead the government authority responsible for regulating national financial markets. Its activity is aimed at protecting the investment public and ensuring financial market participants' transparency and correct behavior.[18]

At present (May 2019), the Italian national legislation does not provide for any specific law or regulation with regard to digital tokens offerings or similar issuing schemes. However, it should be clearly emphasized that the recent release of the first official document on this matter was highly political and symbolically significant.

On 19 March 2019, Consob circulated a public discussion document in order to collect opinions and open a national debate on ICOs.[19] The document is addressed to savers, investors, industry experts, and market players, who were asked to contribute to the debate and give feedbacks on the authority's position. Opinions and comments will be collected through their replies to a questionnaire, which will help Consob shape its position on the general approach to a possible, new legislative proposal on ICOs. At the end of the consultation, the outcome will indeed be presented to the Italian government and will help it to assess the feasibility of taking actions in this respect. Consob is of the opinion that a specific law is necessary to regulate such a peculiar matter, while other countries have taken the opposite approach, classifying crypto-assets under the definition of "financial instruments", as provided for by existing legislation.

The Italian supervisory authority, in Chapter 2 of the discussion document, draws the attention to another recent intervention at legislative level, which also encourages the start of a national debate on technology and regulation. The Italian Parliament, on 7 February 2019, indeed approved the Law-Decree 14 December 2018, No. 135 (so-called "Simplifications Decree"),[20] which establishes for the first time comprehensive definitions of "technologies based on distributed ledgers" and "smart contracts".

"Technologies based on distributed ledgers" are identified under article 8-*ter*, paragraph 1, as

> Technologies and IT protocols based on a shared, distributed, replicable, simultaneously accessible, structurally decentralized ledger, built on cryptographic keys which enable the registration, validation, update and storage of either decrypted or encrypted data, verifiable by each participant and that cannot be altered nor modified.[21]

Paragraph 2 of the same article lays down a specific definition of "smart contract":

> A software which runs on technologies based on distributed ledgers whose enforcement is legally binding upon two or more parties with reference to the relevant terms previously agreed by them. Smart contracts satisfy the written form requirement to the extent that the digital authentication of the parties is made in accordance with the applicable technical standards to be established by the Agency for Digital Italy.

Another point worthy of note is the express provision in the above-mentioned Law Decree of the legal equivalence between storing of information with "Technologies based on distributed ledgers" and electronic time stamps. Article 8-*ter*, paragraph 3 indeed stipulates that the storing of information with technologies based on distributed ledgers produces the legal effects of electronic time stamps in accordance with Regulation (EU) No. 910/2014 of the European Parliament and of the Council of 23 July 2014 on electronic identification and trust services for electronic transactions in the internal market, and thus gives legal certainty regarding the date and time of the related document or information.

Although there is currently an absence of a detailed regulatory framework, and the conclusion of the aforementioned public consultation is yet to be decided, Consob has deemed it appropriate to exercise its firm jurisdiction in relation to initial coin offerings under the Italian Consolidated Law on Finance[22]—the fundamental law governing Italian financial markets—while stating that the possibility of applying these provisions to ICOs needs to be assessed on a case-by-case basis. In particular, Consob considers it possible that a digital token can be qualified as covered by the Italian definition of "financial product", which diverges from the one of "transferable securities", at the core of the European regulatory framework on financial markets.

European financial markets are primarily regulated by MiFID II Directive.[23] Annex I, Section C of MiFID II lays down an articulated list of those products that are regarded as "financial instruments" under such Directive. The list includes "transferable securities", defined in article 4, paragraph 1, number 44 as "those classes of securities which are negotiable on the capital market, with the exception of instruments of payment". The article identifies the following three possible categories of "transferable securities":

(a) "shares in companies and other securities equivalent to shares in companies, partnerships or other entities, and depositary receipts in respect of shares";

(b) "bonds or other forms of securitized debt, including depositary receipts in respect of such securities";

(c) "any other securities giving the right to acquire or sell any such transferable securities or giving rise to a cash settlement determined by reference to transferable securities, currencies, interest rates or yields, commodities or other indices or measures".

The European Prospectus Directive[24] and the Prospectus Regulation[25] similarly cross-refer to the definition of "transferable securities" given in MiFID II Directive. They establish that securities can only be offered to the public in the European Union after prior publication of a prospectus, unless the offer falls within one of the Directive's exemptions.

Lastly, the Regulation on Market Abuse[26]—which establishes rules on "insider dealing, the unlawful disclosure of inside information and market manipulation (market abuse) as well as measures to prevent market abuse to ensure the integrity of financial markets"—also refers to "financial instruments" as defined under MiFID II Directive.

Consob, in spite of its extensive use at EU level, instead of classifying digital tokens as "transferable securities", has chosen to focus on a definition established under domestic laws, using the category of "financial product" to build a strong legal foundation to its action and make it more effective.

In 2018, from October to December, Consob started to decisively intervene in ICO campaigns, suspending for 90 days, as precautionary measure, five public offerings, namely:

- Avarcrypto Investment Plan[27];

- Token TGA[28];

- Crypton[29];

- Green Earth Certificates[30];

- Bitsurge Token.[31]

The underlying reasoning of the Italian regulator—based, as previously mentioned, on the ascription of the digital tokens issued through the above-listed ICOs within the concept of "financial products"—can be explained as follows.

Consob starts its analysis by verifying if the products concerned (digital tokens) meet the requirements specified in the definition of "financial product". Under article 1, paragraph 1, letter (u) of the Italian Consolidated Law on Finance, financial products "shall mean financial instruments and every other form of investment of a financial nature". Indeed, the definition of "financial products" includes not only "financial instruments", but also "every other form of investment of a financial nature".

The notion of "investment of a financial nature", in particular, entails the contemporary presence of three elements:

(a) a capital investment;

(b) an expected financial return;

(c) the exposure to a risk related to the above-mentioned investment.

Consob, in its investigations, concluded that these three conditions were fulfilled with regard to all the above-listed ICOs and therefore the investments advertised should be classified as financial products.

As a second step, after subsuming tokens under the definition of "financial products", it had also to be examined whether the offerings could be considered a "public offering or investment incentive" under article 1, paragraph 1, letter (t) of the Consolidated Law on Finance. This law states: "public offering or investment incentive shall mean every offer or incentive, invitation to offer or promotional message, in whatsoever form addressed to the public, whose objective is the sale or subscription of financial products including the allocation through authorized people".

In all cases, Consob considered that the requirements for identifying a "public offering" were satisfied.

Therefore, the offeror, in each of the five investigated cases, should have published a prospectus (which, similarly to the U.S. legislation, is a document containing all information necessary for investors to make an informed assessment of the issuer's profile and the financial products intended to be sold), giving prior notice to Consob, as required by article 94 of the Consolidated Law on Finance.

Within this framework, the Italian legislation expressly endows the authority with the power to take remedial action "in the event of an ascertained violation of the provisions" of the respective chapter, including the event in which the obligation to release a prospectus is not fulfilled. This includes in particular the power to suspend the offer for a maximum of ninety days with regard to the Italian investment public, as it occurred in relation to the five offerings in question.

All the above-mentioned actions are the sign of Consob's determination to draw the attention to the need to avoid a regulatory and supervisory vacuum in a rapidly evolving sector such as the ICO industry. Given the lack of stable regulatory frameworks, both at national and international level, the market's rapid evolution and the proliferation of different regulatory guidelines and recommendations on a national scale are posing serious challenges to national supervisory authorities. Additional efforts and more suitable procedures will be needed to keep up with the ambition and the pace of development in this industry, in order for supervisory authorities to be able to carry out effective supervision in the challenging and disruptive environment of financial and technological innovation.

13.5.3 Switzerland

Switzerland is another important country that positioned itself as one of the leading hubs with respect to ICOs. This has been possible—as in the case of Malta—by putting in place a legislation aimed at fostering the creation of a favorable environment for investments in blockchain technology and cryptocurrencies.

The authority with the strongest commitment is undoubtedly the Swiss Financial Market Supervisory Authority (FINMA). FINMA took a stance in September 2017 announcing the start of investigations to verify whether some ICO campaigns were in any instances in breach of Swiss laws.[32] Following on from this initiative, FINMA expressed its willingness to outline the structure of a federal regulatory framework for the promotion of ICOs. As a first step, the Swiss authority released its Guidance no. 04/2017 on the "Regulatory treatment of initial coin offerings".[33] This Guidance, dated 27 September 2017, is important as it is one of the first measures that addresses the world of blockchain technology and ICOs, recognizing their innovative potential and underlining the current lack of detailed regulation. On this specific subject, FINMA outlined its considerations on whether ICOs fell within the scope of any of the existing Swiss regulatory laws. In the light of ICOs main characteristics, FINMA believed that several provisions could be relevant, for example provisions on combating money laundering and terrorist financing, whose applicability is connected to the issuance of tokenized payment instruments through an ICO; banking law provisions; provisions on securities trading and collective investment schemes legislation.

On 16 February 2018, FINMA released the "Guidelines for enquiries regarding the regulatory framework for initial coin offerings (ICOs)".[34] In this document, the Swiss authority highlighted that, while the previous Guidance contained its preliminary position on ICOs and references to areas in which ICOs may be covered by existing financial market regulation, the new Guidelines were aimed at providing market participants with all the necessary information on how FINMA would have dealt with enquiries regarding the supervisory and regulatory framework for ICOs. FINMA pointed out that since 2017 several requests for clarification concerning the Swiss law provisions applicable to ICOs were addressed to the authority. Switzerland in fact saw a sharp increase in the number of token offerings in 2017, as more and more companies and start-ups decided to approach this innovative method of raising capital and to do it in the Swiss Confederation. In the interest of both clarity and consistency of Swiss legislation and the development of this innovative market, FINMA decided to release these new Guidelines, in order to help ICO promoters comply with the applicable regulation when launching an ICO.

FINMA noted that (in February 2018) there were no specific regulation addressing ICOs, but several different provisions from different existing legislative and regulatory frameworks could apply to the offerings. There was not even the possibility to take into account the relevant case law, given the recent and rapid development of token offerings. Furthermore, there were several ICOs peculiarities observed, which were reflected in a great variety of tokens issued. These diversities made any generalization far more difficult and meant that the only option was to examine each situation on a case-by-case basis.

In order to respond to this necessity and to be able to ensure coherent and suitable assessments, the Swiss regulator proposed the introduction of an ICO classification, based on the underlying economic purpose of the token issued within the funding campaign. FINMA, in fact, clearly stated that any assessment would have been based on the underlying economic function of the token.

Following this approach, three different token subcategories could be identified:

- Payment Tokens, intended to be used as a means of payment for acquiring goods or services or as a means of money or value transfer;

- Utility Tokens, intended to provide digital access to an application or service by means of a blockchain-based infrastructure;

- Asset Tokens, intended to represent assets such as a debt or equity claim on the issuer and promising a share in future company earnings or future capital flows.

For any of these subcategories, FINMA outlined its considerations on the possibility to classify the corresponding tokens as securities under the Financial Market Infrastructure Act.[35] "Securities" are defined in such law as "standardised certificated and uncertificated securities, derivatives and intermediated securities, which are suitable for mass trading".[36]

With regard to Payment Tokens, FINMA pointed out the existence of different opinions whether these tokens should fall or not under the definition of "securities". The Swiss authority was of the view that not every token should necessarily be classified as security, and given their specific key feature of acting as a means of payment, these tokens were not to be considered among them. However, as previously pointed out, an offering of Payment Tokens would have been subject to the relevant anti-money legislation (the Swiss Anti-Money Laundering Act[37]).

As regards Utility Tokens, FINMA believed that a distinction had to be drawn between those with the sole function to confer digital access right to an application or service, and those with an additional investment purpose. In the first case, Utility Tokens would have not been treated as securities, due to the absence of an underlying investment function. In the second case, on the contrary, the investment purpose could have had no other result than leading to the classification as securities.

Moving on to Asset Tokens, FINMA outlined that they constitute securities if two conditions are satisfied: (i) they represent an uncertificated security or a derivative, and (ii) they have the characteristic of being standardized and suitable for mass standardized trading.

Switzerland has demonstrated a constructive and favorable approach towards the creation of an ICO-related regulatory framework. In its communications, FINMA has always underlined the absence of an appropriate legislative framework or an established case law. Based on these elements and in compliance with the principle of technological neutrality, the Swiss authority has emphasized the need of a strict application of the existing financial markets legislation on a case-by-case basis.

In order to be able to apply this type of comparative assessment, FINMA introduced the first comprehensive token classification—which remains its most noteworthy initiative, in view of the lack of any similar actions in other countries. The Swiss categorization, based on the underlying economic purpose and the specific characteristics of the issued tokens, allows the authority to assess, from time to time, whether the token concerned falls within the scope of Swiss financial market regulation.

13.5.4 Malta

Malta has been one of the countries to lead the way in the transition towards a regulation on ICOs and crypto-activities. National institutions have focused on ICOs and blockchain at a time when it was a fledgling industry with dubious safety features. The country in fact decided to take a firm step in advance, with the goal of becoming one of the principal points of reference in this field. The best way to do this was to provide a first comprehensive regulatory framework and to establish itself as one of the most committed regulators.

Malta had worked similarly in the early years of the online gambling industry boom. This experience allowed Maltese authorities to gain valid skills and experience within the digital environment, always with an eye to the future, pursuing long-term objectives and closely monitoring potential future developments, typical of a "pro-business approach". Blockchain represented the ideal continuation of that path, being a new opportunity to promote the Island's strategic influence in the digital field and relaunch its economy and image as a land of technology and innovation.

Malta's government is currently further developing its national strategy, aimed at embracing the whole innovation process, from regulation and research to market take-up, facilitating cooperation between international market players and operators. In order to do this, harmonized measures have been taken; among the first steps, there are some public consultations on virtual currencies issued by the Malta Financial Services Authority (MFSA).[38]

On 23 October 2017, the Maltese Authority published a consultation document entitled "Consultation on the Proposed Regulation of Collective Investment Schemes investing in

Virtual Currencies".[39] After three months, on 22 January 2018, the MFSA issued a "Feedback Statement"[40] which summarized the feedback that the MFSA received on the Consultation Document, at the same time setting out its responses and positions.

Following the Consultation and the respective Feedback Statement, the Malta Financial Services Authority announced on 29 January 2018 the publication of the "Supplementary Conditions applicable to Professional Investor Funds ('PIFs') investing in Virtual Currencies ('VCs')".[41]

These Supplementary Conditions included provisions to strengthen Maltese regulatory framework and ensure investor protection, market integrity and financial soundness with regard to collective investment schemes investing in virtual currencies. Among the main points of the measure were specific conditions for the authorization procedure as well as requirements on an ongoing basis, necessitating professional investor funds investing in virtual currencies to fulfill requirements concerning competence of the party involved, risk warnings, virtual currencies quality assessment, risk management, investments valuation.

On 30 November 2017, the MFSA issued a "Discussion Paper on Initial Coin Offerings, Virtual Currencies and Related Service Providers",[42] with the purpose of presenting a proposed policy for the regulation of ICOs and virtual currencies. Even in this document, the aim was to combine high levels of investor protection with a reasonable legislation and an orderly development of the market.

Following the publication of the aforementioned Discussion Paper, on 13 April 2018 another document was issued: a "Consultation Paper on the Financial Instrument Test".[43] One of the main aspects of the "Discussion Paper on Initial Coin Offerings, Virtual Currencies and Related Service Providers" was the introduction of a "Financial Instrument Test". The objective of this test would have been to determine whether a specific DLT asset should have fallen within (i) the existing EU legislation and the corresponding national legislation, (ii) the proposed Virtual Financial Assets Act ("VFAA") or (iii) was otherwise exempt.

A test would have consisted in a two-stage process: the first stage concerned whether the relevant DLT asset should be qualified as a virtual token. In case of a negative response, the second step of the process would have determined the possible qualification of the DLT asset as a financial instrument under the EU Markets in Financial Instruments (MiFID II) Directive. In case of another negative answer, then the only admitted outcome would have been the qualification of the DLT asset as a virtual financial asset under the Virtual Financial Assets Act.

On 1 November 2018, three important laws entered into force, providing a comprehensive regulatory framework:

(1) the Innovative Technology Arrangements and Services Act,[44] which defines DLT technology and smart contracts;

(2) the Malta Digital Innovation Authority Act,[45] which establishes a new authority responsible for non-financial innovative activities;

(3) the Virtual Financial Assets Act,[46] which, *inter alia*, deals with ICOs regulation and recognizes the compulsory nature of the white paper.

The Innovative Technology Arrangements and Services Act introduces regulation for Innovative Technology Arrangements (ITAs) and Innovative Technology Services Providers (ITSPs). ITAs are defined under the law as: (i) software and architectures, which are used in designing and delivering DLT; (ii) smart contracts and related applications, including decentralized autonomous organizations; (iii) any other ITA which may be designated by the relevant Maltese Minister, on the recommendation of the MFSA. On the other hand, such act defines as ITSPs the review services and technical administration services, respectively provided by system auditors and technical administrators. Any certification granted to ITAs has a period of validity of two years. The same validity also applies to the registration of Systems Auditors and Technical Administrators.

The Malta Digital Innovation Authority Act provides for the establishment of a new authority, responsible for promoting technological innovation policies, protecting users and encouraging innovation. The Malta Digital Innovation Authority's role will particularly consist in providing regulation and certifying Innovative Technology Arrangements and Services, which represent the key elements of the distributed ledger technology architecture.

The Virtual Financial Assets Act is intended to regulate the field of Initial Virtual Financial Asset Offerings (it is defined as "a method of raising funds whereby an issuer is issuing virtual financial assets and is offering them in exchange for funds", more commonly known as ICOs) and Virtual Financial Assets ("any form of digital medium recordation that is used as a digital medium of exchange, unit of account, or store of value and that is not electronic money; a financial instrument; or a virtual token"), providing a comprehensive regulatory framework aimed at both protecting investors and fostering the industry development. Under the VFA Act, specific requirements applicable to various actors in the field of Initial Virtual Financial Asset Offerings are set out. In particular, the VFA Act regulates the type of assets that can be issued, the procedure for admission to trading on DLT exchanges, the characteristics and the relevant information of a white paper—a document needed for obtaining the approval by the Malta Financial Services Authority—should include.

NOTES

1 Funds raised in 2018 according to statistics supplied by Icodata.io. Available at: www.icodata.io/stats/2018.

2 Funds raised in 2017 according to statistics supplied by Icodata.io. Available at: www.icodata.io/stats/2017.

3 Funds raised in 2016 according to statistics supplied by Icodata.io. Available at: www.icodata.io/stats/2016.

4 Source: Satis Group LLC. Available at: https://medium.com/satis-group/ico-quality-development-trading-e4fef28df04f.

5 FINMA (2018), *Guidelines for enquiries regarding the regulatory framework for initial coin offerings (ICOs)*. Available at: www.finma.ch/en/news/2018/02/20180216-mm-ico-wegleitung/.

6   Financial Conduct Authority, *"Guidance on Cryptoassets"*. Available at: www.fca.org.uk/ publications/consultation-papers/cp19-3-guidance-cryptoassets.

7   Part III of the Financial Services and Markets Act 2000 (Regulated Activities) Order 2001 provides a list of investments that are considered *"specified for the purposes of Section 22 of the Act"*: deposits, contracts of insurance, shares, instruments creating or acknowledging indebtedness, government and public securities, instruments giving entitlements to investments, certificates representing certain securities, units in a collective investment scheme, rights under a stakeholder pension scheme, options, futures, contracts for differences, Lloyd's syndicate capacity and syndicate membership, funeral plan contracts, regulated mortgage contracts, rights to or interests in investments. Available at: www. legislation.gov.uk/uksi/2001/544/contents/made.

8   Securities and Exchange Commission, Release No. 81207/25 July 2017: *"Report of Investigation Pursuant to Section 21(a) of the Securities Exchange Act of 1934: The DAO"*. Available at: www.sec.gov/litigation/investreport/34-81207.pdf.

9   Securities Exchange Act of 1934, As Amended Through P.L. 115–141, Enacted 23 March 2018. Available at: http://legcounsel.house.gov/Comps/Securities%20Exchange%20Act% 20Of%201934.pdf.

10   Phil Daian, Analysis of the DAO exploit. Available at: http://hackingdistributed.com /2016/06/18/analysis-of-the-dao-exploit/.

11   Securities Act of 1933, As Amended Through P.L. 115–174, Enacted 24 May 2018. Available at: http://legcounsel.house.gov/Comps/Securities%20Act%20Of%201933.pdf.

12   Section 2(a), Definitions. (1) *"The term "security" means any note, stock, treasury stock, security future, security-based swap, bond, debenture, evidence of indebtedness, certificate of interest or participation in any profit-sharing agreement, collateral-trust certificate, preorganization certificate or subscription, transferable share, investment contract, voting-trust certificate, certificate of deposit for a security, fractional undivided interest in oil, gas, or other mineral rights, any put, call, straddle, option, or privilege on any security, certificate of deposit, or group or index of securities (including any interest therein or based on the value thereof), or any put, call, straddle, option, or privilege entered into on a national securities exchange relating to foreign currency, or, in general, any interest or instrument commonly known as a "security", or any certificate of interest or participation in, temporary or interim certificate for, receipt for, guar antee of, or warrant or right to subscribe to or purchase, any of the foregoing."*

13   SEC v. Howey Co., 328 U.S. 293 (1946). Available at: https://cdn.loc.gov/service/ll/usrep/ usrep328/usrep328293/usrep328293.pdf.

14   Securities and Exchange Commission, Release No. 81207/25 July 2017. *"Report of Investigation Pursuant to Section 21(a) of the Securities Exchange Act of 1934: The DAO"*. Available at: www.sec.gov/litigation/investreport/34-81207.pdf.

15   Securities and Exchange Commission, Release No. 10445/11 December 2017. *"In the Matter of MUNCHEE INC., Respondent. Order instituting cease-and-desist proceedings pursuant to Section 8a of the Securities Act of 1933, making findings, and imposing a cease-and-desist order"*. Available at: www.sec.gov/litigation/investreport/34-81207.pdf.

16   Securities and Exchange Commission, Release No. 10445/11 December 2017. *"In the Matter of MUNCHEE INC., Respondent. Order instituting cease-and-desist proceedings pursuant to Section 8a of the Securities Act of 1933, making findings, and imposing a cease-and-desist order"*. Available at: www.sec.gov/litigation/investreport/34-81207.pdf.

17   Bank of Italy, official website. Available at: www.bancaditalia.it/homepage/index.html? com.dotmarketing.htmlpage.language=1.

18   Consob, official website. Available at: www.consob.it/web/consob-and-its-activities.

19   Consob, Documento per consultaziome. "*Le offerte iniziali e gli scambi di cripto-attività*". Available at: www.consob.it/documents/46180/46181/doc_disc_20190319.pdf/64251cef-d363-4442-9685-e9ff665323cf.

20   Law-Decree 14 December 2018, No. 135, "*Disposizioni urgenti in materia di sostegno e semplificazione per le imprese e per la pubblica amministrazione*" ("*Urgent Provisions on Supporting and Simplifying Companies and Public Administration*"). Official Gazette No. 290 of 14 December 2018. Availabe at: www.gazzettaufficiale.it/eli/gu/2019/02/12/36/sg/pdf.

21   article 8-*ter*, paragraph 1, Law-Decree 14 December 2018, No. 135, "*Disposizioni urgenti in materia di sostegno e semplificazione per le imprese e per la pubblica amministrazione*" ("*Urgent Provisions on Supporting and Simplifying Companies and Public Administration*"). Official Gazette No. 290 of 14 December 2018. Availabe at: www.gazzettaufficiale.it/eli/gu/2019/02/12/36/sg/pdf.

22   Legislative Decree No. 58 of 24th February 1998, "TUF". Available at: www.consob.it/web/consob-and-its-activities/laws-and-regulations/documenti/english/laws/fr_decree58_1998.htm?hkeywords=&docid=0&page=0&hits=21&nav=false.

23   Directive 2014/65/EU of the European Parliament and of the Council of 15 May 2014 on markets in financial instruments and amending Directive 2002/92/EC and Directive 2011/61/EU. Available at: https://eur-lex.europa.eu/legal-content/IT/ALL/?uri=CELEX:32014L0065.

24   Directive 2003/71/EC of the European Parliament and of the Council of 4 November 2003 on the prospectus to be published when securities are offered to the public or admitted to trading and amending Directive 2001/34/EC, as amended by Directive 2010/73/EU of the European Parliament and of the Council of 24 November 2010 amending Directives 2003/71/EC on the prospectus to be published when securities are offered to the public or admitted to trading and 2004/109/EC on the harmonization of transparency requirements in relation to information about issuers whose securities are admitted to trading on a regulated market. Available at: https://eur-lex.europa.eu/eli/dir/2010/73/oj, https://eur-lex.europa.eu/eli/dir/2003/71/oj.

25   Regulation (EU) 2017/1129 of the European Parliament and of the Council of 14 June 2017 on the prospectus to be published when securities are offered to the public or admitted to trading on a regulated market, and repealing Directive 2003/71/EC. Available at: https://eur-lex.europa.eu/eli/reg/2017/1129/oj.

26   Regulation (EU) No 596/2014 of the European Parliament and of the Council of 16 April 2014 on market abuse (market abuse regulation) and repealing Directive 2003/6/EC of the European Parliament and of the Council and Commission Directives 2003/124/EC, 2003/125/EC and 2004/72/EC. Available at: https://eur-lex.europa.eu/eli/reg/2014/596/oj.

27   Consob Resolution No. 20617 of 10 October 2018. Available at: www.consob.it/web/area-pubblica/bollettino/documenti/hide/cautelari/soll/2018/d20617.htm.

28   Consob Resolution No. 20660 of 31 October 2018. Available at: www.consob.it/web/area-pubblica/bollettino/documenti/hide/cautelari/soll/2018/d20660.htm.

29   Consob Resolution No. 20693 of 14 November 2018. Available at: www.consob.it/web/area-pubblica/avvisi-ai-risparmiatori/documenti/tutela/cns/2018/ct20181119.htm.

30   Consob Resolution No. 20740 of 12 December 2018. Available at: www.consob.it/web/area-pubblica/bollettino/documenti/hide/cautelari/soll/2018/d20740.htm.

31   Consob Resolution No. 20741 of 12 December 2018. Available at: www.consob.it/web/area-pubblica/bollettino/documenti/hide/cautelari/soll/2018/d20741.htm.

32   FINMA, Press release. "*FINMA is investigating ICO procedures*". Available at: www.finma.ch/en/news/2017/09/20170929-mm-ico/.

33   FINMA, Guidance 04/2017. "*Regulatory treatment of initial coin offerings*". Available at: www.finma.ch/en/documentation/finma-guidance.

34 FINMA, "*Guidelines for enquiries regarding the regulatory framework for initial coin offerings (ICOs)*". Available at: www.finma.ch/en/news/2018/02/20180216-mm-ico-wegleitung/.

35 Federal Act on Financial Market Infrastructures and Market Conduct in Securities and Derivatives Trading (Financial Market Infrastructure Act, FMIA) of 19 June 2015 (Status as of 1 January 2019). Available at: www.admin.ch/opc/en/classified-compilation/20141779/index.html.

36 Article 2, paragraph 1, letter b), Financial Market Infrastructure Act. Available at: www.admin.ch/opc/en/classified-compilation/20141779/index.html.

37 Federal Act on Combating Money Laundering and Terrorist Financing (Anti-Money Laundering Act, AMLA) of 10 October 1997 (Status as of 1 January 2019). Available at: www.admin.ch/opc/en/classified-compilation/19970427/index.html.

38 Malta Financial Services Authority, Offical Website. Available at www.mfsa.com.mt/.

39 Malta Financial Services Authority, Consultation Procedure. "*Consultation on the proposed regulation of Collective Investment. Schemes investing in Virtual Currencies*". Available at www.mfsa.com.mt/pages/readfile.aspx?f=/files/Announcements/Consultation/2017/20171311_VCFunds_ExtConsultDoc.pdf.

40 Malta Financial Services Authority, Feedback Statement. "*Feedback Statement issued further to industry responses to the MFSA Consultation on the proposed regulation of Collective Investment Schemes investing in Virtual Currencies*". Available at www.mfsa.com.mt/GetFile.php?type=site&file=Announcements%2FConsultation%2FFeedback%2F2018%2F20180122_VCPIFs_FeedbackStatement.pdf,

41 Malta Financial Services Authority, Circular. "*Circular to the Industry on the Supplementary Conditions applicable to Collective Investment Schemes Investing in Virtual Currencies*". Available at: www.mfsa.com.mt/wp-content/uploads/2019/01/12_1982379302_20180129_VCPIFCircularfin.pdf.

42 Malta Financial Services Authority, Discussion Paper. "*Discussion Paper on Initial Coin Offerings, Virtual Currencies and related Service Providers*". Available at www.mfsa.com.mt/GetFile.php?type=site&file=Announcements%2FPressReleases%2F2017%2F20171130_DiscussionPaperVCs_PR.pdf.

43 Malta Financial Services Authority, Consultation Paper. "*Consultation Paper on the Financial Instrument Test*". Available at: www.mfsa.com.mt/pages/readfile.aspx?f=/Files/Announcements/Consultation/2018/20180413_FITest.pdf.

44 Innovative Technology Arrangements and Services Act, "*An Act to provide for the regulation of designated innovative technologyarrangements referred to in the Act, as well as of designated innovative technologyservices referred to in the Act, and for the exercise by or on behalf of the MaltaDigital Innovation Authority ofregulatory functions with regard thereto.*". Available at: www.justiceservices.gov.mt/DownloadDocument.aspx?app=lp&itemid=29078&l=1.

45 Malta Digital Innovation Authority Act, "*An Act to provide for the establishment of an Authority to be known as the Malta Digital Innovation Authority to support the development andimplementation of the guiding principles described in this Act and to promoteconsistent principles for the development of visions, skills, and other qualitiesrelating to technology innovation, including distributed or decentralized technology, and to exercise regulatory functions regarding innovative technology,arrangements and related services and to make provision with respect to mattersancillary thereto or connected therewith.*" Available at http://justiceservices.gov.mt/DownloadDocument.aspx?app=lp&itemid=29080.

46 Virtual Financial Assets Act, "*An Act to regulate the field of Initial Virtual Financial Asset Offerings and Virtual Financial Assets and to make provision for matters ancillary or incidental thereto or connected therewith.*" Available at www.justiceservices.gov.mt/DownloadDocument.aspx?app=lp&itemid=29079&l=1.

CHAPTER 14

Legal Aspects of Blockchain Technology

Smart Contracts, Intellectual Property and Data Protection[*]

Paolo Balboni and Martim Taborda Barata

CONTENTS

[*] All websites used as sources for this chapter were last visited on 1 February 2019.

14.1 INTRODUCTION

Ever since the system underlying the "purely peer-to-peer version of electronic cash" described in Satoshi Nakamoto's 2008 whitepaper[1] was brought into reality in open source format just one year later, a massive amount of hype around blockchain was created and has only expanded over time. We have seen the value of Bitcoin (BTC) – the most famous form of cryptocurrency transacted over blockchain – peak at close to 20,000 USD towards the end of 2017[2] (and subsequently drop significantly, now being valued closer to 4,000 USD as of the date of this chapter[3]). Other than as a distributed ledger for cryptocurrency transactions, dozens of different potential use cases have been suggested for blockchain technology, ranging from data collection for public health purposes[4] and executing and settling energy transactions[5] to setting up secure and transparent elections[6] and tracking ingredients used in foodstuffs.[7] From 2015 to date, there has been a surge of patent filings for inventions related to blockchain, as recently reported by the European Patent Office in a dedicated conference on "Patenting Blockchain".[8]

Some of the first questions that pop into the mind of a lawyer when met with novel forms of technology most probably include "What potential benefits can this technology bring?", "Which are the legal implications of the use of such technology?" and "How will this be regulated?". Evidence of this can be found, for example, in the vast amount of articles available on the relationship between the law and drones,[9] the "Internet of Things"[10] and artificial intelligence.[11] In this chapter, we ask ourselves the same questions concerning blockchain in a manner that is understandable and useful to both legal and other professionals, focusing primarily on contracts, intellectual property and personal data protection.

14.1.1 Topic, Approach and Methodology

This chapter assumes that the reader already has an understanding of the basic underlying concepts and framework around blockchain systems. The focus of this chapter is, therefore, to explain how the blockchain has been scrutinized under the eyes of various legal scholars and other professionals in varying fields of law, illustrating those fields and legal concepts and describing positions taken concerning benefits or hazards brought about by blockchain, as well as our own take on those positions.

Given the wide variety of legal topics that could potentially be broached on the matter of blockchain, we have decided to narrow the scope of this chapter to three major areas:

(1) contracts (and "smart contracts" in particular),

(2) intellectual property and

(3) personal data protection.

These areas were chosen as they reflect key issues that have been subjected to heavy discussion concerning the interface between blockchain and the current legal framework, although other equally important areas could also have been included (e.g., financial law).

Contracts can be roughly defined as "agreements between parties ... to govern their interactions, either on [a] one-off basis or continuously over a time period".[12] When these contracts are created in a manner that they can be executed automatically (i.e., where the obligations upon one or more of the parties can be performed without further human intervention, once certain criteria are met), usually with the aid of computers, they can be referred to as "smart contracts".[13] In this chapter, we will look at examples of how blockchain technology can be leveraged to create more complex forms of smart contracts, and how these contracts may be affected by blockchain technology during the course of their existence – ranging from their formation (i.e., the moment where a contract is formed), to their performance (i.e., the normal carrying out of the obligations which are included in a contract) and potential breach (i.e., the lack of or defective performance of one or more obligations within a contract), as well as generally addressing the benefits that blockchain may bring towards contract management and litigation costs, while contrasting these with potential issues surrounding lessened flexibility in the drafting of contract terms and an increase in the costs of negotiation.

In turn, intellectual property refers to "creations of the mind, such as inventions; literary and artistic works; designs; and symbols, names and images used in commerce".[14] There are a number of ways in which the law allows for the protection of such creations, depending on the type of creation at stake, including copyright (for literary and artistic works, including computer programs), patents (for inventions), trademarks (for signs used in the marketplace to distinguish the goods of one entity from the goods of another entity, including logos, sound clips and even combinations of colours) and designs (to protect product shapes), among others. In this chapter, we will look at some of the potential specific benefits brought by blockchain, which are relevant to certain forms of protection.

Finally, the subject of personal data protection refers to the rules governing the use of "information relating to an identified or identifiable natural person"[15] (i.e., personal data). We will analyse purported benefits which blockchain may bring to data subjects (meaning, natural persons to whom personal data refers), in particular concerning increased control over how their personal data may be accessed and used by others. This will be contrasted with opinions brought forward by a number of academics regarding potential incompatibilities between the functioning of blockchain systems and the principles and rules laid down in Regulation (EU) 2016/679 of the European Parliament and of the Council, of 27 April 2016 (more commonly known as the "GDPR").[16]

14.1.2 Structure and Arguments

This chapter is organized in three main sections, one for each of the main fields of law assessed: contracts, intellectual property and personal data protection. The first section covers the interaction between blockchain and smart contracts and is particularly focused on how blockchain-based systems may affect phases of a smart contract's "lifecycle" (formation, performance, modification and breach). The second section focuses on intellectual property rights and the benefits brought to rights holders and users through blockchain, addressing, in particular, the implications for copyright, trademarks, designs and trade secrets. The third and final section covers the compatibility (or lack thereof) between principles and rules on the processing of personal data and protection of the privacy of individuals, on one hand, and the use of blockchain-based systems as a means to process personal data on the other, taking the GDPR as a baseline for reference. Each section is complemented with conclusive remarks at its end, summarizing the main points that are expanded upon within the relevant section. In its complexity, the chapter aims to highlight the main advantages and disadvantages that may arise from the use of blockchain and attempts to glean some insight into the meaningful and lawful future applicability of blockchain technology in the realm of smart contracts, intellectual property and data protection, building on the current state of discussions around blockchain and the three fields of law analysed.

14.2 SMART CONTRACTS AND BLOCKCHAIN

Although varying definitions have been proposed over the years, perhaps the best introduction which can be given to the concept of "smart contracts" is to quote Nick Szabo, who coined the term:

> A smart contract is a computerized transaction protocol that executes the terms of a contract. The general objectives of smart contract design are to satisfy common contractual conditions (such as payment terms, liens, confidentiality, and even enforcement), minimize exceptions both malicious and accidental, and minimize the need for trusted intermediaries. Related economic goals include lowering fraud loss, arbitration and enforcement costs, and other transaction costs.[17]

In other words, "smart contracts" are automated agreements, in which certain tasks are performed without the need for further human intervention once certain conditions (e.g., payment of a certain price) have been met.[18]

Developments which have occurred since Bitcoin allow blockchain systems to act more as general computational platforms than simple, decentralized databases.[19] In fact, it has been said that smart contracts have gained prominence due to their use in blockchain and related systems, the primary advantage of which is that, due to the distributed nature of blockchain and, in particular, the system to validate entries recorded on blockchain (relying on consensus between several dispersed "nodes" for this validation, rather than a central authority, such as a bank), the need for a trusted third party to implement and take responsibility for the correct fulfilment of automated transactions is overcome.[20] Though the storage and execution of smart contracts via blockchain can be achieved in many different ways, an example is provided by Guido Governatori et al. which is particularly useful:

> …for example, a smart contract takes the form of a script. The script is compiled into bytecode, and executed in a virtual machine, it is also stored in the Ethereum blockchain [an example of a more complex blockchain system].
>
> The script can be triggered by messages or transactions, resulting into its execution, and the triggered operations (except reading, which is executed on the local copy of blockchain) are executed on every node of the network. As a result, all nodes will reflect the state changes resulting from executing the operations. This replicated execution, which is not particularly efficient, has a cost. To cover this cost, the smart contract can be charged with some amount of resources, so called "gas" in Ethereum. When the operations are executed, the gas is gradually depleted to pay the executions. If the operations cannot be paid anymore, then they halt, otherwise they continue, possibly leading to smart contracts which can be difficult to stop. A smart contract may be also "destroyed", for example Solidity smart contracts in Ethereum have an operation, selfdestruct, which can be triggered to destroy the contract.[21]

It is possible to configure blockchain systems so that they can store contracts in a scripted form, while also allowing the script to automatically execute whenever agreed-upon situations occur (e.g., allowing a certain amount of Bitcoin to be transferred from one individual to another whenever the system detects that a certain price has been paid by the latter to the former). We will now consider the implications that resorting to such form of automated agreements may have concerning certain different points of a contract's "lifecycle".

14.2.1 Impact of Blockchain in Certain Phases of the Smart Contract "Lifecycle"

14.2.1.1 Formation

Given that both smart contracts and "regular contracts" require parties to agree upon a certain set of rules, their initial stage – that is, their formation – occurs in a similar fashion from the legal perspective. However, where a "regular contract" is typically formed when the parties involved accept its terms before starting to perform their respective obligations (for instance, by signing a written document to evidence their agreement), the formation of smart contracts occurs at the same time as the contract's obligations are performed. As noted by Max Raskin, "[a]n individual can say they will initiate a smart contract, which may be a contract in regular law, but until the program initiates, there is no smart contract".[22] Much as with "regular contracts", this assumes that the parties involved are all capable of entering into the smart contract under the applicable law (e.g., that the parties are of age and physically/mentally capable of understanding what they are agreeing to), and that the smart contract is not "unconscionable" (i.e., grossly unfair towards one party compared to another[23]) or illegal, without which the smart contract could potentially be found to be null and void (meaning it produces no legal effects from the start), voidable (meaning its legal effects can be interrupted by court order) or generally unenforceable against one or more of the parties (meaning it specifically does not bind those parties).

Additionally, just as announcing the availability to enter into an agreement can, under certain circumstances, be considered as a legal offer to enter into such agreement (e.g., where someone offers an item for sale, and sufficiently specifies all the contractual terms needed – item, price, method of payment and so on), posting smart contract code on a blockchain system may be interpreted as such an offer.[24] Offers to enter into smart contracts can be made under non-negotiable terms or may be subject to negotiation.[25] Proponents of the implementation of smart contracts via blockchain argue that this method represents a much cheaper system of enforcement (i.e., a system to ensure that other parties hold up their end of the bargain in an agreement), by allowing "finality" to be encoded into smart contracts – it is possible to explicitly configure a smart contract to unavoidably and irreversibly perform a certain task once the triggering condition is met (although it is also possible to build in safeguards to allow one to change their mind).[26] This would allow for lowered transaction costs by removing the need to resort to the courts, or other dispute resolution mechanisms (such as mediation or arbitration), because non-performance would not be an option once the triggering condition is met, which would help the programmed consequence take place.

Additionally, the fact that this approach only allows for the use of specific and precisely-defined terms may reduce the possibility for either party to claim that they misunderstood the contents of the smart contract upon accepting it, or that some other mistake was made regarding the interpretation of its rules. In fact, ambiguities in the programming world are far less relevant than in the "real world", as humans are presently capable of greater semantic understanding than computers (which may lead to the same sentence being interpreted in different manners by humans, whereas this would not necessarily be the case with automated performance).[27] However, as we will see in greater detail in the next section, others have noted that inflexibility is inherent to smart contracts performed over blockchain, preventing easy modifications to agreed terms (unless those are foreseen in the script from the outset)[28] and potentially offsetting the reduction in transaction costs with an increase in negotiation costs. This is because, in more complex contracts, parties will be keen to make sure they very specifically define all the terms used in such contracts, as it is not possible to insert ambiguous terms into the script and foresee all potential cases where modifications may be required in the future.[29]

14.2.1.2 Performance and Modification

The most obvious advantage that is brought by the use of blockchain-based "smart contracts" seems to be the fact that performance is made automatic. These contracts are made up of permanently archived code that will automatically and reliably execute once certain agreed-upon conditions have been met, without any need for any of the parties to carry out any further action.[30] The contract's terms are decentralized and distributed to the various nodes in the blockchain system, granting them nigh-immutability and independence from the contracting parties, who are not able to change their minds or delay performance once conditions are met, as the blockchain will monitor and enable that performance automatically.[31] This is probably the main appeal of this form of contracting, in that it has the potential to lower the costs of the party in monitoring the performance of the other party and having the contract enforced by means of the relevant courts. Additionally, as reported by Eliza Mik, many have touted this characteristic as allowing the overcoming of human contract participants' natural bias and unreliability, as well as the elimination of human discretion regarding the contractual obligations to be met, thereby protecting the parties from a breach of the smart contract.[32]

However, these characteristics also complicate the integration of amendments to a blockchain-based "smart contract" (unless such amendments were foreseen from the outset and programmed into the contracts as "dormant alternatives").[33] This increases negotiation costs between parties, which must ensure that all future states of the contract are completely and precisely defined (to the greatest extent possible),[34] so that the contract will "self-perform" as intended. In fact, it has been said that, in order to preserve the benefits of smart contracts' self-enforcement, it is necessary to not leave any decisions about its performance to humans, meaning that all possible events that may occur during its lifetime and affect its operation must be anticipated and encoded upfront.[35] The specificity required in doing so may further create a risk of discrepancies between the parties' original intent or agreement and its implementation into smart contract form, particularly where the smart contract is programmed by a third party.[36] The immutable nature of blockchain-based smart contracts may also pose a threat to situations where the validity of the contract is affected by changes in the applicable regulatory framework.[37] In fact, it is common for "regular contracts" to be amended in order to adapt their content to changes in external circumstances, including regulatory or commercial changes.[38]

Smart contracts also preclude the use of purposefully ambiguous contractual terms, such as performance standards, which in "regular" contracts allow parties to enter into a full agreement without needing to completely define what is considered adequate performance of that agreement, while also not leaving it undefined or potentially wrongly defined, thereby allowing parties, for example, to gain the benefit of certain mutually understood terms (via references to trade customs or commercial practices) without needing to specifically negotiate them and write them into the contract.[39] Additionally, while it is certain that the use of ambiguous terms in contracts increases potential litigation costs if any disputes on how to interpret such terms arise in the future, it also allows each party to retain flexibility both in performing its own obligations and in monitoring the performance of the other party's obligations.[40] The benefits outlined above cannot easily be reaped in the realm of smart contracts, where definition with precision is key.

Moreover, in many jurisdictions, it is not always necessary for a contract to be perfectly performed in order to be recognized and enforced by the courts (as is the case, for instance, in the United States, under the doctrine of "substantial performance").[41] In other words, as long as there has been a good faith attempt by a party to perform what was required of it under an agreement, that performance may be considered complete by a court even if it does not precisely meet the terms stipulated in that agreement.[42] This "substantial performance" may often represent an outcome which was not, or could not have been, contemplated or specified by the parties, and which a smart contract may not be able to recognise for that same reason (unless some level of discretion is scripted into the smart contract's code from the start, where possible).[43] On a parallel note, very commonly will a party to a "regular contract" accept that the other may deviate in the manner in which it performs its obligations from what was originally stipulated, without the need to resort to a formal amendment. The rigidity of blockchain-based smart contracts, the nature of which does not allow for performance which deviates from original programming to be accepted, runs counter to this and, potentially, to the commercial relationship between the parties entering into the smart contract.[44] It is also self-evident that the very nature of these contracts removes from each party the liberty to withhold performance of their obligations, but also to abstain from enforcing the contract against the other party. While this may seem counter-intuitive at first, as we will see, the complexity of the relationships underlying a contract may make the benefits of unavoidable enforcement questionable under certain circumstances.

14.2.1.3 Breaches of Smart Contracts

A logical conclusion derived from blockchain-based smart contracts' automatic performance is their automatic enforcement, given that the two occur simultaneously. By creating a smart contract tied to a blockchain system, its contractual obligations will be executed without deviation, as the parties become unable to influence or interfere with its operation.[45] Given that standard legal enforcement of contracts, that is, through courts or alternative dispute resolution mechanisms, can be cumbersome, prone to error, lengthy and expensive, the incentive to replace this with automated "algorithmic enforcement"[46] is understandable. The complete execution of blockchain-based smart contracts including, for instance, any transfers of value which are foreseen in such contracts, typically occurs once the trigger conditions have been met without any possibility of interruption (even by the courts!), with the distributed nodes within the blockchain system ensuring this performance. Given that, after such execution has taken place, the transaction becomes irreversibly encoded in the blockchain system, it has been suggested that these smart contracts may come to act as a replacement for the state-based legal system of enforcement.[47]

However, all of this comes at a cost of another type of flexibility afforded to parties of "regular contracts" – enforcement flexibility.[48] Depending on the characteristics of contracting parties and the nature of their relationship, they may prefer to resolve any potential disputes arising from contracts between them in an informal manner – this may include being selective about which contractual obligations to enforce and when, making informal amendments to contractual terms, or even choosing to take on new obligations entirely, among other means.[49] This results from the fact that, in "regular contracts", parties are generally able to choose whether or not to demand that the other party meet what the contract requires of them,[50] while at all times keeping the contract as a means to force the other party's hand through the courts, bringing some stability to the transaction.[51] It may be possible to program blockchain-based smart contracts which allow discretion on the part of one of the parties on whether to enforce one end of the bargain or not (instead of doing so automatically), but this would perhaps defeat their intended purpose, by re-inserting human will as a requirement for complete contractual performance.

Finally, it is also important to consider whether excuses for non-performance (i.e., situations which are recognized by the law as allowing performance of a contract to be frustrated or left incomplete, without a party being held liable for breach of that contract)[52] such as cases of force majeure (where overpowering circumstances, outside of a party's control, prevent it from performing its obligations), impossibility (where performance becomes temporarily or permanently impossible after the contract has been entered into) or unforeseen circumstances or hardship (where circumstances occur which are so unlikely that they could not have reasonably been foreseen by the parties from the outset, and which prevent performance),[53] can be properly built into a smart contract. Eric Tjong Tjin Tai suggests that it may be possible to foresee and program certain causes of non-performance qualifying as excuses into smart contracts (including by using oracles to help determine whether such a cause has taken place), but this may deprive these contracts of one of their main "selling points", that is, the lack of a need for an adjudicator or central authority/third party to enforce them.[54] The issues here seem to come down to what was discussed above in terms of modifications. If it is not possible to configure a blockchain-based smart contract in a manner that allows these excuses to be triggered, halting automatic performance if the conditions of the excuse are verified, then the parties will be deprived of their right to do so. Presumably, the only option at such a stage would be to try to resort to the courts or to alternative dispute resolution mechanisms in order to request a decision capable of reversing or mitigating the effects of the already-executed smart contract.

14.2.1.4 Conclusive Remarks

Some of the benefits brought about by blockchain technology to smart contracts are self-evident and undeniable. These include allowing the secure and immutable archival of smart contracts, the use of specific and well-defined terms (which may reduce friction regarding the interpretation of contractual provisions), and the automated execution of obligations, doing away with the need to take any further actions in order to ensure performance or to enforce contractual obligations. This would allow for the lowering of transaction costs in contractual relationships, removing the need for performance monitoring as well as judicial recourse in order to guarantee that the terms of the smart contract are respected. The blockchain-based smart contract will simply and unavoidably self-execute.

The other side of the coin, however, is that what some see as advantages in terms of reduction of contractual ambiguity, lowering of transactional effort and the encoding of finality, others consider as bringing about greater and less intuitive disadvantages. The lack of an easy manner to make amendments to a blockchain-based smart contract (or, at least, amendments which were not initially foreseen), the increase in negotiation costs derived from the need for all defined terms to be fully specified and agreed upon and the overall reduction of contractual flexibility afforded to parties (for instance, with the use of purposefully ambiguous terms, or the ability to decide on whether to withhold performance or to accept substantial rather than exact performance, precluded) may drive parties away from the more rigid blockchain-based systems to the more "traditional" forms of contracting which preserve the fluidity of the underlying commercial relationship.

In any case, while it seems that blockchain-based smart contracts may not be appropriate to regulate any and all types of commercial relationships, they may still prove valuable in addressing more straightforward transactions between parties, potentially eliminating the need for intermediaries and allowing each person to automatically receive what they are bargaining for in a deal – a record of which will be kept, immutably, on the blockchain system used. As we will see next, contracts related to intellectual property rights, such as licenses, have been claimed as among those types of contracts which could most stand to benefit from blockchain-based automation.

14.3 INTELLECTUAL PROPERTY AND BLOCKCHAIN

As noted in the introduction to this chapter, intellectual property – or, rather, intellectual property rights – can take on many forms, depending on the nature of the intangible asset which is protected by those rights. For example, a song as an artistic creation is best protected by copyright, whereas the shape of a guitar could be protected by means of a registered design. As we will not be addressing all forms of intellectual property rights that may exist worldwide, but only some of those concerning the potential benefits of blockchain systems, we will provide a brief description of each of the rights covered in question.

Copyright (or author's right) is used to describe rights afforded to creators over their literary and artistic works (e.g., books, music, paintings, sculptures, films, computer programs, etc.).[55] Copyright holders are thus given exclusive rights to exploit those works commercially, including by selling copies of those works, translating those works, adapting those works into other formats (e.g., making a film based on a book) and publicly displaying and performing those works. Trademarks are symbols which are used in commerce to distinguish the goods or services of one entity from those of its competitors, and can vary wildly in terms of their underlying assets: word marks, figurative marks, shape marks, position marks, pattern marks, colour marks, sound marks and even motion marks, multimedia marks or hologram marks can currently be registered at the European Union Intellectual Property Office, for example.[56] Trademark owners are the only individuals allowed to use their marks in commerce for certain goods or services (e.g., "Ferrari" for cars) within the countries where they have registered them, and can also block others from using confusingly similar signs or, in some cases, signs which might harm the value of their marks.

The concept of "design" refers to the appearance of a product (or part of a product) resulting from the features of its lines, contours, colours, shape, texture and/or materials of that product, or of any items used to ornament/decorate that product.[57] Examples of items which have been considered as qualifying as designs include the packaging of products, sets of products, computer icons, typefaces, web designs and maps, among others.[58] Designs which are new and have individual character (in short, meaning that they are innovative compared to existing designs) can generally be protected under intellectual property law.[59]

The final intellectual property rights we will discuss in this chapter are trade secrets. As stated by the World Intellectual Property Organization, "[b]roadly speaking, any confidential business information which provides an enterprise a competitive edge may be considered a trade secret. Trade secrets encompass manufacturing or industrial secrets and commercial secrets".[60] Under the EU Trade Secrets Directive, any information which (1) is not generally known among or readily accessible to persons within the circles that normally deal with the kind of information in question, (2) has commercial value due to its secrecy and (3) has been subjected to reasonable measures in order to keep it secret, may qualify as a "trade secret".[61]

All of the above-mentioned intellectual property rights (or "IP rights") can be transferred by their lawful holders to someone else (similarly to how ownership of physical property may be transferred), or can be "lent" to another to make limited use of those rights for a certain period of time, by means of a license (similarly to how physical property may be rented out). These licenses are usually carried out with fixed or variable fees as consideration (sometimes referred to as "royalties"). With the stage set, we will look into some of the benefits that blockchain systems may afford to these different intellectual property rights in greater detail.

14.3.1 Blockchain Applied to Different IP Rights

14.3.1.1 Copyright

In general, copyright protection for literary and artistic works comes into being from the moment of their creation, without any need for additional formal requirements, such as registration.[62] Exceptions exist (e.g., in the United States), and in any case other jurisdictions rely on registration in order to make certain rights available, or otherwise offer voluntary registration.[63] However, in general, it is currently not easy for someone wishing to make commercial use of a copyrighted work to obtain relevant information about the copyright owner in order to, for instance, procure a license from them. Not only is there no central, transparent database which might be consulted (particularly because registration is generally not mandatory, with information left scattered between public registration databases, publishers, record companies, collecting societies and others who may not have much of an incentive to disclose information, at least for free),[64] but also consulting publicly available databases has been shown to usually meet with daunting search costs, formalities and costs in terms of time, significantly reducing its practicality and usefulness.[65] Naturally, however, it will be difficult to validly claim ignorance of the copyright owner as a defence in copyright infringement proceedings brought due to the use of a copyrighted work without a suitable license.

One idea that has been proposed to solve this issue is the creation of "smart IP registries", meaning centralized databases run by an IP office (i.e., an authority in charge of registering and monitoring the use of IP rights), including an immutable record of events in the life of copyrighted works, from creation to expiry of protection.[66] An easily accessible, public and international registration system could therefore provide an easy way to consult and prove the existence of a work and the ownership of the person who created it.[67] By basing such a system on blockchain, it would be possible to create time-stamped, immutable and easily verifiable records of ownership for a copyrighted work, along with subsequent changes[68] – all the rights holders would need to do is encrypt their digital asset as a hash on the blockchain, include relevant details in the records created and report back to the blockchain for evidence of creation and ownership if need be in the future.[69]

The management of copyrighted works and their respective rights is also a field where smart contracts can come into play for the benefit of creators. It is conceivable that a "smart license" could be scripted onto a blockchain, encoding a copyrighted work in digital form (e.g., a song, a film, etc.) and releasing it to those who pay a certain pre-determined amount, as a license fee.[70] Smart contracts can be used to allow automatic and real-time payments to be carried out, as well as to determine the expiration of the license after a given amount of time.[71] This could also apply in the case of more complex transactions, where a single user wishes to purchase licenses from multiple authors or encompassing multiple works, or even where works are created in collaboration by different authors. In such cases, the smart contract could automatically remunerate all copyright owners according to the information encoded on the blockchain as to the ownership percentage belonging to each owner, every time the respective work is acquired and/or used.[72] Connected to this is the matter of "digital rights management" ("DRM") – i.e., access control technology used to protect and license digital IP rights.[73] It has been said that a blockchain-based DRM system would potentially overcome several issues that plague modern-day DRMs, such as their proprietary nature (which can cause issues in allowing interoperability of works bought on one platform with other platforms; a license to listen to a song on Spotify is not transferable to iTunes, for example).[74] A neutral blockchain-based DRM system could function independently of the platform used to engage with the licensed content.

One final connected benefit that we can address is the possibility for blockchain to allow for more direct connections between creators and users, doing away with inter-mediaries brought into the marketplace due to current difficulties for individual rights holders to license their works and monitor/enforce their rights effectively by themselves.[75] This results in rights holders, and in particular artists, receiving progressively smaller cuts of revenue and having less say over how their creative works are priced, shared or advertised.[76] As seen above, it would be possible for individual artists to leverage blockchain-based smart contracts in order to reach out to their fanbase directly, theoretically lessening the need for any intermediaries or platforms and ensuring a fairer price for the artist. An example of steps taken in this direction can be seen with Imogen Heap and her single "Tiny Human", released via Mycelia (Imogen

Heap's "research and development hub for music makers")[77] on the Ethereum block-chain, albeit with limited success.[78]

14.3.1.2 Trademarks and Designs

Trademark holders could also benefit from a centralized, blockchain-based IP rights database being put in place. However, given that full trademark protection is only granted to those marks which have been properly registered at the competent IP office, which will typically establish a public database of trademarks for others to freely consult,[79] the main advantages which might arise for trademark holders would be the ability to provide proof of use and to monitor the distribution of goods containing registered trademarks, assuming that all transactions related to a good containing a trademark would be recorded on the blockchain. Collecting information on the use of a trademark in trade or commerce (e.g., by stamping a certain good with a trademarked logo and putting it up for sale) in such a database could allow nigh-immediate notification of the relevant IP Office concerning such use and provide solid, time-stamped evidence of this.[80] As an example, such evidence could be used to combat a legal claim for revocation of a given trademark due to it allegedly not having been genuinely used for a continuous period of five years,[81] or to support a claim that an otherwise invalid application for a registered trademark should not be denied, as the mark has acquired a "distinctive character" in relation to the goods or services for which it is to be registered in the meantime (i.e., that an initially invalid trademark – for instance, because it is too common or simple to distinguish one company's goods from another's – should not be declared invalid later because it gained the ability to do so, due to, e.g., its repeated use in the market).[82]

Designs can receive protection (of varying levels), whether registered or unregistered, and thus are closer to copyright than trademarks in the benefits which could be gained from a centralized, blockchain-based database of IP rights. Evidence of unregistered designs' conception, use, qualification requirements and current status could then be generated by uploading a time-stamped record to the blockchain containing such information.[83] In fact, considering that designs will only be protected when they are new (meaning, where no identical design has been made available to the public beforehand)[84] and have individual character (meaning, where the design produces a different overall impression on users than any other pre-existing designs),[85] it would be instrumental for potential applicants to have access to such a database of designs made available to the public, in order to understand whether they have legal standing to seek protection.

One additional benefit which blockchain could bring to both trademark holders and design holders in common would be the ability to monitor the distribution of goods containing their trademarks or designs. By means of scannable blockchain-connected tags, tamperproof seals or imprints, products could be tagged along the distribution chain and checked for evidence of their provenance and authenticity by consulting information on their creation, manufacturing process and sources of raw materials uploaded onto the blockchain.[86] The ability to add blocks of data to the chain at every step of the way would allow rightsholders to record details about a product's progress through the various manufacturing and supply stages it must go through, and then to record where goods are placed on the market, allowing them to be distinguished from "grey goods" or parallel imports (as well as identifying where those products left the regular distribution chain, thereby signalling potential leaks).[87]

This could be a potentially more successful solution than the use of radio frequency identification ("RFID") tags in the prevention of counterfeiting, as these tags can still be copied by counterfeiters and are removed at the point-of-sale, making them less effective in verifying the authenticity of second-hand goods sold. Instead, by simply scanning the QR code (or other means used to link a physical product to its blockchain records), it would be possible to check the products entire history in the immutable, irreversible and permanent record created by the blockchain.[88]

14.3.1.3 Trade Secrets

As noted above, under the EU Trade Secrets Directive, any information which (1) is not generally known among or readily accessible to persons within the circles that normally deal with the kind of information in question, (2) has commercial value due to its secrecy and (3) has been subjected to reasonable measures in order to keep it secret, may qualify as a "trade secret".[89] This means that, in order to benefit from such protection, holders of such information have an interest in demonstrating that, on the one hand, they actually hold information which might qualify as a "trade secret" and, on the other, that they have taken reasonable steps to ensure that that information remains secret. This is important so that those holders will be able to react swiftly against any potential breaches of confidentiality, as if they cannot demonstrate either of those points, then there will be no legal standing to, for example, demand that someone be prevented from disclosing certain information or seek damages from that person if it is too late to prevent disclosure.

It must be possible for a company to prove that it was in possession of a particular concept or information at a specific time, in secrecy, in the event of a breach, and that the breach happened in spite of reasonable steps having been taken to ensure such secrecy. Were such a company to store its trade secrets (or a hashed pointer to such information) on a blockchain-based system, subject to encryption, it would be able to generate a time-stamped record that could be used in the event of a breach to prove the first point.[90]

The matter of whether a certain piece of information has been subjected to "reasonable steps" to maintain its secrecy has been called "the biggest hurdle to overcome for trade secrets", in that it requires the following two conditions to occur simultaneously: all reasonable steps to protect such information be taken and solid proof of such information's existence be available.[91] Storing trade secrets on a private blockchain (where there is control over which computers can act as nodes and are allowed to access and validate data entered into the blockchain) may allow the securing of commercially valuable information on a private network through encryption, as mentioned above, which could potentially allow the holder of such information to claim that all reasonable steps to ensure secrecy have been taken, making the blockchain (private or permissioned) a measure through which a trade secret could be held securely.[92] Conversely, the use of public or excessively-permissioned blockchain networks would be likely to compromise the secrecy of the information and, therefore, its ability to legally qualify as a trade secret.[93]

14.3.1.4 Conclusive Remarks

Currently anticipated and upcoming use cases for blockchain-based technology paint a welcoming scene for intellectual property rights holders, as well as for those who might seek to make use of a work protected by intellectual property rights. The ability to set up solid and comprehensive intellectual property registries, allowing the tracking of both registered and unregistered assets and their tagging with accurate information as to, for example, their ownership and licensing terms could provide an effective alternative for those seeking to make use of protected works to the currently cost- and time-ineffective searches through multiple public databases, as well as serving evidentiary purposes for rights holders seeking to prove their entitlement to gains derived from works used. Registered trademark holders could rely on a blockchain-based record logging for the commercial use of their marks to show proof of genuine use of a trademark, or even to support a claim of its acquired distinctiveness, while unregistered trademark (and design) holders could find in blockchain a means to evidence the creation, characteristics, use and status of their assets. In a blockchain-based global registry, those seeking to develop and register new trademarks or designs would find a simplified manner in which to determine whether their creations would meet the requirements for legal protection (such as a lack of likelihood of confusion with earlier marks, or novelty regarding earlier designs).

Blockchain-based smart contracts seem a solid fit for the copyrighted-work licensing market, allowing authors/creators to define their own licensing terms and to directly engage with their intended audience, rather than being forced to accept the interference of intermediaries in order to monetise and monitor their rights. It has also been said that the use of (private or permissioned) blockchain-based systems to simultaneously store and safeguard trade secrets might allow holders to claim that reasonable steps to protect their secrecy have been taken, while also serving as practically unchangeable proof of their existence and contents. The benefits promised by blockchain to the field of intellectual property are promising, notwithstanding the foreseeable hurdles to implementation which might result from the need for their widespread acceptance, use and replacement of current traditional means of handling these intangible assets (and the consequent "shaking up" of the market which may occur, particularly where intermediaries, such as publishers and collective management organizations, are concerned).

14.4 PERSONAL DATA PROTECTION AND BLOCKCHAIN

One major concern that has been expressed by blockchain apologists is whether data protection legislation collides with blockchain-based systems. In particular, whether Regulation (EU) 2016/679 of the European Parliament and of the Council of 27 April 2016 on the protection of natural persons with regard to the processing of personal data and on the free movement of such data, and repealing Directive 95/46/EC (the General Data Protection Regulation, or "GDPR")[94] will render those systems unlawful when connected with the use of personal data. While the GDPR is not universally applicable, with its territorial scope restricted by the rules laid down in Art. 3 GDPR, it is nonetheless a comprehensive regulation on the processing of personal data which, other than representing the main legislative source for rules on personal data processing within the EU, also substantially reflects all fundamental requirements that are present in other regulations on data protection around the world, namely, the principles of openness, collection limitation, purpose specification, use limitation, security, data quality, access and correction and accountability. This allows conclusions drawn from an analysis of the GDPR to apply, either directly or in an analogous fashion, to most other sources of law on the matter of personal data and privacy worldwide, which has led us to rely on it as an international baseline for data protection compliance in this chapter.

Given that blockchain technology was hardly being considered during the debates that surrounded the finalization of the GDPR in 2016,[95] many feel that its provisions are not suited to allow blockchain-based systems for personal data management to properly take hold. The discussion has reached the level of the EU Parliament which, in a resolution passed at the end of 2018 (and which we will look at in further detail ahead), discussed some of the more recurrent questions debated around blockchain and privacy and produced a series of considerations which seem optimistic as to its potential continued use (though focused on private and permissioned blockchain systems, rather than public systems).[96] In this section, we will break down some of the most debated issues regarding the use of blockchain from the personal data protection perspective.

14.4.1 Personal Data?

Before even beginning the discussion, it is important to understand whether information available on a blockchain can be called "personal data" at all, recalling the GDPR's definition given in the introduction: "information relating to an identified or identifiable natural person".[97] Here, we can distinguish between two categories of data stored on the blockchain: transactional data[98] (information uploaded onto the blockchain, which may vary according to the specific use case of that system, also sometimes referred to as "payload" or "content data") and metadata[99] (information related to an upload made onto the blockchain, which may contain the uploader's public key, a time-stamp and other information related to the upload, also sometimes referred to as "header" or "protocol data").

Regarding transactional data, if there is no question that it may, in itself, be personal data—with common use cases being data related to individual behaviour (e.g., Internet of Things, where data on users' activities can be used to profile those users and remember their preferences—consider, for example, smart watches or cars), digital identities/profiles or financial and medical data.[100] The question becomes then if the fact that those data can potentially be stored in different forms on a blockchain-based system, for example, in plain text, encrypted or hashed[101]—allows one to claim that the link between the information and the individual it refers to is severed, to the point where it no longer makes sense to speak of "personal data", but rather of anonymized data. Here, it is worthwhile to quote Recital 26 of the GDPR, broken down into segments[102]:

- "The principles of data protection should apply to any information concerning an identified or identifiable natural person."

As noted above, this is part of the very definition of "personal data" – any information connected to someone who is identified, or who can be identified by using further information, is always qualified as "personal data".

- "Personal data which have undergone pseudonymisation, which could be attributed to a natural person by the use of additional information should be considered to be information on an identifiable natural person."

"Pseudonymisation" is defined in the GDPR as

The processing of personal data in such a manner that the personal data can no longer be attributed to a specific data subject without the use of additional information, provided that such additional information is kept separately and is subject to technical and organizational measures to ensure that the personal data are not attributed to an identified or identifiable natural person.[103]

This definition applies squarely to any personal data that undergo encryption, so long as it is reversible, in that it is still possible to link the encrypted data to the individual it refers to by using the encryption key ("additional information").

- "To determine whether a natural person is identifiable, account should be taken of all the means reasonably likely to be used, such as singling out, either by the controller or by another person to identify the natural person directly or indirectly. To ascertain whether means are reasonably likely to be used to identify the natural person, account should be taken of all objective factors, such as the costs of and the amount of time required for identification, taking into consideration the available technology at the time of the processing and technological developments."

This section reflects the very high standard for anonymization which is present in the GDPR and also reflected in Opinion 05/2014 on Anonymisation Techniques of the

Article 29 Working Party[104] (now currently the European Data Protection Board, an independent European body contributing to the consistent application of data protection rules across the EU and cooperation between EU data protection authorities[105]). In essence, it must be impossible, or at least not possible through reasonably likely means, to link information to an individual for that information to escape qualification as "personal data" – naturally, what is considered "reasonably likely means" may vary over time, as technology develops.

- "The principles of data protection should therefore not apply to anonymous information, namely information which does not relate to an identified or identifiable natural person or to personal data rendered anonymous in such a manner that the data subject is not or no longer identifiable. This Regulation does not therefore concern the processing of such anonymous information, including for statistical or research purposes."

If it is or becomes impossible or sufficiently unreasonable to link information to an individual, that information will be deemed "anonymous" and therefore fall out of scope of the GDPR. The three questions which are asked by the Article 29 Working Party when assessing the matter of anonymizing personal data are[106]:

(1) Is it still possible to single out an individual?

(2) Is it still possible to link records relating to an individual?

(3) Can information be inferred concerning an individual?

Discussing whether personal data that is stored on a blockchain system in plain text continues to be "personal data" is a moot point, as no measures have been applied to those data in order to affect the pre-existing link with an individual. Encrypted data may not be readily accessible to those who do not possess the correct keys, but it is so to those who do – the encryption keys may be considered as "additional information" needed in order to identify the underlying data subjects which, as such, remain identifiable.[107] Additionally, even hashing a dataset, which irreversibly converts it into a fixed-size output, may be insufficient to consider that the dataset has been fully anonymized, as there is still the risk that identification is possible by other means:

For instance, if a dataset was pseudonymized by hashing the national identification number, then this can be derived simply by hashing all possible input values and comparing the result with those values in the dataset. Hash functions are usually designed to be relatively fast to compute, and are subject to brute force attacks. Pre-computed tables can also be created to allow for the bulk reversal of a large set of hash values.[108]

Even adding "salt" to a hash (by adding random values to the output generated), while reducing the likelihood of reidentification, is considered insufficient to prevent the feasible calculation of the original hidden value by reasonable means.[109]

It has been argued that, over time, more advanced cryptographic processes – such as SHA-256 or SHA-3 – may be seen as rendering reidentification so unfeasible that they effectively anonymize the hashed data.[110] The key will be seeing how data protection authorities and courts interpret the notion of "reasonable means" and whether hashing technology available on blockchain systems develops to a point where it becomes practically impossible to single out an individual based on hashed data, to link data related to that individual or to infer additional information on that individual. In this respect, it should be noted that there have been several successful experiments where reidentification of otherwise anonymous individuals was found to be possible simply due to the volume of information available on those individuals outside of a given network.[111] In any case, while these measures may be seen as very effective technical security measures to strive for the integrity and confidentiality of the data they are applied to, one cannot claim with certainty that they allow for anonymization of data in the legal sense (if this is even possible in practice) – therefore, it should be assumed that any transactional data stored on a blockchain system that relates to an individual will be qualified as "personal data".[112]

Metadata, including a blockchain user's public key (which is uploaded onto the chain any time that user uploads data), can also still be considered personal data. Despite asymmetric encryption being applied to public keys, it has been shown that connecting those keys to users' identities by means of additional, off-blockchain information is possible in many ways (including forensic chain analysis) and made easier when users voluntarily provide their public keys.[113] These keys can also, under certain circumstances, be traced back to the IP addresses with which users connected to the blockchain network.[114] Here, it is relevant to point out that EU courts have already ruled that IP addresses, whether static or dynamic, may generally be qualified as "personal data", in that they can either directly or indirectly be traced back to an individual user.[115] In short, while these data on blockchain may be subject to full encryption and unable to link to a given data subject in themselves, they may still be qualified as "personal data" if there is a lawful and not particularly complex means of obtaining information needed in order to complete that link.[116] The same reasoning can apply, in full, to public keys and other metadata.

A simple solution to the issues that may arise with having personal data stored on a blockchain system, and particularly a public blockchain system, is to rely on technical solutions which allow those data to be referenced by the blockchain, but not directly stored on it, by way of a link to off-blockchain data through an on-blockchain hash pointer, for example.[117] This is, in fact, described as a popular workaround to some of the limitations posed by the GDPR to blockchain systems, although it does have its drawbacks (including less transparency regarding the data stored on the blockchain, the potential need to engage a third-party provider for off-chain storage and overall additional complexity).[118] This approach has also been validated by the

French data protection authority, the Commission Nationale de l'Informatique et des Libertés ("CNIL"), which considers that any personal data stored on a blockchain should preferably be stored in the form of a commitment (cryptographic mechanism allowing one to "freeze" data in such a way that it is possible to prove what has been frozen, with additional information, and not possible to locate or identify the frozen data based on the commitment alone), or, for example, in the form of a hash generated using a hash function with a key – the common feature here would be the off-chain storage of personal data in plain text, with only proof of existence of those data stored on the chain.[119] While this is not possible for public keys (with the CNIL considering that these data are essential to the correct functioning of blockchain systems and must remain always visible due to the very architecture of blockchains, thereby concluding that they cannot be further minimized),[120] alternatives such as the use of "zero-knowledge proofs" (which could provide a binary true/false answer regarding whether a certain public key was used, without providing actual access to it),[121] or adding "noise" to data (by grouping several transactions together on the blockchain-based system, in order to make it impossible to discern the respective senders and recipients of a transaction) could potentially be considered as legally anonymizing those keys in the future.[122]

14.4.2 Principles of Data Processing

As noted above, for now we must work on the premise that metadata (or "header data") and transactional data, which refers to individuals either directly or indirectly, will still be considered personal data when stored on a blockchain-based system, regardless of the encryption or hashing measures that may be implemented. In light of this, where the GDPR is territorially applicable (i.e., in the EU and, in some cases, even to entities established outside of the EU),[123] so will be the principles of data processing contained therein.

The principle of **lawfulness**[124] essentially refers to the need for a legal basis for processing to exist in any situation where an entity may wish to make use of personal data, including on blockchain-based systems. There are generally applicable legal bases (consent, need for the performance of a contract with the data subject, need for compliance with a legal obligation, need to protect the vital interests of an individual, need to perform a task in the public interest or in the exercise of official authority and need for the purposes of legitimate interests pursued),[125] as well as more restrictive additional conditions applicable to more sensitive types of personal data.[126] In general, whenever personal data are to be stored or used through a blockchain system, this storage or usage will not be the end in itself, but rather a means to reach a certain end (for example, storing medical records on a blockchain might serve the purpose of allowing the immutable and permanent preservation of those records, and blockchain offers a means of doing so among potential other means which might exist on the market). This is important because the question of lawfulness is directed at the purposes for processing personal data – the *reason* for which data is to be stored or used must fit into one of the aforementioned legal bases, after which the most suitable *means* (e.g., blockchain systems) to process those data should be chosen. This means that the principle of lawfulness is not as relevant to this discussion as it may first appear. The Hungarian data protection authority has previously made a more firm comment on this, stating that the only applicable legal bases for processing personal data stored in blockchain systems are the consent of the data subject or the legitimate interests of the blockchain user.[127] However, situations are also conceivable where, for example, a change in current legislation requires certain data to be stored on blockchain or equivalent systems, or where this storage is technically required in order to perform a contract with an individual.

The principle of **fairness**[128] will be explored in greater detail below. In any case, it is important to note that the functioning of blockchain systems which are to handle personal data should carefully consider whether the privacy, autonomy and integrity of individuals whose information is handled is not stepped on unreasonably, and should offer those individuals practical means to enforce their rights and control access to their information. One of the more effective ways to ensure this, and assess whether or not a given project to process personal data by means of a blockchain-based system correctly and fully addresses concerns related to fairness from the start, is to carry out a data protection impact assessment aligned with the requirements of Art. 35 GDPR, so as to proactively identify potential risks to the rights, freedoms and interests of data subjects and define mitigation measures to address them comprehensively.

The principle of **transparency**[129] requires that it be made "transparent to natural persons that personal data concerning them are collected, used, consulted or otherwise processed and to what extent the personal data are or will be processed".[130] Any entities handling personal data are required to ensure that they provide concise, transparent, intelligible and easily accessible information to individuals regarding their personal data, using clear and plain language, particularly when directed to children.[131] This is generally achieved by means of privacy policies or information notices, gathering all information that must be imparted to a data subject in one document. In theory, one could imagine that a company wishing to handle customers' data via a blockchain-based system could develop a "Blockchain Privacy Policy" meeting the requirements of Arts. 13 or 14 GDPR. However, some of the information which must be disclosed may be difficult to gather, such as "the recipients or categories of recipients of the personal data, if any"[132] (it might be practically impossible to identify individual recipients on a public blockchain, and cumbersome to do so on a private or permissioned blockchain, leading to the need to ambiguously refer to "entities acting as nodes on the blockchain network" as a category, for instance), "the period for which the personal data will be stored, or if that is not possible, the criteria used to determine that period"[133] (as we will see below, the immutability of data stored on blockchain systems runs counter to the idea of maximum retention periods for personal data) or, in particular, "the fact that the controller intends to transfer personal data to a third country or international organization". It is worth to underline that the Article 29 Working Party has stated that, in accordance with the principle of fairness, the information provided on these transfers should be as meaningful as possible to data subjects, which generally requires a naming of each individual third country to which data may be transferred.[134] Given that nodes on a blockchain network may be geographically dispersed, this runs into a similar issue to the one in naming recipients.

The principle of **purpose limitation**[135] requires that any personal data be collected for a specific, explicit and legitimate purpose, and that it is not used for any other purposes (unless they are compatible with the original purpose). This puts an organizational burden upon entities processing personal data to make sure that they map the purposes for which personal data were collected and avoid that those data be reused, combined or repurposed in any way that may be incompatible with the original purpose. The GDPR provides its own "compatibility criteria" with which to assess this.[136] Blockchain does not necessarily collide with this principle, and may potentially find justification for the continuous storage of personal data beyond an initially defined retention period in the qualification of "further processing for archiving purposes in the public interest" as not incompatible with whichever initial purposes may be defined, albeit subject to appropriate safeguards to ensure respect for other data protection principles.[137]

One key principle that may create issues for the use of blockchain to handle personal data is the principle of **data minimization**,[138] which requires any and all personal data to be adequate, relevant and limited to what is strictly needed in order for the purposes for which they are processed to be met. Given that, as stated by the EU Parliament, "in cases where the blockchain contains personal data, the proliferation of copies of data in a blockchain is likely to be incompatible with the data minimisation principle",[139] it must first be assessed whether use of the blockchain is necessary at all, that is, whether there are any less privacy-intrusive alternatives available. The CNIL has noted that blockchain-based systems are not necessarily the most suitable technology for all personal data processing activities, and can be a source of difficulties when it comes to compliance. Therefore, prior thought must be given to the appropriateness of blockchain before implementing it.[140] Adding to this, and as noted by the EU Parliament, even if one concludes that blockchain is appropriate and necessary for a given desired processing activity, it must be accepted that the storage of personal data "on-chain" is at odds with the spirit of this principle, as integral copies of the chain (and the data stored within) will be stored on each full node operating on the network, and cannot in principle ever be amended or deleted from that moment on. As such, it is likely that off-chain storage solutions (as discussed above) are more aligned with this principle.[141]

Tied in to the previous principle is that of **storage limitation**,[142] according to which personal data should not be kept for any longer than necessary to meet the purposes for which they are processed; after this point, those data should be deleted, or otherwise made into anonymous information (save for further processing, e.g., for archiving purposes in the public interest, which may be a point to explore for public authorities seeking to rely on blockchain to handle personal data, as seen above regarding data minimization). As discussed above, the immutable nature of the data stored on blockchain-based systems is profoundly at odds with the GDPR. More precisely, according to Recital 39:

[t]he personal data should be adequate, relevant and limited to what is necessary for the purposes for which they are processed. This requires, in particular, ensuring that the period for which the personal data are stored is limited to a strict minimum. (...) In order to ensure that the personal data are not kept longer than necessary, time limits should be established by the controller for erasure or for a periodic review.[143]

The CNIL has also noted this conflict, determining that, as an inherent characteristic of blockchain systems, once a block in which a transaction is recorded has been accepted by the majority of the participants (nodes), such transaction can no longer be altered.[144] As a means to address this issue, it has been suggested that disabling read and write access of others than the data subject to data stored on a blockchain system might functionally amount to "erasure" of those data,[145] given that they may become permanently inaccessible, depending on the manner in which data is recorded or referenced on-chain. For example, when a commitment scheme is perfectly hiding, deleting the "witness" – the element that allows verification that a given value is committed in a given commitment – and the value committed may render the commitment anonymous under the GDPR; hence, deleting the secret key used in a keyed-hash's function would have similar effects to erasure,[146] though this is not uncontroversial.[147] While some of these issues can be mitigated by keeping transactional data off-chain, public keys cannot be retroactively removed from blockchain systems.[148] However, in this respect, the CNIL has stated that the applicable retention periods to metadata must, due to the natural functioning of blockchain systems, be aligned with the duration of existence of those systems.[149]

The principle of **accuracy**[150] requires personal data to be kept accurate and up to date, with inaccurate data being erased or rectified without delay. Instantly one can think of difficulties in ensuring that this principle is respected when personal data is stored on blockchains, given the fact that recorded information cannot, in principle, be retroactively amended. It should be noted, however, that blockchain systems are not inherently and absolutely tamper-proof. If a majority of nodes participating in a system decide to rewrite the chain, tampering may be possible (and more reasonably achieved on limited, private and permissioned blockchains). Based on an extensive interpretation of Art. 16 GDPR (which enshrines data subjects' right to rectification of inaccurate or incomplete personal data concerning them), it has been further suggested that amendments could be carried out by adding even more data to the blockchain, seeking to rectify previous entries without actually deleting them.[151] This would rely on the possibility for data subjects to exercise their right to rectification via a "supplementary statement".[152] However, this is certainly stretching the letter of Art. 16 GDPR, which seems to intend for these supplementary statements to be used where data is incomplete (to complete those data) rather than inaccurate (where, preferably, inaccurate data would be rectified or destroyed, rather than kept). This seems to be confirmed by Recital 39 GDPR, which states that "[e]very reasonable step should be taken to ensure that personal data which are inaccurate are rectified or deleted", rather than appended-to. In any case, as seen many times above, the simplest solution is to keep personal data "off-chain", allowing transactional data to be amended without the need to touch the blockchain itself.[153]

The principles of **integrity and confidentiality**[154] refer to the need for personal data to be processed in a manner that ensures its appropriate security, in particular against risks of unlawful processing, accidental loss, destruction or damage. This requires those implementing blockchain as a means to, directly or not, process personal data to consider several factors in doing so, such as whether the blockchain offers sufficient measures to ensure the ongoing confidentiality, integrity, availability and resilience of processing systems and services, as well as the possibility to restore availability and access to personal data in the event of an incident.[155] The GDPR does not lay down specific technical and organizational security measures to protect personal data which must be put in place, but rather sets up a risk-based approach to the matter, wherein entities processing personal data must take responsibility in assessing the measures at their disposal, considering a number of factors ("the state of the art, the costs of implementation and the nature, scope, context and purposes of processing as well as the risk of varying likelihood and severity for the rights and freedoms of natural persons"[156]). Therefore, the fact that a blockchain system may offer the possibility to encrypt the data stored therein is not, in itself, a guarantee of compliance with this principle, regardless of the fact that "the pseudonymisation and encryption of personal data" are listed explicitly in the GDPR as examples of security measures.[157] Instead, an in-depth analysis of any blockchain systems used must be carried out to the point where an entity is comfortable that, in light of the type of data it wishes to handle and the purposes for which this is done (among the other criteria mentioned), a reasonable level of security will be afforded to those data. Regardless of the issues which it may cause, the tendentially immutable nature of data stored on blockchain systems may be beneficial concerning data integrity, availability and access, though less so regarding confidentiality (consider, e.g., the issues with storing trade secrets on public blockchains discussed briefly above).

Finally, the principle of accountability[158] requires not only all other principles to be respected, but also that evidence of this is demonstrable at any time. This puts a burden on entities responsible for handling personal data to come up with means to demonstrate that their internal practices are aligned with the GDPR, including policies and procedures, registers of data breaches and responses given to data subject requests, records of their processing activities and so on. To the extent that blockchain systems could keep records of all operations carried out with certain types of personal data (referenced off-chain), including whether or not they are shared with other entities, whether copies or amendments are made, whether they are deleted or anonymized, among other events that may occur during the "lifecycle" of personal data within a company, blockchain records could potentially be leveraged as an accountability tool, either complementing or (if the complexity of the information which can be stored on the blockchain allows) even assuming the role of records of processing activities as required by the GDPR.[159]

14.4.3 Identifying Data Processing Roles

There are two main roles which an entity may play when handling personal data: that of controller (if the entity has any say on the purposes for which personal data is to be handled, as well as the means by which this is done)[160] and that of processor (if the entity merely handles personal data on behalf of a controller).[161] The question of how we can classify the different "players" in a blockchain system therefore arises. In particular, it has been questioned whether it can be said that, in a distributed system such as a blockchain, a controller can be said to exist at all, and, if so, whether each node which acts to validate transactions on the blockchain should be considered as a controller (which, at least for public blockchains containing an indefinite number of such nodes, would seem unfeasible in practice).[162] The GDPR may not even be able to handle this matter well concerning blockchains, as it has been suggested as not having been designed to deal with cases where data is processed without an identifiable entity in charge of doing so.[163] This would, however, mostly be an issue for public blockchains, as it may still be possible to identify central intermediaries "in charge" of private block-chain systems.[164] A binary approach to this issue has increased in popularity. Either no nodes participating on a blockchain system qualify as a controller under the GDPR, or all of them do. The Hungarian data protection authority has firmly stated that "each user who adds blocks and data within them to the system (e.g., one who "mines" in the bitcoin system) simultaneously qualifies as a data controller, as well".[165] In contrast, the CNIL has equally firmly stated that not all of the actors involved in a blockchain must be considered controllers and that nodes responsible for validating transactions (i.e., "miners") are limited to that task, without any possibility to affect the object of those transactions and, as such, the purposes for which any underlying personal data is processed. Interpreting the CNIL's rationale *a contrario*, only those who enter or access personal data on the blockchain, for a given purpose outside of a purely personal or household activity,[166] may be considered controllers.[167]

The approach laid down by the CNIL appears to us as more reasonable than one which considers all participating nodes as controllers – given that those nodes do not actually have any control over the reasons for which personal data which may be uploaded to or referenced on a blockchain system may be used, it would not be fair to impose upon them all of the obligations to which the GDPR binds controllers. It would also not be practicable, given the potential difficulty in establishing the exact number, location and identity of nodes on a blockchain network, and in enforcing any of the controller's obligations on all of those nodes.[168] Instead, the CNIL's solution appears to mostly resolve the issue of an undesirable "accountability gap", the existence of which has been understandably claimed as not ideal for regulators or citizens,[169] by allowing specific entities – the uploader of personal data, if acting outside of a personal or household activity, as well as other entities seeking to use personal data stored in a blockchain-based system for one or more defined purposes – to be identified as controllers and held accountable for compliance with their obligations under the applicable law by supervisory authorities and data subjects alike. Furthermore, this solution appears to be more technically correct than other alternatives proposed, such as that of considering that the data subject/blockchain user might be qualified as the controller for his or her own personal data, which can be seen as conflating the entity responsible for data protection with the individual who needs to be protected.[170]

On the other hand, if one were to give any sort of data processing role to nodes on the blockchain network which validate transactions, it could be reasonable to qualify them as processors, in that they maintain data on the blockchain so that it may be used for purposes determined by others. However, they do not exactly do this on behalf of those entities which we might qualify as controllers (e.g., any company which accesses the blockchain in order to use data stored within for its own purposes) and, more importantly, it may be practically unfeasible to devise contractual arrangements between each and every "miner" node and each and every potential controller – note that Art. 28(3) GDPR requires a written agreement to be put in place between controllers and processors, with a set of minimum obligations. More importantly, Art. 28(1) GDPR puts upon controllers the obligation to "use only processors providing sufficient guarantees to implement appropriate technical and organizational measures in such a manner" that processing will comply with the GDPR – if we were to consider all "miner" nodes as processors, the logical conclusion would be that a controller would not be allowed to legally make use of any data stored on a blockchain without first ensuring that each and every node which may have processed those data is satisfactorily complaint (i.e., a practical impossibility).

These issues regarding public blockchains (with an indeterminate number of "miners") are recognized by the CNIL, which is at present carrying out an in-depth reflection on the matter and has encouraged stakeholders to innovate when it comes to ensuring compliance with processors' obligations under the GDPR.[171] However, they apply the above reasoning to smart contract developers who use the blockchain to process personal data on behalf of others (controllers), as well as "miners" in general, although impliedly only for private or permissioned blockchains.[172] In this latter type of blockchains, it might be possible for the central entity in charge of the blockchain (i.e., the controller) to require "miner" nodes to agree to a certain number of obligations within a "central agreement" or "terms of use", in order to be given authorisation to validate any transactions on the chain, thereby allowing for a written agreement aligned with Art. 28 GDPR to be established. These "miners" could also be subjected to appropriate due diligence carried out by the central entity in order to ascertain whether they meet a certain standard of adherence to data protection regulations and have internal technical and organizational security measures in place to ensure the protection of data subjects' rights.

14.4.4 Addressing International Transfers

One issue which is closely related to the issue of qualification of nodes as "processors" or not has to do with the potential cross-border transfers of personal data stored "on-chain" between those nodes (given that each participating node will obtain a copy of all data lodged on the blockchain). While this does not raise an issue where those flows are contained within the European Economic Area (EEA), the GDPR raises restrictions on the transfer of personal data to "third countries", which may only be done where certain conditions are met.[173] One preliminary issue may be identifying to which countries the data on a blockchain may be transferred. On permissionless (i.e., public) blockchains, participating nodes may be based anywhere.[174] It may be a monumental task to even understand to which countries data may be flowing at any given time, let alone keep track of new "miner" nodes joining or old ones ceasing their participation. Naturally, this issue is not as severe in private or permissioned blockchain systems, where some degree of control over who can become a participating node is possible.

Once these countries are identified, in practice, there is a three-step approach which can be followed when assessing an international transfer of data under the GDPR:

1. Assess whether the recipient country is covered by an adequacy decision[175] issued by the European Commission[176];

2. If there is no adequacy decision, then determine whether it is possible to implement certain appropriate safeguards[177] – such as contracts including approved standard data protection clauses, binding corporate rules (only applicable for transfers within a group of undertakings, or group of enterprises engaged in a joint economic activity) or approved codes of conduct/certification mechanisms;

3. If there is no adequacy decision nor possibility to implement those appropriate safeguards, consider whether it may be appropriate to rely on any of the legal derogations established for specific situations.[178]

In the same manner as it may be possible to bind "miner" nodes in a permissioned blockchain to certain data protection obligations, by means of a "central agreement" or "terms of use", in order to be allowed to participate in that blockchain-based system, it may be possible to incorporate approved standard data protection clauses into that agreement or terms. It is further conceivable that, in the future, a certification mechanism for certain private blockchain-based systems will be developed which might allow for the lawful international transfer of information inherent to their functioning.

Another avenue which has been explored is to rely on the legal derogations, in particular the possibility for data subjects to explicitly consent to such international transfers, after having been informed of the possible risks.[179] This has been seen as a solution which could easily be implemented on private blockchains where access is controlled, though not so much on public versions.[180] It must further be considered that, whereas valid consent is already bound by restrictive conditions under the GDPR, including that it must be a freely given, specific, informed and unambiguous indication of a data subject's wishes, provided by a statement or clear affirmative action,[181] and must further be requested in a clearly distinguishable manner from other matters, in an intelligible and easily accessible form, using clear and plain language,[182] while also generally not being made a necessary requirement in order for the performance of a contract or the provision of a service to be carried out,[183] the requirement in this derogation is for explicit consent (which generally requires that a high individual level of control over what happens to the personal data be afforded to the data subject).[184]

14.4.5 Data Subjects' Rights

Data subjects are afforded a plethora of rights under the GDPR, including (but not limited to) the right to access,[185] right to rectification,[186] right to erasure[187] (or "right to be forgotten") and right to data portability.[188] Controllers are required to facilitate the exercise of these rights, and must provide information on actions taken to address requests to exercise them without undue delay and, as a rule, within one month of receipt of the request.[189] If no action is taken, then this must also be informed to the data subject, without delay and within one month from receipt of the request, along with reasons for this and the possibility for the data subject to complain to the competent supervisory authority.[190] While EU or local laws may allow for restrictions to these rights in certain cases set out in the GDPR, none of these seem directly applicable to blockchain systems *per se*.

Some of these rights do not raise particular issues when it comes to blockchain systems,[191] such as the right to receive concise, transparent, intelligible and easily accessible information on the processing of personal data carried out via those systems,[192] the right of access or the right to data portability.[193] Others, such as the "right to be forgotten", create a conflict of sorts for the blockchain, as the fact that records cannot be retroactively deleted is a key feature of blockchain architecture. However, smart contracts concerning the handling of personal data may have built-in workarounds allowing for the revocation of all access rights to those data upon request of the data subject, thereby effectively making the content invisible to all others.[194] As seen before, this, the CNIL argues, can make those data practically inaccessible, therefore moving closer to the effects of data erasure, and that the material equivalence of these situations should be further evaluated in terms of GDPR compliance.[195]

As also noted above regarding the principle of accuracy, one interpretation of the right to rectification which has been brought forward is that amendments could be made by entering updated data into a new block on the chain, as a form of supplementary statement to the earlier data. Although we note that this interpretation still seems to stretch the wording of Art. 16 GDPR and Recital 39 GDPR, it is noteworthy that the CNIL seems to advocate for this approach, both regarding the right to rectification and the right to erasure:

> As regards the right of rectification, the impossibility to modify the data in a block must cause the data controller to enter the updated data in a new block. Indeed, a subsequent transaction can cancel an initial transaction, even though the first transaction will still appear in the chain. The same solutions as those applied following a request for deletion of personal data could be applied to erroneous data when such data requires deletion.[196]

The right to restriction, which requires a form of blocking of personal data so that it can only be stored and no longer used for most other purposes without the data subject's consent,[197] has also been addressed by the CNIL as one which can be made effective by ensuring that it is programmed into blockchain-based smart contracts from the start.[198] Furthermore, given that the execution of certain smart contracts will necessarily imply "automated individual decision-making", as defined in the GDPR,[199] controllers must ensure that individuals are allowed the possibility to request human intervention from the controller regarding executed smart contracts (e.g., providing the option to request a manual review of a smart contract's performance, which allows the results of that performance to be reversed if the situation merits this) and for the individual to express his or her own opinion on the results of the automated decision made by the smart contract, including to contest it.[200] The implementation of this latter right in particular must be carefully considered by those wishing to enter into smart contracts with individuals, given that it is a reflection of the GDPR's frowning upon decisions based solely on automated processing which may significantly affect an individual, particularly where some form of profiling of that individual is to take place. One point to consider is that having a manual validation step prior to finalization of the performance of a smart contract may allow one to escape its classification as a "decision based solely on automated processing" (and therefore avoid also the application of heavier information obligations, such as the need to provide to data subjects meaningful information about the logic involved, the significance and envisaged consequences of such decisions for data subjects),[201] albeit at the cost of effectiveness and automated finality.

The above has shown examples of solutions brought forward to solve the apparent absolute incompatibility between blockchain and some of the rights afforded by the GDPR to data subjects. These and other solutions must, however, be built into blockchain-based systems, as has been noted before – the EU Parliament has clearly stated that

> in order to prevent the infringement of the fundamental right to the protection of personal data, blockchain technology should not be used for the processing of personal data until the user organization concerned is in a position to guarantee compliance with the GDPR and to specifically ensure that the rights to the rectification and erasure of data are protected.[202]

It is therefore important to understand what concerns need to be at the forefront of blockchain developers and users wishing to handle personal data in order for the design and use of blockchain-based systems to be, ab initio, compliant with data protection principles and, more broadly, ethical in terms of the pressures exerted upon data subjects, which we will shortly address.

14.4.6 Data Protection by Design and Fairness by Design

It has been said that "the technological innovation that brought us blockchains may however turn individuals into data sovereigns that can themselves, copy, change, share, move their data".[203] However, as noted several times before, this is a potential feature in blockchain-based systems rather than an inherent one. Without specifically designing a system to allow for this (similarly to how one must design a smart contract to allow for certain modifications or adaptations) and without carefully planning the use which is to be made of a given blockchain system, it will not be possible to appropriately ensure compliance with the GDPR.

The principle of data protection by design is enshrined in Art. 25 GDPR, along with that of data protection by default. It requires controllers to implement appropriate technical and organizational measures in their systems and activities involving the handling of personal data, so as to ensure that the principles of data processing (in particular, that of data minimization), will be implemented in an effective manner, and that compliance with the GDPR will be ensured. Just as with the selection of security measures, the GDPR offers a risk-based approach to controllers, which must select the appropriate measures to implement those principles

> [t]aking into account the state of the art, the cost of implementation and the nature, scope, context and purposes of processing as well as the risks of varying likelihood and severity for rights and freedoms of natural persons posed by the processing.[204]

Examples of such measures given in the GDPR include the adoption of internal policies, minimizing the processing of personal data, pseudonymizing personal data as soon as possible, ensuring transparency with regard to the functions and processing of personal data, enabling data subjects to monitor the data processing and enabling controllers to create and improve security features. Furthermore, it is stated that any producers or developers of products, services and applications which may be used to handle personal data (e.g., blockchain system developers, smart contract developers) should be encouraged to take these principles into account during design and development.[205]

As described by the European Data Protection Supervisor, there are four equally important dimensions to be considered regarding obligations arising from the principle of data protection by design[206]:

1. Any processing of personal data which is partially or completely supported by IT systems should always be the outcome of a design project – the principle of data protection by design requires appropriate safeguards to be considered at both the design and operational phases of any processing, aiming towards the whole project lifecycle and clearly identifying, as project requirements, the protection of individuals and their personal data;

2. Selection and implementation of measures to ensure effective protection must be done through a risk-based approach (as noted above), considering that the assets to be protected are the individual data subjects and, in particular, their rights and freedoms;

3. Though the GDPR does not lay down specific measures which must be put in place (as this would run counter to the aforementioned risk-based approach), measures which are chosen by controllers need to be both appropriate and effective in ensuring and demonstrating compliance with the GDPR, implementing data protection principles and protecting the rights of individuals;

4. All identified safeguards must be effectively integrated into the processing system and/or activities foreseen – that is, there must be direct protection of individuals, their data and how these are managed, within the systems themselves to the greatest extent possible (although this may be complemented by measures taken via "external means", such as privacy policies given to data subjects outside of the system used to process their data).

The above methodology reflects very important elements which must be considered as a baseline to be met when developing a blockchain-based system designed to handle personal data. The system must be designed, for example, to allow data subjects to easily access their own data, to control disclosure of those data to others, to understand how their data might flow within the blockchain network, as well as to allow for data to be encrypted and/or pseudonymized to the greatest extent possible. It seems inevitable, as a result of the principle of data minimization and the need to ensure an effective ability to respond to data subjects' requests (such as requests for erasure or rectification), that personal data should be stored "off-chain" and referenced "on-chain" via a commitment or hashed pointer, given that the transparency and immutability which is part of the nature of blockchain systems seems to preclude any compliant handling of personal data otherwise. In addition, for public keys and metadata, it has been said that the only way to ensure compliance in this respect "would be to recognize specific key-handling techniques such as particularly strong encryption formulas or zero-knowledge proof as GDPR compliant",[207] which cannot be considered a given at this stage. This may change in the future, however, and it is important for blockchain designers to stay on top of technological developments which might allow for a better accommodation of data protection principles and data subject rights, potentially leading to a solution where personal data can be stored "on-chain" without compromising its confidentiality or the ability for data subjects to exercise effective control over it.

Naturally, this principle does not create obligations only for producers or developers of blockchain systems, but also for those who might wish to make use of such a system (be it to upload data or merely to access data within). As noted before regarding the principle of data minimization, controllers must give prior thought to the appropriateness of choosing blockchain technology to handle personal data, as this may not be appropriate in all cases.[208] This will, in particular, involve the carrying out of a data protection impact assessment which, arguably, is mandatory in any case where a blockchain-based system is intended to be used to handle personal data, given the high risks for the rights and freedoms of natural persons presented by the technology (as discussed above) and, more concretely, due to blockchain being considered as a novel data processing technology.[209] This assessment should be carried out as early as is practicable in the design of the activity which is to rely on a blockchain-based system, even if the full extent of what is intended is still unknown, and should be updated throughout the lifecycle of the project to ensure not only that personal data protection has been considered from the start, but also that compliant solutions are put in place every step of the way and should therefore be seen as a continual process rather than a one-time exercise.[210] All relevant stakeholders should be involved in this process, including the controller's data protection officer (if appointed), any processors which may be involved (such as participating nodes in a permissioned blockchain) and even data subjects or their representatives, where appropriate.[211] The desired end-result is to produce a documented assessment which, as a minimum, contains (1) a systematic description of the envisaged processing operations and the purposes of processing, (2) an assessment of the necessity and proportionality of the processing operations regarding the purposes, (3) an assessment of the risks to the rights and freedoms of data subjects, and (4) measures proposed to address those risks.[212] Ideally, the controller will be able to identify any and all significant risks inherent to the use of blockchain-based systems to handle personal data and implement sufficient measures to lower those risks to acceptable levels. Otherwise, where risks remain high at the end of an assessment, the controller's only choice to remain compliant is either to refrain from carrying out the intended processing activity or to seek a prior consultation from a competent supervisory authority, putting the activity on hold until this opinion is delivered and implemented in full.[213]

Indeed, data protection impact assessments are a key part of complying with the GDPR where high-risk data processing is planned, or is taking place,[214] and are an important means to comply with the principle of data protection by design (in that obstacles to data protection compliance can be detected from the inception of any processing project and dealt with accordingly) and the principle of accountability (as the DPIA itself, documented and subjected to periodic revision, will serve as evidence that data protection considerations have been made from the outset of a project). It is, however, possible to go beyond merely ensuring a blockchain project's compliance with data protection rules by design, to speak of further ethical dimensions concerning that blockchain project's fairness towards data subjects.

The concept of "fairness by design" has previously been discussed in relation to AI and machine learning algorithms, where the concern is to ensure that the end-results produced by those systems are fair towards the individuals which they affect. Researchers from the "Stroke Belt Project" – a project in which a patient-centric platform based on mobile and "Internet of Things" technology is being developed for those at early risk of cardiovascular disease in what is known as the "Stroke Belt" (a region in the southeastern United States, where the incident rates for strokes range from 25% to 40% higher than national average) – have proposed various rules for addressing the idea of fairness from the get-go in projects involving analytics, so as to alleviate the impact of racial, gender and socio-economic biases from their models.[215] These include ensuring the participation of social scientists (to increase awareness of demographic biases), adding fairness measures to traditional machine learning metrics (identifying possible over-generalizations and other biases within certain demographic segments) and being sure to balance representativeness with critical mass constraints (to avoid precluding the fair analysis of statistical minorities in a dataset).[216] Similarly, this concept has been explored regarding dynamic pricing policies, where researchers from BBVA Data and Analytics concluded that such policies may be considered as fair according to their end-results, namely "when the policy provides similarly distributed prices among groups of customers", and appropriate fairness metrics must therefore be implemented to ensure that this end is met.[217]

It can, therefore, be concluded that the objective behind the concept of "fairness by design" is one of results – it will be met if the end-result in a processing activity is balanced and proportionate data processing. To meet this end, developers and companies must consider the interests and reasonable expectations of privacy of the data subjects they may affect from the very design of the data processing systems or activities they wish to develop or carry out including products, services, applications or, in particular, the algorithms underlying those systems. Individuals' privacy, autonomy and integrity should not be unreasonably trodden on, nor should individuals be pressured to provide their personal data against their will.[218] In this sense, "fairness by design" can be seen as a specification of the principle of data protection by design, which seeks to complement legal compliance with an ethical dimension of personal data protection, thereby contributing to the development of a healthy and democratic digital society.[219]

One possible way to achieve this is to develop blockchain-based systems which allow data subjects to effectively control their personal data, from the amount uploaded to the amount disclosed to other entities. As an example, we can analyse the process proposed by Guy Zyskind et al., which can be briefly (and crudely) summarized as follows[220]:

1. Users, that is, persons interested in downloading and using applications, might have an interest in acquiring the services of a provider which, in turn, requires (or desires) some processing of personal data on those users in order to provide its services;

2. Upon signing up for a service delivered by a provider, a new shared identity (referring to the specific user and the provider) would be generated and sent to a blockchain-based platform. At this stage, and later from time to time, permissions would be set and managed by the user for the provider, which will restrict the amount of data related to the user which the provider will be able to access at any given time;

3. Through use of the service, data on the user might be collected and sent to the blockchain-based platform, which will collect those data and re-route them into an "off-chain" storage solution (which can be another blockchain or a trusted third-party storage system, such as a cloud service), retaining only a hashed pointer (SHA-256) referencing those data;

4. Data collected can now be queried by the user (freely) and by the provider (according to the permissions set for it by the user).

This model offers many advantages in terms not only of security, but of sovereignty of the individual as only the user will have control over his or her own data, with the decentralized nature of the blockchain, in combination with digitally-signed transactions, standing in the way of others wishing to pose as the user or corrupt the network.[221] It seeks to allow users to own and control their data, without compromising security or limiting companies' and authorities' ability to provide personalized services to those users.[222] Provided that such a model could be implemented in a sufficiently intuitive way, so that average users would easily understand how to control their data and grant/remove access to it in real-time, as well as where their data is currently being sent to and which entities it is being shared with, it could prove an instrumental example of the concept of "fairness by design" brought to life on the blockchain.

14.4.7 Conclusive Remarks

It is paramount to address the matters raised by personal data protection laws when considering the use of blockchain-based systems, as not only do they offer the possibility for personal data to be directly recorded "on-chain", but also require the use of personal data (in the form of public keys/identifiers) for their very functioning. Given the high standard for anonymization set by the Article 29 Working Party, even encryption or irreversible hashing of personal data stored on blockchain will not suffice to circumvent the discussion (at least, for now).

The interaction between blockchain and internationally recognized data processing principles is not always smooth. While some principles remain largely unaffected by the technology, such as the principle of lawfulness and purpose limitation, and others may even find themselves enhanced by the additional functionalities brought about by blockchain, such as the principle of fairness, others still appear to frontally collide with its "set-in-stone" nature, namely the principles of data minimization and storage limitation which, in turn, may affect the ability to effectively exercise some data subject rights regarding personal data stored "on-chain" (such as the right to rectification or erasure). It is also not a simple matter to identify and agree on the data processing roles played by the participants in a blockchain-based system. An even more complicated matter is to ensure that the formal requirements tied into these roles are met, such as the need for a contract or other legal act containing a set of minimum obligations to be entered into with each processor engaged by a controller, in light of Art. 28 GDPR – this problem currently appears not to have a practically viable solution when considering public blockchains. The matter of international transfers and the implementation of the requirements for their lawfulness raises similar difficulties in light of the decentralized nature of blockchain-based systems.

In general, many of these issues can be solved by storing personal data in an "off-chain" solution, and merely referencing those data (e.g., via a commitment or hash pointer) within the blockchain-based system itself. However, in any case, it must be understood that, while blockchain has the potential to allow individuals to retain control of their data and even to understand, in a transparent manner, who has access to their information and to what extent, this by no means results automatically from the use of blockchain-based systems to process personal data. Rather, those systems must be specifically crafted, in careful consideration of the rules set by the principles of data protection by design and, specifically, of fairness by design, to ensure that individuals' privacy and real control over their data is afforded to them.

The use of blockchain technology as a means to process personal data has been called into question ever since the GDPR was first announced, with doubts solidified by the European Parliament's stance on the matter. For now, it seems that there are manners in which to handle the potential objections raised, at least where private or permissioned blockchains are concerned. We are left to await more practical implementations of blockchain use cases concerning personal data and, in particular, decisions from supervisory authorities and courts on whether the rules on data protection and blockchain can peacefully coexist.

14.5 CONCLUSIONS AND RECOMMENDATIONS

This chapter has addressed three major legal topics, namely, contracts, intellectual property and personal data protection, through the lens of blockchain, attempting to identify potential benefits and issues that have been brought up in the heated discussions taking place across the globe for quite some years now. We began by considering the relationship between smart contracts and blockchain-based systems (Section 14.2), introducing the concept of "smart contracts" and how the blockchain has been leveraged in order to create even more complex forms of automated agreements. We then analysed the impact which implementation of smart contracts on blockchain-based systems can have in certain key points of such contracts' "lifecycle" (Section 14.2.1), including their formation, performance, modification and breach.

In Section 14.3, we moved onto the second topic under discussion, IP, or intellectual property. After a brief introduction as to the different types of intellectual property rights that would be assessed (copyrights, trademarks, designs and trade secrets), we moved onto examples of the practical application of blockchain-based systems to those rights (Section 14.3.1), focusing on benefits which many have claimed may bring the recording, management and enforcement of those rights to the next level. Finally, the last topic proposed for discussion, namely that of personal data protection (Section 14.4), was analysed. In this chapter, after a brief introduction of the initial conflict felt between blockchain and privacy enthusiasts, we isolated several questions to be answered: "Can data on a blockchain be considered personal data?", "How do the principles of data processing apply?", "Can we identify data processing roles on the blockchain?", "How do we address international transfers of data?", "Are data subjects' rights truly incompatible with the blockchain?" and, last but not least, "How can we ensure compliance with the principles of data protection by design and fairness by design?". Each of these issues was tackled individually, aiming to showcase different positions which have been brought forward both by scholars and supervisory authorities, while providing our own commentary when appropriate.

It is safe to say that the jury is still out on whether the benefits brought by blockchain to these three areas of the law will suffice to create an incentive to overcome the hurdles towards their implementation. It seems unlikely that "traditional" contracting will be replaced by blockchain-based smart contracts anytime soon, largely due to the inherent value in the flexibility and ambiguity allowed by older forms of contracting which cannot simply be matched by undoubtedly more efficient automated versions. Conversely, it is likely that the blockchain will see a rise in uptake regarding simpler forms of contracting, including intellectual property license agreements (possibly threatening the existence or livelihood of major platforms and collective management organizations who currently thrive on the inability of individual rightsholders to generate their own revenue effectively). Intellectual property may, in fact, be one of the key areas to benefit from the rise in blockchain-based registries, not only to improve traceability of unregistered rights but also of products containing certain trademarks or built upon registered designs, thereby providing evidence of provenance and authenticity, for example.

In fact, the main area where the potential for blockchain may be hindered to this date seems to be the area of personal data protection. Currently, there does not seem to be a feasible way for personal data to be stored "on-chain" without directly colliding with the principles of data minimization and storage limitation, as well as the inability to respond to requests for erasure in a literal sense (although it may be able to achieve material equivalence by cutting off all access rights to those data other than the data subject's, in practice). There are also serious issues in complying with the GDPR's formal obligations around the engagement of processors (*vis-à-vis* participating nodes, or "miners") and international transfers of personal data – while these are potentially controllable in private or permissioned blockchains, there seems to be few clues to date as to how to manage these and other matters when it comes to personal data stored on public blockchains. Nonetheless, as was illustrated at the end of the chapter, so long as blockchain-based systems are designed with certain key concepts in mind, namely, not only compliance with the requirements set under the GDPR, but also a further ethical dimension of ensuring fairness towards data subjects, affording them as much control as possible regarding their own personal data as the only way of truly making their exercise of the fundamental right to data protection effective, it is possible to think of blockchain-based solutions which go further than any currently available means to ensure the sovereignty of data subjects regarding their personal information. In short, while the blockchain and EU data protection law may currently be seen as enemies, developments over time may show that the blockchain can arise as a means by which to achieve true implementation of one of the main stated goals of the GDPR: the protection of natural persons with regard to the processing of personal data.

NOTES

1   Nakamoto, Satoshi. 2008. "Bitcoin: A Peer-to-Peer Electronic Cash System". Available at: https://bitcoin.org/bitcoin.pdf.

2   Higgins, Stan. 2017. "From $900 to $20,000: Bitcoin's Historic 2017 Price Run Revisited". *Coindesk*. Available at: www.coindesk.com/900-20000-bitcoins-historic-2017-price-run-revisited.

3   "Bitcoin Price (BTC)". *Coindesk*. Available at: www.coindesk.com/price/bitcoin.

4   IBMBlockchain. 2018. "How the CDC is exploring blockchain technology for public health". Available at: https://youtu.be/gDj0kLojxu4.

5   Power Ledger. "xGrid – Product Details". Available at: www.powerledger.io/products/across-regulated-electricity-network.

6   Follow My Vote. "Blockchain Technology in Online Voting". Available at: https://followmyvote.com/online-voting-technology/blockchain-technology/.

7   del Castillo, Michael. 2019. "Blockchain's Moveable Feast: How The Tech Is Changing The Way We Eat". *Forbes*. Available at: www.forbes.com/sites/michaeldelcastillo/2019/01/08/blockchains-moveable-feast-how-the-tech-is-changing-the-way-we-eat-2/#41469cec17f3.

8   Ménière, Yann. 2018. "The emerging blockchain patent landscape". Presentation given at the EPO's "Patenting Blockchain" conference of 4 December 2018. Available at: https://youtu.be/ROwzOLxngsQ?t=525 (08:45 onwards).

9   See, for example: Ravich, Timothy. 2017. "Evolving Law on Airport Implications by Unmanned Aerial Systems". ISBN: 978-0-309-44659-4. Available at: https://papers.ssrn.com/sol3/papers.cfm?abstract_id=3066773; Scharf, Rebecca L. 2018. "Drone Invasion: Unmanned Aerial Vehicles and the Right to Privacy". *UNLV William S. Boyd School of Law Legal Studies Research Paper Series*. Available at: https://papers.ssrn.com/sol3/papers.cfm?abstract_id=3145203; and Hazel, Robert. 2018. "Privacy and Trade Secret Law Applied to Drones – An Economic Analysis". *GMU Working Paper in Economics No. 18-36*. Available at: https://papers.ssrn.com/sol3/papers.cfm?abstract_id=3116378.

10   See, for example: Ni Loideain, Nora. 2018. "A Port in the Data-Sharing Storm: The GDPR and the Internet of Things". *King's College London Law School Research Paper No. 2018-27*. Available at: https://papers.ssrn.com/sol3/papers.cfm?abstract_id=3264265; Busch, Christoph. 2018. "Does the Amazon Dash Button Violate EU Consumer Law? Balancing Consumer Protection and Technological Innovation in the Internet of Things". *7 Journal of European Consumer and Market Law 78–80*. Available at: https://papers.ssrn.com/sol3/papers.cfm?abstract_id=3170985; and Swire, Peter et al. 2018. "Privacy and Cybersecurity Lessons at the Intersection of the Internet of Things and Police Body-Worn Cameras". *North Carolina Law Review, Vol. 96, 2018. Georgia Tech Scheller College of Business Research Paper No. 18-11*. Available at: https://papers.ssrn.com/sol3/papers.cfm?abstract_id=3168089.

11   See, for example: Devarapalli, Pratap. 2018. "Machine Learning to Machine Owning: Redefining the Copyright Ownership from the Perspective of Australian, US, UK and EU Law". *European Intellectual Property Review, 40*(11), 722–728. Available at: https://papers.ssrn.com/sol3/papers.cfm?abstract_id=3293518; Denvir, Catrina et al. 2018. "A New Beginning or a Hastening of the End?: Sustaining the Ideological Evolution of Law in the Age of Artificial Intelligence". *SSRN*. Available at: https://papers.ssrn.com/sol3/papers.cfm?abstract_id=3270728; and Raso, Filippo A. et al. 2018. "Artificial Intelligence & Human Rights: Opportunities & Risks". *Berkman Klein Center Research Publication No. 2018-6*. Available at: https://papers.ssrn.com/sol3/papers.cfm?abstract_id=3259344.

12   Governatori, Guido et al. 2018. "On Legal Contracts, Imperative and Declarative Smart Contracts, and Blockchain Systems". *Artificial Intelligence and Law 26:377–409.* Available at: https://doi.org/10.1007/s10506-018-9223-3, p. 377.

13   Raskin, Max. 2017. "The Law and Legality of Smart Contracts". *1 Georgetown Law Technology Review 304.* Available at: https://papers.ssrn.com/sol3/papers.cfm?abstract_id=2959166, p. 306.

14   World Intellectual Property Organisation. "What Is Intellectual Property". Available at: www.wipo.int/edocs/pubdocs/en/intproperty/450/wipo_pub_450.pdf, p. 2.

15   Article 4(1), Regulation (EU) 2016/679 of the European Parliament and of the Council of 27 April 2016 on the protection of natural persons with regard to the processing of personal data and on the free movement of such data, and repealing Directive 95/46/EC (General Data Protection Regulation), OJ L 119, 4.5.2016, pp. 1–88.

16   Regulation (EU) 2016/679 of the European Parliament and of the Council of 27 April 2016 on the protection of natural persons with regard to the processing of personal data and on the free movement of such data, and repealing Directive 95/46/EC (General Data Protection Regulation), OJ L 119, 4.5.2016, p. 1–88.

17   Szabo, Nick. 1994. "Smart Contracts". Available at: www.fon.hum.uva.nl/rob/Courses/InformationInSpeech/CDROM/Literature/LOTwinterschool2006/szabo.best.vwh.net/smart.contracts.html.

18   It is worth to point out that one does not need to think of blockchain to come up with long-standing examples of such contracts, including those which are executed between a person and a vending machine – *"If the machine is operating properly and money is inserted into the machine, then a contract for sale will be executed automatically [with the chosen item being dispensed]. This is a smart contract."* Raskin, Max. 2017. "The Law and Legality of Smart Contracts". *1 Georgetown Law Technology Review 304.* Available at: https://papers.ssrn.com/sol3/papers.cfm?abstract_id=2959166, p. 306. Smart contracts can thus be individualized, for instance, within the broader concept of "e-contracts" – a term which may be used as covering any and all contracts which can be handled or processed via computer systems, without necessarily having their performance fully or partially automated. (See: Governatori, Guido et al. 2018. "On legal contracts, imperative and declarative smart contracts, and blockchain systems". *Artificial Intelligence and Law 26:377–409.* Available at: https://doi.org/10.1007/s10506-018-9223-3, p. 384) For example, an electronic agreement (e.g., in PDF format) with free-text fields which either party might use to input relevant data (such as their billing address) would be considered an "e-contract", but not necessarily a "smart contract"; the same can be said of the agreements which are formed whenever a user accepts the "Terms and Conditions" of a given website. Additionally, before the concept of blockchain came into the mix, there was the concept of EDI, or Electronic Data Interchange – a *"standardized language to describe and categorize contracts electronically, which encapsulated data like who was covered by the contract, actions accomplished by the contract, and contract conditions."* (Governatori, Guido et al. 2018. "On legal contracts, imperative and declarative smart contracts, and blockchain systems". *Artificial Intelligence and Law 26:377–409.* Available at: https://doi.org/10.1007/s10506-018-9223-3, p. 384) Similarly to the case made for blockchain (as we will see), proponents of EDI claimed that it would allow a minimization in transaction costs, as the use of standardized language in contracts (fully-articulated "if-then" rules) would eliminate (or severely mitigate) ambiguities of interpretation, which could lead to legal disputes over the meaning of a signed contract; moreover, claims were made that requiring a prior logical specification of contractual terms, through EDI's standardized language, would have benefits on managerial decision-making in general, forcing managers to consider potential deals more critically.

(See: Sklaroff, Jeremy M. 2018. "Smart Contracts and the Cost of Inflexibility". *University of Pennsylvania Law Review, Vol. 166,* p. 288) However, in spite of claims that no litigation concerning EDI-formed contracts ever took place for at least forty years since its introduction, EDI failed to fully replace "paper-based" (meaning, human-drafted and performed) contracts in the long run, though it did serve to empower managers in terms of flexibility – EDI systems were expensive and had to be formed bilaterally with other firms, but could be easily and cheaply modified, which forced managers to work together in order to ensure a beneficial deal for all parties involved, by continually optimizing the terms to be agreed upon. (See: A. Cunningham, Lawrence. 2006. "Language, Deals and Standards: The Future of XML Contracts". Washington University Law Review, 313, p. 321 and Sklaroff, Jeremy M. 2018. "Smart Contracts and the Cost of Inflexibility". *University of Pennsylvania Law Review, Vol. 166,* p. 290).

19 Staples, M. et al. 2017. "Risks and Opportunities for Systems using Blockchain and Smart Contracts". *Data61 (CSIRO).* Available at: www.data61.csiro.au/~/media/052789573E9342068C5735BF604E7824.ashx, p. 2.

20 Governatori, Guido et al. 2018. "On Legal Contracts, Imperative and Declarative Smart Contracts, and Blockchain Systems". *Artificial Intelligence and Law 26:377–409.* Available at: https://doi.org/10.1007/s10506-018-9223-3, pp. 385–386.

21 Governatori, Guido et al. 2018. "On Legal Contracts, Imperative and Declarative Smart Contracts, and Blockchain Systems". *Artificial Intelligence and Law 26:377–409.* Available at: https://doi.org/10.1007/s10506-018-9223-3, p. 387.

22 Raskin, Max. 2017. "The Law and Legality of Smart Contracts". *1 Georgetown Law Technology Review 304.* Available at: https://papers.ssrn.com/sol3/papers.cfm?abstract_id=2959166, p. 322.

23 "Unconscionable (definition)". *The Free Dictionary by Farlex.* Available at: https://legal-dictionary.thefreedictionary.com/unconscionable.

24 Raskin, Max. 2017. "The Law and Legality of Smart Contracts". *1 Georgetown Law Technology Review 304.* Available at: https://papers.ssrn.com/sol3/papers.cfm?abstract_id=2959166, p. 322.

25 Raskin, Max. 2017. "The Law and Legality of Smart Contracts". *1 Georgetown Law Technology Review 304.* Available at: https://papers.ssrn.com/sol3/papers.cfm?abstract_id=2959166, p. 322.

26 Raskin, Max. 2017. "The Law and Legality of Smart Contracts". *1 Georgetown Law Technology Review 304.* Available at: https://papers.ssrn.com/sol3/papers.cfm?abstract_id=2959166, p. 323.

27 Raskin, Max. 2017. "The Law and Legality of Smart Contracts". *1 Georgetown Law Technology Review 304.* Available at: https://papers.ssrn.com/sol3/papers.cfm?abstract_id=2959166, pp. 324–325.

28 Sklaroff, Jeremy M. 2018. "Smart Contracts and the Cost of Inflexibility". *University of Pennsylvania Law Review, Vol. 166,* pp. 291–293.

29 Sklaroff, Jeremy M. 2018. "Smart Contracts and the Cost of Inflexibility". *University of Pennsylvania Law Review, Vol. 166,* pp. 291–293, 296–298.

30 Sklaroff, Jeremy M. 2018. "Smart Contracts and the Cost of Inflexibility". *University of Pennsylvania Law Review, Vol. 166,* p. 276.

31 Sklaroff, Jeremy M. 2018. "Smart Contracts and the Cost of Inflexibility". *University of Pennsylvania Law Review, Vol. 166,* pp. 276–277.

32 Mik, Eliza. 2017. "Smart Contracts: Terminology, Technical Limitations and Real World Complexity". *SSRN.* Available at: https://papers.ssrn.com/sol3/papers.cfm?abstract_id=3038406. p. 10.

33 Sklaroff, Jeremy M. 2018. "Smart Contracts and the Cost of Inflexibility". *University of Pennsylvania Law Review, Vol. 166*, p. 291.

34 Sklaroff, Jeremy M. 2018. "Smart Contracts and the Cost of Inflexibility". *University of Pennsylvania Law Review, Vol. 166*, p. 277.

35 Mik, Eliza. 2017. "Smart Contracts: Terminology, Technical Limitations and Real World Complexity". *SSRN*. Available at: https://papers.ssrn.com/sol3/papers.cfm?abstract_id=3038406. p. 12.

36 Mik, Eliza. 2017. "Smart Contracts: Terminology, Technical Limitations and Real World Complexity". *SSRN*. Available at: https://papers.ssrn.com/sol3/papers.cfm?abstract_id=3038406. p. 10.

37 Raskin, Max. 2017. "The Law and Legality of Smart Contracts". *1 Georgetown Law Technology Review 304*. Available at: https://papers.ssrn.com/sol3/papers.cfm?abstract_id=2959166, p. 327.

38 Mik, Eliza. 2017. "Smart Contracts: Terminology, Technical Limitations and Real World Complexity". *SSRN*. Available at: https://papers.ssrn.com/sol3/papers.cfm?abstract_id=3038406. p. 12.

39 Sklaroff, Jeremy M. 2018. "Smart Contracts and the Cost of Inflexibility". *University of Pennsylvania Law Review, Vol. 166*, pp. 281–282.

40 Mik, Eliza. 2017. "Smart Contracts: Terminology, Technical Limitations and Real World Complexity". *SSRN*. Available at: https://papers.ssrn.com/sol3/papers.cfm?abstract_id=3038406. p. 20.

41 Raskin, Max. 2017. "The Law and Legality of Smart Contracts". *1 Georgetown Law Technology Review 304*. Available at: https://papers.ssrn.com/sol3/papers.cfm?abstract_id=2959166, p. 326.

42 "Doctrine of Substantial Performance Law and Legal Definition". *USLegal*. Available at: https://definitions.uslegal.com/d/doctrine-of-substantial-performance/.

43 Raskin, Max. 2017. "The Law and Legality of Smart Contracts". *1 Georgetown Law Technology Review 304*. Available at: https://papers.ssrn.com/sol3/papers.cfm?abstract_id=2959166, p. 326.

44 Mik, Eliza. 2017. "Smart Contracts: Terminology, Technical Limitations and Real World Complexity". *SSRN*. Available at: https://papers.ssrn.com/sol3/papers.cfm?abstract_id=3038406. p. 12.

45 Mik, Eliza. 2017. "Smart Contracts: Terminology, Technical Limitations and Real World Complexity". *SSRN*. Available at: https://papers.ssrn.com/sol3/papers.cfm?abstract_id=3038406. p. 10.

46 Werbach, Kevin et al. 2017. "Contracts Ex Machina". *67 Duke Law Journal 313*. Available at: https://papers.ssrn.com/sol3/papers.cfm?abstract_id=2936294. p. 118, 123.

47 Werbach, Kevin et al. 2017. "Contracts Ex Machina". *67 Duke Law Journal 313*. Available at: https://papers.ssrn.com/sol3/papers.cfm?abstract_id=2936294. pp. 120–121.

48 Sklaroff, Jeremy M. 2018. "Smart Contracts and the Cost of Inflexibility". *University of Pennsylvania Law Review, Vol. 166*, p. 284.

49 Sklaroff, Jeremy M. 2018. "Smart Contracts and the Cost of Inflexibility". *University of Pennsylvania Law Review, Vol. 166*, p. 285.

50 Mik, Eliza. 2017. "Smart Contracts: Terminology, Technical Limitations and Real World Complexity". *SSRN*. Available at: https://papers.ssrn.com/sol3/papers.cfm?abstract_id=3038406. p. 12.

51 Sklaroff, Jeremy M. 2018. "Smart Contracts and the Cost of Inflexibility". *University of Pennsylvania Law Review, Vol. 166*, p. 285.

52 Tjong Tjin Tai, Eric. 2018. "Force Majeure and Excuses in Smart Contracts". *Tilburg Private Law Working Paper Series No. 10/2018. European Review of Private Law 2018/6,*

pp. 787–904. Available at: https://papers.ssrn.com/sol3/papers.cfm?abstract_id=3183637, p. 5.

53 Tjong Tjin Tai, Eric. 2018. "Force Majeure and Excuses in Smart Contracts". *Tilburg Private Law Working Paper Series No. 10/2018. European Review of Private Law 2018/6, p. 787–904*. Available at: https://papers.ssrn.com/sol3/papers.cfm?abstract_id=3183637, pp. 6–7.

54 Tjong Tjin Tai, Eric. 2018. "Force Majeure and Excuses in Smart Contracts". *Tilburg Private Law Working Paper Series No. 10/2018. European Review of Private Law 2018/6, p. 787–904*. Available at: https://papers.ssrn.com/sol3/papers.cfm?abstract_id=3183637, p. 12.

55 "Copyright – What is copyright?". *World Intellectual Property Organisation*. Available at: www.wipo.int/copyright/en/.

56 "Trade mark definition – A little bit of theory". *European Union Intellectual Property Office*. Available at: https://euipo.europa.eu/ohimportal/en/trade-mark-definition.

57 See Council Regulation (EU) No 6/2002 of 12 December 2001 on Community designs, OJ L 3, 5.1.2002, ppppp. 1–24, as amended, Art. 3(a).

58 "Design definition". *European Union Intellectual Property Office*. Available at: https://euipo.europa.eu/ohimportal/en/design-definition.

59 See Council Regulation (EU) No 6/2002 of 12 December 2001 on Community designs, OJ L 3, 5.1.2002, p. 1–24, as amended, Art. 4(1).

60 "What is a Trade Secret?" *World Intellectual Property Organisation*. Available at: www.wipo.int/sme/en/ip_business/trade_secrets/trade_secrets.htm.

61 See Directive (EU) 2016/943 of the European Parliament and of the Council of 8 June 2016 on the protection of undisclosed know-how and business information (trade secrets) against their unlawful acquisition, use and disclosure, OJ L 157, 15.6.2016, pp. 1–18, Art. 2(1)(a) to (c).

62 See Berne Convention for the Protection of Literary and Artistic Works (as amended on 28 September 1979), Art. 5(2).

63 Tresise, Annabel et al. 2018. "What Blockchain Can and Can't Do For Copyright". *28 Australian Intellectual Property Journal 144*. Available at: https://papers.ssrn.com/sol3/papers.cfm?abstract_id=3227381, p. 4.

64 Savelyev, Alexander. 2018. "Copyright in the Blockchain Era: Promises and Challenges". *Higher School of Economics Research Paper No. WP BRP 77/LAW/2017*. Available at: https://papers.ssrn.com/sol3/papers.cfm?abstract_id=3075246, p. 4.

65 Tresise, Annabel et al. 2018. "What Blockchain Can and Can't Do For Copyright". *28 Australian Intellectual Property Journal 144*. Available at: https://papers.ssrn.com/sol3/papers.cfm?abstract_id=3227381, p. 4.

66 Clark, Birgit. 2018. "Blockchain and IP Law: A Match made in Crypto Heaven?". *WIPO Magazine 1/2018*. Available at: www.wipo.int/wipo_magazine/en/2018/01/article_0005.html.

67 Tresise, Annabel et al. 2018. "What Blockchain Can and Can't Do For Copyright". *28 Australian Intellectual Property Journal 144*. Available at: https://papers.ssrn.com/sol3/papers.cfm?abstract_id=3227381, p. 4.

68 Savelyev, Alexander. 2018. "Copyright in the Blockchain Era: Promises and Challenges". *Higher School of Economics Research Paper No. WP BRP 77/LAW/2017*. Available at: https://papers.ssrn.com/sol3/papers.cfm?abstract_id=3075246, pp. 8–9.

69 Tresise, Annabel et al. 2018. "What Blockchain Can and Can't Do For Copyright". *28 Australian Intellectual Property Journal 144*. Available at: https://papers.ssrn.com/sol3/papers.cfm?abstract_id=3227381, p. 5.

70 Clark, Birgit. 2018. "Blockchain and IP Law: A Match made in Crypto Heaven?". *WIPO Magazine 1/2018*. Available at: www.wipo.int/wipo_magazine/en/2018/01/article_0005. html.

71 Savelyev, Alexander. 2018. "Copyright in the Blockchain Era: Promises and Challenges". *Higher School of Economics Research Paper No. WP BRP 77/LAW/2017*. Available at: https://papers.ssrn.com/sol3/papers.cfm?abstract_id=3075246, p. 11.

72 Tresise, Annabel et al. 2018. "What Blockchain Can and Can't Do For Copyright". *28 Australian Intellectual Property Journal 144*. Available at: https://papers.ssrn.com/sol3/papers.cfm?abstract_id=3227381, p. 9.

73 "Digital Rights Management". *Techopedia*. www.techopedia.com/definition/3986/digital-rights-management-drm.

74 Tresise, Annabel et al. 2018. "What Blockchain Can and Can't Do For Copyright". *28 Australian Intellectual Property Journal 144*. Available at: https://papers.ssrn.com/sol3/papers.cfm?abstract_id=3227381, p. 7.

75 Tresise, Annabel et al. 2018. "What Blockchain Can and Can't Do For Copyright". *28 Australian Intellectual Property Journal 144*. Available at: https://papers.ssrn.com/sol3/papers.cfm?abstract_id=3227381, p. 10.

76 Savelyev, Alexander. 2018. "Copyright in the Blockchain Era: Promises and Challenges". *Higher School of Economics Research Paper No. WP BRP 77/LAW/2017*. Available at: https://papers.ssrn.com/sol3/papers.cfm?abstract_id=3075246, p. 11.

77 "Mycelia – About". *Mycelia*. Available at: http://myceliaformusic.org/#about.

78 Gerard, David. "Imogen Heap: 'Tiny Human'. Total sales: $133.20". Available at: https://davidgerard.co.uk/blockchain/imogen-heap-tiny-human-total-sales-133-20/.

79 See, for instance, the European Union Intellectual Property Office's "eSearch plus", which grants access to the Office's public database. Available at: https://euipo.europa.eu/eSearch/#basic.

80 Clark, Birgit. 2018. "Blockchain and IP Law: A Match made in Crypto Heaven?". *WIPO Magazine 1/2018*. Available at: www.wipo.int/wipo_magazine/en/2018/01/article_0005.html.

81 See, for instance, Arts. 18 and 58(1)(a) of Regulation (EU) 2017/1001 of the European Parliament and of the Council of 14 June 2017 on the European Union trade mark, OJ L 154, 16.6.2017, pp. 1–99.

82 See, for instance, Art. 59(2) of Regulation (EU) 2017/1001 of the European Parliament and of the Council of 14 June 2017 on the European Union trade mark, OJ L 154, 16.6.2017, pp. 1–99.

83 Clark, Birgit. 2018. "Blockchain and IP Law: A Match made in Crypto Heaven?". *WIPO Magazine 1/2018*. Available at: www.wipo.int/wipo_magazine/en/2018/01/article_0005. html.

84 See, for instance, Arts. 4(1) and 5 of Council Regulation (EC) No 6/2002 of 12 December 2001 on Community designs, OJ L 3, 5.1.2002, pp. 1–24.

85 See, for instance, Arts. 4(1) and 6 of Council Regulation (EC) No 6/2002 of 12 December 2001 on Community designs, OJ L 3, 5.1.2002, pp. 1–24.

86 Clark, Birgit. 2018. "Blockchain and IP Law: A Match made in Crypto Heaven?". *WIPO Magazine 1/2018*. Available at: www.wipo.int/wipo_magazine/en/2018/01/article_0005. html.

87 Burstall, Ruth et al. 2017. "Blockchain, IP and the Fashion Industry". *Managing Intellectual Property*. www.managingip.com/Article/3667444/Blockchain-IP-and-the-fashion-industry.html.

88 Pun, Hubert et al. 2018. "Blockchain Adoption for Combating Deceptive Counterfeits". *Kenan Institute of Private Enterprise Research Paper No. 18-18*. Available at: https://papers.ssrn.com/sol3/papers.cfm?abstract_id=3223656, pp. 2–3.

89   See Directive (EU) 2016/943 of the European Parliament and of the Council of
      8 June 2016 on the protection of undisclosed know-how and business information
      (trade secrets) against their unlawful acquisition, use and disclosure, OJ L 157,
      15.6.2016, pp. 1–18, Art. 2(1)(a) to (c).

90   Mathias Avocats. 2017. "How can Blockchain and trade secrets support each other?".
      Mathias Avocats. Available at: www.avocats-mathias.com/droit-des-affaires/blockchain-
      trade-secrets.

91   Balbo, Alessio. 2018. "Can Blockchain be a 'reasonable step' to keep trade secrets safe?".
      Trust in IP. Available at: https://trustinip.com/can-blockchain-be-a-reasonable-step-to-
      keep-trade-secrets-safe/.

92   Balbo, Alessio. 2018. "Can Blockchain be a 'reasonable step' to keep trade secrets safe?".
      Trust in IP. Available at: https://trustinip.com/can-blockchain-be-a-reasonable-step-to-
      keep-trade-secrets-safe/.

93   Balbo, Alessio. 2018. "Can Blockchain be a 'reasonable step' to keep trade secrets safe?".
      Trust in IP. Available at: https://trustinip.com/can-blockchain-be-a-reasonable-step-to-
      keep-trade-secrets-safe/.

94   Regulation (EU) 2016/679 of the European Parliament and of the Council of
      27 April 2016 on the protection of natural persons with regard to the processing of
      personal data and on the free movement of such data, and repealing Directive 95/46/EC
      (General Data Protection Regulation), OJ L 119, 4.5.2016, pp. 1–88.

95   Toth, Anne. 2018. "Will GDPR block Blockchain?". *World Economic Forum.* Available
      at: www.weforum.org/agenda/2018/05/will-gdpr-block-blockchain/.

96   European Parliament resolution of 13 December 2018 on Blockchain: a forward-looking
      trade policy (2018/2085(INI)). Available at: www.europarl.europa.eu/sides/getDoc.do?
      type=TA&language=EN&reference=P8-TA-2018-0528.

97   Article 4(1), Regulation (EU) 2016/679 of the European Parliament and of the Council
      of 27 April 2016 on the protection of natural persons with regard to the processing of
      personal data and on the free movement of such data, and repealing Directive 95/46/EC
      (General Data Protection Regulation), OJ L 119, 4.5.2016, pp. 1–88.

98   Finck, Michèle. 2017. "Blockchains and Data Protection in the European Union". *Max
      Planck Institute for Innovation & Competition Research Paper No. 18-01.* Available at:
      https://papers.ssrn.com/sol3/papers.cfm?abstract_id=3080322, p. 10.

99   Salmensuu, Cagla. 2018. "The General Data Protection Regulation and Blockchains".
      Liikejuridiikka 1/2018. Available at: https://papers.ssrn.com/sol3/papers.cfm?abstrac
      t_id=3143992, p. 18.

100   Finck, Michèle. 2017. "Blockchains and Data Protection in the European Union". *Max
      Planck Institute for Innovation & Competition Research Paper No. 18-01.* Available at:
      https://papers.ssrn.com/sol3/papers.cfm?abstract_id=3080322, p. 10.

101   Finck, Michèle. 2017. "Blockchains and Data Protection in the European Union". *Max
      Planck Institute for Innovation & Competition Research Paper No. 18-01.* Available at:
      https://papers.ssrn.com/sol3/papers.cfm?abstract_id=3080322, p. 10.

102   The following quotes all refer to Recital 26 of Regulation (EU) 2016/679 of the European
      Parliament and of the Council of 27 April 2016 on the protection of natural persons
      with regard to the processing of personal data and on the free movement of such data,
      and repealing Directive 95/46/EC (General Data Protection Regulation), OJ L 119,
      4.5.2016, pp. 1–88.

103   Art. 4(5), Regulation (EU) 2016/679 of the European Parliament and of the Council of
      27 April 2016 on the protection of natural persons with regard to the processing of
      personal data and on the free movement of such data, and repealing Directive 95/46/EC
      (General Data Protection Regulation), OJ L 119, 4.5.2016, pp. 1–88.

104 Article 29 Working Party. 2014. "Opinion 05/2014 on Anonymisation Techniques (0829/ 14/EN, WP216)". Available at: https://ec.europa.eu/justice/article-29/documentation/opi nion-recommendation/files/2014/wp216_en.pdf.

105 European Data Protection Board. "About EDPB". Available at: https://edpb.europa.eu/ about-edpb/about-edpb_en.

106 Article 29 Working Party. 2014. "Opinion 05/2014 on Anonymisation Techniques (0829/ 14/EN, WP216)". Available at: https://ec.europa.eu/justice/article-29/documentation/opi nion-recommendation/files/2014/wp216_en.pdf, p. 3.

107 Article 29 Working Party. 2014. "Opinion 05/2014 on Anonymisation Techniques (0829/ 14/EN, WP216)". Available at: https://ec.europa.eu/justice/article-29/documentation/opi nion-recommendation/files/2014/wp216_en.pdf, p. 20.

108 Article 29 Working Party. 2014. "Opinion 05/2014 on Anonymisation Techniques (0829/ 14/EN, WP216)". Available at: https://ec.europa.eu/justice/article-29/documentation/opi nion-recommendation/files/2014/wp216_en.pdf, p. 20.

109 Article 29 Working Party. 2014. "Opinion 05/2014 on Anonymisation Techniques (0829/ 14/EN, WP216)". https://ec.europa.eu/justice/article-29/documentation/opinion- recommendation/files/2014/wp216_en.pdf, p. 20. Available at:

110 Finck, Michèle. 2017. "Blockchains and Data Protection in the European Union". *Max Planck Institute for Innovation & Competition Research Paper No. 18-01*. Available at: https://papers.ssrn.com/sol3/papers.cfm?abstract_id=3080322, p. 11.

111 Salmensuu, Cagla. 2018. "The General Data Protection Regulation and Blockchains". *Liikejuridiikka 1/2018*. Available at: https://papers.ssrn.com/sol3/papers.cfm?abstrac t_id=3143992, pp. 18–19.

112 Salmensuu, Cagla. 2018. "The General Data Protection Regulation and Blockchains". *Liikejuridiikka 1/2018*. Available at: https://papers.ssrn.com/sol3/papers.cfm?abstrac t_id=3143992, p. 21.

113 Finck, Michèle. 2017. "Blockchains and Data Protection in the European Union". *Max Planck Institute for Innovation & Competition Research Paper No. 18-01*. Available at: https://papers.ssrn.com/sol3/papers.cfm?abstract_id=3080322, p. 13.

114 Finck, Michèle. 2017. "Blockchains and Data Protection in the European Union". *Max Planck Institute for Innovation & Competition Research Paper No. 18-01*. Available at: https://papers.ssrn.com/sol3/papers.cfm?abstract_id=3080322, p. 13.

115 See Judgment of the Court of Justice of the European Union (Second Chamber) of 19 October 2016. Available at: http://curia.europa.eu/juris/document/document.jsf?doc id=184668&doclang=EN, paragraph 49 (for example).

116 See Salmensuu, Cagla. 2018. "The General Data Protection Regulation and Blockchains". *Liikejuridiikka 1/2018*. Available at: https://papers.ssrn.com/sol3/papers.cfm?abstrac t_id=3143992, p. 17. Moreover, this argument is in line with Recital 30 of the GDPR, which clearly states that *"[n]atural persons may be associated with online identifiers provided by their devices, applications, tools and protocols, such as internet protocol addresses, cookie identifiers or other identifiers such as radio frequency identification tags. This may leave traces which, in particular when combined with unique identifiers and other information received by the servers, may be used to create profiles of the natural persons and identify them"*.

117 Finck, Michèle. 2017. "Blockchains and Data Protection in the European Union". *Max Planck Institute for Innovation & Competition Research Paper No. 18-01*. Available at: https://papers.ssrn.com/sol3/papers.cfm?abstract_id=3080322, p. 11.

118 Van Humbeeck, Andries. 2017. "The Blockchain-GDPR Paradox". *The Ledger*. Available at: https://medium.com/wearetheledger/the-blockchain-gdpr-paradox-fc51e663d047.

119 CNIL. 2018. "Solutions for a responsible use of the blockchain in the context of personal data". *CNIL*. Available at: www.cnil.fr/sites/default/files/atoms/files/blockchain.pdf, pp. 6–7.

120 CNIL. 2018. "Solutions for a responsible use of the blockchain in the context of personal data". *CNIL*. Available at: www.cnil.fr/sites/default/files/atoms/files/blockchain.pdf, p. 6.

121 In a similar vein, see European Parliament resolution of 13 December 2018 on Blockchain: a forward-looking trade policy (2018/2085(INI)). Available at: www.europarl.europa.eu/sides/getDoc.do?type=TA&language=EN&reference=P8-TA-2018-0528, paragraph 21.

122 Finck, Michèle. 2017. "Blockchains and Data Protection in the European Union". *Max Planck Institute for Innovation & Competition Research Paper No. 18-01*. Available at: https://papers.ssrn.com/sol3/papers.cfm?abstract_id=3080322, p. 15.

123 Art. 3, Regulation (EU) 2016/679 of the European Parliament and of the Council of 27 April 2016 on the protection of natural persons with regard to the processing of personal data and on the free movement of such data, and repealing Directive 95/46/EC (General Data Protection Regulation), OJ L 119, 4.5.2016, p. 1–88.

124 Art. 5(1)(a), Regulation (EU) 2016/679 of the European Parliament and of the Council of 27 April 2016 on the protection of natural persons with regard to the processing of personal data and on the free movement of such data, and repealing Directive 95/46/EC (General Data Protection Regulation), OJ L 119, 4.5.2016, p. 1–88.

125 Art. 6, Regulation (EU) 2016/679 of the European Parliament and of the Council of 27 April 2016 on the protection of natural persons with regard to the processing of personal data and on the free movement of such data, and repealing Directive 95/46/EC (General Data Protection Regulation), OJ L 119, 4.5.2016, p. 1–88.

126 Arts. 9 and 10, Regulation (EU) 2016/679 of the European Parliament and of the Council of 27 April 2016 on the protection of natural persons with regard to the processing of personal data and on the free movement of such data, and repealing Directive 95/46/EC (General Data Protection Regulation), OJ L 119, 4.5.2016, p. 1–88.

127 Hungarian National Authority for Data Protection and Freedom of Information. "*The Opinion of the Hungarian National Authority for Data Protection and Freedom of Information on Blockchain Technology in the Context of Data Protection*". Available at: www.naih.hu/files/Blockchain-Opinion-2018-01-29.pdf, Section 3.

128 Art. 5(1)(a), Regulation (EU) 2016/679 of the European Parliament and of the Council of 27 April 2016 on the protection of natural persons with regard to the processing of personal data and on the free movement of such data, and repealing Directive 95/46/EC (General Data Protection Regulation), OJ L 119, 4.5.2016, p. 1–88.

129 Art. 5(1)(a), Regulation (EU) 2016/679 of the European Parliament and of the Council of 27 April 2016 on the protection of natural persons with regard to the processing of personal data and on the free movement of such data, and repealing Directive 95/46/EC (General Data Protection Regulation), OJ L 119, 4.5.2016, p. 1–88.

130 Recital 39, Regulation (EU) 2016/679 of the European Parliament and of the Council of 27 April 2016 on the protection of natural persons with regard to the processing of personal data and on the free movement of such data, and repealing Directive 95/46/EC (General Data Protection Regulation), OJ L 119, 4.5.2016, p. 1–88.

131 Art. 12(1), Regulation (EU) 2016/679 of the European Parliament and of the Council of 27 April 2016 on the protection of natural persons with regard to the processing of personal data and on the free movement of such data, and repealing Directive 95/46/EC (General Data Protection Regulation), OJ L 119, 4.5.2016, p. 1–88.

132 Arts. 13(1)(e) and 14(1)(e), Regulation (EU) 2016/679 of the European Parliament and of the Council of 27 April 2016 on the protection of natural persons with regard to the

processing of personal data and on the free movement of such data, and repealing Directive 95/46/EC (General Data Protection Regulation), OJ L 119, 4.5.2016, p. 1–88.

133 Arts. 13(2)(a) and 14(2)(a), Regulation (EU) 2016/679 of the European Parliament and of the Council of 27 April 2016 on the protection of natural persons with regard to the processing of personal data and on the free movement of such data, and repealing Directive 95/46/EC (General Data Protection Regulation), OJ L 119, 4.5.2016, p. 1–88.

134 Article 29 Working Party. 2018. "Guidelines on transparency under Regulation 2016/679 (wp260rev.01)". Available at: https://ec.europa.eu/newsroom/article29/item-detail.cfm?item_id=622227, pp. 37–38.

135 Art. 5(1)(b), Regulation (EU) 2016/679 of the European Parliament and of the Council of 27 April 2016 on the protection of natural persons with regard to the processing of personal data and on the free movement of such data, and repealing Directive 95/46/EC (General Data Protection Regulation), OJ L 119, 4.5.2016, p. 1–88.

136 Art. 6(4), Regulation (EU) 2016/679 of the European Parliament and of the Council of 27 April 2016 on the protection of natural persons with regard to the processing of personal data and on the free movement of such data, and repealing Directive 95/46/EC (General Data Protection Regulation), OJ L 119, 4.5.2016, p. 1–88.

137 Arts. 5(1)(b) and 89, Regulation (EU) 2016/679 of the European Parliament and of the Council of 27 April 2016 on the protection of natural persons with regard to the processing of personal data and on the free movement of such data, and repealing Directive 95/46/EC (General Data Protection Regulation), OJ L 119, 4.5.2016, p. 1–88.

138 Art. 5(1)(c), Regulation (EU) 2016/679 of the European Parliament and of the Council of 27 April 2016 on the protection of natural persons with regard to the processing of personal data and on the free movement of such data, and repealing Directive 95/46/EC (General Data Protection Regulation), OJ L 119, 4.5.2016, p. 1–88.

139 European Parliament resolution of 13 December 2018 on Blockchain: a forward-looking trade policy (2018/2085(INI)). Available at: www.europarl.europa.eu/sides/getDoc.do?type=TA&language=EN&reference=P8-TA-2018-0528, paragraph 25.

140 CNIL. 2018. "Solutions for a responsible use of the blockchain in the context of personal data". CNIL. Available at: www.cnil.fr/sites/default/files/atoms/files/blockchain.pdf, p. 5.

141 Finck, Michèle. 2017. "Blockchains and Data Protection in the European Union". Max Planck Institute for Innovation & Competition Research Paper No. 18-01. Available at: https://papers.ssrn.com/sol3/papers.cfm?abstract_id=3080322, pp. 20–21.

142 Art. 5(1)(e), Regulation (EU) 2016/679 of the European Parliament and of the Council of 27 April 2016 on the protection of natural persons with regard to the processing of personal data and on the free movement of such data, and repealing Directive 95/46/EC (General Data Protection Regulation), OJ L 119, 4.5.2016, p. 1–88.

143 Recital 39, Regulation (EU) 2016/679 of the European Parliament and of the Council of 27 April 2016 on the protection of natural persons with regard to the processing of personal data and on the free movement of such data, and repealing Directive 95/46/EC (General Data Protection Regulation), OJ L 119, 4.5.2016, p. 1–88.

144 CNIL. 2018. "Solutions for a responsible use of the blockchain in the context of personal data". CNIL. Available at: www.cnil.fr/sites/default/files/atoms/files/blockchain.pdf, p. 6.

145 Salmensuu, Cagla. 2018. "The General Data Protection Regulation and Blockchains". Liikejuridiikka 1/2018. Available at: https://papers.ssrn.com/sol3/papers.cfm?abstract_id=3143992, pp. 23–24.

146 CNIL. 2018. "Solutions for a responsible use of the blockchain in the context of personal data". CNIL. Available at: www.cnil.fr/sites/default/files/atoms/files/blockchain.pdf, p. 8.

147 Herian, Robert. 2018. "Regulating Disruption: Blockchain, GDPR, and Questions of Data Sovereignty". Journal of Internet Law, 22(2) 1 and 8–16. Available at: http://oro.open.ac.

uk/56264/, p. 13: "*Since throwing away your encryption keys is not the same as 'erasure of data', GDPR prohibits us from storing personal data on a blockchain level*".

148 Finck, Michèle. 2017. "Blockchains and Data Protection in the European Union". *Max Planck Institute for Innovation & Competition Research Paper No. 18-01*. Available at: https://papers.ssrn.com/sol3/papers.cfm?abstract_id=3080322, p. 21.

149 CNIL. 2018. "Solutions for a responsible use of the blockchain in the context of personal data". *CNIL*. Available at: www.cnil.fr/sites/default/files/atoms/files/blockchain.pdf, p. 6.

150 Art. 5(1)(d), Regulation (EU) 2016/679 of the European Parliament and of the Council of 27 April 2016 on the protection of natural persons with regard to the processing of personal data and on the free movement of such data, and repealing Directive 95/46/EC (General Data Protection Regulation), OJ L 119, 4.5.2016, p. 1–88.

151 Finck, Michèle. 2017. "Blockchains and Data Protection in the European Union". *Max Planck Institute for Innovation & Competition Research Paper No. 18-01*. Available at: https://papers.ssrn.com/sol3/papers.cfm?abstract_id=3080322, p. 22.

152 Art. 16, Regulation (EU) 2016/679 of the European Parliament and of the Council of 27 April 2016 on the protection of natural persons with regard to the processing of personal data and on the free movement of such data, and repealing Directive 95/46/EC (General Data Protection Regulation), OJ L 119, 4.5.2016, p. 1–88.

153 Finck, Michèle. 2017. "Blockchains and Data Protection in the European Union". *Max Planck Institute for Innovation & Competition Research Paper No. 18-01*. Available at: https://papers.ssrn.com/sol3/papers.cfm?abstract_id=3080322, p. 22.

154 Art. 5(1)(f), Regulation (EU) 2016/679 of the European Parliament and of the Council of 27 April 2016 on the protection of natural persons with regard to the processing of personal data and on the free movement of such data, and repealing Directive 95/46/EC (General Data Protection Regulation), OJ L 119, 4.5.2016, p. 1–88.

155 Art. 32(1), Regulation (EU) 2016/679 of the European Parliament and of the Council of 27 April 2016 on the protection of natural persons with regard to the processing of personal data and on the free movement of such data, and repealing Directive 95/46/EC (General Data Protection Regulation), OJ L 119, 4.5.2016, p. 1–88.

156 Art. 32(1), Regulation (EU) 2016/679 of the European Parliament and of the Council of 27 April 2016 on the protection of natural persons with regard to the processing of personal data and on the free movement of such data, and repealing Directive 95/46/EC (General Data Protection Regulation), OJ L 119, 4.5.2016, p. 1–88.

157 Art. 32(1)(a), Regulation (EU) 2016/679 of the European Parliament and of the Council of 27 April 2016 on the protection of natural persons with regard to the processing of personal data and on the free movement of such data, and repealing Directive 95/46/EC (General Data Protection Regulation), OJ L 119, 4.5.2016, p. 1–88.

158 Art. 5(2), Regulation (EU) 2016/679 of the European Parliament and of the Council of 27 April 2016 on the protection of natural persons with regard to the processing of personal data and on the free movement of such data, and repealing Directive 95/46/EC (General Data Protection Regulation), OJ L 119, 4.5.2016, p. 1–88.

159 Art. 30, Regulation (EU) 2016/679 of the European Parliament and of the Council of 27 April 2016 on the protection of natural persons with regard to the processing of personal data and on the free movement of such data, and repealing Directive 95/46/EC (General Data Protection Regulation), OJ L 119, 4.5.2016, p. 1–88.

160 Art. 4(7), Regulation (EU) 2016/679 of the European Parliament and of the Council of 27 April 2016 on the protection of natural persons with regard to the processing of personal data and on the free movement of such data, and repealing Directive 95/46/EC (General Data Protection Regulation), OJ L 119, 4.5.2016, p. 1–88.

161   Art. 4(8), Regulation (EU) 2016/679 of the European Parliament and of the Council of 27 April 2016 on the protection of natural persons with regard to the processing of personal data and on the free movement of such data, and repealing Directive 95/46/EC (General Data Protection Regulation), OJ L 119, 4.5.2016, p. 1–88.

162   Czarnecki, Jacek. 2017. "Blockchains and Personal Data Protection Regulations Explained". *Coindesk*. Available at: www.coindesk.com/blockchains-personal-data-protection-regulations-explained.

163   Salmensuu, Cagla. 2018. "The General Data Protection Regulation and Blockchains". *Liikejuridiikka 1/2018*. Available at: https://papers.ssrn.com/sol3/papers.cfm?abstract_id=3143992, p. 11.

164   Finck, Michèle. 2017. "Blockchains and Data Protection in the European Union". *Max Planck Institute for Innovation & Competition Research Paper No. 18-01*. Available at: https://papers.ssrn.com/sol3/papers.cfm?abstract_id=3080322, p. 16.

165   Hungarian National Authority for Data Protection and Freedom of Information. "*The Opinion of the Hungarian National Authority for Data Protection and Freedom of Information on Blockchain Technology in the Context of Data Protection*". Available at: https://www.naih.hu/files/Blockchain-Opinion-2018-01-29.pdf, Section 3.

166   Art. 2(2)(c), Regulation (EU) 2016/679 of the European Parliament and of the Council of 27 April 2016 on the protection of natural persons with regard to the processing of personal data and on the free movement of such data, and repealing Directive 95/46/EC (General Data Protection Regulation), OJ L 119, 4.5.2016, p. 1–88.

167   CNIL. 2018. "Solutions for a responsible use of the blockchain in the context of personal data". *CNIL*. Available at: www.cnil.fr/sites/default/files/atoms/files/blockchain.pdf, p. 6.

168   Finck, Michèle. 2017. "Blockchains and Data Protection in the European Union". *Max Planck Institute for Innovation & Competition Research Paper No. 18-01*. Available at: https://papers.ssrn.com/sol3/papers.cfm?abstract_id=3080322, pp. 17–18.

169   Salmensuu, Cagla. 2018. "The General Data Protection Regulation and Blockchains". *Liikejuridiika 1/2018*. Available at: https://papers.ssrn.com/sol3/papers.cfm?abstract_id=3143992, p. 12.

170   See, e.g., Salmensuu, Cagla. 2018. "The General Data Protection Regulation and Blockchains". *Liikejuridiika 1/2018*. Available at: https://papers.ssrn.com/sol3/papers.cfm?abstract_id=3143992, p. 12, and Finck, Michèle. 2017. "Blockchains and Data Protection in the European Union". *Max Planck Institute for Innovation & Competition Research Paper No. 18-01*. Available at: https://papers.ssrn.com/sol3/papers.cfm?abstract_id=3080322, p. 18.

171   CNIL. 2018. "Solutions for a responsible use of the blockchain in the context of personal data". *CNIL*. Available at: www.cnil.fr/sites/default/files/atoms/files/blockchain.pdf, pp. 5–6.

172   CNIL. 2018. "Solutions for a responsible use of the blockchain in the context of personal data". *CNIL*. Available at: www.cnil.fr/sites/default/files/atoms/files/blockchain.pdf, p. 6.

173   Art. 44, Regulation (EU) 2016/679 of the European Parliament and of the Council of 27 April 2016 on the protection of natural persons with regard to the processing of personal data and on the free movement of such data, and repealing Directive 95/46/EC (General Data Protection Regulation), OJ L 119, 4.5.2016, p. 1–88.

174   Finck, Michèle. 2017. "Blockchains and Data Protection in the European Union". *Max Planck Institute for Innovation & Competition Research Paper No. 18-01*. Available at: https://papers.ssrn.com/sol3/papers.cfm?abstract_id=3080322, p. 19.

175   Art. 45, Regulation (EU) 2016/679 of the European Parliament and of the Council of 27 April 2016 on the protection of natural persons with regard to the processing of

personal data and on the free movement of such data, and repealing Directive 95/46/EC (General Data Protection Regulation), OJ L 119, 4.5.2016, p. 1–88.

176　A full list of the countries which have received such decisions (excluding the more recent Japan) is available at: https://ec.europa.eu/info/law/law-topic/data-protection/ data-transfers-outside-eu/adequacy-protection-personal-data-non-eu-countries_en.

177　Art. 46, Regulation (EU) 2016/679 of the European Parliament and of the Council of 27 April 2016 on the protection of natural persons with regard to the processing of personal data and on the free movement of such data, and repealing Directive 95/46/EC (General Data Protection Regulation), OJ L 119, 4.5.2016, p. 1–88.

178　Art. 49, Regulation (EU) 2016/679 of the European Parliament and of the Council of 27 April 2016 on the protection of natural persons with regard to the processing of personal data and on the free movement of such data, and repealing Directive 95/46/EC (General Data Protection Regulation), OJ L 119, 4.5.2016, p. 1–88.

179　Art. 49(1)(a), Regulation (EU) 2016/679 of the European Parliament and of the Council of 27 April 2016 on the protection of natural persons with regard to the processing of personal data and on the free movement of such data, and repealing Directive 95/46/EC (General Data Protection Regulation), OJ L 119, 4.5.2016, p. 1–88.

180　Finck, Michèle. 2017. "Blockchains and Data Protection in the European Union". *Max Planck Institute for Innovation & Competition Research Paper No. 18-01*. Available at: https://papers.ssrn.com/sol3/papers.cfm?abstract_id=3080322, p. 19.

181　Art. 4(11), Regulation (EU) 2016/679 of the European Parliament and of the Council of 27 April 2016 on the protection of natural persons with regard to the processing of personal data and on the free movement of such data, and repealing Directive 95/46/EC (General Data Protection Regulation), OJ L 119, 4.5.2016, p. 1–88.

182　Art. 7(2), Regulation (EU) 2016/679 of the European Parliament and of the Council of 27 April 2016 on the protection of natural persons with regard to the processing of personal data and on the free movement of such data, and repealing Directive 95/46/EC (General Data Protection Regulation), OJ L 119, 4.5.2016, p. 1–88.

183　Art. 7(4), Regulation (EU) 2016/679 of the European Parliament and of the Council of 27 April 2016 on the protection of natural persons with regard to the processing of personal data and on the free movement of such data, and repealing Directive 95/46/EC (General Data Protection Regulation), OJ L 119, 4.5.2016, p. 1–88.

184　Faber, Stéphanie. 2019. "Does the GDPR Allow for the Use of Consent for the International Transfer of Data?". *Squire Patton Boggs*. Available at: www.securityprivacybytes.com/2019/ 01/does-the-gdpr-allow-for-the-use-of-consent-for-the-international-transfer-of-data/.

185　Art. 15, Regulation (EU) 2016/679 of the European Parliament and of the Council of 27 April 2016 on the protection of natural persons with regard to the processing of personal data and on the free movement of such data, and repealing Directive 95/46/EC (General Data Protection Regulation), OJ L 119, 4.5.2016, p. 1–88.

186　Art. 16, Regulation (EU) 2016/679 of the European Parliament and of the Council of 27 April 2016 on the protection of natural persons with regard to the processing of personal data and on the free movement of such data, and repealing Directive 95/46/EC (General Data Protection Regulation), OJ L 119, 4.5.2016, p. 1–88.

187　Art. 17, Regulation (EU) 2016/679 of the European Parliament and of the Council of 27 April 2016 on the protection of natural persons with regard to the processing of personal data and on the free movement of such data, and repealing Directive 95/46/EC (General Data Protection Regulation), OJ L 119, 4.5.2016, p. 1–88.

188　Art. 20, Regulation (EU) 2016/679 of the European Parliament and of the Council of 27 April 2016 on the protection of natural persons with regard to the processing of personal data and on the free movement of such data, and repealing Directive 95/46/EC (General Data Protection Regulation), OJ L 119, 4.5.2016, p. 1–88.

189 Arts. 12(2) and (3), Regulation (EU) 2016/679 of the European Parliament and of the Council of 27 April 2016 on the protection of natural persons with regard to the processing of personal data and on the free movement of such data, and repealing Directive 95/46/EC (General Data Protection Regulation), OJ L 119, 4.5.2016, p. 1–88.

190 Art. 12(4), Regulation (EU) 2016/679 of the European Parliament and of the Council of 27 April 2016 on the protection of natural persons with regard to the processing of personal data and on the free movement of such data, and repealing Directive 95/46/EC (General Data Protection Regulation), OJ L 119, 4.5.2016, p. 1–88.

191 CNIL. 2018. "Solutions for a responsible use of the blockchain in the context of personal data". *CNIL*. Available at: https://www.cnil.fr/sites/default/files/atoms/files/blockchain.pdf, p. 8.

192 Arts. 12(1), 13, 14 and 15(1), Regulation (EU) 2016/679 of the European Parliament and of the Council of 27 April 2016 on the protection of natural persons with regard to the processing of personal data and on the free movement of such data, and repealing Directive 95/46/EC (General Data Protection Regulation), OJ L 119, 4.5.2016, p. 1–88.

193 Lundqvist, Bjorn. "Portability in Datasets under Intellectual Property, Competition Law, and Blockchain". *Faculty of Law, Stockholm University Research Paper No. 62*. Available at: https://papers.ssrn.com/sol3/papers.cfm?abstract_id=3278580.

194 Maxwell, Winston et al. 2017. "A guide to blockchain and data protection". *Hogan Lovells*. Available at: www.hlengage.com/_uploads/downloads/5425GuidetoblockchainV9FORWEB.pdf, p. 15.

195 CNIL. 2018. "Solutions for a responsible use of the blockchain in the context of personal data". *CNIL*. Available at: www.cnil.fr/sites/default/files/atoms/files/blockchain.pdf, pp. 8–9.

196 CNIL. 2018. "Solutions for a responsible use of the blockchain in the context of personal data". *CNIL*. Available at: www.cnil.fr/sites/default/files/atoms/files/blockchain.pdf, p. 9.

197 Art. 18(2), Regulation (EU) 2016/679 of the European Parliament and of the Council of 27 April 2016 on the protection of natural persons with regard to the processing of personal data and on the free movement of such data, and repealing Directive 95/46/EC (General Data Protection Regulation), OJ L 119, 4.5.2016, p. 1–88.

198 CNIL. 2018. "Solutions for a responsible use of the blockchain in the context of personal data". *CNIL*. Available at: www.cnil.fr/sites/default/files/atoms/files/blockchain.pdf, p. 9.

199 Art. 22(1), Regulation (EU) 2016/679 of the European Parliament and of the Council of 27 April 2016 on the protection of natural persons with regard to the processing of personal data and on the free movement of such data, and repealing Directive 95/46/EC (General Data Protection Regulation), OJ L 119, 4.5.2016, p. 1–88.

200 CNIL. 2018. "Solutions for a responsible use of the blockchain in the context of personal data". *CNIL*. Available at: www.cnil.fr/sites/default/files/atoms/files/blockchain.pdf, p. 9.

201 Arts. 13(2)(f) and 14(2)(g), Regulation (EU) 2016/679 of the European Parliament and of the Council of 27 April 2016 on the protection of natural persons with regard to the processing of personal data and on the free movement of such data, and repealing Directive 95/46/EC (General Data Protection Regulation), OJ L 119, 4.5.2016, p. 1–88.

202 European Parliament resolution of 13 December 2018 on Blockchain: a forward-looking trade policy (2018/2085(INI)). Available at: www.europarl.europa.eu/sides/getDoc.do?type=TA&language=EN&reference=P8-TA-2018-0528, paragraph 22.

203 Finck, Michèle. 2017. "Blockchains and Data Protection in the European Union". *Max Planck Institute for Innovation & Competition Research Paper No. 18-01*. Available at: https://papers.ssrn.com/sol3/papers.cfm?abstract_id=3080322, p. 19.

204 Art. 25(1), Regulation (EU) 2016/679 of the European Parliament and of the Council of 27 April 2016 on the protection of natural persons with regard to the processing of personal data and on the free movement of such data, and repealing Directive 95/46/EC (General Data Protection Regulation), OJ L 119, 4.5.2016, p. 1–88.

205 Recital 78, Regulation (EU) 2016/679 of the European Parliament and of the Council of 27 April 2016 on the protection of natural persons with regard to the processing of personal data and on the free movement of such data, and repealing Directive 95/46/EC (General Data Protection Regulation), OJ L 119, 4.5.2016, p. 1–88.

206 European Data Protection Supervisor. 2018. "Opinion 5/2018 – Preliminary Opinion on privacy by design". Available at: https://edps.europa.eu/sites/edp/files/publication/18-05-31_preliminary_opinion_on_privacy_by_design_en_0.pdf, pp. 6–7.

207 Finck, Michèle. 2017. "Blockchains and Data Protection in the European Union". *Max Planck Institute for Innovation & Competition Research Paper No. 18-01.* Available at: https://papers.ssrn.com/sol3/papers.cfm?abstract_id=3080322, p. 27.

208 CNIL. 2018. "Solutions for a responsible use of the blockchain in the context of personal data". *CNIL.* Available at: www.cnil.fr/sites/default/files/atoms/files/blockchain.pdf, p. 7.

209 Article 29 Working Party. 2017. "Guidelines on Data Protection Impact Assessment (DPIA) (wp248rev.01)". Available at: https://ec.europa.eu/newsroom/article29/item-detail.cfm?item_id=611236, p. 8.

210 Article 29 Working Party. 2017. "Guidelines on Data Protection Impact Assessment (DPIA) (wp248rev.01)". Available at: https://ec.europa.eu/newsroom/article29/item-detail.cfm?item_id=611236, p. 14.

211 Article 29 Working Party. 2017. "Guidelines on Data Protection Impact Assessment (DPIA) (wp248rev.01)". Available at: https://ec.europa.eu/newsroom/article29/item-detail.cfm?item_id=611236, p. 15.

212 Art. 35, Regulation (EU) 2016/679 of the European Parliament and of the Council of 27 April 2016 on the protection of natural persons with regard to the processing of personal data and on the free movement of such data, and repealing Directive 95/46/EC (General Data Protection Regulation), OJ L 119, 4.5.2016, p. 1–88.

213 Recital 84 and Art. 36, Regulation (EU) 2016/679 of the European Parliament and of the Council of 27 April 2016 on the protection of natural persons with regard to the processing of personal data and on the free movement of such data, and repealing Directive 95/46/EC (General Data Protection Regulation), OJ L 119, 4.5.2016, p. 1–88.

214 Article 29 Working Party. 2017. "Guidelines on Data Protection Impact Assessment (DPIA) (wp248rev.01)". Available at: https://ec.europa.eu/newsroom/article29/item-detail.cfm?item_id=611236, p. 19.

215 Abbasi, Ahmed et al. 2018. "Make 'Fairness by Design' Part of Machine Learning". *Harvard Business Review.* Available at: https://hbr.org/2018/08/make-fairness-by-design-part-of-machine-learning.

216 Maestre, Roberto et al. 2018. "Reinforcement Learning for Fair Dynamic Pricing". *Cornell University (arXiv:1803.09967v1 [cs.LG].* Available at: https://arxiv.org/abs/1803.09967, p. 2.

217 Abbasi, Ahmed et al. 2018. "Make 'Fairness by Design' Part of Machine Learning". *Harvard Business Review.* Available at: https://hbr.org/2018/08/make-fairness-by-design-part-of-machine-learning.

218 Balboni, Paolo. 2018. "Cambridge Analytica and the Concept of Fairness by Design". Available at: www.paolobalboni.eu/index.php/2018/07/16/cambridge-analytica-and-the-concept-of-fairness-by-design/.

219   Balboni, Paolo. 2018. "Cambridge Analytica and the Concept of Fairness by Design". Available at: www.paolobalboni.eu/index.php/2018/07/16/cambridge-analytica-and-the-concept-of-fairness-by-design/.

220   Zyskind, Guy et al. 2015. "Decentralizing Privacy: Using Blockchain to Protect Personal Data". *2015 IEEE CS Security and Privacy Workshops*. Available at: https://ieeexplore. ieee.org/stamp/stamp.jsp?tp=&arnumber=7163223, p. 181.

221   Zyskind, Guy et al. 2015. "Decentralizing Privacy: Using Blockchain to Protect Personal Data". *2015 IEEE CS Security and Privacy Workshops*. Available at: https://ieeexplore. ieee.org/stamp/stamp.jsp?tp=&arnumber=7163223, p. 183.

222   Zyskind, Guy et al. 2015. "Decentralizing Privacy: Using Blockchain to Protect Personal Data". *2015 IEEE CS Security and Privacy Workshops*. Available at: https://ieeexplore. ieee.org/stamp/stamp.jsp?tp=&arnumber=7163223, p. 184.

BIBLIOGRAPHY

Abbasi, Ahmed et al. 2018. "Make "Fairness by Design" Part of Machine Learning". *Harvard Business Review*. Available at: https://hbr.org/2018/08/make-fairness-by-design-part-of-machine-learning.

"Adequacy of the Protection of Personal Data in non-EU Countries". *European Commission*. Available at: https://ec.europa.eu/info/law/law-topic/data-protection/data-transfers-outside-eu/adequacy-protection-personal-data-non-eu-countries_en.

Article 29 Working Party. 2014. "Opinion 05/2014 on Anonymisation Techniques (0829/14/EN, WP216)". Available at: https://ec.europa.eu/justice/article-29/documentation/opinion-recommendation/files/2014/wp216_en.pdf.

Article 29 Working Party. 2017. "Guidelines on Data Protection Impact Assessment (DPIA) (wp248rev.01)". Available at: https://ec.europa.eu/newsroom/article29/item-detail.cfm?item_id=611236.

Article 29 Working Party. 2018. "Guidelines on Transparency under Regulation 2016/679 (wp260rev.01)". Available at: https://ec.europa.eu/newsroom/article29/item-detail.cfm?item_id=622227.

Balbo, Alessio. 2018. "Can Blockchain Be a 'Reasonable Step' to Keep Trade Secrets Safe?" *Trust in IP*. Available at: https://trustinip.com/can-blockchain-be-a-reasonable-step-to-keep-trade-secrets-safe/.

Balboni, Paolo. 2018. "Cambridge Analytica and the Concept of Fairness by Design". Available at: www.paolobalboni.eu/index.php/2018/07/16/cambridge-analytica-and-the-concept-of-fairness-by-design/.

"Bitcoin Price (BTC)". *Coindesk*. Available at: www.coindesk.com/price/bitcoin.

Burstall, Ruth et al. 2017. "Blockchain, IP and the Fashion Industry". *Managing Intellectual Property*. www.managingip.com/Article/3667444/Blockchain-IP-and-the-fashion-industry.html.

Busch, Christoph. 2018. "Does the Amazon Dash Button Violate EU Consumer Law? Balancing Consumer Protection and Technological Innovation in the Internet of Things". *7 Journal of European Consumer and Market Law* 78–80. Available at: https://papers.ssrn.com/sol3/papers.cfm?abstract_id=3170985.

Clark, Birgit. 2018. "Blockchain and IP Law: A Match Made in Crypto Heaven?". *WIPO Magazine*. Available at: www.wipo.int/wipo_magazine/en/2018/01/article_0005.html.

CNIL. 2018. "Solutions for a Responsible Use of the Blockchain in the Context of Personal Data". *CNIL*. Available at: www.cnil.fr/sites/default/files/atoms/files/blockchain.pdf.

"Copyright– What Is Copyright?" *World Intellectual Property Organisation*. Available at: www.wipo.int/copyright/en/.

Cunningham, Lawrence A. 2006. "Language, Deals and Standards: The Future of XML Contracts". *Washington University Law Review*, 84, 313–374.

Czarnecki, Jacek. 2017. "Blockchains and Personal Data Protection Regulations Explained". *Coindesk*. Available at: www.coindesk.com/blockchains-personal-data-protection-regulations-explained.

Del Castillo, Michael. 2019. "Blockchain's Moveable Feast: How The Tech Is Changing The Way We Eat". *Forbes*. Available at: www.forbes.com/sites/michaeldelcastillo/2019/01/08/block chains-moveable-feast-how-the-tech-is-changing-the-way-we-eat-2/#41469cec17f3.

Denvir, Catrina et al. 2018. "A New Beginning or A Hastening of the End? Sustaining the Ideological Evolution of Law in the Age of Artificial Intelligence". *SSRN*. Available at: https://papers.ssrn.com/sol3/papers.cfm?abstract_id=3270728.

"Design Definition". *European Union Intellectual Property Office*. Available at: https://euipo.europa. eu/ohimportal/en/design-definition.

Devarapalli, Pratap. 2018. "Machine Learning to Machine Owning: Redefining the Copyright Ownership from the Perspective of Australian, US, UK and EU Law". *European Intellectual Property Review*, 40(11), 722–728. Available at: https://papers.ssrn.com/sol3/papers.cfm? abstract_id=3293518.

"Doctrine of Substantial Performance Law and Legal Definition". *USLegal*. Available at: https:// definitions.uslegal.com/d/doctrine-of-substantial-performance/.

"eSearch Plus". *European Union Intellectual Property Office*. Available at: https://euipo.europa.eu/ eSearch/#basic.

European Data Protection Board. 2018. "Guidelines 2/2018 on Derogations of Article 49 under Regulation 2016/679". Available at: https://edpb.europa.eu/sites/edpb/files/files/file1/edpb_ guidelines_2_2018_derogations_en.pdf.

European Data Protection Supervisor. 2018. "Opinion 5/2018 – Preliminary Opinion on Privacy by Design". Available at: https://edps.europa.eu/sites/edp/files/publication/18-05-31_preliminar y_opinion_on_privacy_by_design_en_0.pdf.

European Parliament Resolution of 13 December 2018 on Blockchain: A Forward-Looking Trade Policy (2018/2085(INI)). Available at: www.europarl.europa.eu/sides/getDoc.do?type=TA& language=EN&reference=P8-TA-2018-0528.

Faber, Stéphanie. 2019. "Does the GDPR Allow for the Use of Consent for the International Transfer of Data?". *Squire Patton Boggs*. Available at: www.securityprivacybytes.com/2019/01/ does-the-gdpr-allow-for-the-use-of-consent-for-the-international-transfer-of-data/.

Finck, Michèle. 2017. "Blockchains and Data Protection in the European Union". *Max Planck Institute for Innovation & Competition Research Paper No. 18-01*. Available at: https://papers. ssrn.com/sol3/papers.cfm?abstract_id=3080322.

Follow My Vote. "Blockchain Technology in Online Voting". Available at: https://followmyvote. com/online-voting-technology/blockchain-technology/.

Gerard, David. "Imogen Heap: "Tiny Human". Total Sales: $133.20". Available at: https://davidger ard.co.uk/blockchain/imogen-heap-tiny-human-total-sales-133-20/.

Governatori, Guido et al. 2018. "On Legal Contracts, Imperative and Declarative Smart Contracts, and Blockchain Systems". *Artificial Intelligence and Law*, 26, 377–409. doi:10.1007/s10506-018-9223-3.

Hazel, Robert. 2018. "Privacy and Trade Secret Law Applied to Drones – An Economic Analysis". *GMU Working Paper in Economics No. 18-36*. Available at: https://papers.ssrn.com/sol3/ papers.cfm?abstract_id=3116378.

Herian, Robert. 2018. "Regulating Disruption: Blockchain, GDPR, and Questions of Data Sovereignty". *Journal of Internet Law*, 22(2), 1, 8–16. Available at:` http://oro.open.ac.uk/ 56264/.

Higgins, Stan. 2017. "From $900 to $20,000: Bitcoin's Historic 2017 Price Run Revisited". *Coindesk.* Available at: www.coindesk.com/900-20000-bitcoins-historic-2017-price-run-revisited.

Hungarian National Authority for Data Protection and Freedom of Information. "The Opinion of the Hungarian National Authority for Data Protection and Freedom of Information on Blockchain Technology in the Context of Data Protection". Available at: www.naih.hu/files/ Blockchain-Opinion-2018-01-29.pdf.

IBMBlockchain. 2018. "How the CDC Is Exploring Blockchain Technology for Public Health". Available at: https://youtu.be/gDj0kLojxu4.

Judgment of the Court of Justice of the European Union (Second Chamber) of 19 October 2016. Available at: http://curia.europa.eu/juris/document/document.jsf?docid=184668&doclang=EN.

Lundqvist, Bjorn. "Portability in Datasets under Intellectual Property, Competition Law, and Blockchain". *Faculty of Law, Stockholm University Research Paper No. 62.* Available at: https://papers.ssrn.com/sol3/papers.cfm?abstract_id=3278580.

Maestre, Roberto et al. 2018. "Reinforcement Learning for Fair Dynamic Pricing". *Cornell University (arXiv:1803.09967v1 [cs.LG].* Available at: https://arxiv.org/abs/1803.09967.

Mathias Avocats. 2017. "How Can Blockchain and Trade Secrets Support Each Other?". *Mathias Avocats.* Available at: www.avocats-mathias.com/droit-des-affaires/blockchain-trade-secrets.

Maxwell, Winston et al. 2017. "A Guide to Blockchain and Data Protection". *Hogan Lovells.* Available at: www.hlengage.com/_uploads/downloads/5425GuidetoblockchainV9FORWEB.pdf.

Ménière, Yann. 2018. "The Emerging Blockchain Patent Landscape". Presentation Given at the EPO's "Patenting Blockchain" Conference of 4 December 2018. Available at: https://youtu.be/ ROwzOLxngsQ?t=525 (08:45 onwards).

Mik, Eliza. 2017. "Smart Contracts: Terminology, Technical Limitations and Real World Complexity". *SSRN.* Available at: https://papers.ssrn.com/sol3/papers.cfm?abstract_ id=3038406.

"Mycelia - About". *Mycelia.* Available at: http://myceliaformusic.org/#about.

Nakamoto, Satoshi. 2008. "Bitcoin: A Peer-to-Peer Electronic Cash System". Available at: https:// bitcoin.org/bitcoin.pdf.

Ni Loideain, Nora. 2018. "A Port in the Data-Sharing Storm: The GDPR and the Internet of Things". *King's College London Law School Research Paper No. 2018-27.* Available at: https:// papers.ssrn.com/sol3/papers.cfm?abstract_id=3264265.

Power Ledger. "xGrid – Product Details". Available at: www.powerledger.io/products/across-regulated-electricity-network.

Pun, Hubert et al. 2018. "Blockchain Adoption for Combating Deceptive Counterfeits". *Kenan Institute of Private Enterprise Research Paper No. 18-18.* Available at: https://papers.ssrn.com/ sol3/papers.cfm?abstract_id=3223656.

Raskin, Max. 2017. "The Law and Legality of Smart Contracts". *1 Georgetown Law Technology Review 304.* Available at: https://papers.ssrn.com/sol3/papers.cfm?abstract_id=2959166.

Raso, Filippo A., et al. 2018. "Artificial Intelligence & Human Rights: Opportunities & Risks". Berkman Klein Center Research Publication No. 2018-6. Available at: https://papers.ssrn. com/sol3/papers.cfm?abstract_id=3259344.

Ravich, Timothy. 2017. "Evolving Law on Airport Implications by Unmanned Aerial Systems". ISBN: 978-0-309-44659-4. Available at: https://papers.ssrn.com/sol3/papers.cfm? abstract_id=3066773.

Salmensuu, Cagla. 2018. "The General Data Protection Regulation and Blockchains". *Liikejuri-diikka 1/2018.* Available at: https://papers.ssrn.com/sol3/papers.cfm?abstract_id=3143992.

Savelyev, Alexander. 2018. "Copyright in the Blockchain Era: Promises and Challenges". *Higher School of Economics Research Paper No. WP BRP 77/LAW/2017.* Available at: https://papers. ssrn.com/sol3/papers.cfm?abstract_id=3075246.

Scharf, Rebecca L. 2018. "Drone Invasion: Unmanned Aerial Vehicles and the Right to Privacy". *UNLV William S. Boyd School of Law Legal Studies Research Paper Series*. Available at: https://papers.ssrn.com/sol3/papers.cfm?abstract_id=3145203.

Sklaroff, Jeremy M. 2018. "Smart Contracts and the Cost of Inflexibility". *University of Pennsylvania Law Review*, 166, 263–303.

Staples, M. et al. 2017. "Risks and Opportunities for Systems Using Blockchain and Smart Contracts". *Data61 (CSIRO)*. Available at: www.data61.csiro.au/~/media/052789573E9342068C5735BF604E7824.ashx.

Swire, Peter et al. 2018. "Privacy and Cybersecurity Lessons at the Intersection of the Internet of Things and Police Body-Worn Cameras". *North Carolina Law Review*, 96. *Georgia Tech Scheller College of Business Research Paper No. 18-11*. Available at: https://papers.ssrn.com/sol3/papers.cfm?abstract_id=3168089.

Szabo, Nick. 1994. "Smart Contracts". Available at: www.fon.hum.uva.nl/rob/Courses/InformationInSpeech/CDROM/Literature/LOTwinterschool2006/szabo.best.vwh.net/smart.contracts.html.

TjongTjin Tai, Eric. 2018. "Force Majeure and Excuses in Smart Contracts". *Tilburg Private Law Working Paper Series No. 10/2018. European Review of Private Law 2018/6*, pp. 787–904. Available at: https://papers.ssrn.com/sol3/papers.cfm?abstract_id=3183637.

Toth, Anne. 2018. "Will GDPR Block Blockchain?". *World Economic Forum*. Available at: www.weforum.org/agenda/2018/05/will-gdpr-block-blockchain/.

"Trade Mark Definition – A Little Bit of Theory". *European Union Intellectual Property Office*. Available at: https://euipo.europa.eu/ohimportal/en/trade-mark-definition.

Tresise, Annabel et al. 2018. "What Blockchain Can and Can't Do for Copyright". *Australian Intellectual Property Journal*, 28, 144. Available at: https://papers.ssrn.com/sol3/papers.cfm?abstract_id=3227381.

"Unconscionable (Definition)". *The Free Dictionary by Farlex*. Available at: https://legal-dictionary.thefreedictionary.com/unconscionable.

Van Humbeeck, Andries. 2017. "The Blockchain-GDPR Paradox". *The Ledger*. Available at: https://medium.com/wearetheledger/the-blockchain-gdpr-paradox-fc51e663d047.

Werbach, Kevin et al. 2017. "Contracts Ex Machina". *Duke Law Journal*, 67, 313. Available at: https://papers.ssrn.com/sol3/papers.cfm?abstract_id=2936294. pp. 118, 123.

"What Is a Trade Secret?" *World Intellectual Property Organisation*. Available at: www.wipo.int/sme/en/ip_business/trade_secrets/trade_secrets.htm.

World Intellectual Property Organisation. "What Is Intellectual Property". Available at: www.wipo.int/edocs/pubdocs/en/intproperty/450/wipo_pub_450.pdf.

Zyskind, Guy et al. 2015. "Decentralizing Privacy: Using Blockchain to Protect Personal Data". *2015 IEEE CS Security and Privacy Workshops*. Available at: https://ieeexplore.ieee.org/stamp/stamp.jsp?tp=&arnumber=7163223.

CHAPTER 15

Prediction of Cryptocurrency Market Price Using Deep Learning and Blockchain Information

Bitcoin and Ethereum

Gulani Senthuran and Malka N. Halgamuge

School of Computing and Mathematics, Charles Sturt University, Melbourne, Victoria, Australia

Department of Electrical and Electronic Engineering, The University of Melbourne, Parkville, Australia

CONTENTS

15.1 INTRODUCTION

Bitcoin and Ethereum are different kinds of popular digital currencies introduced into global financial markets based on their unique specifications. In the last few years, the price of both Bitcoin and Ethereum has been increased gradually. However, a price explosion of around AUD 9,613 in the middle of 2018 has been reported for Bitcoin [1], and a price explosion up to AUD 700 has been noted for Ethereum so far in 2018. [2] These currencies are the leading cryptocurrencies around the world with growing adoption over time. They are making a vast majority in the market capitalization. The blockchain technology helps build trust relationship in the market. It offers an easy tracking of digital exchanges and prevents the possible fraudulent actions. The essential features of Bitcoin and Ethereum were derived from blockchain, which have drawn substantial attention from researchers in different areas including economic fields, Deep learning and cryptography.

Numerous studies have been performed on modelling the time series of Bitcoin price in the market and reported the financial asset capabilities of Bitcoin using GARCH models. Recent studies have also focused on statistical and economical properties of Bitcoin price and its characteristics and investigated the statistical properties of the Bitcoin market [3] and exchange rate of Bitcoin verses US dollar. [4] There has also been analyses of the Bitcoin price model under the fundamental market condition, which were supply demand of Bitcoin, total demand of Bitcoin and equilibrium between Bitcoin supply and Bitcoin demand. [5] In addition, some studies have predicted the Bitcoin price using both Deep learning technique [6] and Bayesian Neural Network (BNN) [7], which analyses the time series of Bitcoin price. Moreover, to tackle the low training sample data issue, a few studies have used a small amount of raw data with Deep learning technique. [8]

The vast majority of the past studies have concentrated on either modelling Bitcoin price without considering its relationship to blockchain information or distinguishing just its linear relationship to macroeconomic factors. An essential inadequacy of previous studies is that they analysed only the prediction price of the Bitcoin currency using different techniques; however, they did not focus on comparing the prediction accuracy for different cryptocurrencies. However, the prediction accuracy is increasingly considered to be a vital parameter among investors and consumers to make more profit from their investments and shares. Therefore, the current study attempts to defeat these restrictions by methodically evaluating the prediction accuracy of Bitcoin and Ethereum currencies.

The main purpose of this study is to analyse the prediction accuracy of Bitcoin and Ethereum using a Deep learning approach. This study employs a Deep learning approach with blockchain and cryptocurrency information on Bitcoin and Ethereum, separately. It should be noted that the application of the Deep learning approach with blockchain information and both currency information extends the accuracy of the process as the blockchain technology is the decentralized ledger for

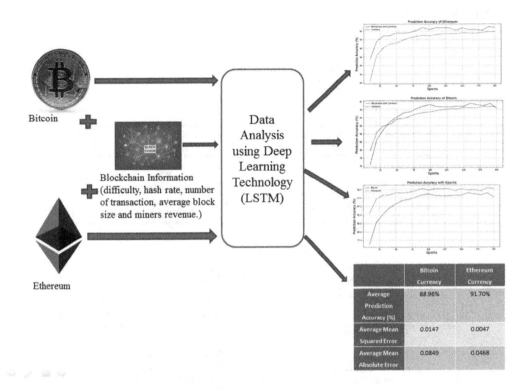

FIGURE 15.1   Graphical abstract

cryptocurrency. [7] This paper presents the application of the long short-term memory (LSTM) model to calculate the error rate of the currencies using blockchain and crypto data. The blockchain information was gathered by monitoring the variables from online websites. The prediction performance obtained in this study substantiates the effectiveness of machine learning with blockchain data. The rest of the article is organized as follows: Section II describes the material and methods used in this study. Section III shows the collection of results of the prediction of the currency. Section IV concludes the analysis, the limitations on the data and the future works of this area.

15.2 MATERIAL AND METHODS

This section describes the material and methods employed in the present study. The method was divided in to the five steps. These are raw data collection, data preparation, pre-processing, data prediction and data analysis. Figure 15.2 schematically illustrates the materials and the main steps involved in this investigation.

15.2.1 Flowchart

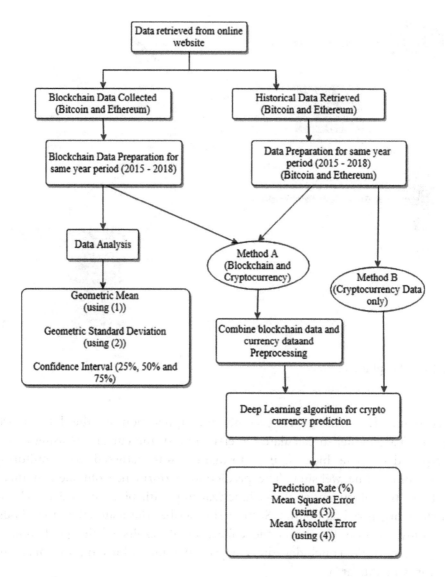

FIGURE 15.2   Proposed analysis for prediction of crypto currency using blockchain and cryptocurrency market price data with the exploitation of Deep Learning algorithm. Method A (blockchain data and cryptocurrency data), Method B (only cryptocurrency data (Bitcoin and Ethereum) were separately studied). Using equations (1) – (4).

15.2.2 Raw Data Collection

The blockchain data were collected from online websites and the retrieved financial information was collected for Bitcoin from 2009 to 2018 and for Ethereum from 2015 to 2018, respectively. These data were based on the reliable source for the data on the Bitcoin and Ethereum blockchain, which was updated every 24 hours. The attributes of blockchain data include blockchain records such as difficulty, hash rate, number of transactions, average block size and miners revenue.

15.2.3 Blockchain

The foremost advantage of using blockchain is the security. The main application of blockchain data of cryptocurrencies demonstrate the perfect automated micro-transactions made between machines.

Decentralization is the esteem sought after by all cryptocurrencies instead of general at currencies being esteemed by central banks. Decentralization can be indicated by the accompanying objectives: (i) Who will keep up and deal with the exchange record? (ii) Who will have the privilege to approve exchanges? (iii) Who will make new cryptocurrencies? The blockchain is the main accessible innovation that can at the same time accomplish these three objectives. Table 15.1 describes of blockchain variables involved in the prediction of Bitcoin and Ethereum.

The blend of blockchain technologies and the financial showcase is a genuine case of a mix of abnormal state cryptography and market economies.

15.2.4 Data Preparation

In this analysis, blockchain information, Bitcoin information and Ethereum information were first retrieved from online websites. A part of the Bitcoin, Ethereum and blockchain data was utilized in the data analysis (i.e., from 2015 to 2018) because the Ethereum information was retrieved only from 2015 to 2018. The Bitcoin data received from the online resource from 2009 to 2018 have been dealt it out manually with-in that period. As a consequence, 6 years of Bitcoin data were excluded from the analysis. In addition, the individual attributes of blockchain raw data were unable to be obtained in the correct format and, therefore, all the blockchain data were set up into matrix arrange.

15.2.5 Processing the Data

Blockchain and cryptocurrency data joined and began to perform the handling to foresee the exactness of the prediction of the currency. Also, simply the currency data were utilized for forecasting. This investigation opened the way to uncover how the blockchain data affects the prediction. In this processing, LSTM model, which is a specific kind of Deep learning, was employed.

TABLE 15.1 Description of blockchain variables involved in the prediction of Bitcoin and Ethereum.

Blockchain Variables	Description
Market price	USD market price of the Bitcoin change
Difficulty	Measurable value of difficult in the new block
Hash Rate	When Bitcoin network is performing the estimated number (Tera hashes second)
Average Block size	Average block size in (MB)
Confirmed Transactions	Number of confirmed transactions per day
Miners revenue	Total mount of coin base block rewards plus transaction fees paid to miners

15.2.6 Deep Learning

Deep learning technique gives effective results on the prediction. [9] This is totally one of the kind ideas to join Deep learning and cryptos. These models can accomplish cutting edge precision, and now and then surpassing human-level execution. Deep learning achieves acknowledgment accuracy at more elevated amounts than ever before. The two main reasons that the Deep learning becomes useful are Deep learning requires lots of labelled data and substantial computing power. [10]

LSTM (Long Short-Term Memory): This task was also achieved with successful results through the implementation of LSTM to compare the predictive performance with blockchain data and without blockchain data.

A LSTM model is used in this study. It is a specific kind of Deep learning model appropriate to the time series data. This enables the network to learn long-term conditions. LSTM cell contains forget and remember gates which enable the cell to choose what information to piece or pass in the light of its quality and significance. Therefore, weak signs can be blocked, which in turn avoids vanishing slope.

15.2.7 Analysis of the Data

In this analysis, blockchain data were used and analysed to find the Geometric Mean (GM), Geometric Standard Deviation (GSD), maximum, minimum and confidence Interval (25%, 50% and 75%). The statistical analysis to find the equations for mean and standard deviation are as follows.

GM_x is given by,

$$GM = \sqrt[N]{\prod_{i=1}^{N} x_i} \tag{1}$$

where N = the number of elements, x_i the value of each elements and GSD_x is given by,

$$GSD = \sqrt{\frac{1}{N} \sum_{i=1}^{N} \left(\ln \frac{x_i}{GM_x} \right)^2} \tag{2}$$

where N = the number of elements, x_i = the value of each elements and x' = mean.

The analysis is performed by using Python 3.6 on MacOS Sierra (Version 10.12.6), 1.7 GHz Intel Core i7, 4GB RAM, 1600 MHz DDR3.

15.2.8 Prediction of the Data

LSTM model was employed in Deep learning to predict the crypto currency prices with 80% of training data and 20% of test data. The mean square (MSE) and absolute errors (MAE) were determined using the relationships given in Eqs. (3) and (4) respectively.

$$\text{Mean Squared Error} = \frac{1}{N} \sum_{i=1}^{N} (y_i - y')^2 \tag{3}$$

TABLE 15.2 Ethereum currency: Statistical analysis on blockchain data (mean, standard deviation, minimum, confidence interval (CI), maximum)

	Difficulty	Hash Rate (TH/S)	Miners Revenue	Transaction	Average Block Size
Mean	6.65e+14	4.52e+13	88.91	1.97e+05	6610.61
Standard Deviation	9.74e+14	6.91e+13	56.02	2.85e+05	8376.69
Minimum	1.47e+12	9.52e+10	31.75	1.32e+03	618.29
25% CI	2.44e+13	1.82e+12	50.62	3.25e+04	1375.02
50% CI	8.25e+13	6.37e+12	73.23	4.69e+04	1672.98
75% CI	1.33e+15	7.70e+13	107.95	2.80e+05	10,444.70
Maximum	3.33e+15	2.67e+14	798.60	1.35e+06	33,683.75

TABLE 15.3 Bitcoin currency: Statistical analysis on blockchain data for (mean, standard deviation, minimum, confidence interval (CI), maximum)

	Difficulty	Hash Rate (TH/S)	Miners Revenue	Transaction	Average Block Size
Mean	5.76e+11	4.47e+06	5.99e+06	237,710.44	0.8254
Standard Deviation	6.70e+11	5.36e+06	9.45e+06	63,978.070	0.1755
Minimum	5.22e+10	3.22e+05	7.53e+05	86,583.0	0.3475
25% CI	1.65e+11	1.24e+06	1.32e+06	195,796.0	0.7081
50% CI	2.59e+11	2.05e+06	1.86e+06	235,084.0	0.8570
75% CI	7.12e+11	5.55e+06	5.79e+06	281,116.0	0.9707
maximum	3.01e+12	2.69e+07	5.31e+07	425,008.0	1.1066

$$\text{Mean Absolute Error} = \frac{1}{N}\sum_{i=1}^{N} \frac{y_i - y'_i}{y_i} \tag{4}$$

where N is the number of samples, y_i is the i-th true objective value and y_i is the i-th estimated value.

15.3 RESULTS

In this study, prediction percentage rates with the different epochs were received from the blockchain data and cryptocurrency data. The LSTM model was used to predict the data and generate following tables and figures were generated on the basis of the predicted data. The data set tables (Tables 15.4 and 15.5) illustrate how the Prediction Rate, Mean Squared Error, Mean Absolute Error for Bitcoin and Ethereum cryptocurrencies with Epochs from 2015 to 2018.

15.3.1 Method A:

TABLE 15.4 Method A: Data set with Prediction Accuracy Rate, Mean Squared Error, and Mean Absolute Error for Bitcoin and Ethereum cryptocurrency using blockchain data and currency data for each Epochs value.

Epochs	Bitcoin Prediction Rate (%)	Ethereum Prediction Rate (%)	Bitcoin Mean Squared Error	Ethereum Mean Squared Error	Bitcoin Mean Absolute Error	Ethereum Mean Absolute Error
10	79.7771	85.4563	0.0093	0.0083	0.0726	0.0657
20	83.4849	89.5449	0.0076	0.0060	0.0644	0.0536
30	85.7657	90.8649	0.0066	0.0052	0.0586	0.0489
40	87.3580	90.8878	0.0058	0.0052	0.0542	0.0487
50	87.6308	91.5374	0.0057	0.0048	0.0534	0.0470
60	88.4970	91.5033	0.0053	0.0048	0.0501	0.0470
70	88.8647	91.6494	0.0051	0.0048	0.0482	0.0467
80	89.1559	92.1144	0.0050	0.0045	0.0465	0.0456
90	89.4391	**92.7736**	0.0049	0.0041	0.0448	0.0437
100	89.6268	92.3007	0.0048	0.0044	0.0431	0.0451
110	90.5844	92.7250	0.0048	0.0041	0.0422	0.0435
120	90.6417	92.7146	0.0048	0.0041	0.0417	0.0438
130	90.7258	92.6955	0.0047	0.0042	0.0410	0.0442
140	90.7218	92.1621	0.0047	0.0045	0.0406	0.0458
150	90.6942	92.6751	0.0047	0.0042	0.0405	0.0438
160	90.6997	92.3011	0.0047	0.0044	0.0404	0.0449
170	90.8374	92.3695	0.0047	0.0043	0.0392	0.0447
180	90.5572	92.0811	0.0048	0.0045	0.0411	0.0458
190	**90.9375**	92.9655	**0.0046**	**0.0040**	0.0390	**0.0432**
200	90.8953	**92.7736**	0.0046	0.0041	**0.0389**	0.0438

15.3.2 Method B:

TABLE 15.5 Method B: Data set with Prediction Accuracy Rate, Mean Squared Error, and Mean Absolute Error for Bitcoin and Ethereum cryptocurrency using only currency data for each Epochs value.

Epochs	Bitcoin Prediction Rate (%)	Ethereum Prediction Rate (%)	Bitcoin Mean Squared Error	Ethereum Mean Squared Error	Bitcoin Mean Absolute Error	Ethereum Mean Absolute Error
10	79.7318	80.4207	0.0094	0.0136	0.0712	0.0888
20	84.5086	86.3979	0.0072	0.0094	0.0616	0.0713
30	85.9785	88.0572	0.0065	0.0083	0.0590	0.0650
40	86.3361	88.9239	0.0063	0.0077	0.0573	0.0609
50	87.6247	89.1827	0.0057	0.0075	0.0554	0.0604
60	87.7773	89.8182	0.0056	0.0070	0.0547	0.0590
70	88.4436	90.4216	0.0053	0.0066	0.0530	0.0566
80	88.9776	90.7671	0.0051	0.0064	0.0518	0.0561

(Continued)

(Cont.)

Epochs	Bitcoin Prediction Rate (%)	Ethereum Prediction Rate (%)	Bitcoin Mean Squared Error	Ethereum Mean Squared Error	Bitcoin Mean Absolute Error	Ethereum Mean Absolute Error
90	89.3036	90.9971	0.0049	0.0062	0.0512	0.0558
100	89.4059	90.8275	0.0049	0.0063	0.0508	0.0568
110	89.7417	91.1079	0.0047	0.0061	0.0502	0.0555
120	89.9779	91.3392	0.0046	0.0060	0.0497	0.0552
130	90.1729	91.3315	0.0045	0.0060	0.0493	0.0554
140	90.1625	91.4165	0.0045	0.0059	0.0494	0.0552
150	90.496	91.5689	0.0044	0.0058	0.0484	0.0549
160	90.3910	91.5347	0.0044	0.0058	0.0486	0.0551
170	90.3943	91.4797	0.0044	0.0059	0.0486	0.0556
180	**90.7275**	91.6283	**0.0043**	0.0058	**0.0481**	0.0547
190	90.6728	91.8279	**0.0043**	0.0056	0.0487	**0.0540**
200	90.6694	**91.8328**	**0.0043**	**0.0056**	0.0483	**0.0540**

The results demonstrate the prediction accuracy of the Bitcoin currency using blockchain data and cryptocurrency data (Figure 15.3). As this figure illustrates, the prediction accuracy is high for Epochs value higher than 30 which obviously demonstrates the high prediction accuracy when the blockchain and cryptocurrency information were employed.

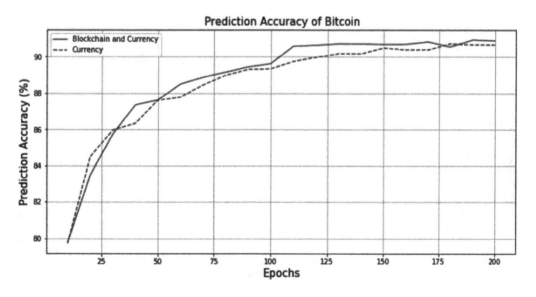

FIGURE 15.3 Bitcoin prediction accuracy of observing influence of blockchain information on prediction accuracy.

The outcome of the analysis demonstrates the prediction accuracy of the Ethereum currency utilizing the blockchain data and cryptocurrency data (see Figure 15.4). As it is evident in this figure, the accuracy is high in all the epochs values. The average increment of the accuracy was 2% contrast with accuracy with the crypto data. The outcomes clearly indicated that the prediction accuracy was high when the blockchain and cryptocurrency information was utilized.

According to the results presented in Figures 15.3 and 15.4, the accuracy of the prediction for the cryptocurrency is more accurate when using the blockchain data and crypto data.

Figures 15.5 and 15.6 show the original and prediction market prices of the Bitcoin currency and Ethereum currency using blockchain data and crypto data respectively when the Epochs value was 100. Both the currencies demonstrate that how the prediction closest to the first esteem. The blockchain data significantly influence the exactness of the prediction.

According to the results, prediction of the market price of the Ethereum currency was very close to the original market price, and the contrary was observed for Bitcoin currency.

The data shown in Figures 15.7 proved that Ethereum currency has highly accurate prediction than Bitcoin. When the epochs value was around 25, the increment of the correctness of Ethereum was 7%. After this epochs value, the increment was down to 2%.

Comparison of Figures 15.8 and 15.9 revealed that the mean squared error and mean absolute error of Bitcoin are higher than Ethereum on the prediction for all the values of epochs.

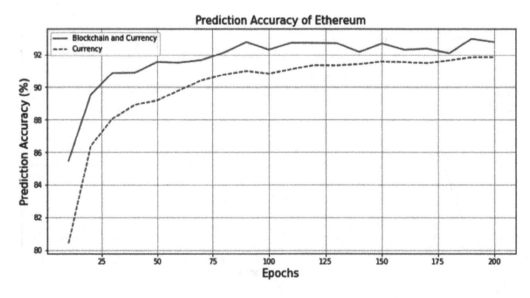

FIGURE 15.4   Ethereum prediction accuracy of observing influence of blockchain information on prediction accuracy.

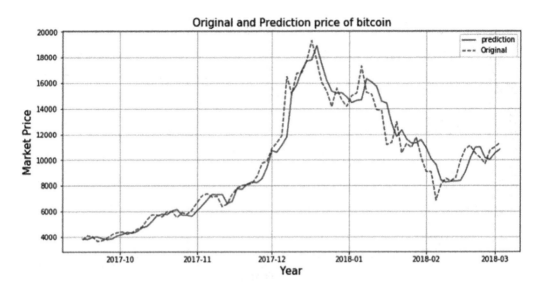

FIGURE 15.5   Original and predicted market price of Bitcoin using blockchain and currency data.

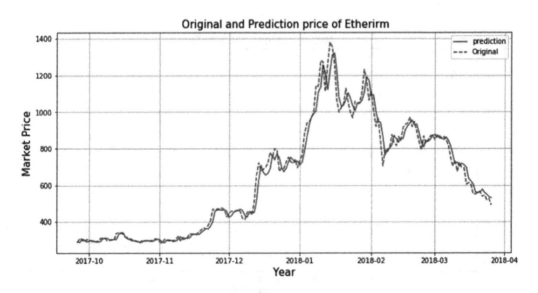

FIGURE 15.6   Original and predicted market price of Ethereum using blockchain and currency data.

15.3.3 Discussion

The main aims of this study are to discern the prediction of the crypto currency prices and to compare the prediction accuracy of two cryptocurrencies (Ethereum, Bitcoin) in the current and future financial market. To the best of the author's knowledge, the present study is the only study till date that reports the prediction

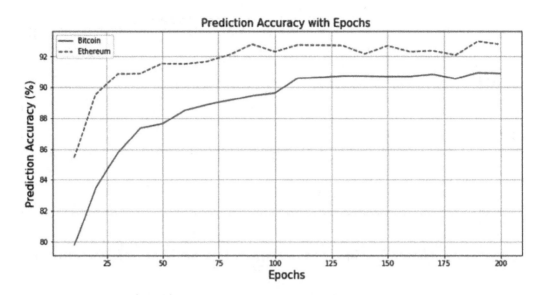

FIGURE 15.7 Prediction accuracy of Bitcoin and Ethereum currencies with different epochs values, when using with blockchain and currency data.

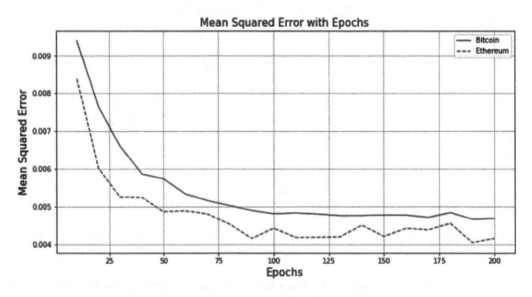

FIGURE 15.8 The Mean Squared Error of Bitcoin and Ethereum currency using blockchain and currency data.

accuracy using Deep learning and blockchain data and compares other currencies to provide the best solution for business, consumers and investors regarding their investments. To accomplish this task, crypto currency data and blockchain data of both currencies were retrieved from online websites and Deep learning model [Long

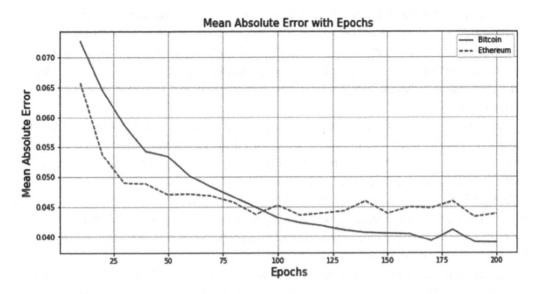

FIGURE 15.9 The Mean Absolute Error of the Bitcoin and Ethereum currency using blockchain and currency data.

TABLE 15.6 Average values for prediction accuracy, MSE and MAE for Bitcoin and Ethereum currencies when using blockchain data and crypto currency data.

	Bitcoin Currency	Ethereum Currency
Average Prediction Accuracy (%)	88.84%	91.70%
Average Mean Squared Error	0.0054	0.0047
Average Mean Absolute Error	0.047	0.0468

Short-Term Memory (LSTM)] was applied to predict the prediction accuracy percentage of the currencies.

Many studies have been conducted on modelling and predicting the cryptocurrency price by employing different technologies, models and statistical analysis. One of the leading outcomes of the present study is that the blockchain data was shown to highly determine the prediction accuracy of the cryptocurrencies. This is owing to the fact the blockchain data keeps the entire history of the cryptocurrency transaction. The blockchain data incorporate significant highlights as primary determinants for pricing Bitcoin. [7] The features of the blockchain information are significant to address the critical issues in the cryptocurrency prediction. [11] The results obtained in this study revealed that Ethereum has higher responsiveness in the current market in long run and short run in contrast to Bitcoin. Analysis of crypto market factors on five different cryptocurrencies, using Autoregressive Distributed Lag (ARDL) showed that Bitcoin and Ethereum are more sensitive. In the cryptocurrency prediction, the use of blockchain data and currency (Bitcoin, Ethereum) data in the Deep learning approach can have a high impact on the accuracy percentage. The use of blockchain data in prediction overcomes the limitations of the poor prediction of currencies and the prediction can be more accurate when the machine learning models are employed. [7] The study by [12] showed prediction accuracy of Bitcoin using blockchain data was 55% with regular Artificial Neural Network (ANN). However, they suggest that there was limited predictability in blockchain data.

The present study used the Deep learning (LSTM) model to evaluate the prediction accuracy. Usually, Deep learning technique is used in the financial market to predict the price [6,11,13] and LSTM is a clear and compelling method of training data and more competent for perceiving long term dependencies. [6]

The prediction accurateness of the market price was found to be close to the original value for the Ethereum currency, while the opposite was observed for Bitcoin. The study by [13] showed that the predicted values of Bitcoin were closer to the actual values. However, they had an issue with in sufficient data.

On the other hand, the average values of mean squared error (MSE) and mean absolute error (MAE) indicated that the error value of Bitcoin is higher than the error value of Ethereum. Application of LSTM model with only crypto data generated an average MAE of about 0.04 for Bitcoin and 0.05 for Ethereum respectively. [13] The LSTM model was able to achieve MSE of the Bitcoin about 0.03. [6] The main limitation of the current study is the data size. Although the Bitcoin data was retrieved from 2009 to 2018, a part of them (i.e., from 2015 to 2018) were employed in the data analysis due to the fact that the Ethereum information was available only from 2015 to 2018. The prediction of the crypto currency price must be calculated and predicted more accurately. To achieve this task, future research should be aimed at using numerous different sample data and applying cloud computing or artificial intelligence. To amplify the financial reward [14], cryptocurrency prediction has become an important field in the past recent years and the analysis of cryptocurrency has received much attention. The blockchain information influenced the secure accuracy on anticipating and Deep learning approach expanded the accurate for the prediction process. This research helps the business to analyse the price prediction of different currencies.

15.3.4 Conclusion

Ethereum and Bitcoin are increasingly significant standards in the current financial market. A great deal of speculators contributes their cash aggressively and it has been widely contemplated in the field of financial matters and data innovation. In this study, the prediction accuracy and the error rate (Mean Squared Error and Mean Absolute Error) on the prediction of Bitcoin and Ethereum currencies were analysed by applying Deep learning algorithm with historical data (blockchain information and cryptocurrency information). The results showed that the prediction accuracy percentage for the financial cryptocurrency is more accurate when predicting with blockchain data and crypto data. In addition, the error rate on the prediction was low when the blockchain and currency data were used for the analysis. Moreover, the prediction accuracy percentage of Ethereum was higher than that of Bitcoin under the same criteria, whereas the error rate in the prediction of Ethereum was lower than that of Bitcoin. Based on the results obtained in this study, it can be concluded that the blockchain information gives high security on the digital trades and it demonstrates the high accuracy of the prediction. In addition, the Deep learning prediction approach can be considered as an effective tool for analyzing the blockchain and cryptocurrency data set. This study provides a reference for researchers who examine the cryptocurrency prediction. Future studies should focus on adapting cloud computing and artificial intelligence, and this would be interesting areas to expose to improve the cryptocurrency prediction rate.

AUTHOR CONTRIBUTION

G. S. and M.N.H. conceived the study idea and developed the analysis plan. G. S. analyzed the data and wrote the initial paper. M.N.H. helped preparing the figures and tables, and in finalizing the manuscript. All authors read the manuscript.

REFERENCES

[1] S. A. Luxembourg. blockchain [Online]. https://blockchain.info/. [Accessed: 2-April-2019].

[2] bitinfocharts. [Online]. https://bitinfocharts.com/ethereum/. [Accessed: 2-April-2019].

[3] M. J. Basgall, W. Hasperué, M. Naiouf, and A. F. Bariviera, "Somestylized Facts of the Bitcoin Market," *Phys. A, Stat. Mech. Appl*, vol. 484, pp. 82–90, October 2017.

[4] S. Nadarajah, S. Chan, and J. Chu, "Statistical Analysis of the Exchange Rate of Bitcoin," *PLoS ONE*, vol. 10, no. 7, p. e0133678, 2015.

[5] M. Rajcaniova, D. Kancs, and P. Ciaian, "The Economics of Bitcoin Price Formation," *Appl. Econ*, vol. 48, no. 19, pp. 1799–1815, 2016.

[6] S. McNally, "*Predicting the Price of Bitcoin Using Machine Learning*," School of Computing, National College of Ireland, Dublin, Ireland, Ph.D. dissertation, 2016.

[7] J. Lee, and H. Jang, "An Empirical Study on Modelling and Prediction of Bitcoin Prices with Bayesian Neural Networks Based on Blockchain Information," *IEEE Early Access Articles*, vol. 99, pp. 5427–5437, 2017.

[8] L. Karlsson, A. Loutfi, and M. Längkvist, "Review of Unsupervised Feature Learning and Deep Learning for Time-Series Modeling," *Pattern Recognition Letters*, vol. 42, pp. 11–24, 2014.

[9] I. H. Witten, and E. Frank, "*Data Mining: Practical Machine Learning Tools and Techniques*," Morgan Kaufmann, 2005.

[10] Mathworks. [Online]. https://au.mathworks.com/discovery/deep-learning.html. [Accessed: 25-April-2019]

[11] S. Saluja, A. Zhao, and I. Madan, "*Automated Bitcoin Trading via Machine Learning*," Computer Science Department, Stanford University, Stanford, CA, 2015.

[12] A. Greaves, and B. Au, "Using the Bitcoin Transaction Graph to Predict the Price of Bitcoin," December 2015.

[13] D. Sheehan. (May 2018) dashee87.github.io. [Online]. https://dashee87.github.io/deep%20learning/python/predicting-cryptocurrency-priceswith-deep-learning/. [Accessed: 2-May-2018].

[14] H. Bettis-Outland, and M. D. Guillory, "Emotional Intelligence and Organizational Learning at Trade Shows," *Journal of Business & Industrial Marketing*, vol. 33, no. 1, pp. 8, February 2018.

[15] A. H. Dyhrberg, "Bitcoin, Gold and the dollar-A GARCH Volatility Analysis," *Finance Research Letters*, vol. 16, pp. 85–92, February 2016.

[16] W. Zhao, "Research on the Deep Learning of the Small Sample Data Based on Transfer Learning," *AIP Conference Proceedings*, vol. 1864, no. 1, p. 020018, August 2017.

[17] S. Valecha, S. Maji, and S. Velankar, "Bitcoin Price Prediction Using Machine Learning," In: *Advanced Communication Technology (ICACT)*, pp. 144–147, February 2018.

[18] Y. Sovbetov, "Factors Influencing Cryptocurrency Prices: Evidence from Bitcoin, Ethereum, Dash, Litcoin, and Monero," *Journal of Economics and Financial Analysis*, pp. 1–27, 2018.

Index